LET ME
BE
FREE

LET ME
— · BE · —
FREE

THE NEZ PERCE TRAGEDY

David Lavender

University of Oklahoma Press
Norman

Library of Congress Cataloging-in-Publication Data

Lavender, David Sievert, 1910–
    Let me be free : the Nez Perce tragedy / David Lavender.
        p.   cm.
    Includes bibliographical references.
    ISBN 0-8061-3190-X (pbk. : alk. paper)
    1. Nez Percé Indians.   2. Nez Percé Indians—Government relations.
    3. Nez Percé Indians—Wars, 1877.   I. Title.
    E99.N5L37   1999
    979.5'.0049741—dc21   99-24427
                                                        CIP

The paper in this book meets the guidelines for permanence and durability of the Committee on Production Guidelines for Book Longevity of the Council on Library Resources, Inc. ∞

Designed by Cassandra Pappas.
Maps by Paul Pugliese.

Published by the University of Oklahoma Press, Norman, Publishing Division of the University. Manufactured in the U.S.A. First edition, 1992. First printing of the University of Oklahoma Press edition, 1999.

1   2   3   4   5   6   7   8   9   10

To Muriel, with cause

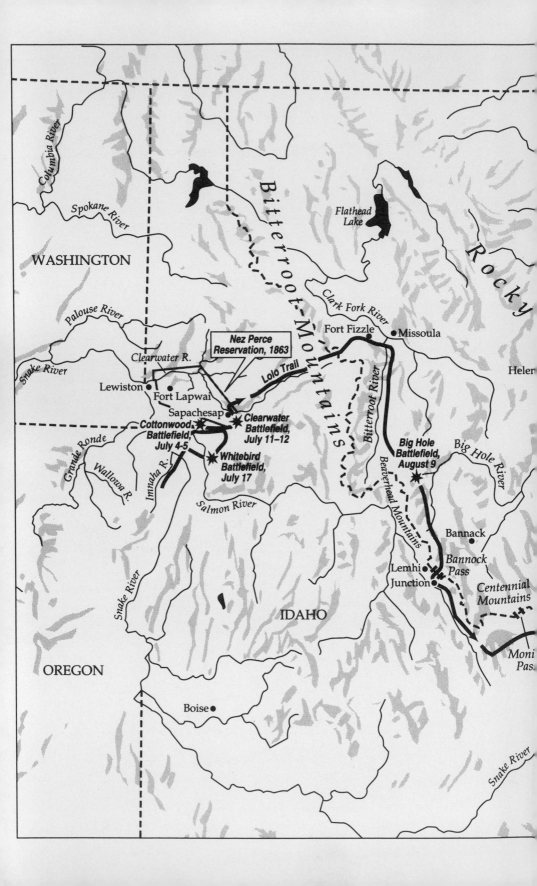

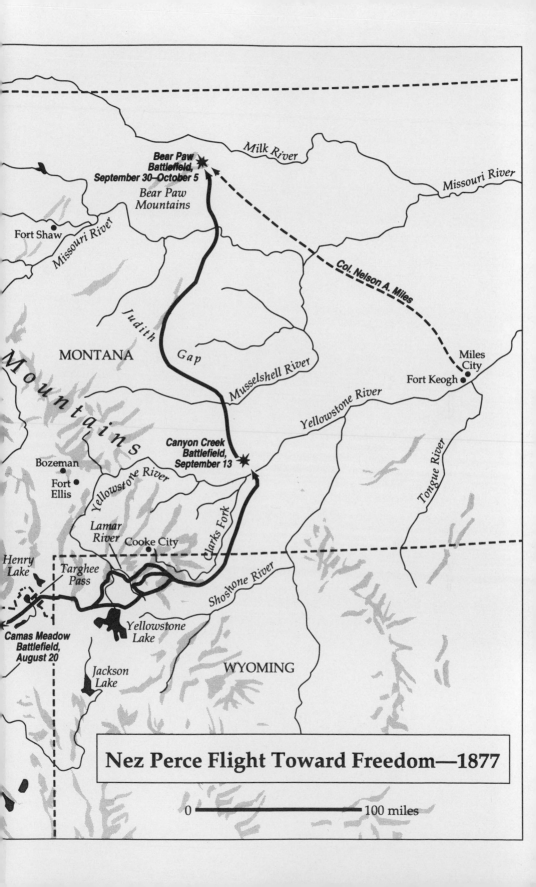

Bear Paw
Battlefield,
September 30–October 5

Bear Paw
Mountains

Milk River

Missouri River

Fort Shaw

Missouri River

Judith

Col. Nelson A. Miles

MONTANA

Gap

Musselshell River

Miles
City

Fort Keogh

Yellowstone River

Canyon Creek
Battlefield,
September 13

Tongue River

Bozeman

Yellowstone River

Fort
Ellis

Lamar
River

Cooke City

Clarks Fork

Henry
Lake

Targhee
Pass

Shoshone River

Camas Meadow
Battlefield,
August 20

Yellowstone
Lake

Jackson
Lake

WYOMING

Nez Perce Flight Toward Freedom—1877

0   100 miles

The civilization or utter destruction of the Indians is inevitable. The next twenty-five years are to determine the fate of a race. If they cannot be taught, and taught very soon, to accept the necessities of their situation and begin in earnest to provide for their own wants by labor in civilized pursuits, they are destined to speedy extinction.

—J. Q. SMITH, COMMISSIONER OF INDIAN AFFAIRS, 1876

Let me be a free man—free to travel, free to stop, free to work, free to trade, where I choose, free to choose my own teachers, free to follow the religion of my fathers, free to think and talk and act for myself—and I will obey every law, or submit to the penalty.

—CHIEF JOSEPH OF THE NEZ PERCE INDIANS, 1879

• CONTENTS •

Illustrations follow page 180.

· 1 ·

THE GRAVE

Early in the summer of 1900, Chief Joseph—his native name was Hinmah-too-yah-lat-kekht, or Thunder Rolling in the Mountains—traveled by steamboat, railroad, and buggy from his place of exile in Washington State to his former home in northeastern Oregon. There, in the incomparable Wallowa Valley, where sentinel peaks rise like a shout out of the grassy plains, his father and mother lay buried. So did the parents of many of the other members of his band. Twice Joseph undertook to win permission to return there from the white settlers of Wallowa County and from the government whose army had crushed him twenty-three years before.[1]

Permission. It is not a word commonly associated with freedom. But incarceration of one sort or another has long been a deterrent used by a dominant society for dealing with transgressors. So it was with Joseph. In 1877 his Wallowa band of Indians, together with several other bands of Nez Perces, bitterly resented the American government's order that they report to a reservation in north-central Idaho that had been assigned as a "homeland" for the entire tribe. In no sense was the land in question a home to the objectors. Still, they might have complied if a few young hotheads had not ridden off among the scattered white settlements of the Salmon River country on a killing spree.

Why didn't the chiefs of the bands to which the guilty belonged surrender them to the army that was already gathering to force obedience to the government's orders? Well, sacrificing a few for the benefit of the many in a

1

case like this wasn't the Indian way. Besides, punishment for the outbreak might be visited on the entire group. For collective vengeance *was* an Indian way. And so most of the Nez Perces who were connected with the perpetrators of the incident chose to avoid retribution by seeking asylum beyond the Continental Divide in Montana. When that hope failed, they turned north toward Canada.

They were caught. Everyone involved in the running fight, except for a few bedraggled escapees, was punished by a long, miserable exile in Oklahoma. Eventually white friends succeeded in pressuring the government into letting half of the surviving exiles return to the Northwest and settle on the Idaho reservation they had once struggled to avoid. The other half, including those under indictment for murders connected with the Salmon River outbreaks, were moved from Oklahoma to equally alien lands in Washington State. But, surely, there was an end to vengeance. With Joseph acting as primary spokesman, they begged for permission to return to their former homes in the Wallowa Valley.

Joseph's first return visit to the beloved valley was made in 1899, twenty-two years after his first clashes with detachments of the United States Army. He delivered his plea to representative white settlers crowded into a second-story meeting hall above a bank in Enterprise, Oregon, seat of Wallowa County. As an interpreter relayed the chief's words, the audience listened with respect. Joseph had become famous in defeat. Military men, seeking perhaps to becloud their own bumblings during the running battles of 1877, had loudly praised the skills with which Joseph had eluded them. His dignity at his surrender and during his later confinements in Oklahoma and northern Washington had stirred widespread sympathy. He had spoken with presidents, cabinet members, and army generals. Buffalo Bill Cody had called him "the greatest Indian America ever produced." The Wallowa settlers had named one of their valley towns Joseph and their newspaper *The Chieftain*.

So they had listened as Joseph told them, during his trip of 1899, that no member of his band had signed the treaty that had relinquished the Wallowa country to the United States government. Would it not be simple justice, then, that the settlers sell—not give, but sell—a portion of that illegally acquired land to the Bureau of Indian Affairs, which would then pass it on to the first dwellers? That way, the Indians could rid themselves of nearly a quarter of a century of despair.

Anderson Smith, a short, wiry, gray-bearded pioneer with whom Joseph had gotten on well before the diaspora, replied for the settlers. Joseph's quarrel, he said, was not with them but with the federal government. An illegal title? Surely, the government would not have surveyed the land and then declared it open for homesteading in the mid-1870s if there had been any substantial doubts about the validity of ownership. Acting on that implied assurance, a steady stream of citizens had filed on their claims according to the laws of the United States and had labored hard to bring their new holdings to the prosperous condition Joseph now saw. They were adamant. They had trusted the government. They would not put a rebellious, nonconforming group of Nez Perce Indians into the middle of their homogeneous white community.

Joseph was used to rebuffs. He was also stubborn. If the quarrel was, in fact, with the United States government, he would take his case there. Somehow he obtained permission and funds for himself and an interpreter to visit the secretary of the interior in Washington, D.C. He was sixty years old by then, and life had handled him harshly. His body had grown heavy. His shoulders sagged so he stood only five feet nine inches tall instead of the six feet that earlier observers had estimated.[2] The twin braids of his hair fell forward across his thick chest. His eyelids drooped a little. An infinite sadness suffused his face.

But pride was there, too, and he had lost none of his eloquence. Impressed by his arguments, the secretary of the interior directed James McLaughlin, chief inspector for the Bureau of Indian Affairs, to study the feasibility of moving Joseph's Nez Perce band from the Colville Reservation in Washington to the Wallowa country.

McLaughlin cut an imposing figure. He was tall and straight backed; his rugged features were adorned with a white handlebar mustache and a heavy shock of white hair. Canadian born, he had spent most of his working years among the Sioux Indians of South Dakota as an employee of the Indian bureau. During the frictions that had led, one icy December day in 1890, to the horrors of Wounded Knee, the Indian police he commanded had killed aging Chief Sitting Bull, principal architect of the coalition that had triumphed over Colonel George Armstrong Custer at the Little Bighorn. Nothing about the tragedy had checked McLaughlin's career or had changed his belief that America's defeated Indians could escape extinction only if they became red replicas of the nation's white majority. Late in the 1890s he declined an appointment as commissioner of the Bureau of Indian Affairs to become chief inspector of field operations, saying that he could accomplish more by mingling with his charges than by sitting behind a desk in Washington.

In 1890 his main task was to check out Chief Joseph's request that his shrinking band of Nez Perces be allowed to return to the Wallowa country. He began the study in the Nespelem Valley of the Colville Reservation, where most of the dispossessed Indians lived. Joseph, the inspector may well have thought during the visit, was uncomfortably like old Sitting Bull of the Sioux. The Nez Perce leader was a persuasive talker. He was hard to budge. He was a Dreamer, a member of a religion whose tenets in many ways paralleled those held by the Ghost Dancers, whose fanaticism (as seen by the whites) had helped precipitate Wounded Knee.

In pursuit of his month-long investigations in Nespelem, McLaughlin talked frequently to the Colville agent, Albert M. Anderson, an obese, balding, round-skulled man who had found Joseph to be a continuing exasperation. The stubborn chief, the agent growled, refused to cooperate with the government's civilizing program—white civilizing. Although the Bureau of Indian Affairs had built a small house on the farm that had been allotted to Joseph, the Indian leader would not live in it. Sneered Anderson: "He with his handful of unworthy followers, prefers the traditional tipi, living on the generosity of the Government and passing away their time in a filthy and licentious way." (One supposes that "licentious" referred to Joseph's two wives. But polygamy was practiced by almost all unconverted Indians who could afford it. And the *tipi*, according to other observers, was not filthy but kept scrupulously clean by those two women.) As for Joseph's nationwide reputation, history was mistaken, Anderson went on furiously. "The appalling wrongs done by him are crying from the bloodstained soil of Idaho for restitution."[3]

McLaughlin, however, found Joseph to be an amiable and cheerful companion as they journeyed, in 1900, from Colville to Wallowa, partly by boat on the Columbia River, partly by railroad, and, on the last stretch, by buggy. Five people covered that final stretch together: Joseph; Inspector McLaughlin; Peo-peo Tholekt, a fierce and devoted follower of the chief; Ed Raboin, the party's interpreter; and Phillip Andrews, camp tender.

The buggy took them out of the deep trench of the Minam River into loveliness. In front of them and to the left (north), the land rolled in broad, soft waves to an undulant horizon. To their right a timbered ridge drew their eyes southeast to an elongated cluster of tall peaks, source of several dancing streams. Two of those streams, Lostine Creek and the Wallowa River, joined in a bright V. Splashing across Lostine Creek into the V, the travelers reached pasturelands and wheat fields belonging to a man named McAlexander—A. V. McAlexander. He and a few other whites, probably riding horseback, joined the buggy as it wound through the grass.

The travelers' goal was an old Nez Perce cemetery located near the toe of a small ridge that thrust well down into the V formed by the junction of the streams. Frequent plowing had obliterated all but one of the scattered graves. The exception was a low mound of rocks, weeds, and random pieces of upright timber surrounded by an unkempt fence. Chief Joseph's father, Chief Tuekakas, generally called Old Joseph by the whites, was buried under that disordered mound—"disordered" being a white man's adjective. Indians saw no reason to prettify the earth to which their people had returned.

Unless Joseph had stopped by the cemetery in 1899, this was probably his first view of his father's grave since 1877, the year in which the Wallowa bands had been driven from their homeland. For Joseph a pause there was natural enough. Still, one can't help wondering. A term that many people used in describing the defeated chief was *shrewd*. Just possibly Joseph was being shrewd there. A constant element in his plea that his band be allowed to return to Wallowa was that his parents were buried there. Perhaps he reasoned that if Inspector McLaughlin actually saw Old Joseph's grave, he would understand its significance more than he did from just hearing the words.

The calculation, if it existed, did not rule out true emotion. Presumably, Joseph stepped out of the buggy to stand beside the ramshackle fence. McLaughlin, who watched him closely, reported that "he melted and wept." And A. V. McAlexander, who owned the land, pressed his horse close and leaned down with what he may have thought were comforting words. He had kept good care of the place, he said, leaving it untouched every time he plowed the rest of the land.

This statement, if reported correctly, was a brazen falsehood. True, the homesteader had plowed around the spot, perhaps because he was too lazy to toss the fence rails and stones aside or perhaps because he had really been sensitive, at first, about disturbing the resting place. If so, the sensitivity had not lasted.

The grave had been vandalized twice. During the first looting, the wrappings had been taken from the corpse. Although McAlexander had not participated on that occasion, he had been involved in the next. The grave robbers that time had been the farmer himself, his wife, his wife's sister, Melinda, and Melinda's husband, L. Pfefferle, who practiced dentistry in Baker, Oregon. During a family outing, the quintet exhumed the corpse and removed its head, which they washed clean of dirt in the nearby stream, so Pfefferle could display the grinning skull in his Baker office.

It is not likely that Young Joseph knew of either atrocity. His tears may well have come instead from memories of his father's last days in 1871. That year the old chief, Tuekakas, would have been well into his eighties—eighty-five if a commonly conjectured birthdate of 1786 is accepted. He was almost blind. If he wanted to ride, a young boy had to sit behind him on the horse and reach around his waist to handle the single bridle rein. Feeling the near-ness of death in August, while the band was camped in the V made by Lostine Creek and the Wallowa River, he had summoned his son and heir. Years later, speaking through an interpreter, Young Joseph recalled his father's words for an article published in the *North American Review* of April 1879. "A few more years and the white men will be all around you. They have their eyes on this land. My son, never forget my words. This country holds your father's body. Never sell the bones of your father and mother." And then young Chief Joseph, speaking out of his first place of exile in Oklahoma, had added, "I buried him in that beautiful valley of winding water. I love that land more than the rest of the world. A man who will not love his father's grave is worse than a wild animal."

Though the magazine article does not say so, there were two burials. The first, a temporary one, had been on a ridge top that commanded a striking view across the plains to the tall Wallowa peaks. Why temporary? Probably to give the Nez Perces time to gather and prepare for the proper rituals. In any event, the body was soon moved from the ridge top to another shallow pit near the base of the ridge, close to a small scattering of other graves. This new site would be the final one.

No mention is made of a casket, although by that time such devices, introduced by Christian missionaries, were fairly common. The missionaries had also emphasized that the body should be placed on its back with its head pointing to the west so that when the corpse stood upright on resurrection day, it would be looking east toward the god that was coming to judge it. But that was Christian. Although Tuekakas—Old Joseph—had been one of the first two Nez Perces to be baptized as a Christian, he had recanted because of the rank dishonesty of the whites, as he considered their treaty actions to be, and he had joined his sons in accepting the Dreamer faith. Dreamer rituals contained many Christian elements, but sometimes twisted them into expres-sions of denial. Thus with burials. After wrapping Old Joseph in buckskin, a cloth blanket, and a buffalo robe and after tying the integuments tight with a spiral of rope, the attendants—surely Young Joseph and his handsome brother Ollokot had been with them—placed the body in the oval grave with its head to the east. That way, when the resurrected body rose, its back would be turned to the oncoming Christian god, if, in fact, there was such a god as the missionaries described.[4]

The grave was filled with earth and covered with rocks as a protection against digging animals. Upright stakes were placed among the rocks and a stout pole was raised. A transverse arm, painted red, was affixed to the pole at a right angle. A bell with a handle on its closed end—a bell like those once used in schools to summon pupils—was tied to the end of the pole, where any strong breeze would set it to sounding. That arrangement, too, was a Dreamer custom.

Because the grave held an important chief, the plot was enclosed by a rude fence of sticks and brush. One of Old Joseph's horses was sacrificed and its skin was draped over the fence. Each summer thereafter, until 1877, Joseph and Ollokot had placed another fresh horsehide at the burial site. On at least one occasion some members of the band—perhaps the brothers—had raised an entire horse's stuffed skin there, bracing it upright with poles.

Standing by the fence, with the buggy just behind him, Young Joseph—not young any longer—remembered those things and, McLaughlin said, wept. Although he noticed that some vandal had taken the Dreamer bell from its support, we can be reasonably sure, as stated earlier, that no white at the grave side told him of the other desecrations. So the memories came without distraction. *I love that land more than the rest of the world.* But the land had been taken, nevertheless. *Never sell the bones of your father and mother.... A man who will not love his father's grave is worse than a wild animal.* Thus his own words, spoken without his knowing that wild humans had been among those bones.

He climbed heavily back into the buggy with the others. The horses plodded on toward the county seat so that Inspector McLaughlin could study the advisability of letting the dwindling band return to its old home. But would he uncover, in his search for what he thought was right, the memories of a race? What would he make of their beliefs and visions? Of their physical and spiritual adaptations to the profound canyons, tall peaks, scabby lava plains, and dark evergreen forests of their homeland? Of a sense of freedom as wide as the rolling prairies? Would he grasp the elusive elements of the humanity that made them, in their own word, *Nimipu*, which, when translated, means the Real People.

Would he? Could he?

· 2 ·

WE, THE PEOPLE

When the season of cold weather and long nights captured the high country of central Idaho, northeastern Oregon, and southeastern Washington, the many bands of Nez Perces moved back to their permanent villages.[1] These were scattered along the bottoms of the profound canyons of the Clearwater, Salmon, Snake, and Imnaha rivers as they rushed powerfully toward their geologically foreordained unions. It was in the cleavages made by Oregon's Imnaha River and in a parallel, high-sided gorge now called Joseph Creek that Chief Joseph; his father Tuekakas; his mother, whose identity is uncertain; and his brother Ollokot spent most of their winters.

Before the catastrophic smallpox epidemics of 1781–82 and another that may have occurred in 1802, the crumpled country of the Nez Perces probably contained more than a hundred of these canyon-bottom towns. Life revolved in tight, accustomed cycles. Village populations were small—from thirty-five inhabitants counting children up to seventy-five or, rarely, a hundred. If larger numbers congregated in one spot, food gathering became a problem.

In general, the dwellings that made up the hamlets were longhouses—A-frames created by leaning small logs against parallel ridgepoles a few inches apart. The buildings—sometimes there was only one to a village—ranged from eighteen to twenty-five feet in width and up to a hundred and, occasionally, a hundred and fifty feet in length. Walls consisted of long, dry, hollow-stemmed rushes tied together lengthwise to form big mats that could be

8

rolled into cylinders for easy transport. During the winter, the mats were laced to the A-shaped frames, which were erected over excavations two or three feet deep. Earth from the pits was piled around the bottom edge of the mats to exclude drafts from the house's dusky interiors. Fireplaces for cooking and heating were spaced ten feet or so apart along the length of the habitation. As a rule two families shared each fireplace. Smoke left the lodge and daylight entered through the slit between the parallel ridgepoles. A less common style of dwelling was a cone-shaped structure that resembled the hide-covered tipis of the Great Plains. Among the Nez Perces these cones were covered with mats, as the longhouses were.

Winter was a communal time. Missionaries of a later day were uncomfortable about it, suspecting that the intimacies of longhouse living led adolescents and adults alike into more casual sex than the stern god of the whites approved of.[2] Perhaps. But it was also a time of bonding the people, especially the children, with oft-repeated tales that expressed, however subconsciously, a tightly woven system of shared values. Young Joseph and Ollokot would remember. A narrator, his wrinkled face changing constantly in the flickering light of the fire, sat surrounded by children munching, as they listened, on bits of dried fish or little cakes made out of the pulverized roots of the kouse plant. Don't worry about being as strong as a bear, the tale spinner said. Think instead about Bluejay and his little friend, Cottontail.

Bluejay and Cottontail were conversing one day at the edge of the forest. Suddenly a starving she-grizzly roared out of the trees and chased the tiny rabbit into a hollow. Determined not to be frustrated, Bear collected pitch from nearby pines, intending to set the sticky stuff on fire and smoke Cottontail out of the den. Anxious about his friend, Bluejay called down from a branch, advising Bear to smear the inside of her legs with some of the pitch so that nimble Cottontail would stick to it as he darted out of the den and tried to dodge underneath Bear to safety. Bear complied, lighted a faggot, and set fire to the pitch in front of the entrance to the hollow. Out came Cottontail. Swift as lightning, he snatched up the faggot Bear had laid aside and set the huge animal's pitch-covered fur ablaze. That ended Bear—a triumph of loyalty and quick wits over mere brute strength.[3]

More important still was the creation myth. The protagonist is Coyote, a favorite character of most Native Americans. At times Coyote is a savior who appears at a scene of trouble in the nick of time. On other occasions he is a scamp, caught up, ludicrously, in the snares of his own cunning. But never is he dull.

Once upon a time—the children's eyes grew big, for they knew what was coming and loved it—once upon a time, Coyote was wandering with his shadow, Fox, along the banks of the Clearwater River in what is now north-central Idaho. Near present-day Kamiah (cam-ee-eye) the pair learned that a gross, vast-bellied monster was devouring, by inhalation, the animals of the valley. Rescue was clearly called for. But how could Coyote get inside the creature to do his work? After thinking long and hard, he secreted five agate knives in his glossy fur. Then he braided several rawhide ropes. With these ropes he tied himself hard and fast to neighboring crags. Thus prepared, he challenged Monster to an inhaling contest. Who would absorb whom? As Coyote had anticipated, Monster drew in a tremendous breath. The ropes snapped, and Coyote landed in the villain's cavernous craw. With one of his knives he cut a hole under Monster's ribs, and the imprisoned animals poured out. Before the Oppressor could inhale them again, Coyote began cutting the heart loose from the body. When one knife grew dull, he changed to another. He disposed of the huge corpse by slicing it into pieces and tossing the quivering chunks in different directions. Wherever a gobbet landed, the progenitors of various Northwestern tribes sprang up—the Cayuses, Yakimas, Spokans, Coeur d'Alenes, Flatheads, and so on.

Not until the butchering ended did Fox remind Coyote that the beautiful Kamiah section remained uninhabited. Coyote thereupon dipped his paws into a pool of Monster's blood and shook the red drops onto the land. Up rose the Nimipu, the Real People, or, more simply, We, the People.* To attest to the truth of the story, Coyote left behind, southeast of the present town of Kamiah, the massive lump of Monster's heart, congealed now into what looks like dead lava. If you visit there, you can see it for yourself.[4]

Almost from birth Joseph, Ollokot, and all Nez Perce children began finding out who they were in relation to the culture that enveloped them. Parturition generally took place in a subterranean, flat-roofed lodge excavated by the band's women. (White anthropologists called such places menstrual lodges.) The shelters were cool in summer, warm in winter. Women repaired to them during their monthly periods. At the onset of puberty girls went

---

*Many tribes identify themselves as "The People." Athabascan groups use a variant of *dinnee: Dineh* (Navajo), *Inde* (Apache). The confederated Blackfeet call themselves *Nitsi-tapi*; like the Nez Perce word *Nimipu*, this word means "the Real People." Compare this with the Delaware *Lenape*, which translates as "Real Men," and the Pawnee *Chahiksichhahhiks*, which means "Men of Men."

there for instruction from older women. If birth labors began while the band was in a temporary camp, a special hut was built for the mothers. Custom kept men from coming closer than shouting distance.

Legend has it that Chief Joseph's birth was different, that he was born in a cave in the bottom of Joseph Creek's deep canyon, close to the Oregon-Washington border. But there seems no reason for his having been born there, except that legend likes to ascribe special births to heroes. Joseph's village, Wawahhiitspe (Wah-wahheets-pa) was close by. Why then, would his mother leave the security of the town's familiar birthing place for the cold, damp embrace of a creek-side cavern[5]—unless, perhaps, the normal menstrual lodge had been damaged?

As with other children, Joseph's umbilical cord was probably dried, put in a small leather sack, and attached as a good-luck talisman to his cradleboard. The cradle (more accurately a carrier) was composed of a baby-size trough of soft hide fitted to an oval piece of wood. The child was laced into the container under a hood that protected the skull from chance blows and excessive sunlight. The portion of the board that rose above the infant's head was lavishly decorated with paint, dyed porcupine quills, and, after contact with whites, a handsome design of colored beads. When the mother needed to walk any distance, she carried the device on her back by means of a tumpline around her forehead. When she rode horseback, she hooked the line around the high pommel of her saddle. Nez Perce babies knew the smell and feel of horses almost from the moment of birth.

A notion has grown up that small children were confined most of the time to the carrier. Not so. For hours at a time they were naked and unrestrained—true freedom, it seems to us now—rolling cheerfully in the grass of the meadows or on mats and furs inside the lodge, watched over by an older brother or sister. Grandparents too, played major parts in the children's upbringing.

Quickly the children learned that by the time spring arrived, the dried fish, dried roots, and dried berries they had been eating throughout the winter were almost gone. As soon as the rocky brows of the lower hills were bare of snow, the band's women, often carrying their infants on their backs, began searching for kouse roots (also spelled "cows" or "cowish"). They dug into the soil with hardwood sticks three to four feet long, one end sharpened to a point, the other fitted with a handle of wood or elk horn, crescent shaped like the top of a crutch. This handle let the digger apply various degrees of leverage when prying a root from the ground. The first roots were welcomed with a traditional ceremony, as were all seasonal foods, and then gulped down, often raw, by a people ravenous for fresh vegetables. Any surplus was pounded into a powder, moistened, and formed into flat cakes that could be threaded onto thongs for transport to the villages.

Fresh kouse roots, new green shoots of other plants, and the flesh of migrating waterfowl tided the people over until they joyfully greeted, again with ritualistic feasting, the great event of the food year, the arrival of the first salmon. Runs of different species—king salmon, sockeye, silver, coho— lasted intermittently from late winter until the next fall. Over the decades the hungry Nimipus had developed a variety of fishing implements and methods that were suited to the different conditions of their streams. On the larger rivers, night fishing was common. While pitch-pine torches spread flickering light from the bank across the water, two men rowed crossways to the current in a shovel-nosed dugout canoe. Behind them they laid out a net of plant fibers, some four feet deep and a few dozen yards long, held more or less vertical by stone weights affixed at intervals to the bottom. Big salmon could not pass through the four-inch mesh. When the men in the canoe and the holders on the bank felt the tug of many fish fighting the obstruction, they pulled in the net and clubbed the thrashing catch to death.[6] Another nighttime method that also employed a canoe and a pine torch was the thrusting of a three-pronged gig into any salmon that came within reach.

Daytime fishing often involved laborious construction work. Young boys—Joseph and Ollokot would certainly have been among them—helped build wooden platforms above rocks that jutted into the stream, creating turbulences. Fish congregated just below such places, readying themselves for their next drive against the quickened water. They could be caught with dip nets or with spears whose detachable heads could be retrieved by the hemp cord tied to them. Where streams were smaller, rock and brush dams steered the fish into weirs and other traps of various sorts. Whatever the method, success was increased, it was believed, by the magical rites of certain shamans, or medicine men, who possessed special power over salmon. Shamans also helped divide the catches among the villagers. Each town controlled certain sites; outsiders could fish there and loll around in the brush-shaded ramadas close by if they asked permission. Generally permission was given.

Occasionally, a few Nimipu families went downstream to meet the fish— down the Snake River to the Columbia River and then down the Columbia to the great cataracts and rapids known later as Celilo Falls and The Dalles. The water along this twelve-mile stretch was fearfully agitated, first by gigantic black-lava boulders that had cracked away from the bordering cliffs and then by a horseshoe-shaped waterfall whose base was lost in a roaring cascade. After that came a series of monstrous whirlpools and compressed narrows that all but stood the entire river on edge.

Two Chinookan tribes claimed the fishing rights to this part of the Columbia, the Wasco on the south side of the river, the Wishram on the north. (Except for Wascos and Wishrams, most Chinookan tribes lived near the ocean.) Incredible numbers of salmon struggled to pass through this gut on their way to the hundreds of miles of headwater streams where they would spawn. The prized fishing place of all was the foot of Celilo Falls. Since the days of antiquity the Indians had maintained rickety platforms that thrust out above the principal eddies below the plunging river. From those mist-slippery perches fishermen swept the foaming water with long-handled dip nets. They felt—not saw—the big salmon that got tangled in the meshes and hauled them out in staggering numbers. During a good day, it was said, one man could land as many as five hundred fish.[7]

Such an overflow of food attracted thousands of Indians. Most came to trade and socialize as much as to fish. Chinooks paddled their high-prowed canoes up the river from the coast, bringing with them wapatoo roots, household implements cleverly fashioned out of wood, dried clams, dentalium shells that they had obtained by trading with natives of the Vancouver area, and abalone shells from California. Other tribes came from throughout the interior sections of the Columbian Plateau—Nez Perces and their closely related allies, the Cayuses, Palouses, and Wallawallas. The Yakimas and Spokans brought for trade dried buffalo, bear, and deer meat; fine baskets made of hemp and bear grass; buffalo robes; and beautifully tanned mountain-goat skins. Paiutes and Shoshonis, the most constant enemies of the Nez Perce, except at trading fairs, rode up from the northern part of the Great Basin with horses and slaves they had captured during their raids.

The many tribes traded these things with each other and bought the dried salmon and fish oil they craved from the river people. They gambled, danced, sang, told stories, and found wives from outside their own bands—one solution to the Nez Perce taboo against marriages between even remote cousins. Cultural influences eddied back and forth. Nez Perce women probably got the striking geometric patterns of their fezlike, brimless hats from the Chinooks. A few Nez Perces may once have sloped the heads of their children to a peak, as the Chinooks did, and may have worn dentalium shells in their noses, another Chinookan custom.

The need for a common language to facilitate trade was met by a simplified lingo made up of words and grammar drawn from the speech of all the tribes of the Northwest coast. On encountering the tongue, white sea traders called it Chinook jargon, although more tribes than the Chinooks were involved. Most of the inland natives of the Columbian Plateau picked up the jabber, as did many early American settlers in Oregon and Washington.[8] Chief Joseph, who spoke no English, though he probably understood a fair amount of it, conversed in Chinook jargon with the pioneer settlers of the Wallowa Valley and adjacent regions.

Finding roots, in this case the bulb of the camas lily, brought into play yet another Indian invention, a rudimentary form of government. A sort of wild hyacinth, camas grew in high, open meadows surrounded by or dotted with pine trees. There were many of these meadows in the Nez Perce country—at Weippe on the plateau above canyon-girt Kamiah; on the undulant prairie southwest of today's Grangeville, Idaho; in the mountain-shaded Wallowa region; or near present-day Moscow, Idaho. As the masses of blue camas flowers faded under the hot sun of summer, the black-skinned bulbs—shaped like small onions—grew edible. In general their growing places were not hard to reach, but individual families seldom went out after them. Partly because of a cultural imperative and partly for protection from enemy raiders, the harvest was an activity of the band.

Each band was governed by a council of elders, who were chosen by their fellows because of their proved wisdom, morality, and leadership. These councillors advised the village's chief. The decisions that came out of the interplay between advisers and the chief were made entirely by consensus. Strong emphasis was therefore placed on persuasive oratory, and it may be that Chief Joseph developed his famed rhetorical powers during his years of argument in his band's council. Consensus among the councillors did not bind individuals or families, however. All who disagreed with the elders' decisions could go their own ways, an ultimate political freedom—except that not many did choose that sort of severance. The constraints of peer pressure were powerful.[9]

Once a decision had been reached—to move from winter quarters to the camas meadows, for instance—it was conveyed to the villagers by an appointed crier, the same person, probably, whose shouts aroused the households each morning. A great bustle followed. Mats were stripped from the dwellings and rolled into bundles for transport. Goods, food, and implements were thrust into carrying baskets; riding and pack horses were saddled; and perhaps some of the town's many vociferous dogs were pressed into service as carriers, for memories still lingered of the prehorse days when dogs had been the only beasts of burden. Horses that were not used on the trip were driven to the meadows by strutting young herders, for it is possible to strut even on horseback. The animals were a family's principal source of wealth and prestige; it would not do to leave them unattended.

Ideally, the chief kept the disjointed flow from unraveling altogether. Arriving at the desired meadow, the cavalcade retrieved last year's dwelling poles from the places where they had been cached. With the men helping, as they did with other heavy chores, up went the frames for longhouses and tipis, the latter being favored in the temporary camps. Mat covers were tied into place. New fires were kindled in the smoke-blackened fire rings; they would not be allowed to go out again until the camp dissolved for the year.

Stability achieved, the women and girls began digging up great mounds of camas bulbs. They removed the thin black skins with their fingers and then arranged several bushels of the cleaned bulbs in a preheated roasting pit. The roots were covered with layers of grass and earth on which another fire was built. After baking for a day or two (or steaming if water had been sprinkled into the pit before it was covered), the roots and bulbs were removed, dried, and pulverized for winter storage. They were consumed either as soup or as a kind of bread. Indians throve on the camas products; in encountering them for the first time, whites were likely to suffer a dreadful flatulence.[10] Meanwhile the men worked at training the horses and repairing or making weapons, especially the choice bows they put together out of the horns of mountain rams, backed by strips of tough sinew held in place by a glue concocted from salmon skins or the boiled and dried blood of a sturgeon. These bows were valuable trade items.

Generally, several bands shared the root grounds. There was a good deal of visiting back and forth, gossiping, storytelling, courting between young men and women, gambling with specially marked bones, racing horses—activities that in their totality confirmed the separate bands as equals in the broader entity called Nimipus. Time drifted by, not as hours or days, but as cycles of living. One cycle was hunting. As the nights slowly grew longer and colder, elk and deer began their annual fall migration from the high country back to the deep valleys. Hunters knew where the animals were likely to gather and rode after them, taut with anticipation. As they neared the target spot, they dismounted, tied the horses, and went ahead on foot. That way they could stalk with greater stealth. They could disguise themselves, creeping toward their prey with skins across their backs and, sometimes, with antlers attached to their heads. Killing an occasional bear, whose claws could be fashioned into a prized necklace, brought fame to the slayer, but the hunters were also content with less dramatic bags—rabbits, porcupines, grouse, and prairie chickens.

Dwarfing all those animals in desirability was the buffalo—more accurately *bos bison americanus*, the smallest and only surviving member of many species of bison that had ranged throughout inland North America before the waning of the last Ice Age. Small the American bison may have been, relatively speaking, but measured at the shoulder, a mature bull stood taller than a man and weighed up to a ton. Cows weighed only half as much, but in general provided tastier and more tender meat. And there were other tidbits—livers, kidneys, tongues, brains, bone marrow, and the fatty lining of cleaned intestines. In addition to food, the buffalo provided leather for dozens of uses—tipis, robes for withstanding winter's cold, bedding, and containers (parfleches) for both dried food and personal goods. Tough bull hides were worked into shields, moccasin soles, and mittens. After sharp steel knives had been introduced by white traders, well-tanned rawhide could be cut into clothing, hobbles for horses, ropes, and saddle straps. Sinew was used for sewing, paunches for carrying water, horns for utensils of many kinds. Rib bones were turned into sled runners; skulls decorated festive gatherings. The tufted hair at the tip of a buffalo's tail was used as a fly brush (as the animal itself had once used it) and for decorations inside the tipi. When wood was unavailable, dried buffalo dung provided a hot, almost smokeless fuel.

The buffalo that the Nez Perces first hunted most likely were small herds that had wandered across the low, grassy passes of the Continental Divide into the northern part of the Great Basin, which bordered Nez Perce country on the south, and into valley glades along the eastern fringe of the Columbian Plateau. Before the advent of the horse, killing the animals had been chancy. A bison that was injured or bogged down in quicksand or winter snow could be dispatched with a stone-headed spear, but luck of that sort was rare. So was encountering herds that could be driven cautiously into extemporized and flimsy corrals. Sometimes the enclosures were made of nothing more than upended travois built to be pulled by dogs. Women and dogs concealed behind this "fence" leaped up with a clamor as the shaggy beasts entered the corral. Startled by the racket, the herd leaders bolted back against the followers. During the confusion, the men rushed in with spears and arrows to kill as many as possible before the animals broke through the thin line to safety. On other lucky occasions, hunters might come across a herd near the brink of a steep bluff. After carefully surrounding the ponderous creatures, they rushed yelling at them and drove them over the drop. Enough would be killed or injured by the plunge to make the hazardous effort worthwhile to a people who had spent much of their lives on the edges of starvation.[11]

The edge of starvation. The edge of terror. To endure such a world, the Stone-Age Indians of North America developed, long before the coming of the horse (which was their first inkling of a different way of life) the concept of a personal, infallible guardian spirit. If properly contacted, these spirits— the Nez Perces called them *wayakins* (wey-a-kin)—would bring to each communicant the essence of all the boons that together constitute a desirable life—safety, physical and spiritual strength, wealth, extra skill at hunting and fishing, and even invulnerability in battle.[12]

Where could these tutelary spirits be found? Like many other North American tribes, the Nimipus regarded their world—its grasses, trees, animals, clouds, and even transcendent human figures—as being animated by mystic powers. Somewhere in the almost endless pantheon was a special spirit that was tuned to each individual's needs. If that enigmatic guardian was especially strong, the person who united with it might become a shaman, or medicine man. He could then prophesy, influence the weather, govern tribal ceremonies, and often cure illness by removing from the patient, during elaborate ceremonies, the evil spirits that caused the malaise. He could also bring evil to others.[13]

Millennia of practice had formulated the method of the search. The first quest was undertaken when a boy or, somewhat less often, a girl, was between the ages of nine and twelve. Whatever the sex, each child had been thoroughly imbued by his or her parents with the importance of the effort. But the quest itself was solitary. Although the territory to be visited was no great distance from the band's village or temporary camp and had been used before, as shown by cairns and carefully arranged circles of stones, the mystic place was nevertheless spooky—in the deep shadows of an overhanging rock, beside an icy lake, or on top of a lonesome mountain.

The neophytes took no food and only a few sips of water with them, for it was well known that hunger hones the senses. After arriving at the chosen place, the individual added his own arrangement of stones to whatever was already there and sat down facing the point where the sun would rise. Shivering in the night's cold, he concentrated with desperate intensity on every sound and movement in the vicinity. The next day, still trying to prevent his mind from wandering, he kept shifting his body so he always faced the sun as it crossed the heavens to its place of setting. The vigil might last five days and nights. Not everyone hung on that long. Lightning storms, animal howls, mysterious night creakings, or imagined footsteps sent some scampering back to the village in fright. Others simply grew homesick.

Those who stayed eventually fell into a hallucinatory sleep. Although, on occasion, a true wayakin did not appear, it usually did. The fundamental nature of the visitor might reside in a yellow bird, a swift-running deer, waving grass, a strange anthropomorphic figure, or whatever. To speak understandably to the child, the wayakin might take on a human shape. It talked of taboos and revealed a secret song that gave power to the singer but would sound like a string of nonsense syllables to other humans. Often, too, the seeker was given a name he was not supposed to reveal until late in life and then only under certain conditions.

During the interview, the child carefully studied the vision for every clue about its identity so he could later wear or carry in his medicine bundle some talisman that would maintain his connection with the spirit. In cases of great need he could call on his wayakin for direct assistance. If no taboo intervened—he would be warned of such circumstances, often in dreams—he would receive the help he had prayed for. It should be noted, incidentally, that a seeker could go on more than one quest and acquire, possibly, additional tutelary spirits. It was this mystic bond between spirit and person that whites later called "medicine." From it came one's true individuality and strength.

Those who failed to find a wayakin might be given one by a relative. If that recourse did not work, the unfortunate seeker was doomed to an undistinguished career, perhaps even to poverty. There was no use lying about the results of one's vigil. Pretense was soon detected—parents sometimes visited the place of the quest to see if a specific object had been left there as proof of attendance—and the pretender was subjected to crushing scorn. Even worse, the wayakin who was lied about might retaliate fearsomely.

A successful neophyte said nothing about his search until he felt ready to participate, some years later, in his first *Wee'kwetset*, or guardian spirit dance. These dances were held only during winter inside large, mat-covered longhouses. They might be convened by a shaman or by some person who wished to honor his tutelary spirit. Essentially, the dances were the principal religious ceremonies of the early Nimipus.

Gift giving was featured at the dances, especially by the host. The guests dressed in their finery, and gorgeous it was—poncho-style shirts and dresses of soft sheep- or deerskin, belted or sashed and enlivened with bits of fur and magnificent yokes created out of beads, shells, quills, colored pebbles, and polished elk's teeth; leggings with fringed and colored seams; moccasins adorned with sunbursts of bead or quill work; earbobs of shells and necklaces of bear's, badger's, or eagle's claws; feather-tipped wands to wave during the dancing; fez-shaped hats of intricately patterned grass for the women; horns and animal heads that had been hollowed out into barbaric caps for the men—all emphasizing the beauty of sinuous glistening bodies decorated with paint made from minerals or clay mixed with fish oil or bear fat.

The days were filled with feasting, gossiping, and gambling. The dance came after sunset in smoky light from the fireplaces in the longhouse. The stamp of feet in time to the insistent rhythm of a drum was an echo of the pulse of each participant's heart-driven blood, and it created a powerful hypnosis. Here each initiate revealed, cryptically, the identity of his or her spirit. Regalias contained symbolic hints, as did the patterns of paint on face and body. On stepping into the line of dancers, the celebrants began bobbing, weaving, and jerking about in ways that were supposedly imitative of their spirit's natural motions. They sang the sacred songs they had been taught. Others picked up the motions and sounds and sang out the same mysterious syllables. As the intensity of the ritual increased, each dancer not only achieved his or her true identity, but welded it into the soul of the community, bringing to the band an exceptional cohesion.[14]

As soon as one band had finished its five-day Wee'kwetset, another began. Participants trooped from site to site, to reaffirm their existence as Nimipus, the Real People. During the interchanges, the participants learned their places in the local hierarchies. Rivalries between individuals often became rivalries between guardian spirits, for the spirits were the sources of power. Shamans were strong enough, it was believed, to put a dancer into a trance just by touching him or her, and by that means, and in other contests, establishing supremacy over other shamans. Gamblers who emerged winners from the incessant games of hand, which were played with marked bones, did so because their wayakins were superior to those of their opponents. Astonishing things happened at the ceremonies: transfigured dancers, we are assured, passed unharmed, like the fakirs of India, through fires burning at either end of the longhouse.[15] But they had to be careful not to abuse their power by engaging in selfish or unethical pursuits, for if they did so, they lost their wayakins.

Like most rituals, the Wee'kwetset was a handmaiden of tradition, designed to preserve the good things of life. And certainly Nez Perce life could be marvelous. Edward S. Curtis, who during the early years of the twentieth century devoted much of his energies to photographing and talking to Indians throughout North America—among those he interviewed was Chief Joseph in his old age—touched eloquently on the uplifting qualities of their existence:

As a [Nez Perce] man passed through the forest the moving trees whispered to him and his heart swelled with the song of the swaying trees. He looked through the green branches and saw white clouds drifting across the blue dome, and he felt the song of the clouds. Each bird twittering in the branches, each water-fowl among the reeds or on the surface of the lake, spoke its intelligible message to his heart; and as he looked into the sky and saw the high-flying birds of passage, he knew that their flight was made strong by the uplifted voices of ten thousand birds of the meadow, forest, and lake, and his heart, fairly in tune with all this, vibrated with the songs of its fullness.... The individual Nez Perce, with his interwoven devotional system communed with almost unlimited nature.[16]

But the sun did not always shine so beatifically. Catastrophe was always imminent, whether from a sudden enemy attack, a murderous bolt of lightning, or failing food supplies. Even innovations that at first seemed to promise good contained the seeds of destruction. This was particularly true of forces emanating from outside the Indian world—from Europeans who claimed to be the discoverers and hence the potential owners of the North American continent, although in actuality the only things that eventually made the land theirs were superior numbers and an overwhelming technology.

· 3 ·

THE FIRST INTRUSIONS

The first horses to reach the American West (they arrived by way of the Spanish ranchers of New Mexico) dazzled the spirits of the Indians who first saw them. Freedom! The animals' very appearance promised it. The horses were small, sleek, and swift. Their classic heads and slender ankles showed the bloodlines of their Arabian progenitors. To the foot-bound Pueblo Indians of the Rio Grande Valley, a Spaniard mounted on a horse flowed like the wind, defying gravity. To have one! Here and there unhappy Pueblos who had been cajoled or forced into working for the invaders ran away to join nearby bands of unsubdued natives, taking horses with them. Once those free tribes realized the animals' potentials, they joined the thieving. Other mounts escaped from the growing herds on the vast ranches, only to fall—some of them—into the hands of the yearning natives.[1]

Such wondrous possessions inevitably became profitable items of trade. The Utes, who were the first tribe on the western side of the Rockies to obtain appreciable numbers of mounts, bartered them to their relatives, the mountain Shoshonis of southeastern Idaho. As soon as the Shoshonis had built up a small surplus, they sought as customers their deadly enemies (except at trading fairs), the Cayuses and Nez Perces. The best guess about chronology suggests that the Nimipus had obtained a goodly number of horses by 1730.

The size of the Nez Perce herds ballooned fantastically, especially in the Wallowa country. Nutrient grasses abounded in the high meadows and on the

21

largely treeless hillsides of the lower country. Canyon bottoms provided shelter from winter storms and predators. The distribution of the animals was not even, however. Over the years a few families acquired hundreds. Others had only a few because, it was thought, of some inferiority attached to their wayakins. But everyone was affected, and nearly everyone learned at least the rudiments of horsemanship.

They taught their mounts to respond to a single bridle rein, one end of which was looped around the horse's lower jaw. They whittled saddles for women out of wood; these sex-oriented seats had high horns on both cantle and pommel so the riders could hang cradleboards and sacks filled with indispensable items on the fixtures. Men's saddles were mere pads stuffed with grass; stirrup leathers were sometimes attached. When they galloped off to hunt or make war, the men often rode bareback to reduce the weight the horses had to carry. On formal occasions horses were painted with bright stripes and splotches, and equipment was encrusted with feathers, quills, and rows of elk's teeth.

Bold Nimipus and equally adventurous members of allied tribes—the Cayuses to the southwest; the Flatheads to the east; the Coeur d'Alenes to the north; and even, in the early days, a few Shoshonis from the south—realized that large parties equipped with many saddle- and packhorses could travel long distances and kill many buffalo. Although a few of the shaggy beasts ranged the high valleys and sagebrush prairies just west of the Continental Divide, a more fruitful place to hunt was the northern plains around the headwaters of the Missouri and Yellowstone rivers. Soon a few parties, each made up of volunteers from several different bands, were venturing across the divide on trips that lasted from a few months to two or three years. Women and children often accompanied their husbands and fathers on these extended journeys. Other tribal members declined to go. Some were too poor. Some were afraid of the enemies they might meet far from home. Conservative elders dismissed the trendy new pursuit as foolish; a family would prosper more in the long run, they said grumpily, by sticking close to familiar fishing stations and root meadows.

Those who did go after the buffalo experienced moments of high exhilaration. Instead of depending on chance to bring him within reach of target, each hunter picked out one of the fattest animals in a bunch, raced his horse close to the fleeing target, and with a sinew-backed bow drove an arrow almost entirely through the massive beast just back of its churning forelegs.

Nor was there any need to be satisfied with one. A single hunter on a top steed could kill five or six buffalo before exhaustion slowed the horse down.

Women followed the trail of carnage with packhorses and skinned the warm carcasses, sometimes helped by the returning hunters. As the excitement subsided, the group ate its fill of raw liver, entrails, and freshly roasted meat from the tender hump that every buffalo carried just behind its shoulders. The feast over, the women built racks of wood on which to dry leftover strips of meat into jerky. They also scraped and tanned the heavy hides, producing a durable leather that could be used for clothing or could be turned into tipi covers to take the place of mats.

Occasionally, the hunters on the plains encountered walking food gatherers from other groups. Some were members of the Piegan, Siksika, or Kaniah tribes, confederated into a "nation" known as the Blackfeet. At some point after 1750 the united bands had began drifting out of the cold valley of the north Saskatchewan into what we now call Montana. Farther south were the Crows. Once the Crows had been part of the semisedentary Hidatsa group of North Dakota and had lived in dome-shaped earthen lodges beside the Missouri. When a quarrel split the tribe, the dissenting bands (the Absoroka, the Bird People, the Crows—all synonyms) migrated into the Yellowstone Valley.[2]

Until the Nimipus and their allies bought horses onto the Plains, the Blackfeet and the Crow had possessed nothing but wolfish dogs to help them hunt and carry their burdens. On glimpsing the tall, hard-hooved animals that did the bidding of the western Indians, the half-starved foot people burned with desire to own some. On spotting a gathering of horse Indians, they would make signs of peace and offer to trade. They were poor, however, and the contemptuous westerners demanded higher prices than most of the pleading customers could afford. Nor could the foot people count on building up big herds from small numbers of breeding stock as the Shoshonis, Cayuses, and Nez Perces had done. The northern Plains were too cold. Horses did not reproduce well, and the colts that were born often died in the blizzards. Their recourse was to steal what they wanted, sometimes even crossing the Continental Divide on their raids.

No stigma attached to the effort. To most Indians, successful brigandage was proof of quick intelligence and high courage—a prime way for a young man to prove his worth. The Nez Perces agreed with the evaluation and were as quick to steal horses as were any other group. But when the lost horses belonged to them, they wanted revenge. Without wasting time searching for the guilty parties, they struck at random and generally in stealth at whatever likely enemy they could track down.

For a time beating up the Piegans, who were the vanguard of the Blackfoot migration, brought joyful interludes to the hunting excursions of the western Indians. Another white man's invention changed that situation, however. Shortly after the middle of the eighteenth century, rival traders pressing into the Saskatchewan region from Montreal and Hudson Bay traded a few firearms to the Blackfeet. In spite of the brass tacks and the replica of a brass dragon that decorated their side plates, the weapons were so trashy that only people who had no guns would lust for them.[3] The guns were smoothbore muzzle loaders. Activated by flint, they discharged at each firing a one-ounce, sixty-caliber ball. Such a slug packed a respectable wallop, but generally missed its target at a range of fifty yards or so. The muskets, moreover, were next to useless on a buffalo hunt. If the first charge failed to fire or if it wounded without killing, as often happened, a second shot was necessary. This meant that a rider, traveling at breakneck speed, had to point the muzzle upward with one hand and with the other sprinkle in powder from a flask made of horn. He then dropped in the second ball, which he had been carrying in his mouth, capped the layers with a wad, and rammed the charge home—awkward on an excited horse. In the same time, a bowman could "throw"—that's the word that was used—a dozen arrows. Bows were easily repaired or replaced, which muskets weren't. Arrows were plentiful; powder wasn't. Accordingly, bows long remained the favorite weapon for hunting buffalo.

Guns were, nevertheless, psychologically overwhelming. They roared horribly, belched smoke and fire, stank acridly. A warrior could see an arrow coming and sometimes duck it. Not so a musket ball. A ball, moreover, could pierce a tough bull-hide shield, whereas a stone arrowhead frequently splintered. With a gun a man could stand up to a grizzly bear, and that was prestige. Wild talk said guns could even punch holes through mountains.

But how could the Columbian Indians get guns? The Blackfeet flatly refused to trade them. Determined to establish themselves on the high Plains, they would not yield to potential enemies any technological advantage that would weaken their hold. Nor was it possible to slip inside a Blackfoot tipi and steal a gun the way a horse tethered outside a lodge could be stolen by an adroit thief. Trying wasn't worthwhile, for the Blackfeet rejoiced in fights they had a good chance of winning. In short, they began harrying their one-time oppressors as they might have harried coyotes.

Sorely hurt by the developments, the Flatheads and Kutenais, small tribes that had once roamed the eastern fringes of the Rockies, retreated across the mountains to havens (they hoped) in wide valleys that drained northward into the Columbia River. The Shoshonis' refuge lay farther south along the upper Salmon River. Eager for horses, the Blackfeet followed, and at times life grew dismal in the extreme.

The more numerous and more distant Nez Perces adjusted to the shock. The Blackfeet, they discovered, had few guns—and less powder. So it was possible to ride in strength to the buffalo grounds on the long-term hunts that so entranced them and, at the risk of a few casualties, hold their own against the enemy. In fact, the Blackfeet helped: Much of what the Nimipus learned about organizing their hunts for greater efficiency came from imitating patterns that their enemy had developed.

The great social need was some way of holding their increasingly large parties together on the trail, during the hunt, and in times of conflict. The difficulty was that the people involved in the excursions came from several autonomous bands. In addition, the Nimipus were often joined in the Bitterroot and Clark Fork valleys of westernmost Montana, by groups of Flatheads. Each band of each nation had its own chief—and often its own council—and that chief could not direct members of another band without the members' explicit consent.

The solution was the formation of a supreme, if temporary, council made up of members of each participating group.[4] This council selected some respected individual to take charge of strategic procedures as soon as the traveling party's scouts discovered a nearby herd or enemy group. The person thus elected was the war chief, even though the party might be searching primarily for buffalo, not enemy Indians. Often his position was signaled by a garish headdress made of the skin taken from a wolf's skull and adorned with bears' claws and birds' feathers.

Another person was elected to oversee the column as it took to the trail or settled into a temporary camp. Delays, strayings, or separations of any sort could be disastrous. The camp chief was supposed to prevent such aberrations while maintaining harmony and morale. (It was as a camp chief, rather than as a war chief, that Young Joseph functioned during the 1877 flight of his and a few allied bands toward Canada.) A qualification should be noted: The new governmental arrangements were ad hoc affairs. As soon as an amalgamated party had returned to its home territory, its members rejoined the villages from which they had come, and the authority of the war and camp chiefs evaporated, to be replaced by traditional forms.

Striking visual changes in clothing also marked the evolving Plains culture. According to Nicholas Point, a Catholic missionary among the Flatheads of a later date, Indians were captivated by anything that fluttered. Feathers were particularly loved. The men tied them to the outer edges of their shields, to long pipe stems, to the shafts of lances. Young warriors wove feathers into their hair and into the manes and tails of their horses, which were kept long so they would stream in the wind. Warbonnets of eagle feathers that circled the head and sometimes reached down the back to the ground were highly prized. A Nez Perce would trade a horse, sometimes two horses, for a particularly ornate headpiece. (One of Chief Joseph's final requests when he was dying was to see his "eagle hat" for the last time.)[5] The seams of clothing were lined with fringe, which also fluttered, as did bright ribbons attached to a variety of articles—once white traders had made ribbons available. Color was equally emphasized. Faces and horses were garishly painted. (One theory holds that Indians, who are not red, were called "red" by early whites because of their penchant for painting their faces that color.) War shirts, women's shifts, and everyone's moccasins were garnished with porcupine quills, animals' teeth and claws, and, eventually, glass beads arranged in intricate patterns. Missionary Point sniffed at the display as vanity. Yet, he concluded, "It must be admitted ... that the costume of an Indian riding through camp at a full gallop is not without its charm."[6]

Tribal misgivings were intensified by yet another deadly Caucasian introduction, diseases against which the Indians had built up no resistance. At the time, the Nez Perces may not have had the least notion about the origins of the trouble, but they were certainly appalled by its results. In 1781–82 an epidemic of smallpox killed seventy-five percent of the Arikaras of North Dakota. Traders from other tribes who visited the gruesomely decimated villages carried the disease to the Blackfeet and Shoshonis. The Nez Perces, who presumably visited the Plains as usual during those deadly years, were scourged in their turn—and again in 1802 or thereabouts—by attacks that may have come up the Columbia from trading ships pausing at the river's populous mouth or even from southern tribes in contact with New Mexico.[7]

Tribal medicine men could not handle the new challenge. Many of them died, too. In desperation the afflicted turned to the balm of sweat houses, which had been soothing every tribe on the continent since time immemorial. Building patterns varied. Some bathhouses were subterranean chambers that were large enough to serve as dormitories for the young men of the town. Those at temporary camps were often little more than frames of bent willows covered with hide. Invariably the sweathouses stood close to running water. A few consisted of basins dug close enough to the low bank of a stream that a small flow could be diverted into them through a shallow ditch.[8]

Rocks heated in a nearby fire were transferred on forked sticks to a cavity just inside the house's entry, which could be closed with a door made of skin. (In the case of stream-side basins hot rocks were dumped directly into the water.) One member of a group inside a covered bath held a buffalo tail. He dipped its tufted end into a container of water and shook a shower on the rocks. Steam filled the chamber. After staying in the dense, humid air as long as possible, the bathers crawled outside and jumped into the adjacent stream.

The process satisfied many needs: pleasant socializing, physical relaxation after times of stress, purification of the soul before undertaking a major enterprise. A thorough steaming while a shaman chanted a magic song was deemed to charm into harmlessness the baleful spirits that caused disease. Probably the baths brought relief from ordinary ailments, but they proved deadly when weak, fever-stricken sufferers from smallpox or measles crawled to the river to dip themselves in the icy water. Watching the ghastly failure of a long-held folk belief increased the terror of the people.

If the sweat baths and the chants, howls, and contortions of a shaman blowing or sucking an offending object from the body of a sufferer did not bring freedom from pain and sickness, then what would? Had the whole world gone awry?

Fear, in short, had become the Indians' unrelenting companion. Later traders caught whiffs of the dread. As Alexander Ross, one of the first whites to be closely associated with the Nez Perces and their neighbors, said: "The Indians with all their independence are far from being a happy people. They live in a constant state of anxiety. Every hostile movement about the frontier excites alarm and sets the whole country on the qui vive." And Bernard DeVoto, in his introduction to *The Life and Adventures of James P. Beckwourth*, another mountain man, added: "His [the Indian's] world was full of daemonic spirits and of natural forces whose malevolence was no less dreadful. [Only] by sacrifice, propitiation, and prophylaxis was it possible to keep his world in equilibrium."[9]

Equilibrium ... some anthropologists believe that the Nez Perces responded to their mounting dreads by embracing messages of hope brought to them by prophets who, during periods of hypnotic trances, had seen visions of better days. The dead, the revelations declared, would return to life; the evil spirits that unleashed diseases would disappear. Mixed in with these optimistic promises were predictions of a new people who would bring marvelous implements to the Nimipus—implements that would put the Nez Perces on a plane with any tribe. All that was needed was for the Real People to purify themselves and then reaffirm their ancient culture and its faiths.

Who were the prophets? They may well have been wanderers from the eastern part of the continent. The last third of the eighteenth century had brought great stress to the native peoples there. First England's victories over France in the French and Indian Wars and then the American colonies' successful revolt against England had disturbed tribal relations everywhere between the Allegheny Mountains and the Mississippi River. Floods of white settlers had poured into the interior. Indian lands were absorbed; Indian villages were uprooted. Some of the displaced Indians took to roaming westward, toward tribes that still maintained some stability. They carried a prophecy of a race of pallid people ever pushing out of the land of the rising sun and bringing with them an array of magical coverings and tools made of new kinds of materials.

Whatever the source, the notion of a new race bearing new hopes seems to have sprung up among all the tribes of the Columbian Plateau. A ritual accompanied the message. It was a special dance—in effect a prayer—that was called the Prophet Dance because of its origin. It was performed outdoors. According to one description, the participants, grouped in a circle, moved seven times around a pole. Although they kept time to the demanding beat of drums, they did not contort their bodies but moved with a profound solemnity. They ended the dance with arms outstretched, palms upward. Or so it is said.[10]

There is an apparent contradiction here. Whites, unseen as yet by the Nimipus, were the genie whose horses and guns had produced the fatal disruptions. Yet the Indians attached no opprobrium to the articles themselves. Evil lay in the way the articles were handled by the enemy. In Nez Perce hands, ah ... that would be different. As for disease, the magical whites of whom the prophets spoke could probably cure it, too, just as rumor said they could return the dead to life. Which is to say that the Nimipus craved, as do all emergent peoples, the very powers they feared.

In September 1805, which, of course, is a Caucasian way of dating, it seemed that the predictions might be coming true. Seven strangers, riding half-starved horses, appeared out of the pine trees bordering a camas meadow called Weippe, located above the canyon-embraced village of Kamiah. They were white men, scouts for a large party that was still working its way through fresh snow on the Lolo Trail, which led westward from Flathead territory in the Bitterroot Valley. Hungry, the strangers asked by means of sign language for food, which they seemed able to pay for.[11]

Clearly they were a race apart. Some of the seven had startling amounts of hair on their faces. All wore odd-looking headpieces. They carried guns that were beautiful to behold, even though the weapons lacked the brass adornments of the firearms used by the Blackfeet. When the main party came up, more surprises appeared—a man who was black all over, a Shoshoni woman and her baby (what could be made of that?), and the biggest dog the Nez Perces had ever seen. Should such people be trusted?

Suspicious members of the root diggers advised that the whites should be killed before they caused harm. At that suggestion, an ancient crone named Watkeuweis spoke up. Many years before, she had been captured by Blackfeet and then passed along from one band to another, each time at a price, until she reached a trading post where she became the property of a kindly half blood, part Indian and part French Canadian. He and his white associates were good to her. Still, she yearned for home. Even though she was burdened with a child by then, she ran away. The flight stretched across hundreds of miles. The baby died. She disposed of it and stumbled on until an unidentified hunting party helped her reach her destination. Remembering the kind treatment she had received from the whites she had encountered during her captivity, she urged the Nimipus to do no harm to these newcomers.[12]

Others agreed, recalling the prophecies about helpful strangers they had heard during the Prophet Dance. Suppose the help included guns like the ones the strangers were carrying. Besides, gift giving and hospitality were more in line with the Nez Perce tradition than was violence. Accordingly, between September 20 and October 9, 1805, the Nimipus succored the hungry, storm-battered, straggling members of the Lewis and Clark expedition. They fed them dried salmon and cakes baked from flour pounded out of camas roots. (The unfamiliar food triggered intense indigestion in some of the men.) They assured the whites that it was possible to travel the rest of the way to the Pacific by water and gave them permission to cut down five trees from which they could hew dugout canoes. Thus aided, the explorers reached salt water just as a miserably rainy winter was setting in. Late the following spring they reached the Clearwater again, this time on their way home. They stayed five weeks with the Nez Perces, waiting for the unusually heavy snow in the Bitterroot mountains to melt.[13]

The only common language, possessed by only a few of the two ethnic groups, was sign talk. In addition, a Shoshoni woman prisoner of the Nez Perces was able to converse haltingly—she had almost forgotten her native tongue—with Sacagawea, the Shoshoni wife of the expedition's French Canadian guide. In spite of the handicaps, the two races exchanged an amazing amount of information. The way to harmony was smoothed by gifts and demonstrations of power. The Indians offered odds and ends of food and a few fresh native horses. The whites showed off their compasses, magnets, and spyglasses. They concocted a salve to relieve eyes inflamed by sun, bright water, alkali dust, and, probably, some cases of syphilis. The Nez Perces displayed their method of gelding obstreperous stallions, a skill that later brought them a wide reputation as the only Indians in America to breed their horses selectively. The young men of both colors indulged in foot races, and most of the whites, William Clark included, bedded with the willing Nez Perce girls. Historians are not sure about Meriwether Lewis's activities.

The two captains compiled Nez Perce vocabularies and asked endless questions about tribal lifestyles, territorial boundaries, populations, and relations with neighboring Indians. Some of the curiosity was purely scientific, some arose from the universal human itch to know how other people live, and some was commercial—a quest for the kind of information that might prove useful to American traders who one day would undoubtedly want to cross the mountains into unexploited regions.

Beyond the quest for information was another mission—one the Nez Perces could hardly have understood. This was the strengthening of America's claims of sovereignty over Oregon, which in those days was deemed to spread from the Rockies west to the Pacific, from Spanish California north to Russian Alaska. Spain had dim claims over the area, as had Russia. The principal contenders, however, were Great Britain and the United States. Except for certain rights of occupancy, the territorial imperatives of the Indians were ignored; they would be dealt with after the whites had their say.

British claims to Oregon were based, in large part, on Alexander Mackenzie's crossing of British Columbia to the sea in 1793. America's strongest claim was based on ship captain Robert Gray's discovery of the mouth of the Columbia River in 1792. Lewis and Clark's journey might become a second major item in the American arsenal if a confrontation between the two powers ever developed. In 1806, however, the vast region was so isolated and so little known that it was not worth the risk of contentious behavior. Yet even though the United States was not then willing to press for sovereignty, there was one nationalistic step the explorers could take. They could strive to create favorable impressions among the Nimipus toward the American nation (insofar as the Indians could understand the abstraction) and toward the American traders, as opposed to British traders who were also working westward at that time.

As they had done all the way up the Missouri River and then down the Columbia River and its tributaries, Lewis and Clark urged peace on the tribes they met, for feuding Indians were not good producers of fur. They announced that the United States would build a trading post beside the upper Missouri where the Nimipus could buy all manner of desirable items. When the Indians said they would be reluctant to go there for fear of the Blackfeet, the explorers promised to carry their plea for peace to that pugnacious tribe. (Actually, the post was never built.)

The captains implicitly downgraded the British by extolling their own government. They gave the leading Nez Perce chiefs they met American flags and silver medals bearing a likeness of President Jefferson, who they said was the Great Father of all American Indians. They proposed that the Nez Perces send a delegation to Washington to meet Jefferson and see for themselves how numerous the Americans were and what great power they possessed. The Nez Perces said no to that; the distance was too great and hence dangerous.

More important than the proposals was the way in which the explorers presented them. The men of the expedition were friendly and sincere. They genuinely liked the Nez Perces, and those of the tribe they contacted responded in kind, vowing they would always be friends of the whites.

The captains' greatest success in personal relations—far greater than they had any way of foreseeing—was with a relatively minor chief called Walammottin because of the way he bunched up his hair above his forehead. The Americans called him Twisted Hair. During their outward trip, Twisted Hair drew, on white elk skin, a rough map of the river system from the Clearwater to the Pacific. Then he and another Nez Perce accompanied the explorers down the Columbia River as far as the roaring Dalles as guides and peacemakers with Indians who were fishing here and there along the river banks. Twisted Hair cared for their horses and horse equipment during a part of the winter. They saw him frequently when they paused in Nez Perce country on their homeward-bound trip in the spring of 1806. They occasionally slept in his lodge and exchanged food with him. As pay for his services, they gave him two guns, ammunition, and powder—princely items, for at that time the entire tribe had only the six guns that specially delegated emissaries had finally obtained during the preceding winter from the Hidatsas or perhaps the Crow Indians.[14]

The association made a profound impression on one of Twisted Hair's sons, who was nine or ten years old at the time. Later the son's Indian name would be recorded as Hallalhotsoot, which translated as "the Bat That Flies in the Daytime." Presumably the image derived from visions the lad received during his quest for a guardian spirit—his wayakin. Hallalhotsoot's mother was of the Flathead tribe, and he grew up speaking both her language and his father's. In time whites who knew him took to calling him the Lawyer because of his sharp wits and skills in argumentation. He would always be a strong advocate of accommodating encroaching Americans, whom he associated with Lewis and Clark.[15]

Eventually, the stance would lead him into confrontations with an equally resolute father-and-son pair, Tuekakas and Hin-mah-too-yah-lat-kekht, known to whites as Old Joseph and Young Joseph. At the time of Lewis and Clark's stay among the Nez Perces, Old Joseph was about ten years older than the Lawyer. Because of the isolation of his homeland in the Wallowa Country, Tuekakas probably did not see the explorers. But he certainly heard of them; news of such strangers was too epochal not to spread throughout the Columbian Plateau.

What Tuekakas thought of the intrusion we have no way of knowing. Probably the reputations the explorers had created among those of the Nimipus who did see them impressed him as well as the Lawyer. For a time, at least, he, too, would try accommodation with the Americans. But as pressures increased, both he and the Lawyer would have to reassess their stands and decide whether compliance or resistance best suited their goals of freedom for themselves and for their followers.

4

RIVALRIES AND SEDUCTIONS

Other bands of whites came within rumor distance of the Nez Perces during the five and a half years that elapsed after the departure of Lewis and Clark in June 1806. A few bold, far-ranging Nimipus, some traveling north and some east, made contact with those pioneering white strangers and returned to hold aloft, as evidence of their daring, the metallic wonders they had obtained—even a gun or two. But no interlopers entered Nez Perce territory—or at least no stories about them found a way into tribal lore. So a great buzz of excitement arose one day in December 1811, when a new group of pale-faced men came walking painfully out of the forested mountains to the south. The men were following an old Indian trail beside the Mulpah River, or, as later traders called it, the Little Salmon, which flows into the main Salmon near the modern hamlet of Riggins, Idaho.[1]

There were eleven of them. Each was armed; each carried a pack on his back. They were gaunt, weary, and, to judge from the way they licked their lips as they looked around, very hungry. They were held in check by two leaders. One was thin faced, wiry, and nervous; he seemed to be about forty years old. The other was hardly thirty, if that, and probably the fattest man the Nimipus would ever see, even though he was so starved at the moment that some of his skin sagged in wrinkles. As Indians will, the villagers asked the names of those two important ones and then repeated the syllables until they could roll off the strange sounds with fair proficiency. The thin-faced one was

Robert McClellan. The big bear of a man was Donald McKenzie. A third bustling young man named John Reed seemed to occupy a place of responsibility somewhere between the leaders and the rest of the men.

People poured out of the mat-covered longhouses. There was a whirl of talk and gesticulation. The Indians wanted to know where the whites came from and what they had to trade. Were they the merchants Lewis and Clark had promised would come? On their part, the whites asked for food, horses, if possible, and directions about how to reach the mouth of a great river they called the Columbia. No, they weren't the government traders Lewis and Clark had spoken of. But the friends they hoped to meet at the mouth of the river—friends who had traveled across the ocean in big canoes driven by wind caught up in cloudlike sails—those friends would send trade goods to the Nez Perces if the Indians worked hard at producing beaver, muskrat, and bear skins to use in exchange. And it was good to have Lewis and Clark as a reference point, for clearly the explorers had impressed the Nimipus. So the newcomers said they were Americans, too.

Mercurial parties of Indians escorted them on down the main Salmon, a busy river winding between high, grassy, wrinkled hills topped with dark timber. At that time of year the weather was probably wet and cold, but there was relief in the smoky mat lodges, located wherever side streams twined into the narrow valley, creating pockets between the hills. Hospitably, the inhabitants in each village drew on their stores of dried fish and dried roots to make appropriate gifts to the visitors. But eleven half-starved men can be ravenous, and with winter coming on the Nimipus may have held back, as during Lewis and Clark's first visit—"very Selfish and Stingey," William Clark had written in his journal in October 1805, thinking of his situation and not theirs.[2]

The newcomers also wanted enough horses to carry their packs, whatever provisions they gathered up, and such men as were beginning to give out. More they could not afford; there were not that many trinkets in their baggage. So there was lots of dickering as they moved along the Salmon toward the point where it begins a big fishhook curve that soon dumps it into the Snake. Settlers later built a tiny town at the start of that curve and called it White Bird after the chief who would be one of Young Joseph's doughtiest supporters during the outbreak of 1877.

At the Indian village that preceded White Bird, a skein of trails branched out toward both the Snake and the lower reaches of the Clearwater. Which river the whites chose to strike for we do not know. A pity. For if they picked the Snake, Tuekakas (Old Joseph), who was about twenty-seven years old at the time, may have met them; the bands of which his mother's second husband had been chief frequently wintered in those sheltered places.[3] In any event, at some unidentified village beside one or another of the rivers—the lower sections of either stream could be navigated—the strangers found a pair of shovel-nosed dugouts they could obtain in trade for their still-new horses.[4]

The white man the Indians probably turned to most often during their conversations was Robert McClellan. McClellan had learned sign language during several years of trading on the central Plains, and buffalo hunters in the Nez Perce villages had mastered many of the same symbols. Also, McClellan improved his discourses through many retellings to many curious groups. Some of the concepts he passed on surely exceeded the grasp of his listeners, just as some of their notions were strange to the whites. (*But isn't destiny the working out of ideas and systems that once seemed incomprehensible?*) Unfortunately, neither side left a summary of the encounters; all we can do is try to imagine, on the basis of our own versions of history, the motes of information that passed back and forth between the races as they groped toward an understanding of the unprecedented events that were beginning to unfold in the once-static Northwest.

The eleven whites who reached Nez Perce country (McClellan could have explained) were members of a sixty-five-person party that John Jacob Astor, a rich chief of the New York City band of Americans, had ordered to cross the continent to the mouth of the Columbia River.[5] There, as McClellan had already said, they were to join another party that had been dispatched by ship to the same destination. Their joint goal was to build trading houses, to be collectively called, Astoria. Merchandise that Indians favored—merchandise gathered from places farther from the Snake River than the Nimipus could even imagine—would be sent there for distribution throughout the Columbia River Basin. At trading posts whose locations were still to be determined, these goods could be exchanged for the beaver, muskrat, and bear hides that the whites were urging the Indians to produce. With guns and iron arrow points that did not splinter—as stone arrows often did on striking a deer's shoulder bone or an enemy's tough, dry buffalo-hide shield—Nimipu men could hunt and fight better than ever before. With sharp steel awls, metal knives, and copper pots, Nimipu women could sew and prepare food with greater ease. With colored beads, ribbons, and vermilion paint, everyone would be handsome at the dances.

The overland party had planned to follow the Lewis and Clark trail through Nez Perce land to the Columbia. As they were toiling up the Missouri in keelboats, however, they met trappers who had preceded them to the river's headwater streams. Blackfeet struck at them—no Nez Perce needed to be told of the Blackfeet's ferocity. After hearing the tales, the chief men of the overland party decided to buy horses and outflank the Blackfeet by finding a new trail across the mountains farther south. The long ride turned into agony. On finally reaching one of the upper tributaries of the Snake—how clear and gentle its water had looked!—they joyfully quit their horses in favor of hewing, out of cottonwood logs, a dozen or so dugouts.

After rushing them south, the current bent west into gray lava canyons resounding with the crash of impassable waterfalls. One man drowned, and others almost did; dugouts split open. Admitting finally that only foot travel was possible, the leaders cached the goods they could not carry in nine onion-shaped holes and then split the oversized unit into smaller parties that might have better chances of finding game and buying food from the Shoshonis of the region. Most of the wanderers managed to cross to the Snake's left bank and strike uncertainly off toward the northwest. McKenzie, McClellan, and their capable clerk, John Reed, however, had clung as close to the right bank as the rugged topography allowed. The trip was unalloyed wretchedness, but they had made it through and, thanks to their red friends, were ready to finish their journey.

The whites asked questions, too. Did anyone in the villages have the least information about the Americans who had gone northwest from the left bank of the Snake? Brown heads wagged negatively. The McKenzie-McClellan group, it developed later, had traveled faster than had the other party.

Well, then, what about the trading houses that were presumably being built at the mouth of the river? Chinooks who lived in the area might have traveled upstream to the great Indian fair at The Dalles, bringing exciting gossip about the shipborne whites with them. And Nimipus who visited the same fair could have carried the talk back home. (There was time enough for the news to arrive. The Astorian ship, the *Tonquin*, which had sailed from New York City on September 8, 1810, had landed in the Columbia's estuary on March 22, 1811, after losing eight men while searching for a way through the formidable bar at the river's mouth. A story like that might spread fast, but there is no record of it reaching Nez Perce country.)

The probability that Astoria already stood at the river's mouth raised questions about Canadian trading houses at its source. In telling the Indians about the incursions of the traders, McClellan probably did not reveal every-thing he knew, not because he was being secretive, but because the story involved matters that were utterly beyond the Nez Perces' experience. There weren't even gestures for some of the ideas involved—ideas emanating mostly from fat Donald McKenzie. Before joining Astor's Pacific Fur Company in hope of better prospects, McKenzie had been employed by the rough-and-tumble, highly competitive North West Company of Montreal. He probably knew David Thompson, the company's famed geographer, and certainly knew that in 1807 Thompson, a partner in the company, had crossed the Conti-nental Divide into what is now British Columbia. From that starting place Thompson and his massive, red-bearded clerk, Finan McDonald, had worked down into northern Idaho and northwestern Montana.

The Nimipus grasped that much. Kept informed by the Indian grapevine, a few of them had ridden north to trade with the Canadians. Elated by the acquisition of a gun or two, they had joined, in the summer of 1810, a war party of mountain Indians that tackled a comparable group of Blackfeet somewhere beside the Clark Fork River in northwestern Montana. McDon-ald and a hard-twisted French Canadian, Michel Bourdon, both of whom many Nimipus would meet later, joined the battle. A victory: the first victory of mountain Indians over Blackfeet, Thompson declared on hearing of the event.[6] The event was less than a year and a half old when the McKenzie-McClellan group reached Nez Perce country. They may have heard boasting about it around the Indian camp fires.

But where was David Thompson trading as 1811 drew to a close? The point was important to Astor's field partners. The New Yorker, who dealt fre-quently with North West Company officials in Montreal, also knew of the new Canadian posts on the upper Columbia. Hoping to blunt their opposi-tion, he suggested the Nor'Westers (as they were called) buy, for fifty thou-sand dollars, a one-third interest in Astor's Pacific Fur Company. His poten-tial trading enemies squirmed angrily. Fifty thousand! They had as much right as he had on the Columbia.

Yes, but Astor had a lever, and he applied it with gusto. In 1809 England and the United States were on the outs again. As part of its cold war strategy, the American government imposed an embargo on all British imports. Although North West Company traders were not a prime target, the law hurt them sorely. Whereupon Astor led them to believe that as an American he could bring into the country, through a subsidiary firm he would set up, the merchandise that would keep them economically alive. All he wanted in exchange was for them to buy deeply enough into the Pacific Fur Company so that competition in the West would be foolish.

The proposal, which amounted to commercial blackmail, rested on shaky ground. The American embargo was as unpopular in New England as it was among the foreign fur traders. An acrimonious debate to repeal the interdiction was under way in Congress when Astor's overlanders started up the Missouri on their journey to the Pacific. What had been the outcome of the congressional arguments? If the embargo was repealed, the Canadians would have no need of Astor. In short, was Thompson a competitor or a friend of the Americans?

Hoping to pick up some crumb of information, McClellan asked if his listeners knew of any white men who had reached the place where the Snake flowed into the Columbia. At that, brown heads might well have nodded vigorously. Several moons ago, just after *hillal*, which meant the time when dense schools of salmon were pushing up the rivers to spawn and the related Shahaptian-speaking tribes were flocking to the banks to fish, a single boatload of whites, floating downstream, had paused in the northeastern triangle formed by the junction of the rivers. Disembarking, they raised a driftwood pole. Fastened to it was a bright object as flexible as a leaf. There was no Nimipu word for cloth at the time, only a comparison. The wavering thing resembled the special gifts Lewis and Clark had given Broken Arm, Twisted Hair, and other special Nez Perce chiefs. Flags! But as McClellan's interlocutors described it, the colors and design were different. A British emblem! That clinched matters. The Nor'Westers would be competitors, not partners.[7]

An itch to hurry seized the Americans—*Soyappo*, the Nez Perces learned to call their race, meaning the "long knives." As the Americans crowded into their two new dugout canoes, they called back that they would soon return with fine merchandise—better merchandise than the British could offer. Let the Nimipus catch many beavers, and they would all rejoice.

Fat Donald McKenzie (he weighed, in normal times, more than three hundred pounds) would learn later that in addition to a flag, the pole carried a paper on which was written, "Know hereby that this country is claimed by Great Britain, and that the N.W. Company of Merchants from Canada ... do hereby intend to erect a Factory for the commerce of the country around. D. Thompson."

Seizing land by proclamation was a ritual the original inhabitants of the New World could not understand. In their view people did not own territory.

You lived on it the way other creatures did. You would fight to protect that living, as the Nimipus fought Shoshoni raiders, but you did not have the power to alienate the land itself any more than you could alienate nature's recurrent rhythms of life—pulse beats, menstrual cycles, sunrise, and sunset. Snow melting, rivers swelling, salmon running. Camas fields flowering as blue as mountain lakes. Larch needles turning golden in the fall. Everything was bonded to everything else.

Each year the councils of the many bands decided afresh how to do what had always been done—overseeing the ceremonies that welcomed the first fish, telling the crier to announce the village's departure for the root-digging meadows, socializing in the sweat baths, planning buffalo hunts, dancing the Wee'kwetset on long winter nights. No one expected or wanted major changes. Life was a sacred hoop. No beginning—no end—at least none the Indians could perceive even when the first flagpoles were raised across the continent: "Know hereby...."

What rights had the whites to do that? Chief Joseph would ask again and again, as did other patriot chiefs.

The whites explained. Each imperial nation owned its share of the continent, in respect to other nations, by dint of discovery, making settlements, or by negotiating with or conquering its rivals. These absorptive whites did recognize that the Indians, who had been there first, had right of occupancy. When ending these rights became desirable, they did it by treaties or purchase, by persuading the inhabitants to move somewhere else, or by defeating them in war. The process was facilitated by regarding the different tribes as nations unified, as white nations were, under an overarching government. The Indians did not understand that social theory either because that wasn't the way they lived. The whites, though, seemed to think that If an Indian could learn to use such products of technology as guns and woven cloth, he could also learn to conduct his political affairs as the whites did.

A symbiotic alliance developed between pioneer fur men and the expanding white nations. When wars broke out between national claimants, Indians could be useful allies. When the daughters of chiefs or of renowned warriors married wilderness traders, they glued their people just a little bit tighter to an encroaching system none of them comprehended. And once the system had been established, the traders could fall back on the authority of government in dealing with their own fractious men—or with any questioning Indians who became fractious.

"Know hereby." The process was so simple. You entered the Indian country, spread out your goods for inspection, and waited for the native people to swarm in with the furs their hunting had produced—especially beaver, from whose dense underfur stylish top hats were made. Your offerings raised the Indians' standards of living. For wasn't iron always better than stone, even if it seduced, even if it diminished freedom by creating dependence?

During the preliminaries few of the enthralled tribes did much resisting. The Nez Perces would prove to be an exception. McKenzie, of course, could not know that they would. As the two dugouts were bobbing out into the current, he called that the Americans would soon be back.

"Know hereby...."

The Nimipus who lived in or near the big hollow where the Clearwater and Snake rivers come together (Lewiston, Idaho, and Clarkston, Washington, thrive there today) welcomed McKenzie and a party of traders once more in August 1812. John Reed and a newly arrived clerk, Alfred Seton, were with the group. Robert McClellan was not, having decided, in a pique, to return to the United States with messengers carrying mail overland to Astor.

McKenzie's rest had fleshed him out and turned him jovial. Using awkward hand talk, supplemented probably by John Reed's gestures, he elaborated on the strength of the post at the mouth of the river, hoping to impress his listeners, for with Indians the trappings of power counted. Nearly all the overlanders had reached Astoria, and as far as numbers went, the settlement was on a sound footing. It was well supplied, too.

Although one ship, the *Tonquin*, had been lost, a second, aptly named *Beaver*, had arrived in May, bringing additional men and sparkling fresh merchandise. Thus reinforced, sixty armed Americans had moved up the Columbia in oared boats to hurl a direct challenge at Thompson's inland posts. McKenzie's unit had been assigned to the Nez Perces living near the lower Snake. On reaching that river, his unit had turned up it in company with grandiose John Clarke, one of the new arrivals on the *Beaver*. The two groups stayed together as far as the Palouse River, which ran through the homeland of the Palouse Indians, a subtribe of the Nez Perces. From the Palouses Clarke bought horses for his people to ride north to the Spokane River, where they would build a post cheek-by-jowl with the Nor'Westers' Spokan House, as the name was spelled. Many of the Nimipus in McKenzie's audience nodded at that. Spokan House was only 125 miles or so from the Clearwater; several of them had ridden there from time to time to investigate trading possibilities. No more need of that, McKenzie told them and spread out his wares. Look at what he had available. The chiefs sat around the display in a semicircle; the lesser people stood behind them. They smoked and talked ceremoniously. All went well until McKenzie priced the items in skins—so many beaver for a gun, so many for a kettle, so many for a paper of beads.

The Indians demurred. Beaver were few in their rough country and hard to hunt with bow and arrow.

Learn to trap, McKenzie urged and showed them one of the heavy devices he had brought along. Traps were more productive and didn't punch holes in the pelts the way arrows or bullets did.

How did they work?

He explained.

A noise of rejection rippled through the listeners. That was the kind of work women and slaves did. Besides, they didn't have time; providing substance for their families and protection for their herds of horses was hard enough at best. If they wanted luxuries, they could get them from American posts they visited when they crossed the Continental Divide into the land of the Blackfeet to hunt buffalo. There was no glory in trapping as there was in slaying Blackfeet or running a frenzied bison bull to the ground after a slambang chase on a good horse. Or they could go up to Spokan House and trade horses for what they needed. No, they were not interested in trapping—especially not when a single iron trap cost six beaver skins. What kind of investment was that?[8]

The Indians meant what they said. A few brought in pelts that were acquired through ordinary hunting, but they did not trap. Beaver, moreover, were not numerous in the nearby streams, as McKenzie confirmed when he sent his own men out to show what could be done. While he was seething with frustration, John Reed returned from a thirty-five-day round-trip to the south to retrieve the goods the overlanders had cached when abandoning the turbulent Snake River in favor of foot travel. He'd found that six of the nine caches beside the river had been rifled. But he came across the handful of men who had dropped out of the party to trap and brought them along with him. From them, from Shoshoni Indians he encountered, and from his own eyes he learned that southern Idaho was crammed with rich beaver streams. Perhaps McKenzie should shift camp from the Clearwater to those more lucrative areas.[9]

Leaving an assigned location was not a decision McKenzie wanted to make on his own. Accordingly, he rode north to Spokan House with an Indian guide and a handful of men to consult with his partner John Clarke. He returned shortly, even more agitated than when he had left. His guide probably filled in the details for the Nimipu as well as he could. The party had scarcely reached Spokan House when two canoe loads of Nor'Westers—King George's men, the Indians had taken to calling them—had paddled up to the neighboring North West Company post. Grinning broadly, their leaders told McKenzie and Clarke, both of whom they had known during the two Astorians' early days with the Canadian company, that the Soyappos and the King George's men were at war with each other.

A strange war. The opponents at Spokan House made no attempt to kill each other. But there might be fighting at the mouth of the Columbia when a ship filled with big guns and many warriors arrived from across the ocean, as the Nor'Westers said it was scheduled to do. England was far away, however, and there might be time to warn the people at Astoria. In great excitement, McKenzie hurried back to the Clearwater. Under cover of darkness he dug holes into which he put his unsold merchandise. After covering the openings of the holes with timber and earth, he had his men drag branches across the raw spots, hoping the Indians would not notice the disturbance. That done, the entire group of whites vanished downstream into the teeth of one of the Northwest's notorious winter storms.

To the neighborhood Nez Perces, it looked as if the Americans were running away. So, on spotting the ill-concealed caches, they pilfered them. In their view, enriching yourself with someone else's possessions was smart—unless you got caught. In this instance they were caught. McKenzie cáme back a few weeks later with a rough-looking crew to retrieve his goods and his handful of furs and to take them to Astoria. All the Americans in the interior were going to assemble there with the fruits of their trading and wait to see what happened. If Astor sent in a supply ship (he might have difficulty getting one through the English blockade), they might try to hang on. If no friendly ship appeared by July 1, 1813, they would load everything on packhorses and try to reach the east by traveling overland.

Finding his caches empty, the bulky trader summoned the chiefs of the nearest village to his camp and demanded the return of his property. The chiefs made a standard reply. Possibly a few undisciplined young men had foolishly lifted an article or two, but for themselves, they knew nothing about the matter.

Furious, McKenzie ordered his hunters to stand on watch with cocked guns while John Reed and he began tearing the nearby lodges apart in a grim, knife-slashing search for the lost articles. Angry and dismayed, yet unwilling to fight because of the wailing women and children in the camp, the Nimipus capitulated.

Most of his goods retrieved, McKenzie turned jovial again, even passing out a few small gifts to the chiefs. Let bygones be bygones. He wanted to buy horses. Lots of horses that he could pick up quickly in some nearby place if they were needed for the cross-continental trek.

The Indians may not have divined the use to which the horses would be put, but they did sense the animals importance to the Soyappos, and it looked to them like a good way to find redress for their humiliation. They refused to sell McKenzie a single animal at any price.

The trader's response astounded them. His men took to stalking horses in the hills, shooting the fattest, and placing beside each carcass a bundle that contained what they thought was a fair price in merchandise. When the infuriated Nimipus prepared to attack the white's camp, they were outwitted. To stop the devastating slaughter, they at last agreed to sell the trader what he wanted at prices both sides agreed were reasonable.

With sour relief they watched the oppressors depart. No more whites for them—an opinion that soon received explosive justification from their relatives who lived at the mouth of the Palouse River. When John Clarke's party paused there to pick up the boats they had left with the Palouse Indians for safekeeping, a young man stole one of the trader's fancy goblets. Aided by the band's chiefs, Clarke recovered the silver cup, but because he had roared in his anger that he would hang the thief if the villain was caught, he felt he had to carry out the threat or lose so much face that all whites would suffer. The Palouses watched the execution in stark disbelief. Outrage swept from their camps throughout the interior. Their friends and relatives took to attacking parties of whites—any whites—that traveled along the Columbia. Far away in southern Idaho, John Reed and a small party of hunters were massacred in retribution, rumor said, for what the Indians of the interior regarded not as punishment but as murder.[10]

Meanwhile the war between the whites—the Americans called it the War of 1812—continued to baffle the Nez Perces, insofar as they heard of it at all. A British gunboat did arrive at Astoria, but again there was no battle, no shooting. Instead the people at the river-mouth post sold, in the fall of 1813, the entire operation to King George's men. Every trading house in the Northwest, all the merchandise, all the furs, passed into Canadian hands. Some of Astor's onetime employees went to work for the Nor'Westers. Some, including Donald McKenzie, went back across the mountains to Lake Superior and then on to Montreal with what developed into the company's annual boat-and-horse transport system to and from the Pacific coast. From Montreal McKenzie traveled to New York to apprise Astor of the disastrous ending of his monumental project.

British flags meanwhile rose above all the trading houses the Astorians had built. No banner was unfurled in Nez Perce territory, however. With reason. The Canadian purchaser had gone over the ledgers at Astoria with care, paying particular attention to entries, dated June 1, 1813, that listed the number of furs the American partners had brought to Astoria prior to the sale. The statistics were startling. Okanagon, which with its satellite houses covered the upper Columbia region as far north as today's British Columbia, had turned in 3,529 beaver pelts, 3,912 muskrat pelts, 147 land-otter pelts, and 42 pelts of other species. John Clarke's Spokan district, which extended into the Flathead country of northwestern Montana, delivered 1,288 beaver pelts, 7,969 muskrat pelts, 175 mink pelts, and 180 pelts of other species. By comparison, McKenzie's returns from the junction of the Clearwater with the Snake were 160 beaver pelts, 5 muskrat pelts, 4 land-otter pelts, and 4 pelts of other species.[11]

Chilled by the figures, the Nor'Westers turned their backs on the area. No one examined whether the abysmal showing was the result of the Nimipus' refusal to trap, the lack of beaver in the plunging mountain streams, or McKenzie's ineptness. Instead, the new masters of the trading posts stayed with what they had and let each day take care of itself. A strange inertia beset them. They felt exiled, cut off from the history-making events east of the mountains—first, the war between the United States and Great Britain and, second, the accelerating clash between the North West and Hudson's Bay companies for control of the land west of the northern Rockies. As compensation for their boring remoteness, the Columbian people adopted the trappings so often associated with British colonialism—dress clothes at dinner, imported niceties for their palates, and a stern social hierarchy that put every man in a place decreed for him by his education and family connections. They also created familiar pleasures for themselves. Those at Spokan House built a racecourse for their horses and a ballroom where local Indian belles learned, without difficulty, the lively steps the Scots and Britons at the post taught them.[12]

Because the masters at Spokan House did no more work than was necessary, neither did the hangers-on. Most were freemen, as they were called, and had worked for the company east of the mountains. Unwilling to return to the settlements when their contracts expired, they drifted to the Columbia with their Indian families and pitched their lodges close to Spokan House. They found occasional work at the post in transporting goods and furs to and from its satellite houses. Because of the fear of the Blackfeet in the Clark Fork region, they traveled in large groups. The show of strength flattered the egos of the masters of the post, but was expensive. Whether the freeman worked or not, they had to be fed. The easiest food was horse meat. Many of those doomed animals were driven north from the Wallowa country, where Tuekakas was by then spending most of his time.

Thus the Nimipus were slowly seduced despite their aloofness toward trapping. The tools they obtained for their horses performed familiar functions far more easily and efficiently then did their traditional artifacts. Metal knives and hatchets cut more quickly than did sharp-edged stones; awls pierced more precisely than did splinters of bone; wool and beads were easier to fashion into attractive clothing than were buckskin and porcupine quills.

A deep-seated uneasiness grew in the Indians. Why couldn't they make such articles? Did the whites have contact with superior wayakins? If so, could the Nimipus learn the magic? If not, then what did the future hold for the tribe? The questions bred tension and led the more conservative members of the bands to listen still more carefully to the sayings their prophets had been uttering ever since the days of widespread disease and intensified warfare.

· 5 ·

MINGLINGS

During the crushing summer heat of 1818, a messenger intercepted a large war party of Cayuse, Wallawalla, and Nez Perce Indians as they were threading a way down the rough, timbered flanks of Oregon's Blue Mountains toward the Walla Walla Valley. Trouble ahead. Many strangers, led by white traders of the North West Company, had just come up the Columbia River in large bateaux. They had disembarked on the barren left (east) bank of the main river a short distance above the mouth of the Walla Walla River. There they had unloaded mountains of equipment for building a post. The Indian fishing camps nearby seethed with uncertainty. What did the principal chiefs of the war party think could be or should be done about the situation?[1]

The question—and the situation—excited the warriors. They had just completed a successful foray into the lands of their inveterate enemies, the Shoshonis, or, as the neighboring tribes and early-day whites called them, the Snakes. They had killed enough hostile Shoshonis to cause great weeping in their villages. They had captured fine horses and had seized several men, women, and children as prisoners. It would be good to be welcomed as heroes by the encampment at the Walla Walla River, to let the women hold their fiercely triumphant celebrations over the captives—and to show the whites how strong the Indians were before they sat down together in council.

The area around the mouth of the Walla Walla was a cheerless expanse of wind-swept, sun-smitten, sandy flats stretching toward basalt cliffs crowned by two monumental columns of rock. The attraction of the region was the salmon in the glittering river. Fishermen were out with long seines made of hemp. Women worked around the temporary huts. Ignoring the dreadful odors and swarms of flies, those without pressing duties helped gut the fish and put the fillets to dry on racks made out of driftwood. Numerous horses, watched by sleepy boys, were scattered about, grazing on such patches of dry brown grass as they could find.

Most of the Indians were Wallawallas and Cayuses, with only a sprinkling of Nez Perces. The whites, however, labeled all as Nez Perces. The related tribes spoke similar Shahaptian dialects, intermarried readily, held similar ceremonies, and fought the same enemies. But the Nimipus, who lived the farthest to the east, were the most numerous and influential. So why split hairs, the whites said in effect, and named their post-to-be Fort Nez Perce, although the Cayuses were the most prominent group in that particular locality.

To the surprise of some of the Nimipus, the leader of the incoming whites was Donald McKenzie—but a much-changed McKenzie from the one who, four years before, had trashed their longhouses while searching for stolen goods near the junction of the Snake and Clearwater rivers and afterwards had shot the horses they refused to sell him. This time he was jovial and conciliatory, even playing a little, when he had a chance, with the black-haired children who flocked around his camp.

During his absence from the Columbian region, it will be remembered, he had gone to New York via Montreal in 1814 to justify to Astor the sale of the Pacific Fur Company. He had hoped he might get another job from the New Yorker, but had been sent packing instead. Back in Montreal, he was hired by the North West Company to go west again and reinvigorate the moribund trade of the Columbian interior.[2] He reached Fort George, as Astoria was known to the Canadians, in October 1816. The people there resented his sudden ascension, his cutting back on their perquisites, and his radical new ideas about increasing fur production by opening up the untouched— and dangerous—Snake Indian country, some of whose resources he had seen during his miserable overland trek in 1811. Because of their ill-natured lack of cooperation, he was not able to begin full-scale preparations for his shake-up of the interior until 1818.

Half a dozen years earlier he would have made trading posts the centers of his campaign. Experiences since then had taught him better. Except when they were hungry for tobacco, beads, or firearms, the western Indians simply would not or could not trap. Even if he prevailed on some of the many bands of Snakes to try, the effort might eat up more than the three years' time still remaining on his contract. To make a showing that would impress the people in Montreal, he would have to hire experienced whites—lots of them—so they could pepper big stretches of water with their traps and still be safe from attacks by opportunistic raiders.

Few skilled trappers were available along the Columbia River and its tributaries in those days. The North West Company and its increasingly relentless rival, the Hudson's Bay Company, had grown rich and powerful by trading with Indians who did the actual trapping. To speed the education of those who were ignorant of the craft, the traders often introduced among them, as role models, trained eastern Indians, mostly Iroquois. Some of these Iroquois had been drifting across the Continental Divide with the whites since 1807 or so, and McKenzie could pick up a few of them at the different posts. Halfbreeds, the offspring of French Canadian *engagés* and native women, were another possibility. A few white Canadians who had learned the craft just from being around it were also available. These varied people, often lumped together under the degrading term *freemen*, were a burden at all the Columbian posts. Trader Alexander Ross, who had arrived in the Northwest with the Astorians in 1811 and who would become McKenzie's principal associate, called them "human refuse."

It was McKenzie's daring vision to defy the doomsaying of his colleagues and gather these unwanted people into a trapping brigade.[3] Nor was that the end of his innovations. Because most of the streams in the Northwest were too violent for water transport, he decided to brush aside another convention and travel not with boats but with horses traded from the obstreperous Nez Perces and Cayuses.

The number of animals he would need staggered the traditionalists at Fort George. Snippishly they pointed out that both riding horses and packhorses would tire on the rough trails and have to be spelled by by fresh animals from a herd driven along with the brigade. Some would go lame. Others would be stolen by the Indians. Why, he would have to have at least three times as many horses along as men.

Each pack animal would have to be unloaded every evening, guarded with the rest of the herd throughout the night, and repacked in the morning. A brigade would look like a freight caravan, for McKenzie planned to take along, in addition to his normal trapping equipment, many bales of trade goods. He would use this merchandise to buy fur and food from whatever complaisant Indians his caravan met along the way. Also, the moving camp had to have caretakers. Custom decreed that they should be women, in this case the Indian wives of the half-breeds and Iroquois. At least some of the women would have babies; indeed, a few babies might be born beside the trail. So along with kettles and knives, there would have to be bags of moss; stuffed into cradleboards, the moss filled the function of diapers.

As for pay, there would be none. The trappers would buy their horses and equipment and whatever their families needed from the company at stiff markups. They would repay the debt by turning into the brigade leader, at set prices, whatever beaver they caught. The squeeze—high prices for supplies, low renumeration for fur—was such that only a few would show a profit at the end of the trip. To the tightfisted partners in the company and to McKenzie, the avoidance of wages seemed shrewd business. Because of the possibility of loss or damage, it also seemed shrewd to let each hunter retain ownership of his catch until it was actually turned in, even though there was always a chance that the notoriously irresponsible trappers would gamble away their pelts in the Indian camps the brigades passed.

Initially, McKenzie would have to take two forces up the Columbia—fort builders and brigade people. The merchandise he carried would always be a powerful temptation to raiders. He would be most vulnerable at the spot where he transferred his baggage from rowboats to horses. The site he selected for the exchange, because it was the closest the Columbia River came to the Snake country, was the mouth of the Walla Walla. There he would build a fort not only to protect his and later brigades but to serve as a staging area and a trading post for horses and any furs the local Cayuses and Wallawallas might bring in. Altogether, he decided, he would need ninety-five men. Even after the resistant managers at Fort George had unloaded their worst freemen on him—twenty-five Canadians and thirty-eight Iroquois—he was still short thirty-two men. To fill the hole, he hired a gentle gang of laborers who had been recruited in Hawaii and were called phonetically Owyhees. (The Owyhee River, which squirms out of southeastern Oregon into southeastern Idaho, would, in time, be named for three of them who were killed while trapping for a later brigade.) This patched-together crew reached what McKenzie hoped would be the site of Fort Nez Perce on July 11, 1818.

The size of the visitation at first alarmed the Indians who had gathered in the vicinity for the fishing. But when the whites proved to be more conciliatory than expected, they grew bold, telling McKenzie that if he wanted to erect a building there, he would have to pass out presents to everyone in the sprawling camp. Still more tribute would be exacted for cutting timber in the mountains and floating it downstream to the workers at the mouth of the river.

Not having goods enough with them to meet the demands, the Nor'Westers piled their baggage into barricades, looked to their guns, and settled down to outwait the Indians. According to Alexander Ross, who left the only account of the episode, the sullen standoff lasted five days. All this while more and more tribesmen galloped in to see what was happening. No eruption occurred, however. The whites were too well entrenched, and the Shahaptians, like most of their race, were reluctant to pay the cost in casualties that would result from a frontal attack. By the time the war party that had been raiding the Snakes came thundering full speed into the camp, the animosities were beginning to thaw. The building could go on.[4]

Construction, however, was only part of McKenzie's problem. He also wanted to carry trade muskets and gunpowder into Shoshoni country, to swap them for beaver pelts and food. The Shahaptians recoiled. Guns to the enemy! If he tried to run the weapons through, the Cayuses and their allies would strike at his caravan as furiously as Blackfeet struck at interlopers in their country.

McKenzie turned to persuasion. If the Shahaptians and the Shoshonis made peace, they wouldn't have to fear each other's guns.

The chiefs who were listening to him in council were offended. Tradition, considerations of honor, and revenge—all stood in the way of amity. As a major leader of the Wallawallas put it, according to Ross, "If we make peace, how shall I employ my young men? They delight in nothing but war, and, besides, our enemies, the Snakes, never observe a peace." He pointed at the booty his warriors had taken. Did McKenzie expect battle-hardened men to throw those things away and become women?

A Cayuse chief spoke next. Ross rendered his name as Quahat, but may have missed the phonetic roll of the syllables. The name could have been Ollokot, which meant Frog. Tuekakas (Old Joseph), whose mother was a Nez Perce and whose father was a Cayuse chief, had a younger half brother named Ollokot. This could have been he.[5] Whoever it was, he pointed to what he considered a simple solution to the impasse. Let McKenzie promise not to give balls or guns to the Snakes, and the Cayuses, at least, would consider granting transit rights to the traders.

Such an agreement would cost McKenzie too much in trade. Sidestepping the proposal, he turned to commercial seduction. He would need hundreds of horses, he said, and he was ready then and there to pay for them with the choicest merchandise—he held up samples as exhibits. The Snakes, he continued, would want the same sort of merchandise; but he'd make them understand it couldn't reach them without the Shahaptian's cooperation and horses. They'd make peace all right, and everyone would prosper.

The Indians capitulated. For the next several weeks the camp swarmed with Cayuses, Wallawallas, and Nez Perces leading horses up to the piles of merchandise on display and pointing out the things they and their wives wanted, all against the background of the rising walls of Fort Nez Perce. Altogether McKenzie bought 280 horses. He reserved 195 for his brigade of fifty-five men and an unreported number of women and children. They must have made an eye-catching sight as they strung out, in disorder, along the trail over the Blue Mountains and into the waving grass of the Grande Ronde Valley. White power? Indians who had accompanied bigger cavalcades across the Rockies to the buffalo plains probably thought the performance amateurish. Their traveling columns were cohesive in spirit and were kept that way by camp chiefs who were chosen to maintain discipline.

McKenzie suffered. Many of the half-breeds and Iroquois of his heterogeneous group were totally irresponsible. Whenever opportunity arose, they left their work to race horses, gamble, or trade their own equipment to the Indians they met along the way—and, if possible, to abduct women. Replenishing supplies was laborious. When dragging laden boats up the canyons of the Snake River proved impractical, McKenzie arranged for reinforcing brigades to meet him in southern Idaho, and that, too, was costly in horses. He had to arbitrate quarrels between the Snakes and Nez Perces and occasionally stand some of them off when they turned on him. Many days he was not sure where the column's next meal was coming from. But each year for three years he kept his quarrelsome, unpredictable people on the move. They trapped as far south as Bear Lake, which straddles the border between Idaho and Utah, and crossed from the Snake River Basin into the enormous, sagebrush-blanketed valley of the Green River in Wyoming. And each year he returned to Fort Nez Perce with thousands of beaver skins—how many thousands we don't really know. When he left the Northwest in 1821, he was well convinced that he had earned every shilling of the annual five hundred pounds his company had paid him.

Meanwhile a new order was on the way. The same year he left, the North West Company and the Hudson's Bay Company yielded to the pressures of an outraged Parliament, gave up their murderous rivalries, and fused into a single entity. Change, most of it aimed at greater economy and higher production, shook the fur country. There was even talk of abandoning the Columbian Plateau, until someone pointed out that if the reorganized Hudson's Bay Company left a vacuum there, the Americans would fill it and jump from there into the far-more-valuable beaver streams of New Caledonia, as British Columbia was then called.

In an effort to improve on McKenzie's routes—but not on the brigade's unruly but inexpensive personnel—the new managers shifted its departure point from Fort Nez Perce to Flathead Post, far to the northeast on the Clark Fork River in northwestern Montana. The reasons were logical enough. There was no big game near Fort Nez Perce, which meant taking along expensive horse meat for food. But a party going south from Flathead Post could drop across one of the low passes in the Continental Divide to the headwaters of the Missouri and find buffalo, along with good trapping in streams still largely untouched. The Blackfeet would be a risk. But so, in the minds of the new managers, were the Nez Perces. The Nez Perces were regarded as "by far the most powerful and Warlike [tribe] in the Columbia ... saucy and impudent," likely at any time to crack down on the brigade "on account of our furnishing them [the Snakes] with the Sinews of War Arms and Ammunition."[6] So the brigade moved away from Fort Nez Perce. True, the fort stayed alive as an ordinary fur-buying post, but its days as the great horse emporium of the Shahaptians were gone.

A question arises. How much contact did young Chief Joseph's father, Tuekakas, have with the rise and decline of Fort Nez Perce? No account mentions him, and yet he knew the countryside well. His father was a Cayuse chief from the Umatilla Valley in Oregon (Pendleton is the principal city there today) who had acquired as a wife a Nez Perce from the Wallowa Valley. Dissatisfied, she left him shortly before their child's birth and returned to her former home. There she married Chief Takinploon of the influential Kallapoon band. We can assume that they had a good life—unexcelled grazing for thousands of horses and, during the summers, rich hunting, fishing, root digging, and berry gathering.[7] Their winters were probably passed in the deep, warm, protected canyon of what became Joseph Creek, near the point where it empties into the Grande Ronde River, many miles below the great circle of the Grande Ronde itself.

When Tuekakas was about seventeen—1803 or so—his mother died. For a brief time he joined his Cayuse father in the Umatilla country. There he came to know his three half brothers, all of whom we will hear about later— Ollokot (Frog), Tauitau (Young Chief), and Pahkatos Qoh Qoh (Five

Crows).[8] Although there is no reason to assume that relations were unfriendly, Tuekakas felt, as his mother had, the tug of the Wallowa and returned to his stepfather's family. By the time McKenzie's brigades began moving back and forth across the Grande Ronde, he was roughly thirty years old and was being groomed for the chieftainship of the Kallapoons. They were, in the context of the times, a numerically strong group, proud, free, self-sufficient, and strongly attached to their isolated land. Their seasonal drift was down the gaping canyons that led toward the Nez Perce towns dotted beside the Snake River between the mouths of the Salmon and Clearwater rivers. But there were also tugs toward the market at Fort Nez Perce, and many of the group, like Tuekakas, had blood relatives among the Cayuse. The ending of commerce must have brought regrets to Tuekakas and his friends. We can imagine them sitting in front of their lodges, the soaring Wallowa peaks at their backs, watching their horses graze on the soft hills. Fingering a gun, hefting a pouch full of powder, running a thumb along the edge of a hatchet blade. Marvelous! They may have reflected, as the great pioneer of the Canadian fur trade, David Thompson, once did, "Without Iron man is weak, very weak, but armed with Iron, he becomes the lord of the earth."[9] Yet to stoop in the mud, grubbing for beaver—No! They were a free people, not slaves to conveniences. Still, it would be good to learn what kind of wayakins the whites had that enabled them to produce such wonders without trapping. If they could learn....

Some of the Nimipus may have remembered dimly the claim stake David Thompson had placed at the junction of the Snake and Columbia rivers. Others of the tribe probably recalled that the people of Great Britain—King George's men—had fought a war with a people who called themselves Americans. Many knew that after the war was over, King George's flags had risen above every trading post on the Columbian Plateau. A few years later the bright red flag of the Hudson's Bay Company was unfurled each dawn beside the British emblem. But they certainly had no idea that the cloth banners were symbols of the way their control over their own destinies was being eroded by the imperatives of something called international diplomacy.

The Treaty of Ghent that ended the War of 1812 between Great Britain and the United States decreed that each of the contending powers was to regain all territory it had held before the conflict began. But what of the vast Oregon country, sprawling between Russian Alaska and Spanish California? The possessory claims each nation had advanced had never been adjudicated. To whom, then, was the territory to be returned? Diplomats from both countries met in a special session in London in 1818 to solve the problem. They agreed that Oregon should be divided. But where? The Americans proposed the forty-ninth parallel, which already marked, as far as the Rockies, the northern boundary of the Louisiana Territory. The British refused. They wanted a line that would follow the Columbia River from the point where it crossed the forty-ninth parallel to the sea. Such a division would give them a buffer of land between the American holdings and the rich fur preserves of New Caledonia (British Columbia). The Americans, who wanted the harbors of Puget Sound, declined.

After weeks of fruitless arguing, the diplomats decided on a ten-year Convention of Joint Occupancy. According to the decree, citizens of both nations would have equal rights to settle and trade anywhere in the disputed territory for the next decade. During that time, the diplomats would try again to work out a viable boundary.

At the time of the decree America's chances of obtaining the boundary it wanted looked slim. The few Yankee ships that plied the coast for furs were making no effort to establish permanent bases. The only white habitations in the interior were trading posts manned by Britons, and they had been strengthened immeasurably by the amalgamation of the North West and Hudson's Bay companies into a continentwide corporation bearing the name of the latter firm. If Americans were kept out of Oregon, the new company would face no competition there, and New Caledonia's profits would stay safely in its hands.

Their power did not render the company officials complacent, however. They were fully aware of the compulsive westward thrust, later called Manifest Destiny, of the aggressive Yankees. They knew that throughout the 1820s Congress considered, but then rejected as too bellicose, several bills to establish military and civil posts in Oregon. More worrisome were the American fur men. After being mired in the economic depression that followed the Treaty of Ghent, they were stirring again. During the early 1820s four companies of them started up the Missouri River. To the relief of the Britons, Blackfeet thoroughly mauled the two that reached the headwaters. The Arikaras of the middle river apparently added to the company's security by throwing a blockade across the stream and then defeating the U.S. Army unit that tried to dislodge them. Out of that impasse, another threat developed. The frustrated trappers of the stalled expedition bought horses and started overland along the trail the Astorians had blazed in 1811. How far the new group had advanced by the end of 1823, the British did not know. It was clear, however, that the company must somehow respond or the managers of their posts might awake one morning to find the Yankees already heading toward New Caledonia.

Devising a way to block them became part of the duties of George Simpson, the dynamic, totally self-assured young governor (he was thirty-one in 1823) of the northern and western reaches of the Hudson's Bay Company in Canada. The best strategy, he decided with his council's concurrence, was to hold the potential invaders east of the Continental Divide—and to do it without resort to force, which would bring the wrath of Parliament down upon them. An instrument stood ready, the Snake Country brigade invented in 1818 by Donald McKenzie. Its still-motley collection of Canadian, half-breed, and Iroquois freemen should concentrate on wiping out all beaver on the western side of the Continental Divide. Deprived of the prospect of profits, the Americans would stay away from Oregon and hence, by extension, from New Caledonia.

Management of the brigade was so "forlorn ... hazardous and disagreeable"—Simpson's words—that the handful of top officers in the Oregon country had declined to take over the job. Until a suitable leader could be found, fill-ins substituted. The first two were former clerks of David Thompson—Michel Bourdon and Finan McDonald. Sturdy men, they performed well, but Bourdon was killed by Blackfeet, and McDonald was so harried that he declared he would not rejoin the brigade until beavers grew skins of gold. Duty then devolved on Alexander Ross, who Simpson considered "empty-headed," but who he had to accept because no one else was immediately available. Before departing from Flathead Post in February 1824, Ross was warned forcefully not "to open a road" for the Americans.[10]

Where did the Columbian Indians fit into all this? As necessary nuisances, mostly. Some of them, including a few Nez Perces, were learning to trap and, of course, the Britons did not want them carrying their furs to the Americans if the latter ever showed up. So it was good business to bring the chiefs into the trading houses and brigade camps to smoke, gossip, and do whatever else might instill loyalty in them toward Great Britain, as represented by the Hudson's Bay Company. Another consideration was enforced conversion. A strong block of benevolent philanthropists, some of them stockholders of the Hudson's Bay Company, thought it was the Christian duty of the monopoly to civilize the heathens among whom they plied their trade. Sending religious missionaries among them was deemed to be the preferable way.[11]

In private George Simpson believed that trying to enlighten Indians simply made them corrupt, idle, and useless.[12] The company's license, however, depended on the government, and in governmental circles right then the voices of the humanitarians sounded loud and clear. Obediently he agreed that steps needed to be taken. He tried to see some advantages. Perhaps civilized Indians could be developed into customers for the Hudson's Bay Company's merchandise; perhaps they could be trained to function as cheap laborers and boatmen for the firm. But establishing mission stations, he thought, would take several years and would be costly. A better way to start, he convinced his directors, was to send a few Indian children to the company's Anglican school at Red River, near the site of today's Winnipeg; educate them there; and let them return as teachers to their people.[13] His superiors agreed to the window dressing.

Thus bulwarked against competitors from the United States in the field and against carping criticism from philanthropists at home, the young governor set out for Oregon in the fall of 1824 on a fast, hard-driving trip of investigation and reorganization.

Totally without his or Simpson's awareness, Alexander Ross became a weaver of fate for most of the native people of the Columbian Plateau. The initial intertwinings came together at Spokan House in late October 1824, and again during the second week of April 1825. The first thread concerned seven of the Americans who had been turned away from the Missouri River by the Arikara blockade—the very Americans Ross had been warned to stay clear of. The second mingling involved Ross's selecting, at Simpson's behest, two Indian boys to be taken to the Red River school for religious instruction and tutoring in reading and writing English. The consequences that would flow from these two episodes would be enormous, not least for Hallalhotsoot, otherwise known as the Lawyer, and for the Lawyer's principal opponents-to-be, Tuekakas and his yet-unborn son, Hin-mah-too-yah-lat-kekht.

Ross had a wretched time with the brigade of "unruly, ill-tongued villains" he led south out of Flathead Post in February 1824. Several of the Iroquois, believing that the party was too large for successful trapping, prevailed on their captain to let them strike off on their own. Snake Indians jumped on them beside one of the sparkling mountain streams of southeastern Idaho, stripped them of everything they had, and frightened them into a blue funk. Salvation, as it seemed to them, appeared in the form of Jedediah Smith and six heavily armed men who had recently been detached from the American party that had come west from the Missouri. Gabbling in broken English picked up during his years with British trapping parties, old Pierre Tivanitagon, the native leader of the stranded Iroquois, offered the newcomers good pay in beaver for protecting them on their way to rejoin Ross's party. The Americans agreed instantly. It was a prime opportunity to learn the country while studying British trading and trapping methods.[14]

The dilemma the newcomers presented when they arrived in Ross's camp was too much for the brigade leader. He was supposed to shun contact with them, and yet if he tried to run them off, they might take some of his volatile trappers with them by offering higher prices for pelts than Ross was authorized to pay. In the end he chose to keep his party whole and let the Americans trail along to Flathead Post, where they arrived on November 24.

A hypocritical letter from Simpson awaited him there. The governor praised his work and then told him he was to be replaced as brigade leader by rambunctious Peter Skene Ogden. If Ross wished, he could transfer to the Red River school as a teacher—but at a lower salary than he had been drawing. "I could wish," Simpson went on, "that two Indian boys of about eight years of age of the Spokan and Nez Perce tribes were got from their relations for the purpose of being educated at the School and taken out with your family."[15]

Thus the weavings: American fortune seekers would press toward Oregon on the heels of Jedediah Smith's trappers, and American religious zealots would be inspired to go in the same direction largely because of forces set in motion by the schoolboys.

Peter Ogden spent three weeks outfitting the brigade for its return to the Snake Country. During that time Smith and his men watched cavalcades of Spokan, Flatheads, and a few Nez Perces ride up to the post to trade, singing peace songs and shooting their muskets into the air to show that they came with empty weapons in their hands and goodwill in their hearts. Both there and on the southward trail, through heavy snows, the Americans spoke quietly to the freeman about the virtues of *their* trade.[16] The seeds they planted sprouted that May 1825, when the brigade ran into the main body of Yankee trappers in luminous Cache Valley, only a few miles north of Great Salt Lake in what was then Mexican territory. By offering higher prices than the Britons paid, the newcomers persuaded several of the freemen and Iroquois to desert, bringing with them seven hundred skins. Loudly, one of the Americans proclaimed his countrymen would soon be driving the British out of all Oregon. That was for the governments to decide, Ogden retorted lamely and withdrew, helpless and furious, blaming Ross for what had happened.[17]

The disaster was not total. Some of Ogden's men returned to his service the next year; in time a few Americans actually followed. Although a few

Yankees did cross the Continental Divide to Clark Fork Valley in Montana and, farther south, to the vast drainage of the Green River and the neighboring mountains of northern Utah, they never managed to do more than dent the fringes of the Snake Country. Ogden's men, motivated by an increase in prices authorized by the company, weren't overlooking enough pelts to make competitive trapping worthwhile. Still, a marked rearrangement of Indian economic patterns had been set into motion. Snakes, Flatheads, and, to a lesser extent, Nez Perces took up trapping in order to buy the manufactured goods they were coming to crave. By 1827 they were familiar enough with the new invaders that a mixed group visited the American trappers' rendezvous at Bear Lake on the Utah-Idaho border and joined wholeheartedly in a kind of boisterous merriment the sterner British tried to discourage.[18] Though firm evidence is lacking, there is reason to assume that during these years of dismayingly swift acculturation, Lawyer, who was then about thirty-seven or thirty-eight, may have joined one of the Nimipu trapping groups. (Plain "Lawyer" now; what had begun as a designation had evolved into an ordinary name.) Tuekakas, then moving into power among the isolated Wallowa bands, seldom associated with the bewhiskered white mountainmen, however, and for the time being was without a white man's name.

While Ogden was moving south with his first brigade, George Simpson continued his headlong inspection trip to the mouth of the Columbia River and back. Aware even in the wilderness of the humanitarian pressures in London, he talked, through interpreters, to several Indian chiefs about religion. He could not detect, he said in his journal, that they had any concept of a Supreme Being.[19] Never lacking in self-confidence, he tried to give them a clue. Because their languages lacked words for God, his interpreters translated the abstraction as "Master of Life." Missionaries became, in the translating process, "messengers from the Master of Life."

When Simpson asked some of the chiefs he talked to whether their people would like to receive the Master's messengers, the response was extraordinary. Yes, yes! Indians as far away as the Thompson River in British Columbia heard of the proposal through the grapevine; in the spring of 1825 they traveled south to the trading post at Okanogan beside the Columbia River to intercept Simpson and discuss possibilities. Two Nimipu chiefs rode north more than two hundred miles to the forks of the Spokane River to ask Simpson whether *he* was a son of the Master.[20] (Warped notions of Christ, perhaps?) When Alexander Ross asked whether two of the Flathead, Kutenai, and Spokan chiefs who were waiting for Simpson at Spokane Forks would

send sons to the Red River school with Simpson and him, they were outraged. Did he think they were dogs that they would part from their children
that way? But when Ross explained that the purpose was to teach them to
know and serve God (the Master of Life), they broke into a clamor. He could
have hundreds of children! but not boys as young as eight, please. Ross chose
two, a Spokan and a Kutenai, as Simpson had suggested, but they were about
fifteen years old.[21]

What, pray, did the phrase *Master of Life* mean to the untutored Indians
of the Pacific Northwest? The revivalists of Great Britain and the United
States, where Awakenings burned hot at times during the decades of the
1820s and 1830s, firmly believed that aboriginal peoples who had not yet
received the Christian message yearned instinctively for the Truth and
responded with pristine exuberance whenever it seemed to be approaching.
And they had received hints of that approach. Some of the masters of the
trading posts had Bibles and read services on Sunday. (Simpson made the
practice compulsory at places like new Fort Vancouver, under devout John
McLoughlin.) Alexander Ross must have had religious convictions or he
would not have been transferred to Red River. French Canadian voyageurs
and Iroquois Catholics, remembering their boyhoods in eastern Canada,
undoubtedly watched many Indian ceremonials and then, sitting around the
camp fires, may have tried to explain some of their own half-forgotten rituals.
The sign of the cross and a few mumbled words would not have been hard for
the Indians to mimic. So they were ready when Simpson came along with his
divine message.

Perhaps.

There is another explanation, based, in part, on material that was
touched on in chapter 2. For centuries, it will be recalled, the Nez Perces and
their neighbors had relied on guardian spirits called wayakins to give each
individual the power needed to control a hostile environment and to assure
personal safety and prestige. In spite of the spirits, however, outside innovations—horses, guns, diseases, and, more recently, influxes of strangers—were
upsetting a once-predictable world. The newcomers established profitable
horse-trading patterns and then abruptly ended them without apparent cause.
They struggled to alter Indian loyalties. They proffered wondrous material
goods that promised an easier life but at prices many could not or would not
afford, as in the matter of trapping beaver. Too often the stresses created on
the Indians by inner doubts and conflicting desires became parts of everyday
life.

Could these stresses be ended by the restoration of ancient purities? A new class of people, whom the whites called Prophets, perhaps after the prophets of the Old Testament, affirmed that such renewals were, indeed, possible. They spoke from hypnotic trances. Frequently, they claimed to have died and gone to the hereafter, where they learned from the dead that if the living returned to their original, unsullied customs, the disappearing game would reinhabit the Earth and the departed people would breathe again. To help these things come to pass, teachers would arrive from the east, the land of the rising sun. The people should hurry this revitalization along with a special Prophet Dance.[22]

A new idea instilled by the Prophets was of a Master of Life. This concept of a Supreme Being may have been brought by wanderers from lands that had been taken from the Indians of the eastern states. But it was not God in the sense the whites used the term. Rather, it was an overarching figure who had mastered the secrets of controlling the environment and making dreams come true by means of magic. "Medicine" was the key. Medicine was secret talismans and incantations. Medicine was the power, in the scornful words of Father Nicholas Point, who lived among the Flatheads in the 1840s, "to acquire, with the least possible effort, the greatest possible abundance of things necessary for life such as fish … game … and the power to win at gambling games."[23] Medicine was the power to dazzle others with great or amazing performances. Medicine could be the power to cause injury to the bodies or fortunes of others. Medicine could restore the earth. It could be learned, moreover, by making proper contact with the Master of Life.

Prophets comforted their people with predictions about such contacts. One example was a Spokan chief, Big Head, whose Indian name an American explorer later spelled Silimxnotylmilakobok. Big Head relayed to his tribesmen a prophecy he had heard a medicine man deliver to his people (Big Head was then ten years old) during a time of great fright. "Soon," Big Head remembered, "there will come from the rising sun a different kind of men from any you have yet seen, who will bring with them a book and will teach you everything."[24] Strangers with a book. That concept—the book—had to have come from observant Indians who had seen the special ways with which whites and possibly a reverent Iroquois or two had touched their Bibles or missals and who had wondered whether these books were the source of the strangers' amazing powers.

Prepared by their Prophets for wondrous visitations, great throngs of Indians gathered to meet Lewis and Clark on their return journey and to lis-

ten to their words about the power of the Great Father (a Master of Life,
rather than President Jefferson?), the Great Father's desire for peace, and the
promise of special trading houses, the last of which failed to materialize, with
what impact on the Indians no record says. The first white man whom the
Indians of the upper Columbia saw was David Thompson during his descent
of the river in 1811. Tribe after tribe danced for him when he landed to speak
to them. Was it an ordinary greeting dance, such as many Indians performed
for important visitors, or a special Prophet Dance? When the Astorians, with
whom Alexander Ross was traveling upstream, also in 1811, reached the
mouth of the Walla Walla, a tremendous concourse of native people welcomed them too with a dance.[25] A customary greeting only?

It is not likely that the questions will ever be fully resolved. The answers
are shrouded in distance and by a mind-set that is totally different from our
own or from George Simpson's. All we can be wholly sure of is that Simpson's
religious adventures in the Columbian region aroused great excitement and
that unguessable results flowed from the boys—renamed Spokan Garry and
Kutenai Pelly in honor of two officers of the Hudson's Bay Company—whom
he and Alexander Ross took to Red River with their cross-country brigade.

· 6 ·

THE QUEST

On returning home from the Red River Mission School in the summer of 1829 for a vacation, Spokan Garry and Kutenai Pelly dropped a cultural bomb. Both were still in their teens and surely they strutted. They let everyone know they had learned to speak, write, and read English—unheard-of accomplishments among western Indians in those days. Furthermore, they brought with them copies of the Book that, they said, explained the Master of Life and the means of reaching Him.

What they and their listeners made of such concepts as predestination, the Trinity, the Holy Spirit, divine grace, the remission of sins, and the Life Everlasting we cannot know. But the young students did demonstrate rituals that could be followed—summons to prayer by a bell, asking a blessing before partaking of food, kneeling during devotions, and reciting from memory translated versions of the Ten Commandments. It was exciting to many of the Nimipus to pick up these trappings of Christianity, but almost surely the purpose remained, to them, what it had always been, the use of magic to enhance their lives and to control their environment.

Few specifics are known about the responses of Kutenai Pelly's home tribe. Spokan Garry, however, demonstrably created a sensation, not only among his own people but among a sprinkling of Nez Perces, Flatheads, Pend d'Oreilles (Kalispells), Cayuses, and Wallawallas. No doubt many of those people sought out the returned convert by walking or riding to whatever village was sheltering him at the time. Garry, too, traveled by foot and horseback. Still, most of his contacts had to be indirect. These were widely scattered, seminomadic band people, deeply involved in the problems of protecting themselves from their enemies while finding enough food, some of it on the faraway buffalo plains, to stay alive. They lacked time to chase after novelties. In addition, Garry stayed in his home country less than a year before returning to the Anglican mission school at Red River. So his message must have been limited, like rumor, to mouth-to-mouth progress, undergoing who knows what transformations on the way.

Such an impact as he was exerting was intensified when the Hudson's Bay Company added five more would-be Indian students to the brigade of 1830 that carried Garry and Pelly back across the Rockies to Red River. The company, of course, chose lads whose allegiances would suit its own interests—representatives of tribes that were strategically located, populous, or in need of flattery. One neophyte was another Kutenai. There was a second Spokan, this one the son of Big Head, the popular medicine man who had relayed to his people prophecies made long ago about a wondrous book. A third was a Cayuse, a nephew of Old Joseph's half brother, Tauitau, and hence of Joseph's. Two were Nez Perces. One of the latter was the son of a chief who lived, as Lawyer did, in the Kamiah section of the Clearwater Valley. He would be renamed Ellice after Edward Ellice, a member of Parliament and of the Hudson's Bay Company's board of governors. We will meet Indian Ellice again as tribal leader whose English name by then was being spelled Ellis.[1]

Bands that had no representatives looked on the choices with envy. How could they reach the place where the books were? The Hudson's Bay Company might never select additional candidates for enlightenment, and if it did, the choice would likely be as random as the last ones had been. Yet for a small party to try to find a way to Red River on its own, risking Blackfeet much of the distance, was unthinkable. Quandaries prevailed around the lodge fires, especially in villages where a few people had had direct contact with Garry and had been stirred by their misunderstandings of what he had said.

One such was Hallalhotsoot, a.k.a. Lawyer. He was then about thirty-four years old and increasingly ambitious. He had actually seen and heard Garry and had brought word of the experience to his home at Kooskia (Idaho), where the south and middle forks of the Clearwater River join—no great distance from Kamiah.[2] Undoubtedly, Lawyer knew of Ellice's departure for Red River and possibly felt a threat in it. But what could he and his followers do to counter it?

An opportunity slowly unfolded during the spring of 1831. Several war-riors and their families from the Kamiah-Kooskia area decided to join some Flatheads and Pend d'Oreille in the Bitterroot Valley for a buffalo hunt on the Plains. Lawyer's mother was a Flathead, and he had many friends in the tribe, whose language he spoke. It is known, also, that he went on several intertribal buffalo hunts during his lifetime. No direct evidence says that he was on this particular trip—or that he wasn't. Let's assume he was.

By the middle of May the hunting party—fifty lodges, or upwards of three hundred people—were camped beside Red Rock Creek, the remotest of the Missouri River's formative streams. Part of the group tangled with some Blackfeet and killed two, only to have the enemy revenge themselves a little later by slaying a hunter, ravishing his wife, gang fashion probably, then hack-ing off her hair and sending her back to her people as a token of how things stood between them. Other wanderers from the hunting party scouted south across the Centennial Mountains, perhaps by way of Monida Pass, a name coined years later by combining the first syllables of Montana and Idaho. There they ran into a party of trappers for the American Fur Company, under the leadership of Lucian Fontenelle and Andrew Drips.[3]

The American Fur Company was still clutched in John Jacob Astor's tightly clenched fist. Although the New York entrepreneur had given up all hope of again challenging the British in Oregon, he was determined to monopolize the fur trade of the upper Mississippi and Missouri River water-sheds, all in American territory. Toward that end, he had either bought out or competitively crushed his rivals along both rivers. His St. Louis associates, working under the name Western Department of the American Fur Compa-ny, thoroughly rearranged the trading posts along the Missouri. Some of the forts were visualized as jumping-off places for supply columns carrying trade goods to company trapping brigades that were sweeping the Plains and as much of the Rocky Mountain area as they could. One such post was located at Council Bluffs, some twenty-five miles upstream from the point where the Platte River flows into the Missouri. Another was Fort Union, built close to the mouth of the Yellowstone. Experiments were also under way to supply the Missouri River posts with a steamboat named *Yellow Stone*.

After moving west from Council Bluffs in the summer of 1830, Fontenelle, Drips, and their fifty or so men toughed out a hungry, snow-smothered winter in Cache Valley (they called it Willow Valley) in northern Utah. In the spring of 1831 they moved north up the Snake River and then up Henry's Fork, catching from forty to seventy beavers a day, most of which they boiled for food after skinning them. Near the source of Henry's Fork, they swung west, weaving through the great belt of pines that slopes gently away from the splendid peaks of the Centennial Range toward the dry, lava-roughened Snake River Plains.

Somewhere near the southern approach to Monida Pass, the whites encountered the scouts from the mixed Nez Perce–Flathead–Pend d'Oreille hunting party. Eager for trade, Fontenelle and Drips suggested that the groups meet a little farther west on Medicine Lodge Creek, where there was ample grass for the horses. The Indians agreed. When they appeared, they were singing a peace song. Halting about fifty yards from the knot of watching whites, they fired their guns in salute, reloaded, and fired again. The trappers returned the salute, and the Indians dismounted. The hunting chief, probably dressed for the occasion, with a wolf's furred skull capping his head, stepped out in the lead. Behind him came four subchiefs. After them marched a long line of warriors in colorful regalia and, at the rear, a subdued but expectant group of women and children. The leader took Fontenelle's hand, raised it, and uttered a prayer. The rest followed suit—more formal greetings, more prayers, until each male Indian had shaken hands with practically every white. The ceremony took about two hours to complete.

The two groups camped side by side for several days. The Indians spent much of their leisure time gambling, in groups segregated by sex, with dazzlingly manipulated pieces of bone. The young men raced horses, not over a course but after the fashion of a chase until someone passed the leader and set his own path. Except for those very Indian pastimes, the native people were disciplined, honest, and gentle, or so they seemed to twenty-year-old Warren Ferris, who many years later wrote a fascinating account of his half-dozen years in the Rockies. He was particularly surprised by certain devout practices he observed and speculated that they had come from a few pious traders and from the handful of Catholic Iroquois who had settled among the Flatheads. If he heard about the school at Red River and its influence, he makes no mention of it.

In mid-June, when the trading was finished, the groups split. Half the whites, led by Fontenelle and Drips, would return to Willow (Cache) Valley to receive the supplies that supposedly were being brought there by pack train from Council Bluffs. At Cache Valley, Fontenelle and Drips would also turn over their furs to the pack train for transport back to the Missouri River, where the pelts would be loaded into mackinaw boats for the rest of the journey to market in St. Louis. Meanwhile the other half of the white group would move into the mountains for more trapping.

The Indians also split. The majority wanted to continue hunting. But twenty men and perhaps a few women decided to go with Fontenelle and Drips to Cache Valley, see what was afoot, and perhaps trade for articles Fontenelle had been unable to provide. It is definitely known that at least four of the party were warriors whose homes were in the Kamiah-Kooskia area. Was Lawyer a fifth? There is no way of saying, though it is certainly a possibility.

They rode south with high expectations. By 1831 the famed rendezvous system of the Rocky Mountain fur trade had explosively outgrown its simple beginnings of 1825. Soaring profits had lured many competitors into the business. These competitors came from Taos in New Mexico, Council Bluffs near the mouth of the Platte River in Nebraska, and the American Fur Company's new trading posts along the upper Missouri River. Increasing numbers of free (independent) trappers joined the influx. Although they often traveled with company brigades for safety's sake, they were not bound to the brigades by wage contracts or debt. At the annual rendezvous they bought from and sold to whatever firm offered the most advantageous deals. The Indians, too, discovered that they could strike better bargains with the competitive Americans than with the Hudson's Bay Company, and they began flocking in.

In 1831 Fontenelle's and Drips's cavalcade of trappers and garishly bedecked Indians were looking forward to the carnival with thirsty anticipation. So when they loped into Cache Valley, ready to fire off their guns and let go their piercing howls, and found only a dwindling number of unsupplied people, they were stunned. They had expected to see Thomas Fitzpatrick at the head of the supply trains of both the Rocky Mountain and American Fur companies, combined that year for greater efficiency. But Fitzpatrick did not appear. When search parties found no sign of his caravan, disappointed customers began drifting away, to make whatever arrangements they could for the coming winter.

Drips and Fontenelle emerged from several agitated councils with a sink-or-swim plan. Using their own employees, they would take their furs at the greatest speed possible to Council Bluffs on the Missouri. After requisitioning supplies from the American Fur Company's post there, Drips would hurry back to Cache Valley. Fontenelle would continue to St. Louis with the furs and during the winter work out a more dependable supply arrangement for the coming year, 1832.

The decision presented the Flatheads and Nez Perces who had accompanied the whites to the shrunken rendezvous with what seemed to them a dazzling opportunity. St. Louis! They had heard of the place; American trappers talked as if it were the very navel of the world. Almost surely they asked Fontenelle whether they could find the Book they wanted there. And he nodded.

Books of their own!—involving a long, possibly dangerous quest into lands of total strangeness. But by then the Indians were comfortable traveling with the Drips-Fontenelle group. They knew that the explorer William Clark, a legendary friend since he and Meriwether Lewis had visited the tribes in 1805–6, lived in St. Louis, and they believed he would help them and perhaps give them good presents. In the end four Nez Perces from the Kamiah-Kooskia area agreed to undertake the trip. Two, Eagle and Man of the Morning, were in their forties. Two, Rabbitskin Leggins and No Horns on His Head, were about twenty, hardly more than boys. Three Flatheads joined them.[4] If Lawyer was there, he held back, even though his contact with Spokan Garry had seeded the idea in the first place.

The trip the seven made to Council Bluffs with the Americans was long, hot, dry, and probably not much fun. The company post, when they reached it, was hectic with many comings and goings. Pressed relentlessly by Andrew Drips, grunting roustabouts wrestled bales of goods together for the return to the mountains. Other workers loaded the brigade's heavy packs of furs into rowboats for transport to St. Louis. In spite of what they had seen of the Hudson's Bay Company bateaux on the Columbia River, the horse Indians of the West were not familiar with water travel. The thought of being cramped in a wobbly boat for many days may have dissolved the resolve of the three Flatheads, who lacked the village ambitions that bound the Kamiah-Kooskia quartet. Anyway, they decided to return to Cache Valley with Drips.

(In spite of furious efforts, winter pinned the Drips party in the Black Hills of Wyoming until the following spring. Before then Fitzpatrick had reached the rendezvous site. Although he brought in less merchandise than expected, the trappers he contacted were able to resume their hunts in anticipation of a truly rousing rendezvous in 1832.)

The Nimipus who continued to St. Louis were battered by incomprehensibility. They stared their way among many houses of unbelievable shapes and materials. Cobbled streets—what a notion!—resounded with the clang of iron horseshoes and iron wagon tires. Masses of people—whites, blacks, Spaniards, French voyageurs, Indians from everywhere except the Far West—gabbled in an infinity of tongues, so that amid all the chatter the Nimipus stayed silent. Steamboat bells and whistles echoed across a wider, browner river than the Columbia. Smells. Tastes. Mistakes. Temptations. Bewilderments and bedevilments.

They found their way to William Clark's imposing home at the corner of Vine and Market streets. Presumably, Clark showed them his famed Indian Hall, filled with trophies from tribes throughout the United States. He would have tried to reminisce with them—through signs—about his visits in their homelands. He might have inquired about people he remembered—Lawyer's father, Twisted Hair, for example. But, and in spite of the legends that have grown up about the meeting, it is unlikely that he gleaned more than a foggy idea of what they were after.

They reached the city's cathedral. Clark may have provided directions and an introduction. Or guidance may have come from Lucien Fontenelle, who was Catholic. Possibly the contact developed after the two older Nez Perces, Eagle and Man of the Morning, fell ill and needed help most desperately during a winter so cold that the Mississippi froze. The priests at the cathedral gave them sacraments and small crosses, which they clutched tenaciously as they died, within three weeks of each other.

Fontenelle kept track of the forlorn young survivors, Rabbitskin Leggins and No Horns on His Head. In the spring of 1832 he let them know he planned to take supplies to the rendezvous, scheduled that year for Pierre's Hole, by a different route—up the Missouri on the steamboat *Yellow Stone* as far as Fort Union and then overland by pack string. The departure was set for March 26, early enough for the boat to catch the high water it would need to cross the river's sandbars.

The two Nez Perces boarded in ample time. Each had a Bible, whether a Catholic or King James version is unknown. Possibly each carried a rosary and a small cross.[5] It is difficult to believe they had learned to read enough during their six months or so in bewildering St. Louis to have mastered ordinary printed English, let alone Biblical sonorities. Realizing their deficiencies, they may—just may—have asked Clark or the cathedral priests or fur-trade officials to send teachers to the Kamiah-Kooskia villages to teach them how to use their new possessions to advantage. If so, they were still thinking in terms of medicine men and magic amulets.

Until they grew used to the *Yellow Stone*, it, too, must have been alarming. A side-wheeler, 120 feet long and 20 feet of beam, it was crowned by two towering, black smokestacks placed in front of the main cabin. The small deck space was crowded with engagés who were bound for the upper river. Another delegation of Indians—Crees and Assiniboins who had gone all the way to Washington to view the might of the Americans—looked down their noses at the two Nimipus.[6] Stops were frequent. Firewood had to be collected from prepared piles and supplies unloaded at company trading posts. Because the boat drew six feet of water, it frequently hung up on sandbars in spite of the early sailing. Occasionally, additional manpower had to be summoned from available trading establishments to free her. During the delays, bored passengers walked along the shore to the next place where they could be picked up. Rabbitskin Leggins probably enjoyed the breaks. No Horns on His Head might not have; the effects of the city winter were showing in his thinness and the sickly pallor of his skin.

Although the *Yellow Stone* had reached as high as Fort Pierre (precursor of modern Pierre, South Dakota) during its maiden voyage the year before, hundreds of Sioux Indians again congregated there to witness the phenomenon. They greeted the traveling members of their race effusively. To the two Nez Perces, who may well have been wearing cast-off city clothing, they gave elaborate costumes so that artist George Catlin, who was also aboard the steamer, could paint them—two horseless Nimipus in Lakota dress—as representatives of the vibrant horse Indian culture of the Plains. The portraits have been used in countless illustrated books on Indians since then.

The upriver trip ended about June 17 at Fort Union near the present North Dakota–Montana border. More excited Indians waited there. During the winter they had brought in seven hundred bundles of tightly pressed buffalo hides to trade for magnificent items of iron, weapons, cloth, kitchen and sewing utensils, decorative baubles, and liquor—part of the *Yellow Stone's* hold was crammed with kegs of pure alcohol awaiting dilution. To the hides, the Indians added fourteen hundred buffalo tongues that would tantalize white appetites in St. Louis. As they sat around waiting for trade to start, and with the two Nez Perces probably listening, the hunters talked gloomily about what seemed to them to be a shrinkage in the number of buffalo on the Plains.[7] Ah, well, if they didn't hunt, how could they obtain the things that freed them from the restrictions of their Stone Age ways of life?

Fort Union, it turned out, was also the end of the road for No Horns on His Head: He died there and was buried, perhaps with his Bible on his chest, while Fontenelle and his new foreman, Etienne Provost, were readying their pack animals for the trip to the far side of the Continental Divide.[8] Some of Rabbitskin Leggins's grief was muted by the joy of being on a horse again. He quite likely helped the caravan's meat hunters as the pack train followed the Yellowstone River (Montana) to the Bighorn River (Montana to Wyoming).

The Bighorn took them to the flanks of the Wind River Mountains (Wyoming), whose southern tip they skirted by way of South Pass. Once the Continental Divide was at their backs, they swung northwest, aiming for lovely Pierre's Hole on the western side of the Teton Peaks. Originally, Fontenelle had hoped to reach Pierre's Hole in time for the annual gathering of trappers, scheduled for the first part of July, but the upriver trip had been too slow. The cavalcade kept pushing hard, nevertheless, for the men of the American Fur Company, who were about to set out once more for the beaver streams, would be badly in need of merchandise and fresh equipment.

Lots happened. As they were spurring their trail-weary horses across the parched, cracked, alkali-streaked plain toward the Seeds-ke-dee (Green) River, they overtook an imposing caravan of about a hundred men and—amazing!—fifteen battered wagons, the first ever to cross the Continental Divide north of Mexico. The commander of the party was Captain Benjamin L. E. Bonneville, on leave from the United States Army for a private fling at the fur trade (combined, perhaps, with a judicious scouting of the geography of the West in case of trouble between the United States and Great Britain over Oregon). The two parties camped together while their jaded horses recovered in riverside meadows. Then, after having lured away some of Bonneville's expert Delaware Indian hunters, Fontenelle and Provost, with Rabbitskin Leggins still tagging along, pressed on up the Green, hunting for the brigade they were supposed to supply.[9]

Along the way they ran into a mixed party—men, women, and children—of Gros Ventres or Atsinas, a tribe so closely associated with the Blackfeet that many trappers called them Blackfeet. The sight of so formidable an enemy was scary at first, but the Indians proved to be meek as well as sullen, and gradually the reason came out. Several days earlier they had stumbled across scattered parties of white trappers and their Indian allies who were about to head for the mountains on the breaking up of the rendezvous. A couple of skirmishes and the treacherous slaying of a Gros Ventre chief by a trapper and his Flathead partner had been followed by a noisy coalescing of the opposing forces. While the whites were pulling their different brigades together, the men and women of the angry Gros Ventre party hacked down enough cottonwood and aspen trees to erect crude breastworks. To them they added a few shallow foxholes. In a sense the fortifications sufficed. They enabled the besieged to hold off an ill-executed frontal attack by a reckless party of the trappers and their allies. Thoroughly subdued, the whites broke off contact, and during the night the Gros Ventre skillfully withdrew, taking most of their dead with them. The total may have been as high as twenty-six, some of them women. Several horses were killed; many were captured. Five whites were slain, six wounded. Seven Indian allies of the trappers died and seven were wounded—approximately. The many contemporary accounts of the battle of Pierre's Hole do not always agree about the number of casualties.[10]

The unhappy Gros Ventres did not tell the whole story to Fontenelle, of course. The whites' versions followed after the supply party had at last overtaken its waiting people and heard their stories, along with those spun by some of the still-excited men of the rival brigades. During the confused, raucous greetings, Rabbitskin Leggins rejoined his fellows. Almost surely he met two of the Nez Perces who had been wounded during the fighting. Both were from the Kamiah-Kooskia area where he lived, and hearing their brags was exciting. One was Tackensuatis, a tall, imposing man who lived on the South Fork of the Clearwater River. Rabbitskin Leggins had probably known him since childhood. Because of his severe, slow-healing stomach wound, Tackensuatis's tribesmen nicknamed him Rotten Belly.

The other was the man who was responsible, in large part, for launching Rabbitskin's saga—Hallalhotsoot, or, as the whites said, Lawyer. He had suffered a wound in his left hip that would lame him for life. The wound also helped bond him tightly to the whites: brothers in battle.[11]

If Rabbitskin Leggins hadn't lost his Bible or his cross (nothing more is ever heard of them), he almost surely showed them off. What he said of their powers or of the possibility that a white medicine man might come to the Nimipus of the Clearwater area to explain how to utilize their magic we do not know. We do not even know whether the young traveler visited his home village before he joined a Nez Perce hunting party that spent the winter of 1832–33 near Bonneville's cold-weather camp in the great, grassy cup where the Salmon and Lemhi valleys come together in east-central Idaho. The town of Salmon stands there today; it is no great distance northwest of Monida Press.

Rabbitskin Leggins's death there was as premature as those of the three other Nez Perces with whom he had journeyed to St. Louis as a naive youth. Spring was touching the mountain air in 1833 when Blackfeet war parties began roaming the hills adjacent to the Salmon, determined to teach a lesson to the Columbian Indians who were showing so much interest in casting their lots with the invading whites. During the involved comings and goings, about three hundred of them trapped thirty or so Nez Perce and Flathead warriors and killed all but one, who happened to be off chasing a horse and escaped to tell the story. When searchers from the camp, accompanied by wailing women, found the corpses, they discovered that all had been savagely beheaded. Among the slain was Rabbitskin Leggins.[12]

Rabbitskin Leggins would have an epitaph. Far to the east, tales of the Nimipus' quest for the Book were being reviewed and reshaped in a most unlikely way.

William Walker was either a half-blood Wyandot Indian or was married to a Wyandot. More to the point, he was deeply religious, fairly well educated, and concerned about the fate, first, of the Wyandots and, more broadly, of all American Indians.

The Wyandots were unhappy remnants of the once-mighty Hurons. The Iroquois had crushed that tribe during the seventeenth-century wars to control the fur trade of the forested Northeast. Some of the refugees had settled in northern Ohio and there, as Wyandot, had become one more element in what North American whites had for two centuries been calling "the Indian problem." The Indians, of course, had been struggling with the white problem for the same length of time.

Frontiersmen who had watched their cabins burn while their relatives were hideously scalped (and who had retaliated by burning Indian towns, ravishing their women, and kidnapping their children) favored ending the problem by exterminating the red obstacles to America's persistent westward thrust. To the more secure citizens of a nation founded on the principles of life, liberty, and the pursuit of happiness for all men, genocide seemed too drastic. Would it not be more civilized to purchase the lands claimed by the eastern Indians and move the sellers west to some remote spot in the newly acquired Louisiana Territory? The vacated lands could then be settled by productive whites, while the displaced savages wandered as they wished through their new homes—once they had come to terms with a new physical environment and new tribes who, in most cases, had not agreed to accept the outlanders.

The removal policy became official in 1830. Within the year President Andrew Jackson forced the first of the so-called Five Civilized Tribes of the southeast to start westward along the notorious Trail of Tears toward what eventually became Oklahoma.[13]

Similar pressures had caught up with William Walker's Wyandots even earlier. Harassed continuously by their white neighbors in northern Ohio, they had agreed tentatively to move to eastern Kansas if the land there seemed suitable for agriculture. William Walker was a member of the committee that was instructed by the tribe to check on the matter. When the examiners reported negatively, the tribe balked against removal and clung to their old homes until 1842.

During his travels to and from Kansas, Walker passed through St. Louis. From someone, possibly Clark, he picked up bits of information about what he was told were four Flatheads who, he wrote later, had walked three thousand miles to the Missouri city in search of the truth, meaning Christianity, Protestant variety. The tale was made still more piteous—and dramatic—by Walker's shocked statement that the skull of one of the searchers had been deliberately deformed in such a way that its front and back parts sloped up to a peak. Ah, if only the Church could rid the benighted of such ungodly ways and in the process save their deformed souls as well!

His plea, which skimmed the possibility of any injustice being visited upon the Wyandot by the new policy of removal, was printed in the *Christian Advocate and Journal* of March 1833—the very time when Rabbitskin Leggins was riding toward his death. Editorials and letters to the editor rang out, urging the American Board of Foreign Missions to get busy. The American Board was addressed because Oregon had not yet been incorporated into the United States and because its native inhabitants spoke foreign tongues, as viewed by the Americans.[14]

Although the spring issues of the Christian Advocate and Journal did not touch specifically on the point, the idea of converting the western Indians to a Protestant religious and social ideology fitted well the yeasty temper of the times. Anything (except Catholicism) that facilitated America's westward march was desirable. Protestant Indians, for example, would be able to accept and adapt to white civilization as it overtook them, and through such accommodations, the centuries-old Indian problem would be solved. What better place to start, moreover, than Oregon, where yearning natives were already seeking the burning light of the Gospel?

Rabbitskin Leggins was dead. Whether he told a Nez Perce or two, before he perished, to expect medicine men—teachers—who would be coming from the place where the sun rose is, ultimately, irrelevant. Times were ripe for the advent. The missionaries, supposing they were wanted, had girded their loins. The Indians of the Northwest were equally ready for a great happening. Spokan Garry had returned home permanently in 1831 and had established a school of his own. A cult based on his teachings, reinforced by oddments gleaned from Catholic Iroquois and Anglican managers of Hudson's Bay

Company posts, had spread with surprising rapidity among the scattered bands. Several fur traders, such as Warren Ferris, Nathaniel Wyeth, and Benjamin Bonneville, wrote of being astonished by the cult's praying, ceremonial dancing, reluctance to fight, and refusal to travel on Sunday. Clearly, such Indians would welcome additional precepts about profitable living from experienced teachers.

This mood was tied in with another expectation. Increasing numbers of Nez Perces, Cayuses, Flatheads, and related tribes were falling under the dazzling spell of merchandise produced by white technology and offered in trading tents at each summer's rendezvous. The appearance at these annual gatherings of anyone who professed to have a key to a better material and spiritual future—the two concepts were tightly interwoven—was bound to stir enthusiasm. The notion that this enthusiasm might turn out to be disastrous never occurred to the celebrants. For who is ever wholly convinced of the grimness of his future?

· 7 ·

REJECTION

The first missionaries to reach the 1834 fur-trade rendezvous in response to the appeals broadcast by the *Christian Advocate and Journal* were five Methodists led by the Reverend Jason Lee. Lee was tall, rawboned, and black bearded, thirty years old, and physically powerful. With him was his twenty-seven-year-old nephew, Daniel Lee, similar in appearance to Jason but so seldom mentioned in contemporary records that one assumes he lived out his first years in the West largely under his uncle's shadow. To teach the Indian children in the mission school they planned to open, the Lees hired sallow, introspective Cyrus Shepard, a thirty-five-year-old bachelor, who sometimes found the day's shocks so unbearable that he retired to whatever secluded spot was available and sought comfort in weeping. Completing the group were two sturdy lay helpers hired on the Missouri frontier—Courtney Walker and Philip Edwards.

By then it was known that church people who were unschooled in wilderness living could reach the mountain Indians only by traveling with a supply column heading west to the annual summer rendezvous of the fur traders. The caravan to which the Lee party attached itself was led by Nathaniel Wyeth, a genial, long-chinned Yankee who had developed a notion that he could successfully invade the Oregon domain of the Hudson's Bay Company as a dealer in furs and salted salmon. His first efforts failed dismally, as much through bad luck as through ignorance. But he felt he had learned enough from his mistakes to risk a second effort. Being a genial soul, he let the missionaries join his column

75

for safety's sake. Also freeloading with him were a pair of Pacific-bound naturalists, twenty-six-year-old John Kirk Townsend, and his mentor, Thomas Nuttall.

The milieu considered, the Methodists adapted well to Wyeth's roughneck
roustabouts. Even so, they could hardly have been prepared for what they saw
as the savageries of the 1834 rendezvous. The meeting, in fact, turned out to be
a turning point in the Lees' careers, but before trying to explain the crisis, it will
be well to look at the famed gathering itself and at the Nez Perces' part in it—or
at least as much as was recorded by the only known diarists who were on hand.
One was John Kirk Townsend; the other was William Marshall Anderson, a
nephew of explorer William Clark. Anderson was traveling west for his health
with the Rocky Mountain Fur Company's supply caravan, led in 1834 by
William Sublette.

The rendezvous that year sprawled over the gray sagebrush flats and dry
hills where Hams Fork twists toward its junction with the Green River—
roughly the neighborhood of today's hamlet of Granger in southwestern
Wyoming. By the middle of June hundreds of men, some of them free agents,
but more working as trappers and suppliers for half a dozen companies, were
coming together with whoops and gunshots and a thunder of hooves. Whites
were only part of the crowd. The diarist, William Anderson, estimated, probably with exaggeration, that fifteen hundred Nez Perces, Flatheads, and
Snake Indians were also in attendance, swarming like flies around the heap of
goods on display in the various trading huts.[1]

Each company had its own tent city, each tribe its own base. Some camps
were as many as eight miles apart. They had to be. The only grass for thousands of horses grew in meadows strung along the stream's banks like widely
spaced emerald beads. When those spots were eaten out, more had to be
found. After moving up the Green River for several miles, the different cavalcades cut back through the sagebrush for fresh, but still widely separated,
meadows beside Hams Fork.

The two tenderfeet riding with the migrants noticed the native women
in particular. Both were struck by their riding astride. Though Anderson considered the Nez Perce women to be homely, he admired their litheness.
"These ladies are very fine riders, mounting and dismounting with the ease
and grace of a cavalier." Townsend was more generous:

Some of the women of this party, particularly of the Nez Perce nation, are rather
handsome.... Their dresses of deer skin are profusely ornamented with beads and porcupine quills; huge strings of beads are hung around their necks, and their saddles are

garnished with little hawk's bells, which jingle and make music for them as they travel along.... Several have little children tied to their backs, sewed up papoose fashion; as they jolt along the road, we not infrequently hear their voices ringing loud above the music of the bells.[2]

Other kinds of clamor were less pleasant. Confined by illness to his tent for part of the gathering's span, Townsend had to listen to the antics of the celebrants outside, and he did not like it.

These people with their obstreperous mirth, their whooping, and howling, and quarrelling, added to the mounted Indians, who are constantly dashing into and through our camp, yelling like fiends, the barking and baying of savage wolf-dogs, and the incessant cracking of rifles and carbines, render our camp a perfect bedlam ... heated by the detestable liquor which circulates freely among them.[3]

The Reverend Jason Lee was also distressed by the revels. "My God, my God," he asked his diary, "is there nothing that will have any effect on them?" Well, the uproar wasn't pretty. But remarks like Townsend's and Lee's reflected more than a little elitism—the educated who had been brought up under strict nineteenth-century social restraints sitting in judgment on uneducated young men who had gone West partly to escape those very restrictions. The young men's work was hard, dusty, dangerous—and exciting. Almost their only chance to hobnob with kindred souls came during the two- to three-week vacation provided by the rendezvous. Many hit the diluted grain alcohol provided by the traders with the exuberance of their youth. But not all did. Many were in debt to the wilderness merchants for their equipment. Others joyfully lavished luxuries on their Indian wives and paramours. Those matters attended to, not much of their meager income was left for drink. What alcohol they bought was often used mostly the way many people use it today, as a social lubricant while exchanging news with old friends. Many did not drink at all, but wrote letters home or went fishing for the fat trout of Hams Fork and other streams.

Be that as it may, the pandemonium of the rendezvous kept the diarists from noticing an item of major significance in the gatherings. During the mid-1830s, more Indians—an aggregate of Nez Perces, Cayuses, Flatheads, Shoshonis, Bannocks, and Utes—attended the sprawling fairs than did whites. They put on impressive parades and dances for the pale-faced visitors to their lands, mingling easily with the boisterous trappers, whose sense of individual freedom was in many ways like their own. From the associations came much of the deep-seated goodwill that kept the Nez Perces and Flatheads at peace with the interlopers long after an influx of a different kind of whites had put a severe strain on the original ties.

Those ties went as far back as the Lewis and Clark expedition and helped account for the dazzling performances of two individuals at the 1834 rendezvous. One was an exuberant young Nez Perce warrior named Bull's Head; the whites called him Kentuck because of his constant singing, in fractured English, of a ballad, "The Hunters of Kentucky," that they had taught him for the joy of listening to his renditions. The other Indian was a Flathead. His compact muscular stature led the mountain men to call him Little Chief. His Flathead name was Insillah (Insula), which has been translated both as War Eagle's Plume and Red Feather. In due time both men would play notable roles in introducing missionaries to the mountains of the Northwest.

Kentuck's feat was a put-up job inspired one evening when William Sublette and he spotted some buffalo near the camp of the Rocky Mountain Fur Company. Their intent was for Kentuck to give William Anderson a show that would be exciting enough for him to take the telling of it home to his uncle William Clark—a remembrance from the Nimipus, so to speak. The next morning the two men managed to cut a huge male out of the herd and catapult it among the tents of the camp. Riding full speed just behind its shoulder came Kentuck in hunting regalia, stripped to his breechcloth, no saddle, bow bent and arrow notched. The camp erupted. Screeches, execrations. Arrows whizzed, guns crashed. Carrying at least nine projectiles in its shaggy body, the buffalo "leaped from the bank and floated, broad side up, down the rapid current of the Green River." All that to please Hi-hi-seeks-tooah, Kentuck's Little White Brother, Clark's nephew.[4]

The second story belongs to Little Chief. The Flathead, wrote Anderson, was reputed to be a splendid horseman. He had once broken a wild horse by vaulting onto it bareback, a flag in one hand and a tambourine in the other. The horse went berserk, bucking and twisting. Whenever Insillah wanted to slow it, he threw the flag across its head, blinding it temporarily. To guide it, he struck it across one cheek or the other with the tambourine, all the while clinging to its heaving back with only his heels and instantaneous shifts of balance. In time the horse just gave up and quit.[5]

Insillah's adventure at the rendezvous came when two Indian boys, who were riding across the face of a hill sloping up from the camp of the Rocky Mountain Fur Company, jumped a grizzly bear and just for devilment chased it downhill, scattering people "as a hawk scatters chickens." Bewildered by so many humans, the huge beast took cover in a dense clump of willows, growling its anger. While everyone else stayed petrified, Insillah loaded his trade musket, crept into the refuge, and dispatched the bear with a single skillful—and lucky—shot. Afterwards he gave the skin, with its ears and claws still attached, to William Anderson. "I don't know that I ever felt so much pride and surprise," Clark's nephew wrote years later.[6] He doesn't say that this gift was also an indirect tribute to the explorer, but would it have been given if Lewis and Clark had not laid the foundations for the goodwill that pervaded the tribe during the 1830s?

On the same day that Kentuck chased the buffalo bull through Sublette's camp, Edmund Christy, a partner in the Rocky Mountain Fur Company, arrived from Fort Vancouver, the Hudson's Bay Company's great bastion on the lower Columbia River. With him were many Snake (Shoshoni) and Nez Perce Indians. Among the latter was Tackensuatis, or Rotten Belly, who had been wounded, as had William Sublette, during the battle of Pierre's Hole two years earlier. "It was curious," wrote Anderson, "to see those two iron men … shouting, laughing, and joking with each other, then winding up by cursing the Blackfeet with a hearty and vicious eloquence."

Again the diarist did not notice a significant trend that lay beneath the boisterousness. Ruthless competition among the whites and relentless attacks on small parties of trappers and Indians by the Blackfeet were seriously reducing the number of beaver available to the fur traders. Hoping to broaden the field of opportunity, three frustrated newcomers—Nathaniel Wyeth, Benjamin Bonneville, and Edmund Christy, a recent investor in the Rocky Mountain concern—had separately decided to break into the interior regions of Oregon, which the Hudson's Bay Company was still determined to maintain as an inviolable buffer to the rich regions beyond the Columbia. None of the three succeeded. But the efforts of two of them were important to the Nimipus of our story. During the winter months of early 1834, Bonneville led three men on a scouting trip across the snow-heaped Wallowa Mountains into the deep canyons that debouch into the Snake River. He was the first American known to have done so. On the excursion he probably met Tuekakas (Old Joseph) and talked to him earnestly and effectively about the virtues of the United States compared to those of Great Britain. Meanwhile, Edmund Christy had a good look at the fertile lands close to Fort Vancouver. Although he came to the rendezvous with few furs, he did bear reports that would help deflect the Lees from the tribes they had been sent forth to convert.[7]

* * *

Word that teachers about God were in Nathaniel Wyeth's camp on Hams Fork was brought to the Nez Perces and Flatheads by some of the mountain men. Whether some of those Indians, stirred by their prophets, had come to the rendezvous hoping for this very event (as some historians believe[8]). The point is irrelevant. What counted was the apparent answer to the earnest prayers of at least segments of the tribes: the God people, powerful medicine men, were here! Several of the Indians rode over to shake hands with them and were not offended when the missionaries, busy putting their tents and liverstock to rights, gave the visitors a brush-off. Later that evening five leaders returned to dine with the Methodists. Their identities are uncertain. All we know from Anderson is that the following leaders, among many others, were at the rendezvous: Rotten Belly, Lawyer, Flint Necklace (the father of the Looking Glass who later fought beside Young Joseph), and Little Chief (Insillah). Undoubtedly some of them shared that first dinner.[9]

The missionaries' schoolteacher-to-be, Cyrus Shepard, thought them "the most cleanly and respectable looking indians I have yet seen." Perhaps they looked too respectable. They were not the exotics Jason Lee had been led to expect by the articles and drawings in the *Christian Advocate*. The Flatheads' skulls did not slope up to a peak; the Nez Perces did not wear shells in their nostrils. And though the Indians seemed favorable, their physical environment did not. Short, dry summers, endless wind, and sterile soil where only sagebrush seemed able to grow would not support the kind of all-purpose farms Lee thought necessary for the civilizing process. Even worse, he would have to contend for control of the Indians with these dissolute whites—more savage, he wrote, than the natives themselves.

There might be an alternative. During their long journey out from the States, Nathaniel Wyeth had surely told Lee that the best agricultural lands he had seen in the West were in the Willamette Valley. The valley lay south of Fort Vancouver, the Hudson's Bay Company's headquarters-bastion on the lower Columbia, in territory that was certain to pass, sooner or later, into the hands of the United States. Edmund Christy, who had just returned from there, may have amplified, passing on to the missionaries what Lee called, without going into specifics, "encouraging information." We can make a guess at some of it. Indians whose heads actually peaked lived in the Willamette Valley, along the lower Columbia, and on the coast. They were completely docile, as were several retired French Canadian servants of the Hudson's Bay Company who, together with a handful of strayed Americans, were beginning to open farms in the Willamette region. Those people also needed religious mentors. If Protestants did not undertake it, Catholics surely would. Here, in short, was a place where true good could be done—a place that, with diligence, could be prepared for colonization by Americans.

The temptation to follow the lead was strong and insidious. The missionaries had to go to Fort Vancouver to pick up the goods that were being shipped to them from Massachusetts around Cape Horn aboard Wyeth's leased brig, *May Dacre*. Why not use the opportunity to compare, with open minds, of course, the opportunities in the Willamette Valley with those in the high, cold, untamed interior? If the situation in the valley did not seem propitious, and surely God would advise them, they would cheerfully load their equipment in rowboats and toil several hundred miles back up the Columbia to ... where? There is no evidence that Jason Lee ever seriously sought, from either mountain men or Indians, information about possible sites for missions in Nez Perce or Flathead country.

The Indians who wanted the kind of power that white medicine men with Books could provide quickly sensed Lee's hesitation and applied such pressure as they could. They told Lee they would pay the missionaries in beaver if they would build white-style houses in their territory. When that approach did not elicit a direct response, they promised to give him children to educate. They would learn to farm if he stayed with *them*. Lee underscored the word in his diary: *them* as distinct from what other Indians? Those in the Willamette?

Vaguely Lee answered that he might return the following year. And on the five went, traveling part way with Wyeth and part with a small company of people from the Hudson's Bay Company. It was tough going—so tough that frail Cyrus Shepard sought relief (some evidence suggests) by attempting to commit suicide.[10] Why repeat these hardships by turning back after reaching what seemed a better goal close to a dependable source of supplies.

Rationalizing thus, they convinced themselves. None of the five ever returned to the interior to stay.

A premonition that they would not return, born of the Lees' evasiveness, troubled the Indian Tackensuatis. As he jogged away from Hams Fork with William Sublette and William Anderson, he remarked gloomily that the Nez Perces needed help. The Blackfeet were grinding them up.[11]

Such statistics as exist support his dejection. In 1805, Lewis and Clark had estimated that the population of the many scattered Nez Perce villages totaled six thousand. After traveling through the heart of Nimipu country thirty years later, Samuel Parker estimated a total twenty-five hundred. (We will meet Parker shortly.) Subsequent guessers reached similar conclusions. The strength of the Nez Perces was shrinking drastically. Disease, which crept up the Columbia from the epidemic-scourged tribes of the coast, no doubt contributed to the toll, but to Tackensuatis, a warrior who had engaged in many fights, the constantly aggressive Blackfeet were the major factor.[12] Of late there had been too many incidents like the one in which Rabbitskin Leggins had died—twenty-nine killed and beheaded, only one escaped. But the men of God, the men with the magic Book, had seemed indifferent. What had gone wrong? What could be done?

William Clark's nephew, William Anderson, responded sympathetically. He would ask the Big Chief of the Whites to protect those incomparable Indians, the Nez Perces and the Flatheads.

There is no indication in the records that Anderson ever did so. One doubts, furthermore, that Tackensuatis was consoled. The White Chief seemed far away, beyond reach. But what of Spokan Garry? He said that the power they needed was as close as a prayer. Many of the Nimipus did pray, very earnestly. To what end? The Lees provided no answer.

What was to be done?

· 8 ·

THE ENERGIES OF HOPE

T he rendezvous of 1835 was held on broad, grassy meadows where Horse
Creek angles into Wyoming's Green River, due west of the snow-
streaked, sky-sawing peaks of the Wind River Mountains, and about a
hundred miles north of the 1834 meeting place. More Indians than
ever were on hand, living in scattered thickets of tipis, among thousands of
horses. Nearby were the canvas or hide shelters of some two hundred whites.
All were impatient, even cantankerous, for the principal supply caravan from
the East was a month late.

When the laden pack animals finally appeared on August 12, they were
welcomed by such a jam of people that Tackensuatis, Kentuck, Insillah, and
many other Indians did not immediately realize that two more men of God,
Samuel Parker and Marcus Whitman, had appeared. This astounding news,
which flashed from camp to camp the next day, quickly dispelled the ignorance, however. One of the white *tewats* (medicine men) was going to work a
cure on perhaps the most famous mountain man at the meeting, James
Bridger.[1]

Tiers of trappers and Indians gathered to watch. Bridger lay stomach
down on a smoothed patch of sun-baked earth. Whitman knelt beside him,
perhaps even astraddle, and with his thumb tested a steel knife blade for
sharpness. He was thirty-three years old. His sturdy body was clad in frontier
homespun, for neither he nor Parker had yet taken to buckskin. Not that the
information would have meant anything to Tackensuatis, but Whitman had

been fairly well educated, for the times in which he lived, at a small medical college in upper New York State. Very religious, he had long wanted to be a medical missionary, but recurrent pains in his side had prevented the American Board of Foreign Missions from appointing him until Parker, bound west and needing a companion, had interceded. Parker, fifty-six years old, a farmer, preacher, and, until recently, headmaster of a girl's school, was clearly the boss of the duo, but this show was entirely Whitman's.

It turned out to be a bloody affair. First, the surgeon made a long incision in Bridger's back—if the trapper had anesthetized himself in advance with diluted grain alcohol, no mention is made of the fact—and gouged hard at the intervening cartilage. Gaped at by scores of pairs of eyes, Bridger held himself motionless. Whitman stayed equally imperturbable as he pried loose and held up a barbed iron arrowhead three inches long that had been lodged in Bridger's flesh since the battle of Pierre's Hole three years before. We can assume the audience's gasps of amazement and then an outburst of raucous whoops and hand clapping.

Inspired by Bridger's example, other patients thronged about. A second trapper had an arrowhead removed from his shoulder, and an Indian, one from an unspecified part of his body. Other kinds of ministrations followed, as did word that several men of the supply train might have died of cholera near the mouth of the Platte if Whitman had not lent his skills.

Strong medicine!—the very sort of power that Rabbitskin Leggins and his three companions had been searching for when they traveled to St. Louis in 1831. Parker and Whitman were equally excited, for here were members of the tribes they were looking for, even though their heads did not fit the descriptions in the Christian Advocate's story about deformed Indians yearning for the gospel. As for Jason and Daniel Lee, who had been put into motion by the same story, well, surely, God's mysterious ways worked for the best.

An adventuring Scot who had seen the Methodists during the winter said they were plowing fields and building a mission school in the Willamette Valley, just as Chief Tackensuatis had suspected. So, there would be no competition along the Clearwater and in the Bitterroot Valley. Praise be!

On August 16 a group of Nez Perces and Flatheads squeezed into the missionaries' tent for an interview. An interview was exactly what it turned out to be. Before founding a mission, the underfinanced American Board of Foreign Missions wanted some assurance of success. Explore the land and examine the people, Parker's directive said. So this became a time of questions and answers. Working through interpreters who stumbled now and then, the whites searched for the necessary pledges. Did the Indians truly want to learn about God? Would they let their children be educated in Christian ways? Would they follow the lead of their teachers in all things related to the Holy Spirit? The Indians said eagerly they would, for was not that the way to power? Happiness filled the tent as whites and Indians clasped hands across a theological and philosophical gulf twenty centuries old, both sides thinking to bridge it solidly with words, a few rituals, and hearts filled with goodwill.

The euphoria touched off a burst of energy on both sides. The whites agreed that Parker should continue his explorations of the land by traveling with an escort of Nez Perces to their home territory. Whitman would return East, taking two Nez Perce boys with him to train as interpreters. After settling formalities with the missionary board, he would marry the woman to whom Parker had introduced him shortly before their departure for the West, recruit helpers, and rejoin his fellow worker at the 1836 rendezvous. By then Parker would have selected the most suitable building site. He would brief Whitman thoroughly and, his assignment completed, would return to his schoolteaching.

The Nez Perces, or at least those aligned with Tackensuatis, were ecstatic. Realizing that the benign but elderly Parker would need special attention, they appointed as his caretaker the singing Indian, Kentuck, who the year before had sought to amuse William Anderson by driving a buffalo through Sublette's camp. Parker himself hired an interpreter, a French Canadian called Compo, who had a Nez Perce wife. No Flatheads were included in the arrangements, for it was not likely that the American could examine the homelands of both tribes before winter set in. So the whites decided, probably on the advice of the trappers, to concentrate on the Nimipus. Theirs was the bigger tribe. A station in their lands could be supplied with relative ease via the Columbia River. Not least, the site would be less exposed to Blackfeet. Reasonable enough, but it put the Flatheads' noses out of joint and may explain why Old Ignace la Mousse, an Iroquois who lived with the slighted tribe, journeyed that year to St. Louis with a delegation that included his two young sons. There he met Bishop Joseph Rosati, urged the Flatheads' case, and thus became responsible for the appearance of Catholic priests in the Bitterroot Valley a few years later.

On August 22, the dominie headed north with three dozen or so of Bridger's trappers and three hundred or more Indians.[2] Loose horses, close to a thousand of them, stirred clouds of dust under a blazing sun. Parker rode the same horse that had carried him most of the way from the Missouri; seeing that the weary beast needed spelling, Tackensuatis gave him an Indian pony. The American's bed, extra clothing, and several religious books were on a pack mule he had appropriated from Whitman; it was the better of the two mules the missionaries had used on their outward journey. During that long ride Parker had never lifted a hand to help with the packing, and it is probable that on his trip with the Indians the daily chore fell to some Nez Perce woman, perhaps Tackensuatis's wife. The women and children also brought him fresh berries and choice bits of meat, saw that he had shade during the lunch stops, and listened attentively as he preached about the grace of God and the salvation of their souls. What the listeners got out of the remarks after they had passed through the sieve of Compo's translation is impossible to say.

At the southern edge of Jackson Hole, Bridger's group, accompanied by a large part of the Indians, split away, intending to go north into the Yellowstone country. As they departed, Parker handed out to the trappers as many religious tracts as he felt he could spare and then swung west across Teton Pass with those of the Nimipus who were returning directly home. He took literally the American Board's behest that he explore the land. He made notes on flora and fauna, studied the composition of rocks through a magnifying glass that amazed the Indians, climbed high places for their views, and recognized the ancient volcanic origin of many of the landforms. But he seems never to have asked the Indians any questions about their own religion.

The trails were difficult at times. Once he found himself riding across a steep, rocky slope above a brawling stream. Muscles tight with apprehension, he tried to guide his Indian pony along what he thought was the best route. The horse, its head tossing angrily, refused to obey. Finally Parker gave it free rein, writing afterwards that the pony's "dashing mode of going ahead, even in the most dangerous places, was preferable to the more cautious management of the American." In hindsight his words can be read as a parable, but Parker never made the transference. He continued pressing his own ways on the Indians even after they had been joined by a large group of hunters under a chief whose name Parker rendered as Charlie. He persuaded the Indians not to travel on Sundays, but to listen to him preach. With painstaking care he taught the Ten Commandments to the chiefs and afterwards tested them, again through Compo's interpretations, on what they had learned.

Somewhere in the vast canyons and among the high, densely timbered ridges of the Salmon Mountains, a fever struck him. He bled himself until he was too weak to dismount and walk across precarious spots, as he normally did. But he would not slow down. As he began to recover, he chafed at the leisurely pace of the Indians and struck ahead with only ten followers. Down to the Clearwater, across the Snake, over bald prairies to the Walla Walla River, and along it to Fort Walla Walla (originally Fort Nez Perce). After enjoying the hospitality of Pierre Pambrun, the Hudson's Bay Company trader in charge of the post, he paid Compo (very stingily, the interpreter later complained), told the Nez Perces with him that he would return in the spring—they promised to care for his horse and mule—and was rowed down the Columbia in a canoe paddled by three Wallawalla Indians.

On April 26, 1836, he was back at Fort Walla Walla. He lingered there for a few days, preaching to Hudson's Bay Company workers in the mornings and to a steadily increasing throng of Cayuse, Wallawalla, and Nez Perce Indians in the afternoons. When he continued up-country in May with his growing flock, news of his approach swept ahead of him. On reaching the wide canyon bottom where the Snake and Clearwater join, he found a multitude waiting. One of the expectants was Chief Tuekakas.

Tuekakas was then about fifty years old. As was noted earlier, his Nez Perce mother had left his Cayuse father shortly before their son's birth. Except for a brief period during his late teens, Tuekakas lived among the bands that roamed the Wallowa region, where his stepfather, Takinploon, had become what has been described as a "divisional" chief.[3]

Nez Perce political organizations were evolving slowly with the changing times. Bands that were decimated by disease and warfare coalesced, with surviving chiefs jockeying for position in the new units. Additional mingling occurred during the winters when several bands congregated in traditional sites in the bottoms of the deep, grassy canyons along the lower reaches of the main rivers. Communal problems led to the elevation of able men to positions of authority over associated groups of loosely structured villages—so loose, indeed, that when spring came, the different bands generally broke apart to attend to their salmon fishing and root gathering as they always had.

The winter villages that recognized Takinploon as their leader lay along the west bank of the Snake River, both above and below its confluence with the Clearwater. Of these villages the most prosperous occupied the mouths of the deeply cupped Imnaha and Grande Ronde rivers. As the latter rushed toward the Snake River, it picked up such affluents as the Wallowa River and, a short distance above the Snake, a tributary later called Joseph Creek.

Heavy snow in the mountains protected the winter villages from enemy raids, whether by Snakes or Blackfeet. The people relaxed. Women wove handsome bags out of twine; the bags were desirable trade items, as well as handy for carrying back to camp the dried camas roots the women dug in the high meadow during summer. The men made weapons, trained horses, and hunted deer and mountain sheep among the crags of the canyons. Winter was a time for teaching children by means of imitation and the repetition of well-tested stories of a type we might call myths. Especially it was a time for courtships and for ceremonies, such as the vibrant guardian spirit dance.

The division chiefs sought to hold their authority during the summer dispersions by appointing subchiefs over the wandering bands.[4] Again, there was a great deal of autonomy, and ambitious young men could maintain their positions best by maintaining their reputations—leading small war or hunting parties, handing out gifts to faithful adherents, showing wisdom in council. Tuekakas was one such chief, appointed by his stepfather to lead a band that summered on the high meadows that rolled northward from the great, gray Wallowa Peaks. The elder man, Takinploon, was generally close by. One of his band's favorite fishing places was along the Wallowa River near the present town of Enterprise. Tuekakas's people made their catches higher up the same stream, where its bright, clean water sparkled out of the north end of Wallowa Lake, near today's town of Joseph. Did Tuekakas keep his position by leading war parties? Did he ever go on buffalo hunts on the plains? We cannot be sure.

By the spring of 1836, when Samuel Parker returned to the junction of the Snake and Clearwater rivers, Takinploon was dead. Tuekakas, who had been carefully trained for the position, inherited the chieftainship of the division. Apparently, however, three chiefs whose bands wintered along the Snake below the entrance of the Clearwater had broken away from the main group. We will hear of all of them again: Apash Wyakaikt (Flint Necklace, or Old Looking Glass), who lived at Asotin in the extreme southeast corner of present Washington State; Tamootsin (Timothy) a few miles down the Snake River at Alpowa Creek; and Hemene Ilppilp (Red Wolf), also near Alpowa Creek. The defections may have worried Tuekakas. He was thoughtful and ambitious and, characteristically, would have sought for ways to prevent further erosion of his influence. If so, white medicine might well have seemed an answer. He had heard of the power of prayer as preached by Spokan Garry, and he almost surely knew of the delegation that had visited St. Louis. His band's piety and friendliness had impressed Benjamin Bonneville when the fur hunter had cross the Wallowa country a few years earlier. For the sake of his own prestige and for the future of the people who still followed him, such a leader would want to be on hand when the white medicine man again visit-ed the river junction.

Tuekakas managed to speak to Parker. Impressed, Parker asked Kentuck for information about him. A good man, Kentuck said. Unlike Charlie, the chief whose band had joined Parker's group during the crossing of the Salmon Mountains, Tuekakas prayed with his heart, not just with his lips, or so Parker understood Kentuck to say. His regard rising still higher, Parker wrote in his journal that Tuekakas had benefited—and presumably would continue to benefit—more from the gospels than would any other Indian he had yet met.[5] Gospels obtained from whom, one wonders. As recited by Spokan Garry? Quoted by Parker? Anyway, here, apparently, was fertile seed for Whitman and whoever came across the country with him.

By then, Parker's explorations were all but over. Faced with the prospect of riding back across the rugged mountains he had threaded the year before, he recoiled and wrote Whitman only in general terms about what he had seen—no mention, strangely, of Tuekakas. He gave the letter to Kentuck to deliver at the rendezvous. For himself, he traveled some distance farther up the Columbia, talking to more Indians and traders, and then dropped back to Fort Vancouver. There he caught a ship bound for the Hawaiian Islands and returned home by sea around Cape Horn. The actual conversion of the Indi-ans of the interior Northwest was now up to Marcus Whitman and whoever Whitman and the American Board of Foreign Missions had managed to gath-er together for the project—a project, the participants were convinced, that would redound to the greater glory not only of God but of all America.

This interlude treats of the obsessions of two born-again Christians. One was Marcus Whitman, whose conversion experience came when he was sixteen and attending a school in Massachusetts run by a famed divine, the Reverend Moses Hallock. (Hallock also taught another youth who was consumed by an obsession, John Brown of Civil War notoriety.) During one of the revivalist meet-ings then sweeping New England, Whitman was, he said later, "awakened to a sense of my sin and danger, and brought by Divine Grace to rely on the Lord Jesus for pardon and salvation."[6] At age sixteen.

Having found the Path, he yearned to show it to others, notably the hea-thens. After completing his medical education and working for a time as a small-town doctor, he began soliciting the American Board of Foreign Missions for an appointment. He was turned down regularly because of his own poor health until Samuel Parker, needing an assistant for his exploratory trip, interceded for him. On returning East from the 1835 rendezvous, he was elevated to leadership of the board's efforts among the Nez Perces and Flatheads. Because it was believed a wife would help spread his message to the Indian women and through them to their husbands, he married, just before his departure and after a scant courtship, twenty-seven-year-old Narcissa Prentiss. She was attractive physically with red-gold hair and a fine singing voice, but there was a reserve and a haughtiness in her that would keep Indians at arms' length. Her reserve may have chilled suitors, also, and turned her passions toward Christ and His work. Still, her marriage to Whitman seems to have flowered into true devotion.

The other true believer was Henry Harmon Spalding. Born out of wedlock and raised in a foster home from which he was violently ejected by his irate foster father when he was seventeen, he experienced his conversion at the age of twenty-two. He testified that he had lived a very wicked life among wicked men until "God in his great mercy raised me from the depths of sin and brought me, as I hope, into his Kingdom."[7] Although that indefatigable biographer of Oregon's Protestant missionaries, Clifford Drury, has not managed to spade up examples of Spalding's self-assigned depravity, his conviction that he had discovered the Light accounts for his fuming temper toward Indians who, later on, did not respond to his teachings as he thought they should.

Until his conversion, Spalding had received scant formal education. Afterwards, supporting himself by menial tasks, he labored through a Presbyterian academy, a college, and a theological seminary. Narcissa Prentiss, Whitman's bride-to-be, lived in the town where the academy was located. Somehow Spalding developed a curdling antipathy toward her, perhaps because (it is sometimes speculated) she refused his offer of marriage. As it was, he wed an acquaintance of his college days, Eliza Hart. Intensely pious, Eliza was coarse haired, thin faced, and homely, whereas Narcissa was pretty; almost scrawny, whereas Narcissa was buxom; and warm of heart, whereas Narcissa was chill.

If it had been possible for the Whitmans to chose anyone other than the Spaldings as co-workers, they probably would have done so. But there was no one. Most pioneers on the frontier despised the continent's first inhabitants as either bloodthirsty savages or drunken louts, idling around trading posts and military stations waiting for handouts. Why try to save them? By contrast, humanitarians in the East admired the Indians as nature's noblemen, yet felt they were anachronisms, wasting intolerable amounts of American land sustaining their hunting economy. It was the great law of God, one theologian declared, that the nation's Indians would vanish from the Earth "*unless* [emphasis added] they adopted those modes of life which would enable them to support the greatest possible number of inhabitants."[8]

Neither Whitman nor Spalding needed to be told what that mode was. Thomas Jefferson had voiced the ideal several decades earlier: "Those who labor in the earth are the chosen of God, if He has a chosen people." All that needed to be done, then, was to transform nomadic savages into sedentary agrarians. By ceasing to be Indians, they could become Americans. Both God and country would be served. Therein, the argument ran, lay true freedom—freedom from ignorance and savagery, as contrasted to the spurious, licentious freedom of wandering around doing as one chose.

The prevailing mood remained skeptical. Little progress toward accommodation between the races had been made since the first European colonists had landed in the New World. It just wasn't in the Indians' nature to settle down in American-style dwellings, till American-style farms, learn American-style political procedures, read English, wear American-style trousers and skirts, have haircuts, and worship in Protestant-style churches. Rather than keep trying to bring such transformations about, the government had adopted as its official policy the removal of whole tribes from the Southeast and Midwest to empty lands beyond the Mississippi, where constant conflict with white frontiersmen could be avoided. Missionaries, however, remained reluctant to follow. The tribes were still— well, Indians. The teeming Orient was a more alluring field. For one thing, the people there were at least civilized.

Whitman could have retorted—and probably did retort—by telling of the eagerness with which the Flatheads and Nez Perces had greeted Parker and him. Remember the delegation to St. Louis. God was working his wonders. The Indians of the Northwest were ready and willing to embrace the truth. The Divine restlessness, moreover, had fallen on lands so remote that Satan's tools, the rough frontiersmen, would not interfere for years. And this point: if Protestants didn't fill that yearning void, Catholics would. For was it not well known that the papacy was engaged in secret and perfidious plots to infiltrate the frontier as one giant step toward making the United States a satrapy of Rome?[9]

Maybe all this was so, but despite nationwide appeals, the American Board of Foreign Missions stayed broke. In 1836 its accumulated deficit was thirty-eight thousand dollars. Three hundred and six missionaries looked toward it for support. Hawaii was the most popular destination.[10] The board's directors felt they could fund, in addition to the Whitmans, only one other couple in the remote and desolate Oregon country. As matters developed, only one couple proved available—the Spaldings—plus, at the last minute, an unwed volunteer who could help with the mission station's endless chores. The single man was William H. Gray, twenty-five, a good cabinetmaker but a dull scholar, enormously self-assured but just as enormously quarrelsome. He would not suffer authority gladly, but that point did not emerge until after there was no turning back.

By pinching pennies, Whitman was able to buy, for $3,063.96, one large wagon (Spalding had a light dearborn of his own) eleven horses, six mules, four milk cows, several beef cattle to eat along the way if necessary, saddles (sidesaddles for the two women), harnesses, tools, clothing, books, seed, medicines, provisions, and camp equipment. The two Nez Perce boys Whitman had taken East to learn English helped with the livestock. To serve as roustabout as far as the rendezvous, the missionaries hired a young man named Dulin. More aid came from a sixteen-year-old redhead who attached himself to the party at the jumping-off place. Also along, his coming and going unrecorded, was a grown Nez Perce named Samuel Temoni. Temoni proved useful in supplying the party with buffalo meat during its long weeks on the Plains. (Narcissa relished the wild meat, but the daily diet of it sickened Eliza.[11]) For protection along the way they joined, in the face of some hostility, the American Fur Company's annual supply caravan. That year the caravan consisted of about seventy men, four hundred animals, and six heavily loaded wagons. The latter, like the Whitmans' big wagon, would be dropped off at Fort Laramie in Wyoming, but the missionaries would cling to the light dearborn as far as Fort Boise in Idaho.

It was a hard trip, but exceptional only in that two women were making it. Inexperienced and slow, the missionaries generally dragged along at the end of the column. As they toiled down the west side of South Pass toward the Green River—the rendezvous that year was held again at the junction of Horse Creek and the Green River—they were as much as two or three miles to the rear. The gap allowed for a bit of pageantry and an unspoken agreement between at least some of the Nez Perces and their would-be reformers. Apprised by messengers from the supply column that women and God-people were coming along behind, four or five mountain men and perhaps twice that many Indians came howling out to greet them, firing their guns into the air as their horses leaped high over the sagebrush. During the tumult, Whitman recognized three of the Indians Parker and he had met the year before. One was Kentuck, who carried a letter from Parker. The other two were Tackensuatis (Rotten Belly) and Hallalhotsoot (Lawyer).

Years later Whitman said angrily that the letter contained little information about the crucial point that Parker had gone forth to discover—suitable sites for missions.[12] As a consequence Whitman and Spalding would have to spend time searching the wilderness for proper sites. That meant relying on Indians whose trustworthiness they did not know. Where should they look? How should they get there?

As an opening gambit they invited Tackensuatis and Hallalhotsoot to dine with them that evening in the conical community tent the women had sewn together shortly before their departure from the frontier. (Kentuck was not involved, probably because he was not a chief.) With the two Nez Perce boys and perhaps Samuel Temoni interpreting and Lawyer adding such English as he knew, communication stumbled along fairly well.

No record was kept, but underneath the talk surely ran the terms of an implied contract. "Give us help," the missionaries said in effect, "and we will bring you God." "Give us power," the Indians replied in effect, "and we will do whatever you ask." It was an open contract, freely entered into by both parties. Biographer Drury insists that the missionaries did not force themselves on the natives at the rendezvous.[13] But can any contract be open and free when neither side understands the other's basic premises?

The Indian camps lay about six miles up Horse Creek from the Green River. When the hundreds of Indian men, women, and children clustered there learned that white women had reached the rendezvous, they decided to put on a show. The males stripped to their breechclouts, wove feathers into their hair, and tied feathers to their lances. They painted bold, slashing designs onto their bodies and onto the flanks and faces of their horses. The women donned soft buckskin dresses, garnished with beads, quills, and fringe, and swung easily into their saddles. Down the valley they charged, screeching, blowing eagle-bone whistles, shooting. The Indian women kissed Narcissa and Eliza enthusiastically; the men contented themselves with shaking hands all around. Tackensuatis and Hallalhotsoot introduced their wives. High prestige!

Meanwhile a dozen or so mountain men pranced around the missionaries' camp, stirred by who knows what memories of home, what dissatisfactions with their roving lives. The surest way to attract the women's attention was to ask for a Bible or a tract. "This is a cause to live for," golden-haired Narcissa exclaimed in a letter to her parents.[14] The excitement that accompanied the exchanges was not lost on those Indians who were concerned about such things. The Books had arrived!

As departure time neared, Tackensuatis and Lawyer grew anxious. Lack of a destination had created uncertainties in the whites' minds about which route to follow. Many of the Indians wanted to lead them due north over the trails the Nimipus had used with Parker. Some would leave the road to hunt buffalo, but many others would swing west across the Salmon Mountains to the Clearwater, and it seemed to them a logical way for the God-people to travel. Trappers said, however, that the light wagon could not cross the mountains. Some of the Cayuse women also objected. They wanted the missionaries to settle in Cayuse country, but the whites would not do so if they first went into the land of the Nez Perces.[15]

The decision was taken out of the Indians' hands by the arrival of a small group of traders from the Hudson's Bay Company who had ridden to the rendezvous to pick up whatever furs they could. Their leader, John McLeod, carried another letter from Parker to Whitman, advising the missionaries to travel as far as Fort Walla Walla under the protection of the British. Such a route would take them west to the Snake River. They would follow the turbulent stream through southern Idaho to the head of its vast chasms and then slant northwest across the Blue Mountains—the heart of Cayuse country. Those Cayuse who were concerned about having white teachers settle among them were delighted. The Nez Perces with similar interests were not.

The best way to counter the Cayuse's unexpected advantage, Rotten Belly and Lawyer decided, was to accompany the God-people to Fort Walla Walla, showing their sincerity in every way they could. (Kentuck shared in the effort for a while, but then left for unrecorded reasons.) Opportunities to impress the missionaries were frequent. By the time the travelers had reached the Snake River, the majority of the Nez Perces and Flatheads had departed by various trails for the north. Those who remained, mostly Nez Perces, were then in a good position to call attention to themselves. They went at it with unflagging energy.

Tackensuatis gave the missionaries two horses to replace animals that had been lost on the outward journey. He and his followers accepted the strictures of the Sabbath, staying in camp and praying. Realizing that the whites were shocked by the physical labor performed by Indian women, he began helping his wife pack their camp horses every morning and set up their lodgings every evening—degradation in the eyes of Indian warriors everywhere.[16] Later, when the sore-footed cattle began to lag during the rough crossing of the Blue Mountains, he and a few of his people stayed behind with Spalding to push them along, foot by dreary foot. When William Gray collapsed of heat exhaustion on the way to the Snake River, Lawyer was the one who came back, hoisted him into the saddle, and supported him until they reached camp. But nothing could help Spalding's light wagon when it collapsed—the *chick-chick-shauile-kai-kash*, as the Indians called the hateful vehicle from the noise it made lurching across the lava cobbles that littered the sun-baked earth. Determined to take the dearborn to the Columbia River— no wagon had ever gone so far—Whitman and Spalding ingeniously turned it into a two-wheel cart. To no avail, even with the Indians' help. They abandoned it at Fort Boise, along with some of Narcissa's and Eliza's cherished personal possessions.

The crisis for Lawyer's and Rotten Belly's Nez Perces did not end at Fort Walla Walla. The missionaries announced they were going to descend the Columbia in a Hudson's Bay Company boat to Fort Vancouver to buy supplies and consult with Dr. John McLoughlin, the Hudson's Bay Company's chief factor in charge of the Oregon country. Fearful that the whites would not return, as Jason and Daniel Lee had not, the Nez Perces promised, just before the missionaries started downriver, to carry their goods to the Clearwater and build houses for them if only they would return and settle there. The Indians then went to their villages to await the outcome.

In the end, both the Nimipus and the Cayuses gained what they wanted, but for reasons of which they knew nothing. The antipathy that had begun with Spalding's and Narcissa's dislike for each other had grown so consuming that the couples knew they could not spend the rest of their lives cooped up in one station. After writing their superiors that they could reach more Indians with the Christian message if they manned two stations, one serving each of the competing tribes, Whitman and Spalding prepared to separate. Leaving their wives temporarily at Fort Vancouver, they and William Gray rowed their new supplies up the Columbia River to Fort Walla Walla. No Indians were waiting at the dock; the whites had returned sooner then either the Nez Perces or the Cayuses had expected. Escorted only by a worker from the fort, they poked along up the Walla Walla valley for twenty-two miles, finally selecting a building site for Marcus and Narcissa. The Cayuses called the place Waiilatpu for the tall reeds that grew there—the place of rye grass.

At that point Tackensuatis appeared with two dozen or so excited tribesmen, ready to lead the whites to the Clearwater, about a hundred and ten miles to the east. Was Tuekakas (Old Joseph) with them? In view of the deep interest he had shown in Parker's plans just that spring, it would have been logical for him to join the bodyguards—if he had heard of the program. But there was jealousy among the chiefs about who should possess the God-people and learn from them how to manipulate a greater power than any of the Nez Perces had yet possessed. So Tuekakas may have been kept in darkness even though his band's Wallowa country was closer to Waiilatpu than was any other section of the Nimipus' land.

Be that as it may, Tackensuatis and his shocked tribesmen tried to persuade Whitman not to waste himself on the volatile Cayuses. Whitman refused for reasons they of course did not understand. On top of that they learned that young William Gray would first help the other missionaries build their houses and would then go to the Flatheads to establish his own station. Again they did not understand the reason—Gray's prickly ambition and his constant troublemaking. All they saw was that three of the five whites were disregarding their homeland. So they clung hard to the last couple, Henry and Eliza Spalding, both along the trail and at the spot Tackensuatis had selected for them. The site lay on a broad meadow beside Lapwai Creek, about two miles above its junction with the canyoned Clearwater.

Mystery surrounds the choice. Tackensuatis's home was at Stites (Idaho), sixty or so miles farther to the southeast.[17] Perhaps he feared that the missionaries would refuse to settle at a place so distant from the lifeline of the Columbia and accordingly had persuaded a chief whose small village was at one end of the meadow by Lapwai Creek to accept the two whites. The chief's name was Hin-mah-tute-ke-kaikt—Thunder Strikes or, variously, Big Thunder or Thunder Eyes. Spalding later renamed him James.

Convincing himself that the site would do, Spalding returned to Fort Vancouver for Eliza and Narcissa. When they reached Fort Walla Walla on their return, more than a hundred Nez Perces were waiting. The Indians raised a shrill welcome and then rode with them through chilly November weather to Waiilatpu. There Spalding dropped off Narcissa (with what kind of farewell we know not), picked up Gray, and continued to Lapwai. Ensconcing himself and Eliza in a buffalo-hide tipi, he launched construction on what was to be a combined community hall and home.

Rotten Belly and his fellows worked like gold prospectors scenting a mother lode. No wood that was suitable for building a cabin grew anywhere nearby. To obtain what they wanted, the Indians had to go to the Clearwater. There they collected driftwood, for the valley's steep hillsides were also bare of timber. Pieces that were relatively straight they chopped into logs about ten feet long and a foot in diameter. These they carried to the cabin site, twelve Indians to a log, spelling each other along the two-mile slope. From time to time Rotten Belly wielded an axe, but was so clumsy that his wife took the tool from him and swung it herself. For their labor they were paid in tobacco, to which they were addicted. Indians from Chief James's nearby village of mat houses stood around and stared in mingled envy and disapproval. What was their world coming to?

By December 23, 1836, after three weeks of intensive labor, the cabin was finished. It was eighteen feet wide and forty-two feet long. A blanket served as a partition between the Spaldings' living quarters and the much larger section that served alternately as a meeting hall, a church, and a schoolroom. The roof consisted of sticks placed closely side by side and slanting up to the ridgepole. A layer of grass was spread on the sticks and a layer of earth on the grass. Presumably Spalding orchestrated a dedication, whites and reds side by side on their knees, their hearts rising in joy to the different gods they were addressing. In spite of the dour looks they received from some of Big Thunder's people, they had no premonition that after eleven years of service, violence at Waiilatpu would force the mission's abandonment. Nor could they possibly have imagined that the cleavages they were creating in the Nez Perce tribe by their intrusion would long outlast the century in which they lived.

· 9

THE STRUGGLE FOR SOULS

In November 1838, two years after reaching Lapwai, Henry Spalding began a hit-or-miss journal, recording some of the events that transpired at his hectic station. His report for Sunday, December 2, says that he preached to a congregation composed mostly of Indians about the Samaritan woman who had five husbands and yet had none, polyandry, like polygamy, being against God's laws. Among his listeners was fifty-two-year-old Tuekakas. As chief of a considerable band of Wallowa Indians, Tuekakas had been wed at least four times, not always serially.[1] In societies where there was a shortage of men because of war and hunting accidents, the custom made good cultural and economic sense, but Spalding either had not learned that yet or chose to condemn the heathenish custom out of plain intolerance.

Because the missionary was still not proficient in the Nez Perce tongue, he often used supplementary devices to convey his messages. One was for his wife, Eliza, to draw pictures illustrating the talk's theme. Spalding then explained the drawings to a "crier." A crier's normal function—the institution was common to many tribes—was to listen to discussions in tribal councils and afterwards ride around the camp shouting out the purport of what he had heard. Because audiences at Lapwai were small and tight, Spalding's crier probably remained stationary, but may not have translated literally. Probably he was coached to convey emotions at fitting points. He had a good model. For Spalding, as an evangelical missionary from a pulpit-pounding society, surely laced his sermons with hellfire-and-brimstone rhetoric. It worked. On numerous occasions, his diary reports, he—and the crier—drew floods of tears from some of the supposedly stoic Indians.[2]

On December 2, Spalding's histrionics and the crier's booming translation brought Tuekakas, four times wed, to the stand, riven presumably by guilt and determined to reform. From the pulpit he spoke, says his mentor, "most affectively" and urged his listeners, the majority of whom were, like him, still unconverted, "to give their hearts to Jesus Christ without delay."

In his account Spalding calls the speaker Joseph. Although it is the first time the name appears anywhere in print, the offhand way with which it is dropped into the diary entry indicates that Joseph had been favorably known to Spalding for a far longer time than the preacher had been keeping his journal.

What's in a name? Well, for one thing, the English forms of Biblical names were easier to pronounce and spell than were multisyllabic Indian names. More important, a new name can be a strong statement of a new identity. So with Tuekakas. He had been making hard choices in a difficult context, and Spalding used the new name to show his appreciation.

It could not have taken the middle-aged chief long to attach himself and those of his bands who would follow him to the mission. His winter camps in the lower Grande Ronde canyon and its deep tributaries were only a long day's ride from Lapwai. His spiritual orientation was equally close. As the fur trader, Benjamin Bonneville, had remarked after visiting the area a few years earlier, the Nez Perces were good-hearted, helpful to strangers and each other, and given to following Christian rituals as best they could without the aid of trained professionals. Now there was a God-person in the area. Tuekakas splashed his horse across the Snake and rode up the Clearwater to learn what he could. His mood was as fresh and eager—and as apprehensive—as when he had left his parents' mat house as a boy to search for his own personal wayakin.

At the mission he immediately ran into tasks that awoke deep cultural clashes—as deep as the one about polygamy. He surmounted his hang-ups because God, speaking through Henry Spalding, told him to. Here was a new way to heaven—or at least away from the flames of hell, which was, by the nature of things and Eliza Spalding's pictures, a more easily visualized concept. And so he and many other Indians who visited the mission out of a variety of motives—fear, curiosity, hope of gifts, or true piety—found themselves doing many things that violated their ancient standards.

Spalding's unbending convictions lent impact to his demands. He probably tried to explain those convictions to his confused visitors with the exuberance he used in explaining spiritual themes during his sermons. Non-Christians, he would have thundered, could not achieve the salvation they hoped for without being converted. They could not be converted until they had achieved a true understanding of God's nature and His will—that is, until they had been civilized. And they could not be civilized until they abandoned their nomadic ways of life. Or, as Spalding put his theory in a letter to the American Board of Foreign Missions, "No savage to my knowledge has ever been christianized upon the wing."[3] To Tuekakas and the other Indians who stayed to listen to him, Spalding was equally emphatic if less metaphorical. Stay at home. Learn to farm so you need not split into small bands wandering about the wilderness most of the year like starving coyotes, searching for fish, roots, and game, especially buffalo, for buffalo hunts were Spalding's particular ogre. Gather instead into stable communities. Put your faith in God. Live the way white Christian Americans live. For your Indianness can lead only to doom.

Tuekakas quickly learned that in pursuing these ideals, Spalding worked as hard as he wanted the Indians to work. To obtain seed needed for planting during his and Eliza's first spring at Lapwai, he rode with a few Indians 200 miles north to Fort Colville, a supply depot of the Hudson's Bay Company, far up the Columbia River.[4] (Fort Walla Walla was only 120 miles to the west, but Whitman's mission at Waiilatpu drew on its stores.) The party, and we have no way of knowing whether Tuekakas was with it, left too early; snow caught the travelers, and the trip became perilous as well as exhausting. When much of the seed he planted failed to mature, he repeated the journey in the fall, this time with twenty Indians and eighty pack horses, for he needed enough food to keep prospective converts close to the mission throughout the winter. He succeeded, paying for his purchases with drafts issued on the American Board of Foreign Missions.

To enlarge the mission's farming operations and to reduce his drain on the board, Spalding contrived, during the winter, thirty hoes. In the spring he passed the tools out to thirty Indians who had set up their mat houses and tipis around the mission compound. Energetically they hacked away the weeds and flaked up the earth for seeds. They prepared about fifteen acres for themselves and half that many for Spalding. He had hoped, unrealistically, for a hundred-acre total.[5] But what he achieved would have seemed, at the onset, equally unrealistic to a mountain man who knew the Nez Perces. Digging in the ground for roots was quintessentially and immemorially women's work. Yet now at Lapwai men were digging side by side with women, stirred by the promises of the new religion. Almost certainly, Tuekakas participated in the hacking, probably in the company of his latest wife. Many visitors must have dropped by to see this radical innovation with their own eyes. Not everyone was won over—certainly not members of the ultraconservative cult which declared that Mother Earth should not be deliberately wounded by humans. (Digging roots was acceptable because roots were indigenous, whereas crops grown from imported seeds were alien to the soil. Many societies live by thus splitting hairs.) In spite of objections, however, a core of the mission's supporters did take shape, some of it centered on Tuekakas and some of it on a gentle chief named Tamootsin, who grew so devout that he christened his home village Alpowa, meaning the place where the Sabbath is observed.

The dark side was Spalding's ferocious temper.[6] He was overworked. He handled the Nez Perce language clumsily. As a result his orders were not always carried out as he directed. The mistakes sparked unreasonable furies in him. He was giving up his life to bring salvation to these people—people he tended to regard as contrary children, rather than as responsible adults who were trying to adjust to a totally new set of values. They *had* to obey.

The difficulties were brought to a critical point by the suffocating heat and swarms of mosquitoes that turned the first summer at Lapwai Creek into a hellish torture. Rather than face the ordeal again in 1838, Spalding determined to move the station down to the Clearwater. The air beside the river might be cooler, the neighboring lands less swampy, the mosquitoes fewer, and space for an expanded mission more attainable. Several Indians were persuaded to help, and here Tuekakas, his wife, and their children were definitely involved.

Because the two-story house Spalding wanted to build needed better timber than the driftwood used in the original station, the Nimipu men and women who were capable of heavy work were sent upstream to forests containing suitable evergreens. There the volunteers felled trees and rafted the trimmed logs to the new site. They adzed the sides flat and piled the timbers up cabin fashion. They gathered stones and built chimneys at either end of the new house and schoolroom, where, during the coming winters, Eliza would teach reading, writing, and scripture, all in Nez Perce (she invented a special alphabet) to as many as a hundred noisy but generally intent children and such adults as wished to join the classes. Until a separate church could be built, the room would also house Sunday services. Outbuildings went up, some of unburned adobe bricks. In addition to this intense burst of construction, there were horses and a few cattle to care for, and the little farm plots on Lapwai Creek to till and irrigate. A few of the Indians may have put together small huts of mud to live in, but most set up buffalo-hide tipis. Out of necessity, they often dropped their work to ride to the high meadows for camas roots and game or to their fishing stations for salmon.

As they toiled in the heat at unfamiliar tasks, small mistakes exploded into crises. Too often Spalding snarled in a passion at whatever Indian he believed was at fault. Sometimes he struck the supposed delinquent. If he was defied, he brought out a whip and flogged the obstructionist.[7] Although whipping was still common in many American schools and in most maritime fleets, physical punishment was alien to the Nez Perces. Nevertheless, most of them endured it, thinking perhaps that this was a test on the road to God, just as the frightening experiences they had encountered while seeking their wayakins had been tests. As for Tuekakas, he was cooperative enough to have avoided the flail and been rewarded with the name of Spalding's favorite Old Testament character, the Joseph who was sold into slavery in Egypt. At about the same time, Tamootsin of Alpowa became Timothy. Together they felt highly responsible for helping the mission succeed by living as models for their tribesmen.

Unexpected stress soon appeared in the monumentally self-assured form of William Gray. Gray had gone East in the furtherance of his own ambitions (more of that in a moment). On his return he brought with him a wife, Mary Augusta, and three sanctimonious religious couples named Cushing and Myra Eells, Asa and Sarah Smith, and Elkanah and Mary Walker. With them was a bachelor, Cornelius Rogers, who was desirous of spreading the Word, and a tagalong trapper, James Conner, who had joined the missionary party at the rendezvous. Conner was married to a Nez Perce and could speak her native language.[8]

Well before the new missionaries reached Whitman's station at Waiilatpu, the hardships of the trail and their own better-than-thou natures had put them at swords' points. Their one focus of agreement was their aversion to William Gray. Inasmuch as Whitman and Spalding were already on the outs, it was evident that care concerning assignments had to be taken. In the end the Walkers and the Eellses opened a station among the Salish-speaking Spokans at a place called Tshimikain. The Smiths landed, in time, at Kamiah, some sixty miles up the Clearwater from Lapwai. Since neither pair knew the language of the people they would be serving, Hallalhotsoot (Lawyer) was hired to teach Salish to the Eellses and Walkers and Shahaptian to the

Smiths. The red tutor found the job prestigious and the pay acceptable, but he steadfastly refused to be converted.[9]

The appointment that grabbed Chief Joseph's attention—he was no longer Tuekakas to the whites and will not be to us—was William Gray's. Gray was sent to Lapwai. The place had taken on added importance. Shortly after the reinforcements arrived at Waiilatpu, the missionary group as a whole had voted to designate Spalding's establishment their "Central Station." As such, it would be the home of a major blacksmith shop and of a water-powered gristmill and sawmill that would be built as soon as finances allowed. Lapwai would also house a printing press that had been offered by the Presbyterian Church's Hawaiian mission. As soon as the press arrived, the Central Station could print badly needed schoolbooks and gospels, using an improved version of the Nez Perce alphabet that Eliza Spalding had already invented. By overseeing some of this extra work, Gray would enable Spalding to concentrate on spiritual affairs.[10]

The job, which caused hackles to rise throughout the Indian community at Lapwai, was a step down for William Gray. Gray had gone East the year before to recruit helpers for the Oregon missions, to raise funds, and to obtain permission from the American Board of Foreign Missions to open a station of his own. Shortly before his departure from Oregon, he came up with the not-altogether-zany idea of driving cheap Nez Perce horses to Missouri, trading them for cattle, and driving the cattle west when he returned with the reinforcements. Spalding agreed. He had noticed how the mission's small herd of cattle fascinated his charges. Owning livestock would advance them another step toward civilization and might wean them away from buffalo hunts. Accordingly he prevailed on four Nez Perces—Ellis, Blue Cloak, the Hat, and a fourth whose name has not survived—to round up a herd from whoever was willing to take the risk and help Gray drive the cattle east.[11] Ellis was chosen because he had been sent as a boy to the Hudson's Bay Company school at Red River in Canada. There, under the name Ellice (spelled Ellis by Spalding), he had learned some English, a plus for any horse trader.

The quartet left Lapwai for the annual fur-trade rendezvous in the early summer of 1837. With them, they drove about fifty horses for sale. Gray, who had been exploring the Flathead country for a mission site, would meet them at the rendezvous and they would continue east with the supply caravan, loaded now with furs. Annoyed by a long delay in the train's departure, Gray decided to hurry ahead in spite of grave warnings from the trappers against such recklessness. The Nez Perces listened, however. All except the

Hat pulled out and returned to Lapwai with about half the horses.

Spalding was furious. Feeling that his vision of launching a great cattle industry among the Nez Perces had been betrayed, he sentenced each Indian to a whipping and fined them a horse apiece, to be delivered to the mission. Ellis and the unnamed Indian simply rode away. That left only Blue Cloak to absorb Spalding's bile. When no Indian would do the flogging, Spalding administered the fifty lashes himself, presumably with vim.

Meanwhile Gray had put together a small party to help him and the Hat with the remaining horses. One of the recruits was Big Ignace, an Iroquois who lived among the Flatheads. Big Ignace was a Catholic and wanted to bring priests to the Northwest. Either Gray, a Protestant, did not know this at the time or was willing to overlook it to obtain Ignace's strength and experience. The decision looked good. Because of Ignace four Flatheads agreed to join the group. Also along were three whites, one of them the young son of Francis Ermatinger, a trader with the Hudson's Bay Company. Gray had promised to deliver the boy to an uncle in the East for tutoring.

Because of the trappers' warnings of danger, they rode as if fiends were pursuing them, often after dark. To no avail. A war party of Sioux Indians jumped them at Ash Hollow in what is now Nebraska. After a brief skirmish, a French trader who was traveling with the Sioux arranged a truce. Gray and the whites were given the worst of the horses and let go. Not so the Hat and Ignace or the four Flatheads. The Sioux wanted their scalps—literally. Although the western Indians killed three Sioux in a frenzied struggle for survival, they were annihilated.

News of the happening reached the mountains before Gray did on his return trip with the three new missionary couples. The trappers who knew him believed his escape was a sellout: his and his white companions' lives traded for the five Indians. Or perhaps Gray had seized the opportunity to rid himself of the Catholic Iroquois's embarrassing presence. In any event, he seems to have dropped his idea of setting himself up among the Flatheads— did he fear them now?—and agreed to render his services once more to the Nez Perces.

A hostile crowd greeted him at Lapwai. The Hat was dead, Blue Cloak had been humiliated, and many horses were gone. After yammering at him about these things for awhile, they shifted their anger to Spalding. Spalding was scared stiff. The Indians, he wrote David Greene of the American Board of Foreign Missions, were determined to have either his head or all his property. A not-always-reliable Catholic source says the whites at Lapwai were so terrified they barricaded themselves inside Spalding's new two-story house.[12]

In the end the uproar was settled by Spalding's turning over a few cattle from the mission's small herd to the Indians who had lost their horses. Although none of the skimpy records mentions the names of either Joseph or Timothy, it is not hard to visualize them as the peacemakers. So when Spalding did begin his diary, his references to the two men were warm and friendly. If his new associates in the mission body had been willing, he would have baptized them in the spring of 1839 and, as a corollary, have inducted them into the newly founded (August 18, 1838) First Presbyterian Church in the Oregon Territory. The deprecators of the idea said loftily that the two Indians were not yet suitably familiar with the church's principal doctrines.[13] The charge was probably true. In general, untutored Indians from the mountains and plains were not at ease with pure abstractions.

William Gray having been appointed overseer of Lapwai's temporal affairs, Spalding was ordered by the local board of the Oregon church to "itinerate" with his charges. That way, it was hoped, the Indians would not let the teachings they had been exposed to during the winter slip away when they left the mission to hunt and fish. As an example, in June 1939, less than a year after his arrival in Oregon Territory, the bachelor Cornelius Rogers had been sent to the Plains with a party of buffalo hunters, a tremendous, but unrecorded experience. As for Spalding, he chose July of the same year to escape Lapwai's oppressive heat by visiting both Timothy and Joseph in the Wallowa Mountains.

Timothy and some of his Alpowa people acted as guides as far as the lower canyon of the Grande Ronde, a chasm that Spalding called a gulf. There they were met by some of Joseph's band. Although the heat was intense, as many as could do so crowded into Joseph's movable tipi to hear the white God-person talk on one of his favorite topics, the Ten Commandments.[14]

In the morning Joseph led the cavalcade, a numerous one now with many spare horses, up a precipitous, zigzagging trail onto a plateau covered by sweet-smelling forests dotted with meadows. Several of the men rode off to hunt, returning with deer, mountain sheep, a wolf, and a bear to eat. When an infant died along the way, Spalding wrote sadly in his journal, "How much these wandering people suffer & how they are wasting away." Yet life persisted. The next day Timothy's wife, seeking partial shelter behind a bush, gave birth to a child and shortly thereafter rejoined the caravan.

Angling southwest, they entered rolling prairies where grass grew thickly and hundreds of horses grazed. Ahead rose the tall, snow-streaked summits of the Wallowa Mountains. Glistening streams poured out of the gaps between the peaks; uniting, the streams formed the deep-pooled Wallowa River. Many of the Indians dropped out to fish. During the three days Spalding was in the area, they caught fifteen hundred or more big salmon. Although his diary does not say so, most of the women of the party undoubtedly stayed busy from dawn to dark, gutting the fish and slitting the flesh into flat pieces for drying on wooden racks.

While all this activity was going on, Joseph rode with his missionary friend into one of the gaps between the peaks, along the shores of a dazzling lake, whose head nestled among evergreens and whose lower end was bounded by the granite boulders of a glacial moraine. As a fillip, the chief, who was fifty-three or so, climbed a pine, seized a nearly grown white-headed eaglet from its nest, and presented the large wings to Spalding. The enthralled missionary named the place Spalding Lake; inasmuch as he wrote the name in parentheses in his diary, he may have taken the liberty without asking Joseph's permission. No matter. The name did not last, and the mountain sapphire is still known as Wallowa Lake.

When it was time for Spalding to return home, the Indians were still fishing, so Joseph and two other male Nez Perces led the way across plunging mountain canyons to Lapwai. Both the missionary and the chief carried guns. As they rode along, they held a shooting match, using blue grouse as targets. The contest ended in a tie at four each. After two weeks in the mountains Spalding reached home as relaxed and contented as Joseph had yet seen him.

By November 1839, Joseph, Timothy, and their wives were also back in Lapwai, braced to be catechized on their fitness for baptism and membership in the First Presbyterian Church in Oregon Territory. James Conner, the American mountain man with the Nez Perce wife, was scheduled to undergo the same soul-searching examination at the same time. This welcoming of the mission's first two native converts was a red-letter occasion. Marcus Whitman rode 120 miles from Waiilatpu to help Spalding conduct the spiritual investigations.

It was not smooth sailing. The Indian wives failed to give satisfactory "evidence of having been born again." But when Joseph's turn came, he persuaded the catechists that, in his own words, God's law had entered his heart like an arrow. Timothy and Conner were equally convincing, and the ceremony of induction was set for November 17.[15]

One theological objection remained. Joseph and Timothy had not yet been united to their mates as Christian ritual specified; therefore, they were not eligible to receive the sacrament of baptism. Marriages were accordingly scheduled to precede the other ceremonies. On the appointed day Spalding summoned the Nez Perces in the vicinity to assemble around the door of the small schoolroom that also served as the church. Loudly he asked whether anyone in the gathering knew of any evil perpetrated by the couples before them during the preceding year. When no one answered, he solemnly married Timothy and his mate according to Presbyterian custom and gave her the Old Testament name of Tamar. After Joseph and his spouse had been similarly linked, the woman was rechristened Asenath, after the Egyptian woman whom Pharoah gave in marriage to the Israelite Joseph. Cohabitation having thus been legalized, Joseph, Timothy, and Conner received the holy waters of baptism and were taken into the church. That evening they all feasted joyfully in the Spaldings' living quarters. Still suffused with triumph, Spalding wrote afterwards, "Oh what a glorious thought to have lived to see two of the sons of the Red man brought into the fold of Christ. To God be all the praise forever and forever. Amen."[16] Outside, a whole lot of unbaptized Indians still wandered around bound for Hell.

Added excitement came the next Sunday, November 27, when Spalding baptized Timothy's two and Joseph's four young children. (Young children were not required to expound on church doctrine before receiving the sacrament.) Joseph's four young ones were rechristened Mary Noyes, Abigail, Hannah, and Manassa (Spalding's spelling of the biblical Manasseh). Manassa, whose Indian name was Sousouquee, was the only boy. His name, also derived from the book of Genesis, had originally been applied to the first son of the biblical Joseph and Asenath. Nor did the ceremonies end there. At the time of the baptisms, Asenath was carrying another child. The baby was born, probably, in early April 1840. Baptized on April 12, he was named Ephraim, who, in Genesis, was Joseph's second son by his Egyptian wife. The timing raises a small question. Was that second son born in Joseph Canyon, as legend attests, or at Lapwai? Since the two places are only a day's ride apart and Indian women were accustomed to transporting infants on horseback very early in their lives, either spot was possible.

Ephraim did not stick as a name any more than Spalding Lake did. Asenath borrowed from one of her brothers a sound Nez Perce name: Hin-mah-too-yah-lat-kekht, or Thunder Rolling in the Mountains. Later, during a search for a wayakin, the lad may have achieved another, secret name. Finally, white settlers, often seeing father and son together and needing a way to distinguish them, took to calling them Old Joseph and Young Joseph.[17]

Beset by so many powerful examples of Christian correctness, Asenath and Tamar struggled to learn enough doctrine to be admitted into the magical church. Studying with them from time to time was Old Joseph's half brother, the Cayuse chief Pahkatos Qoh Qoh, or Five Crows. Heaven (let the word be read literally) knows what they got out of it, but it was enough that Spalding wanted to baptize and take all three of them into the church in December 1841. Whitman vetoed the suggestion. Back to their lodges the trio went, to be coached afresh by their husbands and relatives in the hope that light would soon descend on them. It would be hard to overestimate the impact these multiple ceremonies had on this handful of Stone-Age people who were trying diligently, for their own sakes and those of their people, to understand the then-modern world.

Although affairs at Lapwai were degenerating by 1840, the friendship between Spalding and his Indian converts stayed warm. When Joseph, taken ill while summering in Wallowa, sent an urgent summons to Lapwai, the missionary immediately responded with a hard two-day ride to the chief's encampment. He administered his favorite cure-all, first a stout dose of calomel and jalap, then bleeding. After "a copious passage," as Spalding put it in his diary, "Joseph's fever broke and his pulse rate return to normal." Spalding stayed on guard, however, using the Sabbath to preach on the evils of envy before dining on bear meat cooked in a pit partially filled with preheated stones and covered with hemlock boughs and earth. One imagines that, to the convalescent chief, Spalding may have sounded—that stentorian voice—and even looked—that great spade beard and a receding hairline above a bulging forehead—a little like God himself. As his strength returned, Joseph offered a horse in payment. Spalding demurred. He didn't want to seem like an Indian medicine man exacting compensation for his "conjuring," as Spalding called their healing practices. But when Joseph and the Indians around him kept insisting that no one in the tribe would regard this particular gift in so unfavorable a light, he accepted and returned home to the hot, hard work of harvesting the Lapwai grain fields.[18]

Joseph soon found an additional way of repaying the debt. During the December following his illness, Spalding called on a group of Nez Perces to go with him and two white mountain men who had chanced by to the forests upstream. There they would cut timber for a church building. A few of the loggers traveled by dugout canoe. Joseph and the others rode. They cut and tied into rafts twenty-eight big, "beautiful" logs. After coupling the rafts in tandem, Spalding, Timothy, and an Indian called Luke boarded the first one. A few other workers settled down on the ones behind. Joseph and the bulk of the loggers returned to Lapwai on horseback.

All went well until twilight. Then, exactly opposite the mission station, the lead raft crashed into the head of an island. Momentum piled the following rafts onto the paralyzed leader. The whole mass took to bucking and rolling in water so frigid that chunks of ice were floating by.

Alarmed for Spalding, Joseph rode out leading a spare horse, "on which," the missionary wrote, "I reached the shore in safety, thankful I trust for the preservation of life." Timothy and the rest were taken off by canoes. Three days' work amid bobbing chunks of ice was needed to bring the timbers ashore. Not a log was lost.[19]

Joseph and Timothy were rapidly becoming the showpieces of the mission. Entries in Spalding's diary tell of them plowing, digging ditches to take water to their grain, speaking at church services, holding religious observations in their own homes, and attending classes with a few other chiefs at the school run by Spalding's wife. The men's behavior impressed five members of a United States exploring mission who visited the establishment in the summer of 1841. After touring the mission and riding up Lapwai Creek to look over the Indians' small fields of corn, wheat, potatoes, and watermelons and the little houses some of them had built with adobe brick, the visitors praised Spalding's leadership. Then one of them singled out Joseph for special notice, saying he would not have expected so much from a "savage."[20]

There was much the visitors did not see, however. As the novelty of the Christianizing program wore off and hard labor failed to produce the material gains most of the Indians had counted on, many drifted away. One such loss, dismaying to Spalding, was Tackensuatis, the chief who, with his wife, had been notably helpful on the missionaries' arrival from the East in 1836.[21] Other Nimipus turned actively hostile. One was Big Thunder, headman of a band whose winter village lay a few miles up Lapwai Creek from the Mission. In the beginning he had been cooperative enough to win the name James from Spalding. Then his daughter came home with William Craig, a mountain man she had married. Coached by Craig, Big Thunder began complaining that back in the country of the rising sun, the whites paid for the land and water and air they used. But here the God-people took what they wanted and required the Indians to work like slaves and then turn over to the whites, without recompense, part of what they produced. They were even supposed to forget their cherished beliefs about reaching power through private wayakins. Soon Big Thunder's followers were hooting, shoving, and doing their unpleasant best to halt the influx. Get out! This was not the newcomers' land to wound and tear apart at a white man's bidding![22]

Another uproar involved the multitude of dogs that helped keep the Nez Perces' encampments clean. The Indians liked the animals and let them roam unrestrained. But as the dogs' attacks on the sheep that Spalding was slowly gathering together increased, he demanded that the owners get rid of the predators. The Indians ignored him. At that he paid some of his followers (Joseph among them?) to kill the offending dogs—or so Asa Smith charged as he brooded unhappily at Kamiah, hating Spalding for being more successful than he was.[23]

Gradually, the incidents evolved toward real violence. Big Thunder led some of his people in breaking a dam Spalding and a crew of Indian laborers had built for bringing water to the mission's new gristmill. On another occasion, two of the chief's men dressed in war costumes and streaked their faces with paint. Invading the schoolhouse, they offended Eliza Spalding with threatening glares and obscene gestures. When Spalding asked Big Thunder to intervene, he refused.[24]

The ill will spread. One day an emissary arrived from Asa Smith at Kamiah, saying that his and his wife's lives were being threatened by men who were being goaded by a doughty old war chief and buffalo hunter, Apash Wyakaikt. (He was the elder Flint Necklace, later known to whites as Looking Glass from a small trade mirror he wore hanging from his neck like a pendant. On his death, Looking Glass would pass his names and the talisman to his son, one of Young Joseph's principal allies.) Without hesitation Spalding called on Joseph and Timothy to ride with him to the rescue, sixty miles through a drenching rain, only to find on their arrival that the troublemakers had vanished.[25]

Less physical but more worrisome to the Presbyterians was the setback that resulted from the arrival of Catholic missionaries. The first to appear, in 1838, were Fathers Modeste Demers and François Blanchet, responding to a call from French Canadian voyaguers who, on retiring from the Hudson's Bay Company, had settled in the Willamette Valley. In 1839 the priests moved in their long gowns up the Columbia River from Fort Vancouver to Fort Walla Walla, where the trader currently in charge was Pierre Pambrun, an ardent Catholic. After enjoying Pambrun's hospitality, the proselytizers rode due south to the Umatilla River, on whose banks, near present Pendleton, Oregon, stood the village in which Tuekakas (Old Joseph) had been born to a

Nez Perce mother and a Cayuse father. Joseph's half brothers, Tauitau (Young Chief) and Pahkatos Qoh Qoh (Five Crows) inherited their father's position and served as joint chiefs of the local band of Cayuses. Tauitau lived in a house that Pambrun had built for him, partly to improve trade and partly to turn him into a Catholic. There the priest baptized one of Tauitau's children in a ceremony that made its Presbyterian counterpart look drab.[26] Meanwhile, and reflecting perhaps the influence of his half brother Joseph, Five Crows, whom Spalding had renamed Hezekiah, was studying hard for the privilege of entering the Protestant church at the Lapwai mission.

The Catholic noose, as the Protestants regarded it, grew swiftly tighter. Jesuits, under the supervision of famed Father Pierre Jean De Smet, entered the Bitterroot Valley through southwestern Montana, set up a mission among the Flatheads, and from there spread out, thinly to be sure, among other Salish-speaking tribes north of Nez Perce country. If rumors trickling back from buffalo hunters, as well as from Cayuses and Wallawallas were to be believed, the interlopers were easily winning far more converts than were their rivals. The Presbyterians scoffed defensively; becoming a Catholic was altogether too easy for the Indians. They were baptized first and only afterward were they given instruction about the significance of what they had done. Still, it hurt Henry Spalding and his wife when they heard indirectly that Chief Tackensuatis and his spouse had embraced the Romanish way.[27]

Wars of words and images developed. The Jesuits sneered at the Protestants for having wives and wearing clothes like the ordinary people they were. The Presbyterians sneered back that the long gowns were used to hide the fact that the wearers were in truth false teachers; irreparable harm would befall anyone who heeded them. As part of the battle for souls, the Spaldings invented what were later called "ladders." These were pictures about six feet tall and two feet wide. Eliza's brightly colored drawings showed two routes rising from a fiery pit toward a serene blue Heaven above. Beginning with the Pope, all who chose the Catholic way were represented, in Spalding's words, "as falling back into hell at the approach of the Lord Jesus Christ who is coming through the clouds of heaven with his holy angels." The Catholics retorted with a drawing of a tree; non-Catholics were shown dropping from withered branches into the same consuming abyss.[28]

Some Indians were frightened when they saw the renditions, and many were confused; a few may have been converted to one or another of the faiths. Joseph, who was having to face a soul-searing split in his family— Young Chief favoring the Catholics, Five Crows favoring the Presbyterians—

was deeply perturbed. Soon, however, the religious rancors were overshadowed by the arrival of a letter from the American Board of Foreign Missions, addressed to Marcus Whitman.

That year the first substantial train of white immigrants—more than a hundred men, women, and children, some carrying their household goods in wagons—entered Oregon from the United States. Their trail led right past the Waiilatpu mission. Among the newcomers was Dr. Elijah White, given to stuttering and somewhat fuzzy of mind. White had first gone to Oregon in 1837 as physician for a group of Methodists who had been sent by ship to reinforce the mission that Jason Lee had established among the listless, disease-ridden Indians of the Willamette Valley. There he had picked up Lee's vision of serving not Indians but whites, whose population was bound to increase, he believed, when the Northwest was finally divided between its claimants, Great Britain and the United States. Returning to Washington, D.C., after a quarrel with Lee, he had bulled his way into an appointment as American subagent for the Indians of the Oregon country. The meagerness of the job, which probably was not Washington's to grant, did not worry him, for he saw in it promises of greater things to come.[29]

As a courtesy White carried with him the letter from the American Board had addressed to Whitman. Its contents, of which he knew nothing as he continued down the Columbia River, sent Whitman scrambling to call his fellow workers to attend an emergency meeting at Waiilatpu on September 26, 1842. The announcement he made to them after they had assembled was shattering. Spalding was fired; Gray and Rogers were advised to withdraw; Smith was let go without prejudice because of his wife's failing health; and the Whitmans were transferred to Tshimakain, where the Eellses and Walkers had not yet made a single convert. Waiilatpu and Lapwai, where Joseph, Timothy, Five Crows, and several others were struggling to change their lives, were ordered closed.

Why? Why? Gradually the stunned listeners put together the reasons. During the past few years various members of the group had been firing off poison-pen letters about each other to the board in Boston. Most of the output had come from Asa Smith, sulking at Kamiah. Gray and the bachelor, Cornelius Rogers, had added their share; even Whitman had stooped occasionally. While no one among them had escaped the shotgun scattering of charges, the principal target had been Spalding. Again and again he had been damned by his fellow Christians for his and Eliza's inadequate teaching, his fiscal mismanagement, his temper and use of the lash, his authoritarian ways, and unjustified exaggerations about what he was accomplishing.

Cruel ironies underlay the orders. The Smiths had already left for the lower Columbia, hoping to catch a ship for the United States. Gray and Rogers had accepted jobs in the Willamette Valley and would soon be departing. Of much greater importance was the emotional reconciliation Whitman and Spalding had held in May, pledging to work thereafter in amity. And while Spalding did indeed exaggerate, none of the other workers had attained results comparable to his. Only a few months earlier he had engineered an eight-day religious revival at Lapwai that had drawn, by his count, two thousand Indians from a broad area. Joseph and Timothy had performed like prodigies caring for the "multitude," to use Spalding's word. Meanwhile Eliza's school was flourishing, and the printing press had turned out, in the Nez Perce language, a primer for children and a Nez Perce grammar. Although the number of acres under cultivation and the number of sheep and cattle owned by the Indians remained small, still the trend was upward. Letters announcing these improvements had been sent to the board, but obviously had not arrived in time to halt the order to close. Now the work would go for nothing and the salvaged souls would be lost—unless the powers in the East could be induced to change their minds.

Whitman proposed just that. He would take his plea across the continent in the face of winter. His sole companion would be A. L. Lovejoy who had reached Waiilatpu only two weeks earlier with the migrants but was willing, for reasons still unknown, to turn back, risking his life with Whitman's.

The missionary knew he was riding to meet the future. In 1840 he had watched three mountain men, Caleb Wilkins, Robert Newell, and Joe Meek, accomplish what he had failed to do—bring two wagons as far as Waiilatpu. The next year he had helped a few all-white families with supplies and information when they had paused at the mission on their way to the farmlands of the Willamette Valley. And then there was that new catalyst, Elijah White. On returning East after his quarrel with Jason Lee, he had listened with amazement to the new resonances being stirred by the word Oregon. Although Congress, unwilling to offend Great Britain, had rejected bills that proposed the occupation of the Northwest, the average citizen felt no such restraint. Emigrant societies, White told Whitman, were springing up here and there throughout the nation. White himself had added to the drive by addressing audiences wherever he could. Although only a handful of people had been able to get ready to travel with him in 1842, there would be more the following spring, when the new grass was tall enough to support livestock. Whitman, he said, could depend on that.[30]

And so the missionary started for Boston, intending to return with the rising tide. That he reached Massachusetts is a wonder. Learning at Fort Hall that war parties of Sioux were prowling the standard route down the North Platte, Lovejoy and he took a snow-plagued, thousand-mile detour through southwestern Colorado into New Mexico. Lovejoy played out at the edge of the Plains; luckily Whitman was able to continue along the Santa Fe Trail with traders bound for Missouri. Arrived in Boston at last, he told his story to the American Board. Plus this: Waiilatpu, he said, had outgrown its role as an Indian mission; it was also needed as a rest- and supply stop for American emigrants. Moreover, Catholics were at work in the Northwest. If no one opposed them (and the failure of the Methodist missions near the coast was imminent), the papists would spread far and wide—a long step toward completing what many people of the day believed was a nefarious plot to use the frontier as a starting point for winning control of the entire country.

The board revoked its order. Whitman hurried to his home in upper New York State for a brief rest. Then he was off again, accompanied by a thirteen-year-old nephew, Perrin Whitman (we will hear more of Perrin later), as he rushed to catch up with the 1843 migration. It was big, all right—about 1,000 people with 120 wagons pulled by hundreds of head of work stock and supplemented by many pack animals and riding horses. More than 3,000 head of milk cows and range cattle trailed along behind. A mountain man named John Gantt was hired to act as the guide and coordinator as far as Fort Hall.

When Gantt dropped out, Whitman took over his role as leader. His first block was psychological. The Hudson's Bay Company's trader in charge at Fort Hall sent ripples of panic through the column by saying that so unwieldly a mass of men, women, and children could not take wagons across the southern Idaho deserts and the Oregon mountains to the Columbia River. Whitman contradicted him. He knew better, he said, and proceed to show the way while holding the mass together at a pace fast enough to outdistance the onset of winter. He had knowledgeable help from a group of Christian Nez Perces, identities unknown, whom Spalding had sent to meet the train with several packhorses laden with flour. Because the demand was high and the supply was small, Whitman was able to ask higher prices than some of the disgruntled buyers liked to pay.

At Grande Ronde a messenger handed him a letter saying that both Spalding and his wife were gravely ill. Turning the guiding over to a skilled and amiable Cayuse, Chief Sticcus, the doctor hurried ahead, past Waiilatpu to Lapwai, where he found that nature and a long rest in bed had served his associates well.

By November 1843 the greater part of the travelers were safely in the Willamette Valley. Writing the Reverend David Green of the American Board of Foreign Missions, Whitman singled out what he considered his greatest accomplishments. In 1836 he had set a powerful example for future travelers by bringing the first two white American women across the Continental Divide. He had kept the train of 1843 from breaking apart under pressure, and he had opened a wagon road to the Columbia River.

He meant to continue serving the Indians, he said, for they were highly at risk. Civilization had caught up with them sooner than anyone had expected. Now, more than ever, their salvation, both spiritual and physical, would depend on their accommodating themselves to the new order—in effect, transforming themselves into whites with copper skins. Indians, such as Sticcus, Joseph, Lawyer, and Timothy, made the quantum leap seem possible. But the likes of Big Thunder, Old Looking Glass, and the more intransigent Cayuses cast shadows. To Whitman's distress, those people were in effect preaching that freedom lay in retaining their identities as Indians, rather than in bowing to the forces of change.

· 10 ·

CATASTROPHE

As Old Joseph, Timothy, and other Christian Nez Perce chiefs must have known, Marcus Whitman's sudden departure for the East had been followed by fresh eruptions of violence at both Lapwai and Waiilatpu. Anti-Christian Nez Perces had subjected Eliza Spalding to more obscene taunts outside the schoolhouse and in the mission compound. In an unrelated affair, a disgruntled Indian had held a cocked gun against her husband's body for three or four minutes that must have seemed as long as a polar night. Meanwhile the Indian grapevine rustled with rumors of worse assaults at Waiilatpu. An unidentified Cayuse had tried to break into Narcissa Whitman's bedroom. She saved herself by screaming loudly enough to waken a Hawaiian worker who was sleeping in another part of the main building, and the intruder disappeared. Completely unnerved by the incident, Narcissa fled for sanctuary to the Hudson's Bay Company's post at Fort Walla Walla. Not long afterwards an arsonist set fire to the Waiilatpu gristmill, destroying part of the structure and much of the grain stored there—a considerable monetary loss.[1]

Reports of the disturbances went down the Columbia River to Dr. Elijah White, the new United States subagent for the Indians west of the Rockies—whatever that title meant. At once he came up the river to investigate. Fearful of his intentions, most of the Cayuses faded away. Unable to find enough chiefs at Waiilatpu to deal with, he sent an express to Spalding, asking that the Nez Perce chiefs be gathered for a meeting at Lapwai. Spalding promptly relayed the summons throughout the countryside.

During the closing days of November 1842, twenty-two chiefs, most of them accompanied by their families and retinues, converged on the mission. There they found that White and his party had arrived ahead of them. While awaiting their arrival, the agent had inspected the Indians' fields and lodges and Eliza's school. He was voluble in his praise, and that helped smooth away some of the arriving chiefs' aloofness. Relaxing a little, they examined the agent's party in their turn and were impressed. Six French Canadians served as guards; during the ascent of the Columbia, the sextet had doubled as boatmen.[2] There were two interpreters. One was Cornelius Rogers, whom Joseph and many of the chiefs knew from his short period of work at Lapwai and Kamiah. The other interpreter was the half-breed Baptiste Dorion, whose father had come west with the Astorians and had been slain by Snake Indians. Finally, there was the formidable figure of Tom McKay, who had also been in Oregon since the days of Astoria. Governor George Simpson of the Hudson's Bay Company once described McKay as "cool and resolute among the Indians; has always been employed on the most desperate Services in the Columbia and the more desperate it is the better he likes it.... His name alone is a host of strength."[3]

The conference began on December 5. Among the assembled chiefs was Joseph's half brother, the Cayuse Hezekiah (Five Crows), who was spending his second winter at Lapwai. He was neatly attired "in English costume." (One mark of the cultural transformation sought by the missionaries was the wearing of white-style trousers, coat, and hat. Was Joseph so dressed on this cold December day? It is likely.) White told his attentive listeners that he wanted them to formulate and write down in both Nez Perce and English a set of laws governing their relations with each other and with the whites. He promised that if the code was adopted, fitting punishment would befall any white man who murdered, stole, or sold the Indians damaged goods. Other speakers chimed in, but the clincher was Tom McKay, speaking in the kind of rolling parallelisms favored by Indian orators.

"I have mingled with you in bloody wars and profound peace; I have stood in your midst, surrounded by plenty and suffered with you in seasons of scarcity; we have had our days of wild and joyous sport and nights of watching and deep concern.... Will you hear what [the great chief of the whites] says? Surely you will hear. But if [you are] disposed to close your ears and stop them, they will be torn open and you will be made to hear."

Free choice? Elijah White insisted later that nothing was forcibly imposed on the Indians, and, indeed, Hezekiah, clad in his western duds, and six or eight missionary-oriented Nez Perce chiefs spoke out in favor of the proposal. Joseph? Timothy? We don't know. The only Nez Perce named was ninety-year-old Red Grizzly Bear, the grandfather of Ellis. Red Grizzly Bear had talked to Lewis and Clark when they had urged peace on the tribe thirty-five years before. Since then the Nimipus had expected good advice from the Americans. Now, said Red Grizzly Bear, the time to heed them again was at hand.

Made confident by the murmurs of assent that greeted the remarks, White read aloud the nine rules he had composed in collaboration with Henry Spalding. They dealt with the sort of wrongs the missionaries had experienced—arson, the taking of property without the owner's consent, entering fields or houses without permission, and making threats with lethal weapons. Later the Indians added a tenth rule looking to control dogs that injured the sheep some of them were trying to raise, as was the mission.[4]

Only one sentence covered the vital point of enforcement. "If an Indian break these laws, he shall be punished by his chiefs; if a white man break them, he shall be reported to the agent, and punished at his instance." The retribution to be exacted for murder and arson was hanging, a procedure foreign to the Nez Perces and their neighboring tribes. Other infractions were to be punished by fines and whipping. In the case of the Christian Ten Commandments, obedience was exacted by fear of Hell's fire. In the case of Elijah White's ten rules, nothing was said about handling culprits who defied the authority of the chiefs. Nor did White say how he expected to handle belligerent Caucasian lawbreakers in a land where neither police forces nor courts existed.

No one raised disturbing questions, however. The agent's rules were accepted, and the meeting was adjourned for three hours. The chiefs were instructed that when they assembled again they should elect one of their number head chief. This dignitary was to be assisted in his work of maintaining order by twelve subchiefs, each of whom was to be attended by five guards. White asked that the head chief be chosen by ten o'clock the following morning. As an inducement to promptness, he said he would celebrate the election by purchasing a fat ox from the mission as the foundation for a grand feast. For as Spalding had told him, few things put the Nimipus, whose diet was often spartan, in better humor than the prospect of a bountiful meal of fat meat.

The notion of a head chief with tribalwide authority violated the Nez Perces' traditional form of government. Except during buffalo hunts or times of war, each semiautonomous band had its own chief. Each chief's rule rested not on coercion but on suasion, and it did not extend to other bands. Baffled by the shock of going against tradition, the electors asked White to pick a man for them. He refused, at least ostensibly. He did let Cornelius Rogers and Tom McKay consult with the chiefs, however, and at length they emerged with a decision that suited, probably not by chance, both Spalding and White. The new head chief was Ellis. Undoubtedly, some of his grandfather's popularity had rubbed off on him. As for his own attributes, he had attended the Red River Mission School in Canada, where he had learned to speak, read, and write a limited amount of English. He was pro-Christian. He tilled a small farm near Kamiah, owned a few cattle and sheep, and possessed, it is said, a huge herd of horses—1,100 head. But he was young, only thirty-two, in a society where age and wisdom were equated. Probably he was younger than any of the twelve chiefs who were selected to be his assistants, Old Joseph among them, and it is hard to believe his election did not create the kind of envy that would militate against success. It is significant, too, that in this first faltering move toward an American-imposed government, the ordinary Indian was given no voice.

His revolution of another people's laws completed, White started back to the Willamette Valley via the Walla Walla Valley. Failing again to assemble the fearful Cayuses, he said he would return in the spring to settle accounts concerning the burned mill and grain. Narcissa, still alarmed and very ill, stayed away from Waiilatpu. Stepping into her and Marcus's place at the mission were two independent preachers, William Geiger and Philo Littlejohn. They had come to the Northwest in 1839, but, lacking church support, had been unable to establish missions of their own and had accepted a variety of jobs to make ends meet. After helping Geiger for a time at uneasy Waiilatpu, Littlejohn moved on to Lapwai.

Alone of the missionaries, Spalding was showing some success with the native population. As he took pains to write White, the introduction of the laws had gone a long way toward restoring order. Attendance at church was good. The drawing power of the school was even greater. Nearly all the leading Nez Perce chiefs attended classes, as did the Cayuse, Hezekiah. Joseph was a principal assistant in the educational program. Since the mission lacked textbooks, Eliza and her husband printed out the day's lesson with pens on pieces of paper. These originals were passed around among the pupils so they could make copies to take home for studying and committing assigned parts of the material to memory. The only subjects covered were White's laws and the Gospels.[5]

To speed things along and spread the word still farther, Spalding was already preparing to print, in Nez Perce, on the mission's small press, a few hundred copies of an eight-page edition of the laws. That done, he would turn to a far more ambitious project, the printing, also in Nez Perce, of the Gospel of Matthew. In fact, the only sour note was the new head chief, Ellis, whose election had filled him, Eliza Spalding wrote, with "pride, vanity, and great swelling words." And even these faults were cured by having Ellis carry a letter to White, in which the agent was urged to rein him in. Somehow White succeeded.[6]

But if the Nimipus—or at least the Christian faction of the Nimipus—were quiet, the Cayuses were not. They had no way of understanding that Marcus Whitman's sudden departure for the East was to persuade his church's missionary board not to close Waiilatpu and Lapwai and not to fire Spalding. Many of the Indians believed that Whitman would return with an army of whites to seize their lands for distribution among an advancing migration of white settlers. Others focused their resentment on White and vowed not to lose their independence by accepting his laws. Apprehension and their pride in their prowess as fighters led them to give vent to great swollen words of their own about carrying war throughout the Northwest. Rumors of the threats flew down the Columbia River to the tiny American and French Canadian colony in the Willamette Valley. Panic seized the people. Many who lived on outlying farms sought protection by moving to more populous centers, and cries went up for Agent White to build fortifications out of government funds—money that, in fact, he did not have.[7]

Clearly the time had come to confront the Cayuses. Putting together a somewhat larger force than he had led before, but lacking the support of Tom McKay and Cornelius Rogers (the latter had drowned in the Willamette River during the winter), White moved into the Walla Walla Valley during the early days of May 1843. As he had surmised, the Indians had been fighting a war of words. The prospect of actual gun fighting alarmed them, and as soon as they were convinced that White was not coming after their scalps, the chiefs agreed to meet with him. They remained belligerent enough, however, to refuse his laws. All he could get from them was a promise that if Ellis and a group of Nez Perces would come to the Walla Walla Valley and describe how the laws worked, they would listen. Agreeing, White sent word to Spalding, asking him to assemble a convincing delegation. He then followed at his leisure. With him went two lower-country Methodists, Gustavus Hines and H. E. W. Perkins. Hines's account of subsequent events is all we have.[8]

A "convincing" delegation!—Spalding hurried a messenger to Kamiah, asking Ellis to clothe the men, women, and children of his neighborhood in their finest gear, mount them on spirited horses, and come to Lapwai to stage a grand entry. Old Joseph meanwhile flew eagerly to work in the Lapwai area preparing a comparable force of greeters.

To show off his accomplishments to the agent and his Methodist guests, Spalding arranged to baptize and take into the First Presbyterian Church nine Native Americans. Leading the list of aspirants were Joseph's and Timothy's wives, Asenath and Tamar. With them were three other women and four men. One of the men was a good friend of Joseph's whom Spalding had renamed Lyman after Lyman Beecher, who had been one of the missionary's hell-roaring teachers at the Lane Theological Seminary in Cincinnati, Ohio. The Indian Lyman had been captured as a child during a Nimipu raid on a Snake encampment. After growing up as a slave, he had been adopted into the man-short Nez Perce tribe and, through processes now unknown, had become Joseph's boon companion.[9] Now he had a place with the others on center stage. A crowd of more than two hundred people gathered with the American visitors in an enclosure behind Spalding's house to watch the transformation by baptism. The impact was what Spalding had hoped it would be. Gustavus Hines later reported enthusiastically, "This is evidently the most promising mission in Oregon."[10]

Now for the circus. At the appointed time Joseph drew up, more or less in line, an estimated seven hundred mounted, garishly dressed Nez Perces and faced them toward a comparable number of riders led by Ellis. At a signal, the head chief's people charged. Guns fired, drums beat, war whistles shrilled. Just short of a collision, the chargers split left and right and raced back and forth in front of Joseph's line, so close that foam from the mouths of the plunging horse spattered the faces of the watchers. The Spaldings' little daughter, named Eliza for her mother, was so frightened she almost went into hysterics. Then another signal produced an almost magical quiet, and Ellis's newcomers, pressing close and grinning broadly, shook hands over and over with Joseph's greeters.

Next the mingled, milling throng rode to a nearby meadow. There they formed a circle around a warrior who, in stentorian tones, described his slaying of twelve Blackfeet; while he talked, his followers held aloft on the tips of their lances twelve scalps as evidence. The boasting finished, several Indians replaced the speaker in the center of the ring and reenacted the battle of Pierre's Hole, where the Nimipus had fought on the side of the whites at the

close of the fur-trappers' rendezvous of 1832. Lawyer, who had been permanently lamed by a hip wound incurred during the battle, played a star's part in
the reconstruction. Possibly he was joined by his wife. She deserved a part, for
during the real battle, while she was bringing a horse to her stricken husband,
a bullet had pierced her doeskin skirt, bringing her a new name, Shot-
Through-the-Dress. To wind up the show, Lawyer led a big troop of excited,
befeathered men in a war dance, possibly to the discomfiture of Spalding,
who stood almost unnoticed among the spectators as spokesman for the
Christian Prince of Peace.[11]

A shrewd man, this Lawyer. He was not a chief, but had started his career
as a crier charged with riding through his band's camp calling out directions
for the day's activities or relaying to the people the decisions of the group's
council. Ambitious and gregarious, he had early recognized the advantages of
staying in the limelight, for hadn't his father achieved lasting fame by helping
Lewis and Clark along their way to the western sea? Sometimes he called
himself Aleiya, which is said to have been one of his father's names. (Is
Lawyer a corruption of Aleiya?) Often he was known as Hallalhotsoot.[12] Having seen how fascinated many Indians were by Spokan Garry's account of
Christianity as taught at the Red River Mission School, Lawyer had helped
put into motion the famed delegation to St. Louis. When missionaries at last
arrived, he had parlayed his knowledge of English, picked up from American
mountain men, into teaching Salish—his mother was a Flathead—and Shahaptian, the language of the Nez Perces—to the God-people. It was quite in
character, then, for him to have used his Pierre's Hole experience as a way to
draw to his crippled self the attention of the potentially important Americans
who were finding their way into Oregon. It was also in character for him to
ride up front with Joseph, Timothy, Spalding, Elijah White, and Ellis when
some five hundred mounted Nez Perces and twice that many horses swam
across the spring-swollen Snake on their way to Waiilatpu.

There the earlier script was repeated. The two groups—Nez Perce visitors
and Cayuse greeters—rushed at each other with such thunderous abandon
that some of the whites feared a real conflict might result this time. To cool
things down, Spalding called for a prayer meeting at the Whitmans' house,
where a pallid Narcissa was again in residence. Joseph, still sweating from the
"battle," was probably among those who attended.

The visit put heavy pressures on the Cayuses. After long speeches by
both whites and Indians—Ellis and Lawyer thought they deserved extra pay
for doing so much translating—and after Elijah White had assured the local

Indians that he had not come to catch them like beavers in a trap, the bad-gered Cayuses assented to the laws. Joseph heard with pleasure that his half brother, Hezekiah, aka Five Crows, was elected head chief. On June 16, after White's party had returned to the Willamette, Spalding baptized Hezekiah as a Protestant. (The Cayuse's full brother, Tauitau, who had almost been elect-ed head chief, was a Catholic.) The law, so it seemed, was now safely in the hands of the pro-Christian Nez Perces and Cayuses, as opposed to what Spalding called the "heathen party" of the tribe.

We come now to a small but puzzling omission. In June 1844, a year after Hezekiah's baptism, nine Nez Perces and one French Canadian were admitted to the First Presbyterian Church at ceremonies held at Lapwai. Marcus Whit-man, who by then had returned from his trip east, assisted in the rituals. Later he wrote to the head of the American Board of Foreign Missions that Old Joseph, as an elder of sorts, distinguished himself with "discretion and Chris-tian zeal."[13] Such matters were important to the Wallowa chief, who by then was about sixty years old. Spalding had baptized him and three of his children in 1839. He had baptized "Ephraim" (Young Joseph) in 1840 and Joseph's wife and Joseph's friend Lyman in 1843. But what of Ollokot, another son of Joseph? It is believed that Ollokot—the Cayuse word means Frog—was born two or three years after his older brother "Ephraim."[14] If the estimate is accu-rate, he could have been baptized at either the 1843 or 1844 ceremonies. Yet there is no evidence that he was, in spite of his father's meticulousness about the rite. Perhaps the child was younger than supposed. Perhaps he was absent because of illness. The point, however, is this: He missed his chance. For nearly a quarter of a century after 1844, no more Nez Perces would be taken into the First Protestant Church. The strange new world that Old Chief Joseph had chosen for himself and his family was falling apart.

The first explosion came, by coincidence, in 1844. By that year the tribes of the interior had come to look on cattle as a source of wealth. Learning that the animals could be obtained at small cost in California, a large group of Cayuses, Wallawallas, Nez Perces, and Spokans made the long ride there to trade horses and furs for a herd. During a quarrel with some roughneck Americans in Califor-nia, the son of a prominent Wallawalla chief Peo-Peo Mox-Mox, was wantonly murdered. The angry Indians demanded that Elijah White punish the murderer, as White's own code said he must.

The subagent's authority, such as it was, in no way extended to California. He soft-soaped Ellis when the Indians approached him and then, for unrelated reasons, departed permanently from the Northwest. Feeling hoodwinked, the frustrated Indians talked of taking the law into their own hands and slaying objectionable whites everywhere—the red man's code did not limit vengeance to the actual perpetrators of a wrong—but finally the threat sputtered out, along with the Indians' trust in the white man's promises about justice.

On the local scene, too, the laws were falling into disrepute. Head Chief Ellis and some of his deputy chiefs were accused of being too severe in the whippings they administered. Defiance grew, especially among members of the heathen party. When their resistance went unpunished—after all, what enforcement powers did the chiefs have?—the code and, by extension, all things introduced by the whites were subjected to raucous scorn.[15]

Meanwhile, the immigration of whites over the Oregon Trail had grown phenomenally. While returning to Waiilatpu in 1843, Whitman had accompanied a column of about a thousand persons. By 1847, the year after the United States had acquired the present Northwest by treaty with Great Britain, the annual influx had risen to more than four thousand. Opportunists among the Cayuses made quick profits by swapping, at favorable terms, fresh horses for exhausted livestock, which they then fattened and sold again. They dealt in grain, flour, and vegetables. A few even hired whites to plow additional farmland for them.[16] Although many of the interracial meetings were pleasant and mutually advantageous, more were scarred, on the part of the rough American frontiersmen, by a dark mistrust and arrogance that the Indians resented.

Thoughtful Cayuses soon began to wonder how long it would be before the whites began yearning for the land itself. From occasional half-breeds traveling with the wagon trains, they heard of the dispossession of the Indians in the East. They noticed that Whitman was paying more attention to the newcomers than to the tribesmen he was supposedly serving. He sold the travelers produce that he and faithful Cayuses had grown on land the Indians considered theirs, yet he paid no rent. Each winter he housed from thirty to fifty trail-weary immigrants. He and Narcissa adopted orphans. His school, once operated for the native populace, now concentrated on white children. The Indians, he wrote in one letter, were doomed. "[They] have in no case obeyed the Biblical command to multiply and replenish the earth, and they cannot stand in the way of others doing so."[17] Sensing that stance, unfriendly Cayuses (not all were), increased their harassment of mission property and even of Whitman's person.

The disgruntlement reached out to Lapwai. Attendance at the Spaldings' school dropped from over two hundred to eight and, finally, during the notoriously frigid winter of 1846–47, to zero. The dam that held water for the gristmill was torn out. The closest call came late in 1845. A noisy group of gamblers outside Spalding's house settled down to one of their stick games. Their yelling and chanting he could stand, but when they began feeding their fire with his wooden fence rails, he put on a heavy buffalo-robe coat and rushed outside to stop them. They threw him into the fire. The coat held off the flames long enough for him to crawl out and defiantly drag some of the rails from the blaze. With scornful yammers the Indians withdrew, but Spalding was so discouraged that he went into the house and wept. Later, after toughs had thrown rocks through the meeting-house windows, he wrote that there was no use trying to repair anything. It would just be smashed again. The Indians, he finished miserably, were demanding that he pay them not only for the water he used and the land on which the mission buildings stood, but even for the air he breathed.

The crisis came when some American families, traveling in the long, disjointed wagon trains of 1847, brought measles with them. Some of the whites stopped at Waiilatpu to rest and nurse their sick. The disease spread to the Cayuses, most of whom had not developed an immunity to it. One estimate declares that half the Cayuse tribe died during the epidemic that followed.

Unaware of the situation, Spalding loaded seventeen packhorses with grain for sale to the migrants and set out for Waiilatpu on about November 20, 1847. With him, in addition to an Indian helper or two, was his ten-year-old daughter Eliza, whom he intended to enroll in Whitman's all-white school. He was stunned by what he found. Close to seventy whites, many ill with measles and suffering from dysentery, were crowded into the mission. To help out, Spalding carried such small medical skills as he possessed to some Wallawallas who were camped nearby. On his return he agreed to join Whitman on a hurried errand of mercy of Hezekiah's village of Cayuses, twenty-five or thirty miles to the south. Near Hezekiah's settlement was another village, presided over by Hezekiah's Catholic brother Tauitau (Young Chief). A Catholic mission had recently been established there at the chief's invitation. The Protestants blamed much of the restiveness among the Nez Perces and Cayuses on the machinations of the papists, but during those times of acute trouble, members of the two sects were extending helping hands to each other.

To save time, Whitman and Spalding rode all night through a cold rain. As they dropped, at dawn, down a hill leading to Hezekiah's village, Spalding's horse fell, painfully injuring him. Because of the discomfort of riding, he decided to lay over a day or two after Whitman started home. When at last he was jogging along the trail, he saw one of the priests, Father Jean Baptiste Brouillet, and two Indians coming toward him.

Brouillet told Spalding that he had recently gone north with an interpreter to give help and administer Catholic sacraments to Cayuses who were camped near Waiilatpu. While the priest had been at his work, the village chief, Tilokaikt, told him proudly that the Indians had just attacked Waiilatpu.

Essentially, the bloodletting had been defensive. One wild rumor that many Cayuses believed was that the missionaries wanted the Cayuses' lands and were administering poisons disguised as medicines as a way to get it. Another motive for the uprising sprang from cultural imperatives. Disease, the Indians believed, was transmitted by evil spirits. A strong shaman could kill a person just by concentrating his thoughts on the victim's death. That was what Whitman and his followers were supposedly doing. No Cayuse shaman had come forward who was strong enough to deflect the lethal scheme. To save the tribe, warriors had stepped in and had used their hatchets and guns to eliminate the threat. Tied to this reasoning was the compulsion for revenge; a close relative of a patient who died while under the treatment of a medicine man was entitled to slay the inept or malicious tewats. And so Whitman had died, a pipe tomahawk buried in his brain.

Shaken by Tilokaikt's revelation, Brouillet had ridden on to Waiilatpu. "What a sight did I behold! Ten bodies lying here and there, covered with blood, and bearing the marks of atrocious cruelty."[18] The only woman killed was Narcissa Whitman. During the days following Brouillet's visit, four more men would die, a count that included one man who drowned while trying to flee down the Columbia. Another who escaped in spite of a wounded hip was a recent immigrant named William Canfield. He set out on foot to warn Lapwai that the next blow might fall there. Three of the many sick children of Waiilatpu died for want of attention. Forty-seven people, most of them just past puberty, were distributed among the victors. Christian Hezekiah (Five Crows) restrained himself for a time, but, wanting to know what a white woman was like, asked that one be delivered to him through the priests at the new Catholic mission. Powerless to intercede and anxious about their own lives, the fathers complied, giving him a frantically terrified adolescent as a "wife."[19]

Much of this had not yet transpired when Brouillet reached Waiilatpu, administered sacraments to the dying, and helped dig graves for those already dead. Hoping to warn Spalding to stay away from Waiilatpu, the priest asked the Cayuses for permission to return home with his interpreter. The Indians let them go, but delegated a young warrior to ride along to see what they did.

Late in the afternoon the trio saw Spalding jogging down the trail toward them. He was unarmed; the warrior with Brouillet wasn't. Earnestly, the priest urged the glowering Cayuse to let the missionary go. Torn by uncertainty—didn't both these whites claim to be God-people?—the youth galloped back to Waiilatpu to tell the warriors where Spalding was. Fearful for his mission, his wife, and his younger children, Spalding began a flight that can't be believed—except that it happened.

Thick fog that rolled in with darkness hid him from the Cayuses who set out in pursuit. The next day he spent cowering in thick, wet brush, taking to the trail once more at nightfall. Again he eluded his pursuers, but while he was resting, his unhobbled horse wandered off, and he was too frightened to wait for daylight to look for it. On he went on foot. His stiff boots had served while he was in the saddle, but pinched unbearably when he walked. Discarding them, he limped ahead with his feet wrapped in leggings. After four days and nights of piercing December cold, he reached the Snake. In spite of a new downpour of icy rain, he managed to cross the river in a purloined canoe. On the sixth day, starving, bracing his steps with two sticks, and half incoherent from pain and exhaustion, he reached the mission. Indians swarmed everywhere.

Friends among them bandaged his feet, fed him, and let him sleep. Then they took him three miles up Lapwai Creek to William Craig's homestead. Craig had harassed the missionaries in the past, but when the wounded Canfield brought word of the attack on Waiilatpu, he offered shelter to the frightened mission staff. Now he took in Spalding as well. There the missionary listened in despair as Eliza told him that the mission had been looted and that some of Joseph's band had been among the thieves.

A strong guard of Nez Perces, mostly from Big Thunder's village, surrounded Craig's homestead. This was for the Indians' protection as well as for the whites'. If revengeful Americans sent troops into their country, the white prisoners could be used as hostages during whatever dealings followed.

Nez Perce oral tradition insists that Old Joseph was in the Wallowa country—probably in one of its canyon-cupped winter villages—when the massacre occurred.[20] But where was he during the half dozen critical years that followed? Because mentions of him are few, all we can do is resort to assumptions, slippery though they are, as substitutes for historical documents.

Certainly, Old Joseph learned soon of the killings at Waiilatpu and of the withdrawal of Mrs. Spalding and the handful of other whites at the mission to William Craig's homestead on Lapwai Creek. Certainly, he was aware of Spalding's dramatic return and of his friend Timothy's ride to Waiilatpu to rescue little Eliza if he could.

He could hardly have helped knowing, further, that some of the non-Christian members of his own band had participated in the looting of the Lapwai mission. Later Spalding would claim that Old Joseph, too, had participated in the thieving. Such an action on the chief's part is hard to believe. What probably happened is that Spalding, hurt at not seeing Joseph among his supporters at Craig's, had decided that his onetime friend had joined the mission's enemies. Unlikely ... yet, for whatever reason, Joseph does seem to have stayed aloof during those uneasy days.[21]

The active Indian grapevine next brought him word that Peter Skene Ogden, in command of a strong party of Hudson's Bay Company men, had landed at Fort Walla Walla near the point where the Walla Walla River runs into the Columbia. All the tribesmen in the vicinity either knew Ogden personally or knew of him. Ogden was shrewd, far traveled, tough, fair, and better versed than were most whites in the characteristics of the native peoples. When he summoned the Cayuse chiefs to confer with him at the fort on December 23, they came, as did two unnamed Nez Perces. He said he was there to ransom the captive Americans. He offered to do what he could to calm the Americans of the lower Columbia region, but he would not promise to halt any war of retaliation they might launch.

The power of his personality and the might of the huge trading monopoly he represented carried the points. The Indians surrendered their captives in return for a not-very-generous quantity of blankets, clothes, guns, ammunition, and tobacco. By letter Ogden urged the Spaldings and the few whites with them to leave the country with the onetime captives. Fifty Nez Perces escorted them to the dock at Fort Walla Walla, where they rejoined little Eliza, sick and gaunt from her long ordeal. There is no indication that Joseph was with the escort, although he again certainly knew about the departure of the white friend who once had played so large a part in his life.

Nearly two months later, Joseph's half brother, Hezekiah (Five Crows) appeared at one of the Wallowa band's canyon camps. He was nursing an arm whose bone had been splintered by either a rifle ball or a load of coarse buckshot from a shotgun blast. His spirits were as sore as his flesh, and from him Joseph learned of the steps the Oregonians were taking to avenge the Wai-ilatpu killings.

As soon as word of the massacre reached Oregon City, "capital" of the Willamette Valley settlements, the provisional government authorized the mustering of five hundred militia volunteers. Although what we call the Northwest had been acquired by the United States in 1846, Congress had not yet formed a territorial government. Accordingly, the Cayuse war had to be financed by contributions and loans from private individuals and businesses. (Spalding committed the American Board of Foreign Missions to five hundred dollars.)[22] The whites' strategy was, first, to offer peace to the Cayuses in exchange for their surrender of the actual murderers of the thirteen people at Waiilatpu. Fearing that the Indians would not agree to the terms if they could reinforce their disease-depleted ranks with allies from other tribes, a peace commission of three men was appointed to isolate the Cayuses. The pivotal tribe whose neutrality had to be assured because of its numbers and the skill of its warriors was the Nez Perce.

All three members of the commission were acquainted, to some extent, with the Nimipus. All three may have met Joseph at some time or another. One was Joel Palmer, a leader of the big Oregon Trail immigration of 1845. Wanting to buy horses, he had visited Lapwai for a week in 1846, a time when Joseph might well have been planting new crops just outside the mission compound. Another member was Henry A. G. Lee, who had arrived in Oregon with Whitman in 1843. He had taught in the Lapwai Indian school during the winter of 1843–44, when Joseph and Asenath were deeply involved in it, and then had moved on to the Willamette. When the militia were mustered, he was elected one of its majors.

The third member of the commission was Robert Newell, a onetime trapper and a great friend of William Craig's. Both had roamed the mountains at times with Nez Perce hunters. Both had Nez Perce wives. Newell's spouse—he called her Kitty M—was reputed to be one of the most beautiful women of the tribe.[23] She bore him five children and moved to the Willamette settlements with him in 1840, only to die in 1845. Remarried quickly to a fifteen-year-old Caucasian, Rebecca Newman, who later bore him eleven more children, Newell took an active part in local political and economic affairs. Because of his familiarity with the Nez Perce tongue, he, like Lee, was a logical choice to deal with the Cayuses.

Spalding sought to boost the commission's chances as much as he could by giving the commissioners a note to the Nez Perce chiefs he knew best—even some antagonistic ones, but also including Old Joseph—urging them to listen to the commissioners before they decided how to align themselves in the coming disturbances.[24] The note was placed in a sealed packet, presumably to convince the Nimipus that Spalding had really written it and that the whites weren't trying to gather the chiefs into one locality before slaying them.

To increase their appearance of peacefulness, the commissioners proposed to move out ahead of the main army, accompanied only by a small escort. The army's commander, Cornelius Gilliam, a domineering frontiersman spoiling for a fight, refused permission. However, he did let the commissioners entrust Spalding's letter, along with some mail for Fort Walla Walla, to a Nez Perce whom Newell had picked up in Oregon City. The fellow was known as Old Elijah. He was instructed to deliver the packet to the Nez Perce chiefs, along with his own urgings that they meet with the commission at the ruins of Waiilatpu.[25]

During the latter days of February 1848, the undisciplined, haphazardly equipped militia moved with its constrained commissioners across the barren lava plains east of The Dalles. At a place called Sand Hollow, about twenty-five miles west of the Cayuse villages on the Umatilla River, they were confronted by about four hundred Cayuses, both men and women. Adopting standard tactics, the army bunched its spare horses and the cattle it was driving along for food in a makeshift corral and then formed a wide circle around the pen. Meanwhile the commissioners advanced cautiously toward the Indians, Newell holding up a large American flag as an invitation to a parley, for it was evident from the way the Cayuses were milling around that they were not united in favor of battle. Gilliam, however, sent orders for the would-be negotiators to come back, and when some of the Cayuses made gestures to the same effect, they reluctantly complied.

Abruptly, a long-distance duel, rifles against muskets, began. The little cannon the whites had wrestled along with them boomed ineffectively. Trying perhaps to stir the Cayuses into a charge, two warriors all of a sudden spurred headlong toward the whites. One was a medicine man called Gray Eagle; he had consulted his wayakin and believed its power would make him invulnerable. The other was Five Crows, roaring defiance. You bet, he was the despoiler of a white virgin—a victorious warrior's prerogative—and what were the whites going to make of it?

Two shots gave the answer. Gray Eagle dropped dead. Five Crows reeled back with a shattered arm. In the stunned pause that followed, the militia advanced, the red men howling along their flanks. The noisy affair ended with eight Cayuses killed and half a dozen whites wounded.[26]

Not long after Five Crows had finished telling Joseph the tale of the fruitless conflict, messengers arrived in the Wallowa country with word that Timothy and an Alpowa neighbor of his, Red Wolf, were urging the chiefs to come to an important meeting at Lapwai to discuss their place in the coming war. On arriving at the meeting, Joseph learned the story of the packet of letters Old Elijah had been carrying. Cayuses had stopped him and had appropriated the gifts he bore for the Nez Perce chiefs. But they had sent the mail on to Fort Walla Walla. By good fortune, Red Wolf and Timothy happened to be at the post at the time. Noticing the packet Spalding had addressed to the chiefs, the trader at the fort summoned the pair to watch while he broke the seal. He then read the contents aloud. Would the Nez Perces meet the white commissioners at Waiilatpu to discuss peace? Straightaway Timothy and Red Wolf rode to the Clearwater to lay the proposal before as many chiefs as they could bring together.[27]

Some of the chiefs were suspicious. This was an American trick. The whites wanted to lure the principal Nez Perces into one place where they could kill them all and take their land. Timothy and Red Wolf calmed them, saying that the message truly came from the big chief in Oregon City. They had seen the seal broken. The trader had assured them everything was honest.

Thus reassured, most of the Nimipu leaders, strongly aware that the Nez Perces had never battled with the Americans, decided to go to Waiilatpu and hear what the peace commission had to offer. Because Ellis and the Lawyer had not yet returned from the Plains, where they had been hunting buffalo with a large group of Nez Perces and Flatheads, the assembly elected Old Joseph to act as temporary head chief during the meeting with the whites, who were already nearing Waiilatpu and a hoped-for showdown against the Cayuses.

About 250 Nez Perces made the journey. Many were women, for it was their job, during trips, to set up the lodges and prepare the meals. Almost certainly, Asenath was with them. This meant that the youngsters trailed along, as they did on journeys to the camas meadows for roots and sociability and to the streams of the high Wallowa country for salmon. Adventures, games, stories, work with horses, and practice with little bows and arrows filled those happy days. But this time there was a seriousness to the elders. It sobered the children, especially Young Joseph, who was more thoughtful by nature than his siblings. His eighth birthday was just around the corner—not too young for him to start noticing things that mattered.

When the cavalcade was close to Waiilatpu, the chiefs called a halt so the people could don their finery, paint their horses, and make an impressive entry. When all was in readiness—it was the morning of March 6—Robert Newell, of the peace commission, and his good friend William Craig, who had sheltered the Spaldings during the days of fear following the massacre, arrived to usher the Nimipus to the appointed council ground. Awed by the stateliness of the Indians whom they had supposed they would soon be fighting, many of the militia broke into cheers. Surprised into relaxing, the Indians cheered back.[28]

The council ground selected by Colonel Gilliam and the peace commissioners lay roughly between the army's camp and the ruined structures that had once marked the heart of the mission compound. Although the soldiers had done some policing after their arrival, trash still cluttered the area, much of it lying sodden in the irrigation ditches. Although Catholic priests helped by loyal Indians had fenced off the communal graves and the one where the Whitmans lay, wolves had managed to unearth some of the bones. According to one gruesome tale, hanks of Narcissa's blond hair had been cut loose from the scalp and were circulating among the curious militia men. The buildings, their outer walls consisting mostly of adobe brick, had been gutted by fire. Troopers had carted off load after load of the blackened adobes for constructing a barricade four to five feet high around their own camp.

On the morning of March 7, Gilliam and the peace commissioners marched formally to the council ground and sat down facing the Indians across a table that had probably been retrieved from the mission. As was customary, the Nez Perces sat on the ground in concentric semicircles, facing the white negotiators. The main chiefs occupied the first curve; the others filled in the rest of the rows according to rank. The pipe of friendship, Newell wrote later, "passed back and forth until all our hearts were good and our eyes were watery." Young Joseph, placed far to the back with the other children, probably watched and listened with care, knowing his father would be the first to speak for the Indians.

It was a short speech. Old Joseph stood and adjusted his blanket while the crier who would translate his words into English for the whites made ready. Dramatically, then, the chief held aloft a small, crudely bound volume. It was one of the copies of the Gospel according to Matthew that Spalding had translated into Shahaptian and printed on the little press at Lapwai. It was part of the much larger Bible that only fifteen years or so earlier Spokan Garry had said showed the way to heaven—the book Rabbitskin Leggins and his friend had gone to St. Louis to find. This is what Joseph said as he held it:

When I left my home, I took the book in my hand and brought it with me. It is my light. I heard the Americans were coming to kill me. Still, I held the book before me and came on. I have heard the words of your chief. I speak for all the Cayuses present, and all my people. I do not want my children engaged in this war, although my brother is wounded. You speak of the murderers. I shall not meddle with them. I bow my head. *Kopet* [This much I speak.][29]

"I held the book before me and came on": powerful magic surely. Other chiefs followed Tuekakas. Each in his own way insisted that the Nez Perces bore no responsibility for the massacre. They had known nothing of it until after it had occurred. They had not forgotten that Lewis and Clark had told them to live in peace. They had agreed to the law Elijah White had laid down: Anyone who committed a murder would forfeit his own life. No, they would not fight to protect the murderers.

In answer Joel Palmer appointed William Craig to act as the Nez Perces' agent. He told the Indians that Craig would listen to their grievances and help them with their farming. He promised that the government would send them a blacksmith and a schoolteacher if they wished. He urged that they always do what they knew was right.

So far, so good. The Nez Perces would not ally themselves with the Cayuses. But why not press for more, now that the chiefs were in a cooperative mood? Robert Newell made the pitch, extemporizing on the religious theme Old Joseph had introduced. A crier translated the words and shouted them out to the audience of Indians:

The laws of God have been broken here on this ground. Look at those walls, see how black they are, look at that large grave. He is angry at those people who broke His laws, and spilt innocent blood. How can we have peace? This way, my friends, and no other. All join together, and with good hearts try to get those murderers and do by them as the great God commands, and by so doing this ground will be purified, and in no other way will we have peace.[30]

Newell capped the exhortation by giving a large American flag to the Nimipus, handing it in trust, probably, to Old Joseph as the temporary head chief of the Nez Perce tribe. That night the Indians showed their hearts with a war dance. The next morning many of them started with the avenging army toward a Cayuse camp several miles away. The march was interrupted by Cayuses bearing a white flag and asking for a council. The plea was granted, but negotiations were soon aborted by the Indians' adamant loyalty to their own people; they would not unconditionally surrender the warriors the army command named as the killers it wanted.

The records make no mention of Joseph's whereabouts. One assumes, on the basis of his own speech to the commissioners, that he had deliberately removed himself from the punitive expedition. His father had been a Cayuse; his half brothers were Cayuses. He had lived with his father's band for a time. He could understand what Five Crows meant when he declared that the warriors whom the whites called murderers were in truth heroes who had struck a blow for freedom. For had not Whitman been using evil spirits called measles to kill the Cayuses so he could give their land to the whites he so clearly favored?

And yet, as the commissioners had said and as Spalding would have confirmed, the laws of God and man were absolute. The Christian God would cause the souls of murderers to perish in the flames of hell. White men would help the inexorable process along by putting a rope around the necks of the guilty and hanging them until they were dead.

How did one reconcile the quandary? Perhaps Lewis and Clark had been wisest when they had told the Nez Perces that the Great Chief in Washington wanted his children always to live in peace. Talk everywhere reported that this Great Chief was now in control of the land between the high mountains and the ocean and would soon send his agents into the territory to establish the ultimate rules by which men should live. Surely, this was the time for patience.

Like Timothy and other Christian Nez Perces, Joseph probably continued with familiar routines, farming his plot of land near Lapwai, discussing agricultural processes with Craig, intermittently traveling with his family to the vast rolling meadows of the Wallowa Mountains when the summer heat at Lapwai grew unendurable, and in winter taking his horses to the shelter of the deep canyons that sliced through the uplands. It was not possible, though, to stay wholly isolated. He undoubtedly heard of the militia's indecisive, two-day battle with the Palouses, close relatives of the Nez Perces and the only allies the Cayuses had. He learned that Gilliam had mortally wounded himself while pulling a loaded rifle out of a wagon. And he heard, with intense shock, of a ruling laid down by Henry Lee, the former commissioner who had succeeded Joel Palmer as the provisional government's superintendent of Indian Affairs.

The edict came about this way: The morale of the militia had sagged dismally under the boredom of aimless marchings and fruitless skirmishes with the Cayuses. To bolster their spirits and encourage new enlistments, Lee had declared that the Cayuses' land was forfeited and open to homesteading by participants in the campaigns. The proclamation did not define the boundaries he was talking about. What was to keep whites from using the pronouncement as an excuse for settling on whatever bits of Umatilla, Wallawalla, or Nez Perce lands that suited their fancy? In this proclamation, Lane cited no enabling treaty, offered no payment, made no mention of the Great Chief in Washington. He simply reached out and took, confirming what Five Crows and others had been saying. Land was the only thing the whites really cared about.[31]

Surely Old Joseph talked to his friend Lawyer about the threat. Lawyer was rising rapidly in the Nez Perce world. Not long after the council at Waiilatpu had ended, he had returned from the Plains with the dreadful news that measles had swept through the buffalo hunting party he and Head Chief Ellis had been traveling with. Ellis and sixty others had died, a staggering loss to the tribes involved. Just before his death, Ellis had urged Lawyer—so Lawyer said—to keep the goodwill of the all-powerful whites by obeying their laws.

The statement, which lacked corroboration from any third party, sounded as if Ellis had wanted Lawyer to inherit his mantle. Either the whites did not understand the gesture or ignored it. Instead they chose as their new head chief a young follower of Whitman's named Richard. Richard was an amiable person who could speak English, and evidently that was the main reason he was named. The Nez Perces paid little attention to him. Meanwhile, Lawyer spread word throughout the tribe, particularly the Christian part of it, about his own claims. When an announcement at last arrived, in March 1849, that Oregon was a part of the United States and that a territorial governor named Joseph Lane had arrived to assume charge, he was ready. Taking a small group of followers to Oregon City, he won an interview with Lane, who told him, as Ellis had, to keep the Nez Perces in line by holding firmly to the laws of the whites. In effect, Lawyer was now head chief of the Nimipu, although there is no record that he was ever elected as such by a vote of the whole tribe.

Not long after Lane's inauguration as governor, a strong column of uniformed regular U.S. Army soldiers marched along the Oregon Trail to the Willamette Valley. Clearly, those warriors would be much more effective than Oregon's bumbling militia had been. That prospect, along with a general weariness from fighting and hiding, led the Cayuses to come to terms with the new order, and they surrendered five men wanted by the whites as the Whitmans' murderers. Rumors abounded that the five were inveigled into going along by false promises of leniency. There was even some doubt that all of them had actually participated in the killings. Be that as it may, all five were tried by a jury that took forty-seven minutes to find them guilty. After being baptized by Catholic priests, they were hanged on June 3, 1850. The white law had triumphed.

The verdict left many Indians, several Nez Perces among them, deeply resentful. The whites, they felt, not justice, had been served. Many who had tried the civilizing process and then had recanted after not finding the material gains they had expected, mocked Old Joseph for his loyalty. So did a number of others who had clung to the old ways in villages far back in the hills. Was the debacle at the missions what he had traded his life for? Where had the white God hidden when He had been needed? Better the wayakin, which was the true way of reaching the pervading spirits that dwelt with Mother Earth and Father Sky. So which was Joseph going to choose now? How was he going to raise his children?

We can only imagine the doubts and sorrows in Joseph's heart. He missed Spalding, his mentor, and, especially, the gentle Eliza, who had opened for him a crack in the door of the white man's knowledge and in whose school he had taught. He missed praying and singing hymns in unison in the church. He missed reading Bible stories to the congregation.

Now those things were gone. But he still remembered how it had been when Spalding had married him and Asenath according to the Christian way, creating bonds the missionary said would last as long as they lived. He remembered his childrens' baptisms, another magic ritual and an admission to secret sources of power they could call on, through prayer, even as heathen children called on their wayakins—only better, perhaps, with surer contacts to What Lay Beyond.

He looked at his three sturdy sons—Manassa, whose Indian name was Sousouquee; Ephraim, who at some point became Hin-mah-too-yah-lat-kekht (Thunder Rolling in the Mountains), but who generally would be called Young Joseph by the whites; and Ollokot, the Frog. He would teach them if he could, if they would listen, the ways of peace. That was the path that would open a safe passage through the entanglements lurking in both the red mens' religion and the whites'. That and not blood, as Robert Newell had claimed, was what would purify the ground.

· 11 ·

BACK HOME

In 1850 the Congress of the United States passed a pernicious measure known as the Donation Land Claim Act. The aim of the act was the rapid settlement of Oregon Territory, an enormous entity from which the present-day states of Oregon, Washington, Idaho, western Montana, and much of Wyoming would later be carved. Scheduled to expire in 1853, a date later extended to 1855, the new law handed out such generous amounts of Oregon land to white Americans that a wild rush developed. In 1852, for instance, more people poured into western Oregon than went to California's glittering gold-fields.

Legally, the act's promises of free land were premature. American law, like the British colonial law that had preceded it, recognized that the Indians held occupancy rights to their traditional homelands. Before outsiders could move in, those rights had to be extinguished. Generally, this was done by treaty. Often those treaties specified that the original inhabitants could hold back a part of their lands, called reservations, for themselves. Reservations were unpopular with the whites of the East, however, and during the second quarter of the nineteenth century, another method came into vogue: the United States would purchase, by treaty, all a tribe's holdings and then remove the dispossessed natives to new "homes" in Indian Territory—today's Oklahoma and much of Kansas.

The process did not suit the Northwest. By 1850 Indian Territory was almost full of eastern, southeastern, and midwestern tribes. Besides, Oklahoma was a long way from Oregon, past deserts and towering mountains. But perhaps the broad, dry, thinly populated Columbian Plateau could serve as a substitute. Let the tribes whose homelands lay between the Cascade Mountains and the Pacific relinquish their holdings to the United States and resettle themselves east of the mountains. Legislation authorizing the necessary treaties was passed on the heels of the Donation Land Claim Act, and a man named Anson Dart was sent west, as superintendent of Indian affairs for all of Oregon, to rearrange the living patterns of the northwestern tribes.

Dart arrived in the Willamette Valley in the fall of 1850. Preliminary investigation indicated that the coastal tribes were willing to sell their holdings—the annuities mentioned to them during the cold, rainy winter looked mighty good—and Dart turned to preparing the next step. What would the tribes of the interior think of playing host to their relocated brethren? In the spring of 1851, scarcely six months after his arrival in this strange new world, he set out to learn.

Having obtained a small escort from the military, he began looking for interpreters. Henry Spalding seemed, briefly, to be a logical choice. As a sop for losing his mission at Lapwai, he had been appointed agent for the Indians of southern Oregon. He seldom visited them. Some, like the Rogues, were notoriously quarrelsome. He was distraught over the recent death of his wife, Eliza. His temper remained explosive. He fomented trouble by carrying with him everywhere he went a crazed conviction that Catholic priests working in secret with the minions of the Hudson's Bay Company, were responsible for the Whitmans' massacre and the closing of the Protestant missions in the interior. For all these reasons, Dart found him unacceptable—they never did get along—and the superintendent turned instead to Elkanah Walker, former missionary, with Cushing Eells, to the Spokan Indians.[1] Both had left the area, with their families, after the Whitman catastrophe.

As a backup for Walker, Dart chose Perrin Whitman, Marcus's nephew, who had come to Waiilatpu in 1843 at the age of thirteen. A job at The Dalles had let him escape the killings at the mission. Although he was only twenty-one in 1851, he was a hard-twisted young man and had a working command of the Shahaptian dialects used by the Cayuse and Nez Perce tribes.

After a toilsome trip up the Columbia, the whites held an unfriendly, inconsequential meeting with a few Cayuses. Hoping for better from the Nez Perces, Dart sent an emissary to them, requesting a meeting in the Lapwai Valley close to the squatter's claim occupied by their agent, William Craig, and his Nez Perce wife. It is possible that Perrin Whitman carried the message to Craig. If so, it is also possible that he said something about land being the topic to be discussed—a subject that was sure to stir apprehension among the Indians. In a letter to his wife Mary, Walker estimated that four hundred warriors met Dart's party in a broad section of the Lapwai Valley near Craig's homestead. If the missionary's conjecture about numbers was correct, more than half the able-bodied males of the tribe were on hand. Old Joseph—Tuekakas—was one of the leaders, as was Timothy—Tamootsin. In fact, those two were the only Nimipus named by Walker in his letters.[2] Almost surely, then, the younger Joseph was also on hand, well mounted and watching wide-eyed with excitement.

Sensing the importance of the occasion, the gathering bands decided to greet the visiting whites with an impressive entrance, much like the one they had put on in 1842 when Elijah White had come to them with his proposals concerning tribal laws. They caught their best horses from the herds they had brought to Lapwai Creek, painted the animals lavishly, and wove hawk and eagle feathers into manes and tails. Stripping themselves to their breechclouts, the warriors streaked their brown bodies with color and wove more feathers into their long black hair. By midafternoon of June 26, they were ready. Yelling, shooting, blowing whistles, beating drums, and cheered on by their families, who were also mounted, they charged at full gallop onto the meadow where the whites stood grouped in front of their tents. The display of horsemanship finished, the riders dismounted and danced, bending, straightening, and stamping their feet to rattle the strings of little deer hooves and small brass bells attached to their ankles.

Christian Timothy was one of the wildest of the dancers. Disgusted and disappointed both with him and with the amused whites, missionary Walker wrote, "[T]o what a low state human nature has fallen when it requires such vanities, and delights in such mean low excitements."[3] But because most whites enjoyed the spectacle and the Indians relished showing off, "war dances" (more properly greeting dances) became standard features at important powwows between the two races.

Inasmuch as Superintendent Dart was only scouting the region, he was able to turn aside questions from Joseph, Timothy, and, probably, Apash Wyakaikt (Old Looking Glass) about land cessions. No, he assured his listeners, the whites were not interested in gobbling up Nez Perce land, though perhaps some day in the future they would ask the Nimipus to provide living space for a migrating coastal tribe or two. The Nez Perces didn't like the idea—fat, fish-smelling, disease-ridden canoe Indians from a land of dripping skies and heavy forests—but since no immediate threat was involved, the meeting ended on a friendly note. As the Indians returned to their several little villages, they probably thought they had let the pale, bushy-bearded American chief know that their revered homelands were not to be treated lightly.

Homelands. For Joseph that meant the Wallowa country. When he learned from Dart that Eliza Spalding was dead and that her husband would not be returning to Lapwai, the last bonds holding him to his tiny farm near the empty mission buildings began to slip away. To be sure, he had never completely left the sunny meadows and cool forests beside the Wallowa peaks or the deep, warm canyons of the winter country. But now these areas took on a new focus where, as he thought, he could resume the age-old patterns of his life, modified and sweetened by what the white medicine men had taught him.

For Young Joseph, who was eleven at the time of Dart's visit, and for Ollokot and their brothers and sisters, the shift back to Wallowa was a release into fuller "Indianness" than they had yet known. Not that they had become wholly Westernized during their years at the mission. As far as we know, for one example, none of them had cut their hair, which to the missionaries was a primary mark of successful acculturation. They had experienced ritualistic sweat baths during which some of the band's elders spun long tales of tribal history and lore. They had heard the plaintive notes of flutes as youths only a little older than themselves wooed the girls who had caught their fancy.

More exciting for a boy of eleven, or twelve, or thirteen—for time did pass—was Young Joseph's growing responsibility with the herds of horses. Each morning, after the crier had awakened the village, either beside one of the purling high-country streams or in the profound winter canyons of Joseph Creek and the lower Imnaha River, he would ride out nearly naked with the other boys to round up the animals and drive them to a nearby corral. After the men had caught the mounts they wanted for that day, the youngsters returned the rest of the cavorting steeds to the grazing grounds that were currently being used. Very early Joseph and Ollokot knew the thrill of wild races across the meadows; the prickling exhilaration of scouting the area's ravines and hollows for signs of raiders; the slow growth of confidence in their equestrian skills until no horse in the village band was more than they could handle and almost no bog or timber-strewn hill or rocky river ford was too rugged to be crossed.

Did Young Joseph ever go to the buffalo plains as a young man? No record indicates that he did. The Wallowa lands were rich enough in camas and salmon, deer and elk, bear and mountain goats to absorb the people's energy and provide them with the food they needed. If they craved cultivated vegetables, they could get occasional pack loads from the shrinking number of farms at Lapwai or even Kamiah, where, in Old Joseph's absence, Timothy, Lawyer, and other Christian chiefs were consolidating their influence over the still-loyal converts.

Almost certainly Young Joseph did go on a search for his private wayakin, or source of power. Spalding had considered the ancient custom an ungodly superstition to be exorcised. But the Indians' need for direct contact with the immense forces of the natural world ran deep, and with the missionary's influence removed, a reversion to this basic cultural trait was inevitable. Where Young Joseph went, utterly alone in the vastness, or how many days and nights he searched is unknown. In what form the wayakin appeared to him remained his own secret. Possibly it came as a lightning bolt or crash of thunder rolling from the valleys up to the great peaks—a phenomenon described by the phrase *Hin-mah-too-yah-lat-kekht*. But Hin-mah-too-yah-lat-kekht was also a family name, borrowed for him from an uncle shortly after his birth. He may well have had another, secret designation, given him by the wayakin and revealed, with many ambiguities, at the guardian spirit dance, the Wee'kwetset, a winter ceremony in which he certainly participated as a young man. So in spite of his early training in a white-style school and in spite of the English he read and spoke somewhat but gradually lost through disuse, Young Joseph—Hin-mah-too-yah-lat-kekht, a name almost impossibly hard for Anglos to pronounce—Young Joseph was thoroughly Indian. The same may be said of his younger brother, Ollokot. As for their older brother, Manassa (Sousouquee) almost nothing is known, perhaps because he was killed during a brawl a few years after the family's return to the Wallowa country.[4]

The brothers' education was not untainted by Western materialism. The Oregon Trail crossed the Grande Ronde River about twenty miles from its confluence with the Wallowa River. The Nez Perces, like the scattered Cayuses, traded with the emigrants for worn-out horses that could be fattened and for the cattle that were increasingly becoming signs of Indian affluence and prestige. They acquired and grew dependent on a host of what seemed to them magically fabricated items—glass beads of the purest blue, harness buckles and bridle bits, comfortable American-style clothing, soft blankets, new kinds of groceries, and even canvas to use on their tipis instead of heavy buffalo hides.

Deep down there awaited potential crises of identity in the psyches of a people, who, on the one hand, were impatiently desirous of the new power presented by these imports and yet who also sensed, as many did, that too much accommodation with the outsiders who brought the goods might, in the end, destroy a culture that went further back toward the beginnings of life than even the oldest grandmother in the tribe could say. Nimipu, they called themselves—the Real People. What good could come from surrendering that conviction?

During the summer and fall of 1853, only two years after the Nez Perces' meeting with Superintendent Anson Dart, units of the U.S. Army Corps of Topographical Engineers began closing in on the Columbian Plateau from unexpected directions. The supreme commander of the various detachments was Isaac Ingalls Stevens, in whose small body were embedded many of the big ambitions of his young and expanding country.

Born in Andover, Massachusetts, in 1818, Stevens graduated at the top of his West Point class, was commissioned a lieutenant in the Engineer Corps, and won recognition for his fighting during the Mexican War. He was also wounded in the foot. The injury, which never healed properly, pained him for the rest of his life, as did a lingering hernia incurred when, as a twelve year old, he was pitching hay on his father's farm. He had stubby legs. His head was larger than average, but he was handsome, with piercing dark eyes and a precisely trimmed mustache and beard. What struck his contemporaries was the intensity of his ambitions and the unflagging energy with which he pursued them.

Following the Mexican War, he became second in command in the U.S. Coast Survey. Though he worked faithfully and well at reorganizing the department, he did not want to be second to anyone. Openly disobeying army regulations, he worked hard at helping his friend Franklin Pierce win election as the Democratic party's dark-horse candidate for the presidency of the United States. His reward was the governorship of Washington Territory, which Congress carved out of Oregon in the spring of 1853. The dismemberment left Oregon with the boundaries it still has; the rest—today's states of Washington and Idaho plus much of Montana and Wyoming—went to the new territory. Most of the four thousand whites who lived in the huge sprawl were clustered in a strip of land west of the Cascades, between the lower Columbia River and Puget Sound. Everything else, as the bulk of the nation saw it, was a howling wilderness.

This emptiness did not bother Stevens. He was looking at the future, when the first transcontinental railroad would, in his imagination, bring thousands upon thousands of homesteaders into the region. The first step toward such a railroad had already been taken. Congress had authorized, also in the spring of

1853, a four-pronged reconnaissance to determine the most satisfactory rail route from four different points in the Midwest to the Pacific Coast. Working again through President Pierce, who recognized and valued the little soldier's undeniable talents, Stevens won, along with his governorship, command of the party delegated to explore the northern route from Lake Superior to some suitable terminus on the Washington littoral.

He knew the two jobs would bring him face to face with potentially rugged Indian problems. Largely because of the intransigence of such interior tribes as the Yakimas, the plan of buying the holdings of coastal Indians and moving them en masse onto the Columbian Plateau had been abandoned. As a substitute, officials who were appointed to deal with the Indians—Anson Dart, mentioned earlier in this chapter, was one—had decided on their own authority to concentrate on requiring the Indians who lived between the Cascade Mountains and the Pacific to sell only a part of their traditional homelands to the United States while "reserving" the rest for themselves—reservations, in short, like those that had been tried, unsuccessfully, in the East in earlier times.[5]

When Stevens moved west, only a few of the treaties had been entered into, wholly in southwestern Oregon, and Congress had not yet ratified any of them. Stevens thought the idea sound, nevertheless, and wanted a similar program introduced not just among the small tribes of coastal Washington, but throughout the broad reaches of the Columbian Plateau as well. Working yet again through President Pierce, the new governor had himself appointed superintendent of Indian affairs for Washington Territory. Normally, governors did not hold both jobs simultaneously, but Stevens, being Stevens, was determined to exert as much control as possible over what he envisioned as the new rush to the Northwest.

He divided his exploratory force into several detachments. He took some of the men directly west through Montana and over the Continental Divide. Lieutenant George B. McClellan meanwhile led another group across the Isthumus of Panama and north by steamer to Fort Vancouver on the Lower Columbia River. There McClellan's explorers switched to horses and moved laboriously to the east side of the Cascade Range, intending eventually to meet Stevens.[6] The many crisscrossings of the countryside by armed American soldiers filled the Indians with apprehension. What was happening?

Young Joseph was well into his thirteenth year—in late August 1853— when the first rumors about the army's penetrations reached the Nez Perces. It was root-digging season, a time of sociability. The Wallowa bands may well have been camped with other groups from the upper Clearwater on the broad, pine-dotted meadows at Weippe or near the site of present-day Moscow, Idaho. While the women unearthed the small, onion-shaped bulbs with their pointed, crutch-like digging sticks, the children played and the men gambled, raced horses, talked of buffalo hunts, and looked to their weapons. Joseph and Ollokot, who was eleven, scampered around with the younger ones at times, but the elder lad was mature enough by then to feel stirrings that made him look at the budding girls while pretending not to and to hang, with deep yearning, around the circles of seated warriors as they talked about stealing horses and fighting enemy Snakes or Blackfeet.

A brand new topic opened up with the arrival of messengers from the Yakima country at the western part of the Columbian Plateau. They said that certain Klickitats (neighbors of the Yakimas) had been acting as horse packers and guides for six dozen or so soldiers under an officer named McClellan. Along the way a few of the troopers had boasted to the Klickitats that a chief more important than McClellan—Stevens—was on his way from the east to take whatever Indian land and horses the Americans wanted.[7]

On being informed of the threat, the best known of the Yakima leaders, Kamiakin, and several fellow chiefs had ridden out to talk directly to McClellan. They even followed him around for while, trying to divine his purpose. He dodged the Indians' questions, saying simply that he was looking for a railroad pass across the Cascade Range. Railroads meant nothing to Kamiakin, but the officer's demeanor during the interviews so upset the chief that he sent word of his doubts to all the Shahaptian-speaking tribes. Something bad was afoot. Stay alert. The boys shivered with excitement. Their elders were in turmoil. What did it mean? Would there be fighting?

Hard on the heels of Kamiakin's exhortation came more news. White soldiers were passing through Cayuse country on their way east to meet Stevens. At that news, several Nez Perce chiefs donned their ceremonial costumes, joined some of their Palouse neighbors, and rode out to meet the troops, who by then had reached the junction of the Snake and Palouse rivers. Lieutenant Rufus Saxton, the leader of the detachment, spoke just as smoothly as McClellan had. Don't worry. Then he had his men demonstrate their skills with the army's new rapid-fire rifles. The crackling burst of explosions awed the Indians. It worried them, too, and that word flashed through the villages.[8]

Meetings between soldiers and Indians continued during the fall and early winter. Stevens himself skirted the north end of the Bitterroot Mountains, encountering several groups of buffalo hunters on his way, and then cut south through Spokan country to Fort Walla Walla. There he put his party into canoes for a dash down the Columbia River on his way to the new capital of Washington Territory at Olympia. About the only definite thing he did say about his intentions was that he was going to make peace between the Blackfeet and the Plateau Indians so that all tribes could hunt on the Plains in safety.

The Nez Perces agreed that peace with the Blackfeet would be fine if it came about. Meanwhile, they could not help linking Stevens's passage to Olympia with another development. During the summer and fall of 1853, hard-working white settlers from the Pacific side of the Cascades hewed a road 235 miles long through thick forests, over a mountain pass a mile high, and through the heart of Yakima country to Fort Walla Walla, where an already existing road sliced off to join the Oregon Trail. Washington boosters who were stationed at the junction diverted several score wagons from the more familiar trail and lured them, straining and creaking, over the Cascades to homesteads close to Puget Sound.[9]

Kamiakin was vocal about it. The way West was becoming too easy. Too many whites were entering the country. If the Indians of the Columbian Plateau did not form a common front against the invaders, they would indeed lose much of their land.

Like children everywhere, Young Joseph and Ollokot picked up more of what was agitating the tribe's adults than their parents realized. Out of their own forebodings, they probably began to formulate their own concepts of home and of the land that surrounded them. They remembered the farms their father and other Christian Indians had tilled at Lapwai, but those farms had been on land they had borrowed, so to speak, from Spalding's God. They had used it with no thought that it could be severed from the earth of which it was a part and turned over to other users in exchange for desirable merchandise, such as horses.

The white people who each fall poured over the horizon in long lines of white-topped wagons felt differently about the land. Their chiefs came out of the Light (the East) and measured what they wanted and took it the way the traders in the Bitterroot Valley or beside the Missouri River took buffalo hides, giving beads or gunpowder in exchange and then putting private marks on the pelts and shipping them away in big bundles.

Land was different. Land was space. Land was life. It was where the grass grew and the trees spread their shade for everyone who was tired and hot. It was where bright streams flowed so that salmon, beautiful with their sequined sides, could come to the people and nourish them. It was where, when you killed a deer, you thanked its spirit for the gift. Did the whites do that? The boys thought not.

There were no seams between the land and the people it supported. Land was the power you felt rising in you when you saw a strong ridge shouldering against the sky. Knowledge of the land was what came to you with your wayakins. Land was the All-Mother. But did the whites have wayakins? The boys thought not.

Now Kamiakin, the Yakima, a tall, strong, grave man with heavy, dark, grave features, was saying that the chief of the whites, the one named Stevens, was going to take part of each tribe's ancestral holdings and divide it among his followers to do with as they liked—wound it with plows, scar it with roads, imprison it with wooden fences slashed from the trees of the forest. The Indians would have only what was left.

Although only a few explorers appeared in the interior during 1854, village talk swirled continually around the problem. If the land takers really did appear, as Kamiakin predicted, how should they be met? Hard-core conservatives and buffalo hunters who bore wounds from encounters with the Blackfeet spoke for war. Young Joseph and Ollokot shivered with excitement when they heard that sort of rhetoric. War was a young man's road to fame. But war was not the road their father and those who had worked and studied with him at Lapwai had chosen. They said God was peace. They said the Nez Perces had never fought with Americans, who were too strong to be beaten, in any event. Tension filled the villages, and the young people were alternately exhilarated and afraid as they heard the uncertainties and discord that sounded in their elders' voices.

Early in April 1855—almost on Young Joseph's fifteenth birthday, an age that among the native people was practically manhood—a small party of Indian-guided whites arrived at Lapwai. At the head were James Doty, Governor Stevens's secretary, and Andrew J. Bolon, whom Stevens had appointed his subchief for all the tribes living in Washington east of the Cascades. The two said they were arranging for a great council of all Shahaptian-speaking Indians, to be held late in May. The topic was to be the one the Indians dreaded—the sharing of their lands with the whites. If the Nimipu chiefs would come to Lapwai, Doty and Bolon would work out details for the meeting with them.

After a number of anxious chiefs had gathered, the white emissaries set about impressing them with the importance of what lay ahead. The council would be very grand. Kamiakin of the Yakimas had agreed, reluctantly, to attend and had suggested that the meeting should be held at a traditional gathering place in the Walla Walla Valley, not far from the ruins of Whitman's Waiilatpu mission. Wily Peo-Peo Mox-Mox, whose son had been murdered in California, would be there. So would Old Joseph's half brothers, Young Chief and Five Crows of the Cayuses. But, Doty said, the council could not succeed without the Nez Perces, the most numerous and influential of the Plateau tribes. Negotiating for the whites would be Governor Stevens of Washington and Joel Palmer, superintendent of Indian affairs for Oregon Territory, an old friend of the Nez Perces.

On April 18, when it appeared that the Nez Perce chiefs would approve the plan, an incident occurred that James Doty saw fit to record in his journal. Nimble youths stripped the branches from a pine tree growing near the meeting ground and attached an American flag to its top. It was the flag Robert Newell had given to the Nez Perces during the Cayuse War, most probably handing it to Old Joseph as caretaker. Presumably, then, it was Old Joseph who brought it to the meeting, and it is not hard to imagine Young Joseph clambering up the ladder of branch stubs to help with the unfurling—an unfurling that was also a statement.[10]

In 1805, while pausing at one of the Clearwater villages, Meriwether Lewis and William Clark had given an American flag as a token of friendship to one of the tribe's chiefs. Half a century later (less five months) the Nez Perces were replying with another unfurled flag—the one statement that could bind the tribe's factions together. We have been friends for fifty years, the banner said. Do not let the brotherhood be broken now.

Those chiefs who listened to Doty and Bolon at Lapwai carried the proposal (and, no doubt, the story of the flag) back to their people. The response was electrifying, cultures considered. The Nez Perce tribe was a linguistic, not a political, group. Each of its many bands could go whichever way it chose, as could each individual within a band. But on this occasion there were few divisions. When the people gathered late in May for the trip to the Walla Walla council, fifty-seven chiefs and subchiefs showed up. Of the best-known leaders only testy Old Flint Necklace (Looking Glass) was absent; for the past two years he and a few minor chiefs had been in the buffalo country. Twenty-five-hundred people—warriors, women, children—appeared with the chief, according to one American observer. (Surely the figure is too large. The population of the entire tribe could not have been much more than thirty-five hundred in 1855. Of that number, about four hundred were in the buffalo country, and there must have been many old people, ill people, women with young children, loners, and malcontents who chose not to join the pack. So cut the estimate of those going to the council to two thousand; it's still a huge number for the time and place.)

Plus many thousands of horses. And baggage—tipi poles and covers, lodge mats, arms and ceremonial clothing, household utensils, and food. Confrontations with Anson Dart when he had arrived in 1851 with the first official hint of the whites' intentions had given the Nimipus some experience in mass logistics. But Dart had met the Nez Perces in their own territory, at Lapwai. To meet the whites this time, the unwieldy crowd of people had to travel on horseback, driving their extra mounts with them, 125 miles or so to the Walla Walla Valley, setting up and taking down camp each of the four or five days they spent on the way.

Young Joseph, Ollokot, and (probably) their older brother were almost certainly watching the Wallowa part of the huge herd of horses as it moved ahead, reveling as the animals did in the freshness of the rain-washed grass, the spring flowers, and the brawling streams. But when the American encampment came in sight, anxiety replaced some of the holiday atmosphere. Feeling the strain, the young people let the horses graze untroubled while they drifted close enough to the leading chiefs to overhear their plans for a grand entrance. What came to them made excitement surge again. The Nez Perces wanted the whites to see unmistakable evidence both of the Indians' pride and of their basic friendliness toward these interlopers.

Messengers galloped forward with the same flag that had been flown from the pine tree at Lapwai. From a distance the boys watched the whites accept it and place it on a staff hastily erected on a low knoll in front of their camp. Certainly, there was no pomp or circumstance there. Ordinary tents had been pitched for Stevens, Palmer, and a few officers. The hundred or so soldiers and civilians with the negotiators sheltered themselves against the frequent showers in hutches made of pack-mule covers spread over bent willows. A small log cabin had been built nearby to hold the provisions and gifts that would be distributed among the more important Indians. In front of the officers' tents was an arbor formed of branches spread on top of a rectangular wooden frame. In the coolness of that shade, the chiefs and white leaders, eating off tin plates, would share some of their meals. The rough-hewn tables nearby would be used by Doty and other recorders to transcribe the proceedings of the council.[11]

As soon as the flag had been flown from the staff, the principal whites gathered around it on foot, except for Stevens and Palmer, who were mounted. Simultaneously and with slow dignity, the chiefs rode forward in the order of their importance—Lawyer, the politician, first; then Timothy; Old Joseph; James (Big Thunder); Eagle-from-the-Light; and the rest. William Craig introduced them one by one to the two negotiators for the whites. That done, the moment came that the boys had been itching for—the parade of the warriors. Altogether and counting eager youngsters who were fudging a little on their status, there were between six hundred and a thousand riders (estimates vary). They were stripped to their breechclouts. Their bodies and their horses' bodies were garishly painted and adorned with plumes. Jostling into lines, single file in some places, double in others, they charged toward the white reviewers, firing muskets into the air, singing, and beating drums. At a signal they reined in abruptly and, glistening with sweat, formed a big ring around the flagpole. There, a score or so of them dismounted and danced while the rest, still mounted, beat out the time with their drums—an extra-special greeting ceremony. The performance completed, Old Joseph and several other chiefs went to Stevens's tent for a ceremonial smoke. The rest, the women included, retired half a mile or so to their campsite, screened from the white's bivouac by a line of creek-side trees.

On the following day, a mixed group of Cayuse, Wallawalla, and Umatilla warriors appeared. Four hundred strong, they came in truculently, yelling and whooping as they met with the Nez Perces but growing grimly silent around the whites, whom they pointedly slighted by rejecting offers of provisions and tobacco. Kamiakin and his small delegation, who arrived still later, were equally aloof.

Actual business deliberations did not begin until the afternoon of May 29, 1855, nearly a week after the arrival of the Nez Perces. Of the five thousand Indians who are reputed to have come to the council grounds, about one thousand turned out to hear the whites' proposals. It was an onerous experience. The listeners sat on the ground in concentric semicircles, the chiefs occupying the first rows. Although the main part of the audience spoke dialects of Shahaptian, each tribe wanted its own interpreter, as a matter of trust. (Observers from the Flatheads, Spokans, and other Salish-speaking tribes were also on hand, but it does not appear that special interpreters were provided for them.) At least two translators operated at once. After each sentence the speaker on the podium would pause while the interpreters translated it for the crier of the tribe they were serving. The crier then bellowed it out, sentence by sentence, to his part of the audience. When the Indians spoke, the process was repeated in reverse.

Obviously the method was subject to errors, for the interpreters were not well educated in their own language, let alone in the complex subtleties of Shahaptian. Sitting still through the cumbersome process was vastly boring for anyone who was not vitally concerned with what was being said. At least twice one crusty chief scolded young people for the disturbances they were making. Many youths never showed up, preferring to join in the gambling games, horse sports, and foot races in the camps. Others went off fishing and hunting. How Joseph's three sons passed the time we do not know. Almost certainly, they heard, at the evening camp fires, the unrestrained opinions their elders offered about each day's proposals.

During the first days, Stevens and Palmer spent hours telling long lies about the friendship the whites felt toward the Indians. As an example they cited President Andrew Jackson's movement of the southeastern tribes from their original homelands to the lovely countryside of Oklahoma, out of the way of the whites. The listeners, who had heard the truth of those brutal episodes from migrant Indians and half-breeds, somehow managed to stay polite. They stayed polite when the speakers shifted into blatant, though perhaps unconscious, racial superiority. The Indians' future, Stevens and Palmer implied, depended on the natives becoming like whites. Listen to the logic. Hunting was wasteful of land; furthermore, game was growing scarce. So turn to white-style agriculture and home industries, which did not use so much land. Crowd themselves onto reservations, in short. The benign government would help them pick the reservations and then would pass on to white settlers whatever was left over. Carefully segregated from the whites, the red men would then learn to be imitation whites. The Great Father would help the process along by spending up to sixty thousand dollars on the Nez Perce reservation for building schools, fences, carpenter and blacksmith shops, gristmills, and so on—the old missionary program, it must have sounded like to the Indians, but minus God.

Another part of the bribery was a promise of two hundred thousand dollars worth of annuity payments. These payments would take the form of clothing, tools, food, teachers' salaries, and the like, all distributed by the Indians' agents over the course of twenty years—that being time enough, presumably, for the Indians to complete the program of acculturation. Head chiefs would have houses built for them and receive annual salaries of five hundred dollars each, a sure way of stirring jealousies.

There would be marvels as well. At one session Palmer tried to explain a locomotive hauling a train of "waggons." He tried to explain the telegraph. These improvements, as he called them, would run through the Plateau area if the Indians agreed and would benefit them, as well as the whites—who, he threatened at another session, would descend on the area "like grasshoppers on the plains ... You cannot stop them." What he did not say was that his fellow commissioner's most passionate commitment was to building a railroad that he believed would speed the development of the territory of which he was governor. But Palmer's listeners had no trouble divining that the proposals being held out to them were intended for the good of the invaders—not for the native inhabitants of the land.

Angered by the whites' crass efforts to manipulate them, many of the Columbian Indians grew increasingly angry at the Nez Perces and at Lawyer. The Nimipus' land, it was widely believed, was not going to be as severely affected as was the land of the other Shahaptian tribes. Stevens had wanted the Nimipus at the council because their acquiescence to the government's program would influence the other tribes. His main tool in securing their cooperation was Lawyer, who had been steadily maneuvering his way upward to recognition as the head chief of all the Nez Perce bands. But the other tribes, in their own opinion at least, were not fooled. As Peo-Peo Mox-Mox of the Wallawallas snapped, the whole course of events had been prearranged. Craig and Lawyer, working together, were trying to rush things to a conclusion without giving the other tribes time to think.[12]

Perhaps the estimate was unduly severe. Consider Lawyer's hat, for instance. Drawings of it today look absurd. It was a tall stovepipe of the sort worn during that era by American dignitaries—by Abraham Lincoln, for one. Lawyer had probably picked up the headgear during one of his opportunistic trips to Portland to talk to white officials. To it he affixed, in upright position, three striking hawk or eagle feathers.[13] The hybrid may well have been his own form of statement: He wanted to link the two races, for his own gain, no doubt, but also for the good of the Nimipus, who he believed could not survive if they did not come to some sort of accommodation with the onrushing Americans.

Many of the other Indians did not see it that way. Resenting Lawyer's unctuousness and resenting even more the pressures the hypocritical negotiators were applying, the angry Cayuses, Wallawallas, and the few Yakimas who were in attendance with Kamiakin hatched a plot. It is not certain who was the target. Perhaps Lawyer was to be murdered. Perhaps Stevens and Palmer were the intended victims. If Old Joseph or any other Nez Perces were aware of the scheme, they apparently stayed quiet, thus perhaps giving tacit approval. In any event, in the middle of the night of June 2–3, Lawyer slipped with his wife and children to the center of the whites' compound, where he snuggled his tipi close to Stevens's tent.

The next morning he told the governor he had done so as a sign to the plotters that if they struck at the head negotiators, they would have to kill Lawyer, too, and that would bring the entire Nez Perce tribe down upon them. Stevens evidently believed the tale, and his son (who was at the conference as a thirteen-year-old boy) included it in the biography he later wrote of his father. Lawyer bashers scoff. They speculate that the chief invented the whole tale to curry additional favor from Stevens. Or if there was a plot, it was directed at him and he fled to Stevens's compound to save his own skin. At this late date a definite conclusion is impossible.[14]

Shortly after Lawyer's move, the negotiators finally got around to describing the specific boundaries of the reservation they wanted the Indians to accept. Two tracts were involved, one in Nez Perce country, one in Yakima land. In addition to agreeing to a shrinkage of their territories, both tribes would have to make room for outsiders. Spokans, Cayuses, Wallawallas, and Umatillas would be moved into enclaves among the Nez Perces. The Yakimas would have to take in several small tribes scattered from the southern slopes of Mount Adams far north to the upper Columbia River. Most of those small tribes were not represented at the council and thus were unable to have any say about their futures. Munificent benefits would be given the dispossessed peoples, Stevens promised, as if price were the point.

The storm broke. Speaker after speaker from the tribes that would be moved to Nez Perce land rose to declare that the earth, nourisher of all life, should not be clipped into pieces, sold for perishable goods, and the fragments tortured with unnatural implements—which was what Stevens's proposals came down to. A second, passionate objection revolved around love of one's native land. People should not be uprooted any more than plants. Just as the earth provided for the Indians, Young Chief declared, so the Indians were expected to care for that portion of the land on which the Great Spirit had placed them.

Lawyer, whose old battle wounds were paining him severely, stumbled through a speech supporting the proposals. No other Nez Perce spoke up. Lacking their support and fearing that an uprising might really be in the making, the outnumbered commissioners gave ground. The Cayuses, Wallawallas, and Umatillas, they said after conferring throughout most of the night, could go to a joint reservation of their own along the Umatilla River. The move, which quieted those Indians, also isolated the Yakimas and the few delegates from the distant tribes who would have to join them on their shrunken reservation.

The Nez Perces remained worried. They might be asked to compensate for the withdrawal of the Cayuse group by yielding more of their own territory to the insatiable whites. Several chiefs, Old Joseph among them, spoke earnestly to Stevens about this possibility, each in an effort to protect his own band's territory. How much influence they had is problematical. Stevens had wanted a Nez Perce reservation primarily as a holding ground for Indians who were dispossessed of lands suited to quick settlement. So he granted the Nimipu a favor that did not cost him much and snipped off only some of the more remote edges of the territory they claimed as theirs.

Relieved that the Wallowa country would remain untouched, Old Joseph spoke out in full council for the first time. He and his fellow chiefs had been stubborn not for themselves, but for their children. "It is good for the old people [he was about seventy] to talk together and straight, on account of our children on both sides."[15] Of all the speakers who poured out their hearts during the long deliberations, he is the only one on record who spoke of future generations.

One more dramatic interruption remained. On his way home from the buffalo plains, Old Looking Glass had heard the Nez Perce chiefs under Lawyer were selling his band's home territory. The report was garbled. No Nez Perce leader would presume to sell the land on which another group customarily ranged. Nevertheless, Looking Glass raced in a fury to the council grounds with a small party of hunters, one of whom was waving a freshly lifted Blackfoot scalp at the end of a long stick. At a hurriedly convened meeting on the council grounds, the other Nez Perces tried to calm him. But, as the tribe's most influential buffalo chief, he disliked having any negotiations made without him, and he particularly distrusted Lawyer, of whose rise to prominence he was more than a little envious. For two tumultuous days he tried to supplant his rival so he could reopen the negotiations. Lawyer's strong network of Christian Indians held him off, however, but at the cost of deepening factional wounds that would persist long after the principals in the fray had passed on.[16]

By the time the internecine struggle was over, the Indians were ready to go home. Hoping perhaps to soothe hurt feelings, Stevens asked Lawyer to sign the treaty first as head chief, followed immediately by Looking Glass. Lawyer wrote firmly "Aleiya," Looking Glass made an X beside his name. Later he claimed he had not signed but had touched the pen just barely as a gesture of courtesy to Lawyer. Stevens then called on Joseph. Although Joseph could write, he, too, made an X, as did Timothy and every other signer. After the Congress of the United States and the president had ratified the agreement, the Nez Perces would own roughly 7 million acres of land onto which the general run of whites could not come without the tribe's permission. The rule would last for as long as the grass grew. Stevens solemnly said so.[17]

When representatives of the other tribes followed suit, their expressions were so grim that some people jumped to the conclusion that the signing was treachery, intended simply to give the whites a false sense of security. The Indians' angry hearts, proponents of this theory maintained, did not guide the hands that held the pens.[18]

Stevens stayed at the council grounds for a few more days while writing his reports. Many Nez Perces also lingered. As a sign of amity, they performed a scalp dance, during which the trophy that one of Looking Glass's men had brought from the Blackfoot country was grossly abused. Next a circle of young women formed inside a ring of spectators and moved slowly around, "chanting a mild and plaintive air." Young warriors, gaily clad, pressed inside that circle. As the girls revolved, a youth would place a token on a shoulder of the one who pleased him most. If she let it stay there, his approach was favored. Young Joseph? He was only fifteen ... but he may not have felt too young to play.

Meanwhile Old Joseph was working on a love affair of his own, a parchment map, sixteen by eighteen inches, drawn in pale green ink that delineated the Wallowa country.[19] He devised his own set of symbols: a drawing of a fish indicated Wallowa Lake; figures of deer indicated mountains; almost microscopic images of horseshoes showed main trails. His reason for making the map was implied in an earlier remark to Stevens. It was for his children. He showed the map to them. Their home, forever. The government of the United States had promised.

· 12 ·

UPHEAVAL

Restlessness, indecision, prejudice, fear, anger, and eventually violence shook the Northwest during the latter part of the 1850s as the two races struggled for control of the country. Much of the turmoil was precipitated by the deliberate perfidy of Governor Isaac Ingalls Stevens. Stevens knew perfectly well that the Indians of the interior would continue to hold possessory rights to all their accustomed homelands until the treaties negotiated at Walla Walla had been ratified by the Congress and the president of the United States. Entry before then, unless the Indians granted permission, was trespass. Stevens, however, needed an influx of settlers for the sake of his railroad. (He did not believe that the tensions between the American North and the South over routes would continue to stall it for long; he had a marvelous ability to see things the way he wanted them.) So when Palmer and he sent copies of the treaties from the council ground to their territorial legislatures, they included notices to the newspapers that land east of the Cascades was now available for homesteading and mining. The disgruntled tribes of the Columbian Plateau would not like that, but he'd handle them.[1] Then off he rode, across the Continental Divide, to treat with Blackfeet. During his absence Charles H. Mason, the twenty-five-year-old secretary of Washington Territory, would also serve as acting governor.

Other angers and uncertainties about the future contributed to the Indians' malaise. Many small tribes that had not been represented at Walla Walla suddenly found they had already been "documented" out of their lands and were expected to crowd onto the severely shrunken Yakima reservation. Hot words

155

were thrown at the tall, smoldering Yakima chief, Kamiakin: He had sold them out. Kamiakin denied the charge with equal vehemence: He had not signed the treaty. The whites were the false ones and must be resisted.

Kamiakin occupied a strategic base for spreading his war propaganda. His lands commanded the eastern approaches to the passes that crossed the Cascade range. He was related to influential tribesmen both on the Pacific side of those mountains and in the country that swept from the eastern banks of the Columbia River up to the Bitterroot Mountains. With grim diligence he set about putting those advantages to work. He rode endlessly from tribe to tribe, frequently offering a large number of horses to those who would join him as allies. Ground that he lacked time to cover himself he assigned to family members and ardent followers.[2]

The whites' lust for gold provided unexpected substance for his rhetoric. For several years, traders, explorers, and Catholic missionaries had known that the rivers of the Colville, Spokan, and Pend d'Oreille country contained small, shallow, scattered deposits of placer, or "float," gold. Obstacles to mining were great, however. Transportation of supplies up the Columbia River was expensive because of the roaring rapids at The Dalles and the Cascades, and the rugged horse trails across the mountain passes and through the country of the Yakimas did not offer an attractive alternative—until 1854. Late that year an economic depression spread gloom across the Northwest. When Stevens illegally announced that, thanks to his treaties, the interior was open for exploitation, scattered groups of desperate and unencumbered men began crossing the passes and trickling through Yakima territory on their way east.[3]

Several got through. Some did not. One who failed was the subagent for the Yakimas, Andrew J. Bolon, a friend of Stevens and former member of Washington Territory's legislature. After picking up tales of murder on the reservation, he decided to investigate. Thinking (recklessly, it seems now) that the Yakimas would talk more freely if he went among them without the threat of an armed escort, he rode out alone on his errand. Along the way—the mid-September day was cold and rainy—he fell in with a small, mixed group of Yakimas. They seemed friendly. At noon all halted and built a fire for warming themselves. Relaxing, the agent offered to share his ample lunch with his new companions. As they were eating, the male Indians suddenly threw the white man to the ground. While one seized his beard and pulled his head back, the other cut his throat. Hoping to conceal what they had done, they rolled his corpse over the edge of a nearby cliff into a talus-bordered pit, partially hidden by a leaning pine tree. (Others say they burned the body on the bonfire around which they had been eating.) They then took his horse to the brink of the same cliff, shot it, and pushed the corpse into the pit.[4]

Not surprisingly, the killers boasted. An Indian spy sent out from the military fort at The Dalles to learn why Bolon had not appeared on schedule picked up the tale and reported to the post commander, Major Granville Haller. On October 3, Haller marched forth with eighty-four federal troops to teach the Indians a lesson. The Indians drubbed his troops soundly, killing five men, wounding seventeen, and capturing many wagon loads of supplies. The Yakimas said only two of their warriors died during the fighting. Four were wounded.

Such a defeat had to be avenged. Major Gabriel Rains, in command at The Dalles, rushed requests for reinforcements to the small U.S. Army posts in western Washington and Oregon. He also asked the acting governor, young Charles Mason, for volunteers, although federal troops in general scorned the short-term militiamen.

The emergency gave Mason the quivers.[5] Aroused, in part, by the events in the interior, the coastal Indians were breaking out of the reservations into which Stevens had pushed them and were spotting nearby hamlets with blood and fire. Mason wanted to keep all available troops close to the settled regions, but he could not override a federal commander. Miserably he watched a part of the area's regulars march to the Columbia to board steamboats for the first leg of the journey to The Dalles. Even more miserably, he let go of some of his volunteers, consoling himself with recently arrived information that a sizable contingent of Oregonians had been mustered for service in Washington.

But even this reinforcement might not be enough. Governor Stevens was expected back shortly from his peace council with the Blackfeet near the headwaters of the Missouri, east of the Continental Divide. Confident that the Walla Walla treaties had calmed the Plateau tribes, he had taken only a handful of soldiers with him. Traveling to the same Blackfoot conference was a large contingent of Nez Perce buffalo hunters led by such crusty chiefs as Old Looking Glass, Eagle-from-the-Light, Three Feathers, and Plenty Bears, the last-named being one of Old Joseph's neighbors from the Grande Ronde River. But, Mason wondered, could the often-antagonistic buffalo hunters be counted on in times of trouble? He thought not.

Trouble was in the making. Exhilarated by the Indians' victories on both sides of the Cascades, Kamiakin and his chiefs were urging Peo-Peo Mox-Mox, Five Crows, and Young Chief, acting as the heads of a loose coalition of Wallawallas, Umatillas, and Cayuses, to join in an attack that would cut off and destroy Stevens while he was riding back to his territorial capital at Olympia.

Apprised of this threat by friendly Indians, Mason wrote the governor a frantic letter. Not enough troops could be mustered to break a path through the hostiles. Stevens should therefore retreat to New Orleans, catch a steamer to the Isthmus of Panama, cross it, and take another ship to Olympia. Anything else would be suicidal and touch off a massive Indian uprising.

The dispatch was handed to William H. Pearson, an expressman who merits a short digression.[6] A native of Philadelphia, small, wiry, and as tough as a stub of baling wire, Pearson had been a Texas ranger, an Indian fighter, and a guide. Stevens may have met him first during the Mexican War. Be that as it may, Pearson somehow landed in Washington State and was hired by the governor as a man who was qualified to carry important dispatches on horseback long distances at improbable speeds. After hurrying the Walla Walla treaties almost entirely across the land that now makes up the state of Washington, Pearson had turned straight around with messages for the far-ranging governor. He caught up with Stevens at Hell's Gate near today's Missoula, Montana, where Stevens was winding up yet another treaty conference, this one with the Flatheads, Pend d'Oreilles, and Kutenais. Back to Olympia the former ranger galloped with those papers. Now he was returning nine hundred miles to Montana with Mason's warning at a time when winter storms were likely.

According to Stevens's son, Hazard, Pearson usually drove two extra horses with him. When the one he was riding became tired, he changed his saddle to a fresh one. But at the start of this last journey, he had no extras, for unstated reasons. When his mount tired in the Umatilla Valley, he roped a half-broken bronco grazing with a herd he passed, spurred the kinks out of it, and outraced a group of pursuing Indians. He rode all that day and night without stopping. When he reached Red Wolf's and Timothy's contiguous villages, located where Alpowa Creek runs into the Snake River, his bronco was done in. Not Pearson. Saying nothing about the warning he was carrying—the word might spread—he borrowed a fresh mount from Red Wolf and rode on to Lapwai. There he rested a day. Lawyer gave him fresh horses and recruited a young Nez Perce to guide him over the difficult, shortcut Lolo Trail into the Bitterroot Valley. Somewhere between there and Fort Benton on the Missouri River, he expected to contact Stevens.

Meanwhile emissaries from Five Crows, Peo-Peo Mox-Mox, and Kamiakin (whose Indians had not yet tangled with Gabriel Rains's storm-buffeted slow-moving army) were seeking Nez Perce help in setting the trap for Stevens. Their efforts were frustrated by the absence of the buffalo hunters, especially Looking Glass and Eagle-from-the-Light. Stevens had persuaded those rugged chiefs and their followers to cross the mountains with him, not to isolate them from potential troublemakers, but to help him make peace with the former enemies they knew so well. Such a triumph would bring new safety and prosperity to the Nez Perces, and in the end a huge delegation did make the trip. Estimates of the number of Nez Perces at the Blackfoot peace parley range as high as one thousand.[7] This left the pro-white elements who stayed on the Clearwater largely unchallenged, and there was little chance that they would join Kamiakin's conspiracy. Thus, Old Joseph, whose devotion to Christianity had been thoroughly diluted by the whites' activities since the days of the Whitman massacre, became a key figure in the plans of the hostile tribes. His support could carry the day for them.

The posttreaty years were wrenching ones for old Chief Joseph. Over and over he asked himself: How is it possible to resist the whites? He had watched their numbers grow ever since the exciting days of Lewis and Clark's visit. And though he had come to doubt that praying to the white man's god would bring him the power Spalding had said it would, he still respected the missionary's teachings about peace. He tended to agree with his onetime friends, Lawyer and Timothy, that the Nimipus' best hope for the future lay in following the Law, as laid down by the Americans.

Still, Joseph told himself, and probably Lawyer as well, the Americans were unfair. They did not obey their own laws, but acted as if their strength and abundance of material goods were enough justification for pushing the Indians aside, onto reservations, in their search for still greater wealth. Should the Nimipus simply give way in the face of such aggression?[8]

Stevens and Palmer had said, while arguing for their own good at Walla Walla, that their people were no more to be resisted than was the flow of the Columbia River. But was that statement really true? The Indian world of the Plateau buzzed joyfully over word of the Yakimas' thrashing of Major Haller. Most of the tribes had not yet heard of Rains's avenging march, and the eyes of the ambassadors from Kamiakin and Peo-Peo Mox-Mox burned with fervor as they sought out Joseph. The whites were not invincible. Join us! Join us! Help cut off Stevens! Make him return the lands he has taken! That done, Peo-Peo Mox-Mox boasted, he himself would lift the governor's scalp.[9]

Joseph and his band's council, we may be sure, discussed the matter at meeting after meeting. Criers listened to what was said and called out the arguments to the people of the villages. Among them were Old Joseph's sons, listening intently—Manassa, Young Joseph (although he was not yet called that), and Ollokot, one of whom would probably be the chief's heir. Think, my sons. It was for them that their father had prevailed on Stevens to draw the reservation's boundaries to include all the Wallowa winter and summer ranges and part of the Grande Ronde. Protected by those lines, they could continue in the old ways, calling not on the white man's god, but on their own wayakins for strength while building up their herds of cattle and horses, both of which found ready markets among the whites. Yes, a man did hate to seem a coward in the eyes of his sons, but ... and so they debated, taking ample time to think things over, as Indians preferred to do when choices were hard.

The deliberations were interrupted by a messenger from the Clearwater, sent probably by Lawyer. William Craig, interpreter and subagent for the tribe, had just arrived at Lapwai with an appeal for help from Stevens. The story went like this: The expressman, William Pearson, had reached Stevens on the far side of the Continental Divide. The governor was in good humor. In spite of bungling by the agents in charge of supplying the Blackfoot council with gifts and food, he had concluded a peace between the prairie raiders and the mountain Indians, all to the future good of his railroad. Now Mason expected him to run away! Cockily ignoring the advice, he selected Craig, Pearson, a soldier or two, and four Nez Perce chiefs as his escort. Counting on speed and surprise to carry him through, he dashed off ahead of his pack train and the bulk of his small squad of troops, bucking through deep snow drifts and floundering across ice-choked rivers.

The scheme worked. The first tribe he reached, the Coeur d'Alenes, had supposed the drifted trails to the east were impassable. When he and his men stormed headlong, rifles cocked, into the first of their villages, the chiefs were completely rattled. Before they could solidify a counter plan, he had bluffed fresh promises of allegiance from them. He also heard more about the plot to waylay him in the Walla Walla Valley and set about countering it. When the rest of his troops came up, he sent Craig and three of the Nez Perce chiefs to Lapwai. There they were to ask Lawyer to recruit enough Nez Perce warriors to force a way through the enemy tribes. That message dispatched, the governor hurried on with his reunited force to outface the Spokans.

As the Nimipus instantly realized, Stevens's request was tantamount to asking them to turn against people who spoke the same language and followed the same customs they did, people who had been their allies for as long as anyone in the tribe could remember. Highly stirred and wanting to discuss the matter, they flooded into the canyon of Lapwai Creek, 208 lodges of them, approximately two thousand people, of whom several hundred were said to be capable of bearing arms.[10] Their tipis and mat-covered lodges spread over small meadows and along the banks of the creek for more than a mile below Craig's place. The house they prepared for a meeting of the leaders was a hundred feet long and could hold two hundred people.

While waiting for Stevens, they argued heatedly, in long orations. Many of the younger people and many of the buffalo hunters, just back from the Blackfoot council, were enraged by the white man's presumptions. He had prevailed on them to make peace with their enemies. Now he wanted them to fight *his* enemies—their friends. No, this was a time for Indian unity, for helping each other.

Lawyer answered with patient logic. Joining the Wallawallas and Cayuses at this particular moment could not bring the Nez Perces any good, he said. They had fared well at the Walla Walla council. Most of their homeland was intact; they should not put it in jeopardy now. For if they let anger lead them into conflict with the whites—conflict that might well end in defeat—they could expect to have great portions of their territory taken from them.

Old Joseph, who was related closely to the Cayuses, surprised the advocates of war by backing Lawyer. Thinking of the Wallowa country, he asked his listeners to picture their combustible villages overrun by furious aliens brandishing guns and firebrands. Many lives as well as great expanses of land would be lost. Lawyer was right. The belligerents' prime goal—the death of Governor Stevens, who would be quickly replaced—was not worth the risk.[11]

Passions simmered down. When Stevens and his men reached Lapwai on December 11—his force was still undersized, although he had picked up a few miners and stray governmental employees along the way—he was greeted affably. Sensing from the multitude of Indians surrounding him that there had been a heated discussion about his request for help, he changed tactics. Instead of blustering, he turned meekly to the Nimipu's head chief, and asked, "My friend, Lawyer, what shall I do?" To which Lawyer replied, "My friend, Governor Stevens, we will take you in our arms as a child and as a child shall deliver you safely to your own people."[12] Stevens, sensitive about his diminutive stature and the implied putdown of his military abilities, could hardly have liked that, but presumably he was wise enough to swallow his resentment.

Planning for the rescue had to wait until after the obligatory feasting. With proper pomp the white officers joined the leading chiefs around the fires in the longhouse. Young men passed around plates of roasted meat, a service of honor. (Was Young Joseph one of the attendants? The records mention no names.) During the speeches that followed, the Indians promised Stevens, in the words of his son and biographer, "250 of their bravest and best warriors, stark buffalo hunters and Blackfoot fighters every one." When dour Looking Glass declared, "I will get up and go with him," the last opposition to accommodation with the whites collapsed—at least for that day.[13]

Almost immediately thereafter, news arrived that Nimipu fighters were not needed. Five hundred Oregon volunteers had recently encountered, near the Touchet River, a strong force of Indians under the general direction of Chief Peo-Peo Mox-Mox. Perhaps the size of the white army gave the Indian leader pause. Or perhaps he really wasn't as hostile as whites said later when trying to justify their military scouring of his country. In any event, he did not seem to be spoiling for a fight as he and five companions approached the commander of the volunteers, Colonel James Kelly, under a flag of truce and asked for a parley. When the talks proved inconclusive, Kelly either violated the truce by seizing the Indians as hostages—or (accounts vary) Peo-Peo Mox-Mox and his companions stayed voluntarily in the white camp, hoping that their presence there would stave off a fight. It is said that the chief even offered to feed the whites a meal of Wallawalla beef if they would go to his village.

Whatever the truth, a long, sporadic shooting affair did develop. Finding that the ground his troops were on was untenable, Kelly withdrew toward Waiilatpu. The retreat galvanized the Indians into charging on horseback. According to accounts by whites, Peo-Peo Mox-Mox and his companions began yelling, cheering, and waving their people on. This behavior angered the nearby whites, who started to tie up the Indians. During the scuffle that developed, Peo-Peo Mox-Mox was clubbed to death with a rifle barrel. The others were shot as they fled.

Heavy casualties at last led the attackers to break off the battle and vanish into the rugged countryside. Some of the tired volunteers, savagely excited, used the respite to mutilate Peo-Peo Mox-Mox's corpse, dividing his scalp into small pieces so that many people could have trophies. They also cut off his ears and removed enough of his skin to make a razor strap.[14]

News of the ghoulishness evidently did not accompany word of Kelly's victory to Lapwai, for the Nez Perces there stayed calm. In fact, many were disappointed. Stevens's way was clear now, and Nimipu help was not needed. Sensing the anticlimax, the governor, ever expedient, said he would show his gratitude by taking an honor guard of sixty-three Nez Perces with him as far as the Walla Walla Valley. This troop was formally mustered on December 15, 1855. William Craig was their captain. Their native leader—presumably he, too, was given a rank—was Spotted Eagle, a buffalo hunter but a devoted follower of Lawyer's. Others in the guard included Old Looking Glass and Old Joseph.[15] Lawyer did not go along, most likely because the wounds he had received while fighting beside American fur trappers at the Battle of Pierre's Hole were troubling him so that he could not walk without a cane.

In spite of bitterly cold weather—the thermometer dropped at one point to twenty-seven degrees below zero—Indians and whites had a good time, chattering and showing off to each other as they followed the ancient trail connecting the Clearwater and the Walla Walla. Arrived in the valley, where Stevens conferred at length with Colonel Kelly, the Nez Perces almost certainly heard the details of Peo-Peo Mox-Mox's death. They probably learned also that Major Gabriel Rains, striking hard to avenge Haller's defeat, had sent Kamiakin's Yakimas scattering throughout the snowy countryside. Whatever distress these bits of information brought to the Nimipus, they did not show it—not away from home, surrounded by a victorious army of Oregonians. After thanking them for their friendship, Stevens promised that the U.S. government would pay them for their service. (It never did.) Bill Craig then took them to Lapwai, where he made a list of their names so they could be summoned back to service if the army so desired. Then, on January 20, 1856, he formally mustered them out.[16]

Within two months most of them—and more besides—were back. Brush-fire wars were erupting throughout the Northwest. Although Stevens and his Washington volunteers easily quenched a flare-up by the desperate, disorganized tribelets along the coast—some of these little tribes actually had the temerity to attack the infant town of Seattle—the Indians of the interior continued to blister him. Yakimas and a few river people struck the installations that guarded the transportation portages around the Cascade Rapids of the Columbia. They killed fourteen, wounded eleven, and sent shivers of terror through the white settlements. Although federal troops under Colonel George Wright, who scorned the unruly volunteers, chased the Indians off, the men in blue could not bring them to grips. Restlessness spread and, in Stevens's opinion, had to be checked before it tore apart the peace he supposed his fast-paced diplomacy and Kelly's smashing of Peo-Peo Mox-Mox's people had imposed on the Plateau.

In pursuit of his plan of containment, Stevens sent fresh companies of volunteers into the Walla Walla Valley and, James Kelly having returned to civilian life, put them under the command of Colonel Thomas R. Cornelius. Feeling still more strength was necessary, he asked Lawyer to recruit as many Nez Perce warriors as he could. The head chief of the tribe, a rank he held mostly in the eyes of the whites, responded with 113 men. Old Chief Joseph was one.[17] The date of their mustering was March 11, 1856. Were any of Joseph's sons included? Again the records are silent.

Seventy of the new group were attached as auxiliaries to Cornelius's volunteers and marched straightaway across the Snake River, east of the Columbia, in a guerrilla-style chase after the scattered Yakimas. The remaining forty-three—and this group was where Old Joseph landed—were formed into what was designated as Company M of Washington Territory's Second Regiment of volunteers. Company M's duty was to patrol the broad, unmarked swath of canyons, lava plains, and mountains that lay across the western approaches to Nez Perce country. Their aim was to keep disaffected Indians from reaching the Nez Perces and establishing alliances with that tribe's hostile elements. The patrol's white captain was Henri M. Chase, who a few years earlier had settled on Lapwai Creek close to William Craig. Either Company M or Spotted Eagle's auxiliaries—or perhaps each in turn—proclaimed their prowhite allegiance by carrying, as their banner, the American flag first given the tribe for its help following the Whitmans' massacre and later raised over the Walla Walla council of 1855.[18]

Old Joseph soon found himself caught between two emotional millstones. The flag spoke to him of loyalty and peace, as Spalding had preached peace, and of his march with the honor guard that had escorted Stevens part way home after his triumphant council with the Blackfeet. But Cornelius's volunteers, fortified by Spotted Eagle's auxiliaries, also carried an American flag on their slashing zigzags north of the Snake. As they marched, they ravened. Their indiscriminate shootings and illegal appropriations of livestock so frightened the Indians that many fled for refuge among the Nez Perces farther west—exactly what Stevens had not wanted. Crowning the atrocities—if "crown" is the right word—was the hanging of an inoffensive Nez Perce whom Cornelius wrongly suspected of being a spy. By the time Company M was mustered out on July 12, Old Joseph (who may have left even before then) was increasingly reluctant to support Lawyer, Timothy, Spotted Eagle, and William Craig's exhortations that the Nez Perces should aid the cause of peace by supporting the whites' efforts.[19]

Joseph went home to a seething tribe. A reputed twenty-five-hundred Indians from throughout the interior had gathered with the Nimipus to discuss measures to take in resisting the invaders. Their autonomous form of government by band, their disagreements, jealousies, and sudden doubts of a sort that were all too frequent in American Indian affairs crippled them, and they formed no coherent plan. The Nez Perce dissidents, however, did make their feelings plain by driving off a white-led pack train that was bringing in supplies that had been promised them at the Walla Walla meeting.[20]

A crisis came on July 17. A strong company of volunteers, led by gaunt red-bearded, remorseless B. F. Shaw, surprised a camp of Cayuses in the Grande Ronde Valley. Many of the warriors were off hunting, and the uncontrolled volunteers had, for them, a joyous time massacring dozens of people, most of them old men, women, and children.[21]

The reaction among the Nimipus was twofold—hate and fear. Looking Glass gave up his pretense of cooperation and began preaching war. Supporting him, according to express messenger William Pearson, were such firebrands as Three Feathers, Eagle-from-the-Light, and Old Joseph. Tensions grew so intense that Henri Chase, the white captain of Company M left his home on Lapwai Creek and fled with his family across the mountains to safety in the Bitterroot Valley.[22]

There was also fear. The carnage in the Grande Ronde had struck close to home—painfully close to Old Joseph's Wallowa home. Adding to the shock was its confirmation of what he had warned about a few months earlier when urging the Nimipus to visualize hate-filled whites rampaging through their villages. How could he risk bringing this horror on his own band? If he really had been the incendiary Pearson declared, he reassessed his stance. The fluctuations agonized him and must have had a profound effect on his sons, especially the most thoughtful of the three, Hin-mah-too-yah-lat-kekht, Young Joseph, whom whites would soon be calling by the name they used first for his father.

Old Joseph and the tribe's uncertainties played into Steven's hands, or so the governor thought. He asked for, and Lawyer promoted, a second council in the Walla Walla Valley where all the tribes could air their grievances and a settlement could be reached. Many Indians no longer trusted Stevens, however, and the gathering, scheduled to begin deliberations on September 11, 1856, was much smaller than its predecessor had been. Among those who did attend was Old Joseph. Again families were involved, as they had been at the first council, and probabilities are high that Young Joseph, five months past his sixteenth birthday, rode with his father.

Another who openly and vigorously mistrusted Stevens was aged General John Ellis Wool, commander of the U.S. Army's Department of the Pacific. It was Wool's conviction that the little governor–Indian superintendent–railroad surveyor was far too full of himself. His treaties—the ones Stevens had pushed down the Indian's throats at the first council—said that whites were not to enter the ceded lands until Congress had ratified the documents. (Wool wrote Congress that in his opinion the trouble-breeding papers should not be ratified.) In spite of the prohibition, whites were trespassing freely. When the tribes objected, forming alliances to uphold their rights, the governor summoned hard-bitten, Indian-hating, short-term volunteers to break their resistance. (Wool ordered the volunteer companies disbanded. Stevens and the governor of Oregon defied him, declaring the federal army had no control over territorial officials appointed by the president.) To prove his authority, Wool dispatched Colonel E. J. Steptoe and four companies of regulars to Walla Walla, evidently to keep an eye on Stevens, rather than on the Indians. Stevens sought to compromise by keeping only one company of volunteers with him at the council. Steptoe obligingly camped some distance away, but what stance he would take if the powder keg Stevens was walking into blew up was, in the minds of some of the governor's retinue, a dangerously unpredictable point.

The council's discussions, punctuated each night by war dances and the beating of war drums, lasted a week. Stevens defended his treaties by expatiating again on the benefits they would bring to the tribes. Lawyer and Timothy supported him, saying that the documents, duly signed by the chiefs, were the law of America and had to be obeyed.

The Nez Perce chiefs of the antiwhite faction—Old Joseph, Looking Glass, Eagle-from-the-Light—retorted that Lawyer had no right to speak for the whole tribe. They said they had not understood the treaties as translated by the interpreters and bellowed out, clause after clause, by the criers. They wanted their land back.[23]

Stevens became impatient. He had offered to talk about remedying grievances concerning parts of the treaties, not about canceling the treaties entirely. It was nonsense for the chiefs to say they had not understood what they were signing. Old Joseph, for one, had seen to it that the boundaries of his band's portion of the reservation had been drawn as he wished. Brusquely he snapped that land which had been legally sold could not be unsold. Period.

Listening to this talk, Old Joseph realized afresh that Stevens was the one who did not understand. Land could not be parceled out the way white people wanted to parcel it, one fenced plot here, another there. Land was as continuous as the air. It could not be alienated from the trees that grew in the high country or from the deer that browsed in the canyons. It was openness, available to all. It was where the people and the horses moved as they needed, to the places of grass, of roots, of undivided streams where the salmon flashed on their way to the sources of new life. Land was freedom. No, Stevens did not understand. Shamefully, neither did Lawyer, who had let expediency turn him away from the path of his fathers.

As positions hardened, the governor moved the meeting ground close to Steptoe's camp, a shift intended to make the rebellious Indians more careful. It did not work. The nighttime beating of drums grew more feverish, and on September 17, Stevens broke off the talks, telling the Indians scornfully that those whose hearts spoke for war should go ahead and try.

Thinking they might be foolish enough to do just that, he formed his columns for the march downcountry to The Dalles with military precision. With him he had sixty-nine volunteers, fifty loyal Nez Perces under Spotted Eagle, and fifty teamsters and herders, some of them Indians, who cared for the unit's wagons, and five hundred head of horses. Mingling with their dust was smoke from the autumn-dry grass the Indians had fired to deprive Steptoe's horses of the grazing they needed. Hundreds of dissident warriors yammered around the flanks of the plodding column. It was like a reckless circus performance. They screamed obscenities, fired their guns wildly, and dashed about with dazzling displays of horsemanship, but they never quite attacked. Indian spectators rode along beside them to watch the performance.[24]

Old Joseph? His sons? It is safe to say they weren't with Stevens's loyal group, and he makes no mention of them as being among the 120 hostile Nez Perces who made up a considerable part of his harassers. Old Joseph was probably content to stay with the spectators. But it would be strange if Young Joseph—and Manassa as well—excited by the war talk and dances of the previous evenings and eager to show they were sons of a respected chief, did not indulge themselves.

On entering a saucerlike basin about six hundred yards in diameter, Stevens threw his wagons into a defensive circle—he called it a corral, perhaps because his horses were penned inside—and prepared to challenge the Indians. They could not have been very serious about fighting back, for a white courier was able to race off to Steptoe's camp, about three miles away, with an appeal for joint action.

The colonel thought it would be better if Stevens joined him. Because most of the grass around his bivouac had been destroyed, he needed to move camp but lacked wagons and teams. Would the governor return with the necessary vehicles? Stevens agreed—all this being arranged by messengers passing back and forth at will.

As soon as night offered concealment, Steptoe sent twenty-four mounted dragoons and a mountain howitzer to Stevens's camp to facilitate the retreat. The retreat, too, was carried out in the dark, unimpeded by Indians. At sunrise, perhaps feeling a little foolish, a part of the hostile natives charged across the burned grass to attack the newly combined forces. An answering charge by Steptoe's dragoons and the roaring of the howitzer drove them back. During the entire affair, the whites lost one man killed and one seriously wounded. But Stevens boasted, "We killed and wounded thirteen Indians."

Leaving one company behind to guard the establishment (it grew, after minor shifts, to be the modern city of Walla Walla) Steptoe marched toward the coast with Stevens. The Indians scattered, Joseph's family most probably going to the high Wallowa country to gather their horses and cattle for the annual drive into the warm canyon bottoms for the winter. After that, for awhile, the battles that were fought were paper battles.

Convinced by the collapse of the council that Steven's program bred trouble, rather than soothed it, General Wool directed Colonel Steptoe to issue a proclamation closing the Plateau country east of the Cascade Mountains to whites—with a few crucial exceptions—until the 1855 treaties were ratified. Simultaneously, he continued doing what he could to prevent ratification.

Stevens's pen sputtered with furious replies, as did the pens of many Northwest pioneers. To cool them, the War Department recalled Wool—but replaced him with General Newman S. Clarke, who made no move to alter Wool's policies. The territorial legislature of Washington meanwhile voted to censure Governor Stevens for his mishandling of Indian affairs, but the populace retorted by electing him Washington's delegate to Congress. There he did what he could to push the treaties through while promoting his railroad, not realizing apparently that Southern interests could block the northern line as long as they had a voice in the national Congress.[25]

Steptoe's proclamation that closed the interior was aimed at agriculturists. Farmers imprisoned land, fenced it, tore it with plows, and attracted town promoters and road builders. Of course, the Indians objected. So keep settlers away, Wool (and Steptoe) reasoned. But then the proclamation added exceptions. Employees of the Hudson's Bay Company, which still maintained a few trading posts in the interior, could enter the area. Missionaries (this meant Catholics, who had established themselves among most of the tribes except the Nez Perces) were allowed to stay at their stations. Then came the sticker. Miners could pass through the Indian country on their way to the new goldfields in northern Washington and British Columbia. Miners did not want land as such. So let them seek the gold that would boost the region's economy. Troops in the area would keep them moving, meanwhile acting as referees when disputes arose between the prospectors and the Indians.

No problem. No problem at all.

· 13 ·

A TOUCH OF GOLD

At the start of the second week of May 1858, the Christian Indian Tamootsin, renamed Timothy by Henry Spalding on the day of his baptism nineteen years before, noticed a column of American dragoons approaching his little farm and apple orchard, located where Alpowa Creek runs into the Snake River. He rode out to meet the soldiers, probably wearing, as he often did, American-style clothing.

Counting officers, there were 158 dragoons in the column. Their commander was Colonel E. J. Steptoe, whom Timothy had most probably met during the fracas that had followed the ending of the second Walla Walla council in September 1856. Accompanying Steptoe's regulars was a laden pack train of 85 animals. The Snake River was running high and the colonel was not sure the heavily burdened horses and mules could breast its current long enough to reach the river's northern bank.

He explained his presence. Gold prospectors who were crossing the territory to reach the northern mines, as the army's closure order had said they might, were complaining of difficulties with the region's Indians—Spokans, Coeur d'Alenes, and the Yakimas who frequently visited them. Steptoe was going to march that way to investigate and sound a warning. Just a demonstration. But first he had to get his detachment across the river. Would Timothy and his people lend a hand?

They did. The village's women rowed armament, food, spare accoutrements, and some personnel to the far side in canoes, many of them shovel-

170

nosed dugouts that were mostly employed for setting salmon nets. Each dragoon, still mounted, swam his own horse across. Mounted Nez Perces helped drive the unloaded pack stock into the current. Other Indians stripped off their clothing and swam among the animals to keep them from milling and turning back.

The crossing completed, Timothy, some of his kin, and a few warriors joined the expedition as scouts. It was a shocking experience for them. Near the site of today's Spokane, upward of six hundred painted and plumed Indians challenged the Americans. The clash developed into a running, chaotic battle of swirling fragments, handfuls of attackers charging frenziedly at splintered targets, shooting, swinging war clubs, and then dashing away, only to whirl and charge again—a typical Indian conglomeration of many individualistic skirmishes that gave each brave a memory he could boast about for years. At dark the American soldiers and Timothy's scouts struggled up a low hill that gave them some defensive cover. The attacking Indians, busy sorting through booty and dancing in triumph to their drums, let big holes develop in their siege lines. The whites slipped through and made their way back to the Snake, carrying their wounded on improvised litters. Again Timothy's people ferried them across the river, this time to safety.[1]

Steptoe's superior, Colonel George Wright, was furious—twenty-five men killed; at least that many wounded; and two howitzers, many horses, and piles of equipment lost. He himself led the war of reprisal. With him that August he took 680 well-trained, well-disciplined men equipped with powerful new rifles for fighting at a distance and sabers (which Steptoe's people had lacked) for hand-to-hand combat. Some 200 packers and herders handled a supply train of 400 mules. Thirty Nez Perces, commanded by Spotted Eagle and dressed in army uniforms to distinguish them from adversaries, went along as scouts. Timothy, apparently, did not accompany them. This time his band's help at the Snake River was minimal; after waiting out a violent storm, the troopers used hastily built flatboats to ferry themselves across the river.

They crushed the Indians without losing a single man. They burned whatever Indian food they seized and, in a particularly gruesome incident, shot several hundred horses to death after reserving 130 of the best animals for their own use. "Nothing," explained one officer, "can more effectively cripple the Indians than to deprive them of their horses."[2]

As the defeated Indians began surrendering, Wright demanded that the perpetrators of offenses against the whites be handed over to him. He gave the designated ones the barest trials—or none at all—and hanged them in front of their horrified fellows. When a large group of thirty-five confessed to having fought against him, he pointed, wholly at random, to four of them and had them executed as an example of what not to do.[3]

The Nez Perces, who quickly learned what was happening—and who knew some of their own people had helped it happen—were stunned and frightened. Throughout the difficulties they had remained unscarred because none of the main trails to the mines crossed their homelands, and largely for that reason no clashes had arisen to demand retaliation. But how long could their immunity last?

The question acquired new urgency on October 31, 1858, twenty-six days after Wright completed his last executions. The treaties Stevens had pressed the Indians to sign remained unratified. Hence, title to the land the Indians had agreed to cede still rested with the Indians. In spite of that, General W. S. Harney, the newly appointed commander of the area, declared the interior open to settlement. People responded in swarms, particularly in the Walla Walla area. Now the need for ratification truly was vital to the Nimipus, for the invisible line of the still-unsurveyed reservation was the only defense for keeping invaders at bay. Lawyer sensed this need clearly when he wrote to delegate Stevens in Washington, D.C., that for three years "we have been waiting to hear from our Big Father ... and I would like to hear what he has to say. If he thinks our agreement [the treaty] good, our hearts are thankful."[4]

Although there were good places in the Wallowa region for digging camas bulbs, Joseph's band still liked to round up large numbers of their horses and ride from their own high meadows down to the junction of the Snake and Clearwater rivers. From there, they followed the Clearwater some fifty-five miles past Lapwai to a steep trail that climbed out of the river's canyon to the pine-encircled, bulb-rich reaches of Weippe Prairie. Each summer many bands met there, as much for the socializing as for the numerous roots the women dug.

Life was good there on the tattered carpet of bunch grass, beside the tall trees, their needles smelling faintly of resin under the hot sun. The campers ate well, danced, played games, gambled, gossiped, and, above all, raced and traded horses. The Weippe Prairie was also the place where the warriors laid plans for buffalo hunts on the far side of the mountains. There is no telling how often, if at all, Old Joseph and his sons participated in the dangerous excursions. Temptations must have been frequent, for it is known that the Wallowa people, whose band was the largest in the tribe, came so regularly to the prairie that they had been accorded, by tradition, their own private camping site near the same three trees.[5] White Bird's band from the lower Salmon River (White Bird was a noted buffalo hunter) generally camped nearby. The two chiefs were good friends, as will become evident later. But if they hunted together, the fact has eluded the records.

This we know, however: The easygoing day of July 22, 1859, as the whites reckoned time, was interrupted by the arrival of the tribe's new agent, accompanied by a small retinue of Indian guides, interpreters, and soldiers from new Fort Walla Walla. The agent's name was A. J. Cain; his office was a political plum, and he was replacing William Craig, who had been serving pro tem while the Walla Walla treaty was in abeyance. The document had been finally ratified, thanks to ex-governor Stevens's work with the big chiefs in council in Washington, D.C.—the Congress, as Americans called the gathering. Wanting to bask in the excitement of his revelation, Cain had picked crowded Weippe as the place to make the announcement.

The Indians' pleasure was not unalloyed. Where, asked some of the chiefs as Cain finished his story, were the annuities the treaty had promised— the plows and blankets and clothing, the material for shops and schools, and the teachers who were to show the Nimipus how to run them? Where was head chief Lawyer's loghouse and the five hundred dollars in annual salary due him for his extra work dealing with the government?

Cain tried to explain. Congress had adjourned before making the necessary appropriations. Next year, he promised breezily, the goods would arrive. The main point right then was the knowledge that the treaty was in effect.

To Old Joseph, that was indeed the main point. Trespass was now forbidden. The Wallowa country as he had mapped it for Stevens was forever secured to him and his children. "This is where I live," he proudly told Cain, pointing to the chart, "and there is where I want to leave my body."[6]

Not all the Nimipus were as optimistic as Joseph and Lawyer about Cain's assurances. The premature opening of the Plateau to settlement had already lured hundreds of restless whites. Much of the stimulus had come from the army's decision to make Fort Walla Walla an important frontier post. To meet the establishment's need for supplies, a smoke-belching steamboat, named *Colonel Wright* to honor the conqueror of the northern Indians, had been launched in February 1859. It carried small mountains of cargo up the Columbia River from the rapids near The Dalles to the mouth of the Walla Walla River. From there the piles for matériel were moved to the fort by hordes of teamsters and pack-train operators. Farmers followed to raise horses, beef cattle, wheat, and vegetables for the military. Crude tents and log shacks that furnished beds, meals, and drink to speculators, salesmen, and rovers sprang up just outside the military reservation. Like the fort, the rowdy town was named Walla Walla. Could the Nimipus truly believe, the worriers asked, that none of those people would venture southeast into the Wallowa country or due east to the Indian villages strung along the Clearwater River?

Mixed with the opportunists swirling around the fort were many miners, whose insatiability a few of the Nimipu had first noticed during horse-trading trips to California. Since then, the prospectors' energies had shifted northward to tempting goldfields in northern Washington and southern British Columbia. Now that the Northwest was peaceful again, still greater numbers were on the move. A favorite jumping-off place was the ford across the Snake River near its junction with the Palouse. Already an American army lieutenant, John Mullan, was beginning work on a wagon road that would run north and northeast through the Palouse country to the Continental Divide and on to the headwaters of the Missouri. As soon as it was finished, travelers could come as easily into the Plateau from the east as from the west. Was it likely that none of those people would find their way into the new Nez Perce reservation? Was the army really strong enough—and its commanders conscientious enough—to hold them back? Look! The *Colonel Wright* had already thrashed up the Snake as far as the Palouse to test the practicability of bringing mining supplies and passengers that far into the interior. The still-unsurveyed, invisible line that was supposed to guarantee the reservations' integrity lay only a few miles farther upstream. For the past two or three years, vague rumors had been whispering that there was gold beyond the line. Would no one try to find out?

During the winter of 1859–60, the usual winds lashed the tall Wallowa peaks. Drifts piled up beside streams where salmon spawned in the summer; crusted snow lay in windrows on flattened bunch grass that in spring would straighten up fresh and green for the horses. But snow turned to rain before it reached the profound canyon bottom of the Imnaha River, which joined the Snake just above the mouth of the Salmon. It was rain, too, that fell, not frequently, into the abyss that became known as Joseph Creek; that stream entered the hard-pushing Grande Ronde hardly a rifle shot from its melding with the Snake.

Those interlocking canyon bottoms, dotted with small meadows and bordered by steep, grassy hills almost devoid of timber, were Joseph country. On reaching the area at the beginning of cold weather, the band broke into extended families that scattered to where shelter and resources were adequate. Each family took up its residence in a mat-covered longhouse, down whose interior cooking fires shone like glowing eyes. In the smoky dusk there were stories for children, gossip and games for the family elders, meals for everybody. In separate houses there were dances. Horses and small herds of cattle found what grass they needed on the pale tan hillsides. There was fine hunting back among the crags, where mountain sheep, deer, and elk came down below the snow line in their search for feed.

As the arc of the sun turned back toward the north and snow melted into gurgling water, the people began pushing their animals up precipitous trails to the evergreen forests that covered the hilltops and on through the mottled shadows to meadows that lay like ruffled skirts around the peaks. Mobile tipis were pitched at favorite spots, and life slid easily into its summer routines. The people worked together to build fish weirs; the women scraped and tanned deerskins to a soft, lovely whiteness. Children who were approaching adolescence went anxiously into the lonely nights to find their private wayakins. Young warriors searched for round, unshatterable stones they would wrap in rawhide and attach to handles as war clubs. They made magic whistles from the hollow wing bones of cranes. They practiced war, riding concealed like buffalo hunters on the sides of their horses. "Some of us," said Yellow Wolf, a relative of the Joseph family, "would ride by where friends were standing or sitting and fire at them under the horse's neck, but not to hit. I have done that myself in play."[7] And so surely did Joseph's sons play in their youth—Manassa (whose Indian name Sousouquee meant Brown), Hin-mah-too-yah-lat-kekht, and Ollokot.

The summer of 1860 again took the Wallowa bands back to the Clearwater and on to the Weippe Prairie. (According to General Oliver O. Howard, Young Joseph's adversary during later years, the Wallowa Nez Perces made the trek every summer.[8]) But other attractions than custom also pulled the band north and east from Wallowa, and all were associated with Lapwai, both the creek and the Indian settlement at its mouth. One tug was the dislike that both Old Joseph and Chief Big Thunder felt toward Lawyer. He was a pushy one, that Lawyer. His home was Kamiah, but when A. J. Cain chose the mouth of Lapwai Creek as the site of the headquarters of the U.S. government's new tribal agency compound, he moved there. He strutted. He wore his befeathered plug hat and sported a tobacco pouch decorated with three dangling squirrel tails.[9] He boasted of the white-style cabin the government was going to build for him close to Spalding's old missionary buildings, some of which still stood. He lorded it over Big Thunder, who was chief of the band that had occupied the area since time immemorial, and, of course, that behavior raised Big Thunder's hackles. As for Old Joseph, he mistrusted Lawyer because of his quick subservience to Stevens at the Walla Walla conference. No doubt Joseph also felt envy. There had been a time following Ellis's death when Joseph had wanted to be named head chief.[10] So growling about Lawyer became a pastime of sorts for the two lesser chiefs.

Beyond that were family attractions. One of Old Joseph's wives had a brother in Lapwai, a subchief called Reuben. Although Reuben had once been a dashing buffalo hunter, he had joined the prowhite faction, an aberration that could be forgiven now that the Walla Walla treaty had been ratified. In addition, Lapwai was the home of Ta-ma-al-we-non-my, daughter of yet another subchief in Big Thunder's band. Hin-mah-too-yah-lat-kekht was smitten by her, and she by him. Young Joseph, as he would soon be known among the whites, was powerfully built. Some accounts say, with exaggeration, that he was six feet two inches tall.[11] Handsome and adept with horses, he carried his deep-chested body with an innate dignity and gentleness that contrasted notably with the harum-scarum impetuosity of his younger brother, Ollokot. In time both Old Joseph and the girl's father gave their consent to a wedding. As custom decreed, Old Joseph provided a feast at which lavish presents, including many horses, were given to the family of the bride. These gifts were not a purchase, but the cementing of an alliance between two families in a culture in which kinship ties were vital. After the marriage—and we do not know exactly the day or even the year when it occurred—the parents of the bride had their turn at putting on a present-giving feast for the groom's family.[12]

These connections—Big Thunder, Reuben, and Ta-ma-al-we-non-my's family—added important sources of information to the grapevine that carried news throughout the Indian country. During the summer of 1860, Old Joseph heard through this network that the fears of some of the chiefs had been confirmed. A handful of prospectors had penetrated the Clearwater Canyon as far as the river's North Fork. Moreover, they had been welcomed by several of the naive Indians of that region, most of whom had been friendly toward the whites since the days of the missionaries. Why not? Unlike farmers, miners would not stay. They would dig up a little soil and then move on. Meanwhile the local people, who did some farming themselves, would sell the newcomers food and horses in exchange for tools; oddments of woolen clothing; and decorative items, such as beads, vermilion paint, and dentalium shells. Didn't that make sense?

For a time the question did not have to be answered. The reservation agent, A. J. Cain, who lived in Walla Walla, and his subagent, Charles Frush, who was settling in at Lapwai, ran the white interlopers off the reservation, as the treaty of Walla Walla said they should. The prospectors, however, kept returning at intervals throughout the year. Late in the fall they eluded the government's watchers by swinging far north of the Clearwater and then cutting across the river's North Fork to a small stream they named Orofino Creek. Fine gold—very fine, in the sense that it appeared, as the Indians themselves learned by panning some of the gravel, in tiny, thin flakes of "float" metal.[13]

Fine though it was, it became the base of exuberant stories that trickled back to the rough trading center of Walla Walla, and probably into the deep wintering canyons of Joseph Country as well. The North Fork Indians were growing excited, as well they might. In December 1860, the whites established, at Orofino Creek, a town named Pierce after Elias Davidson Pierce, the man who had brought in the discoverers. The fever grew so intense that Old Joseph's relative, Chief Reuben, entered into a partnership with William Craig to build a ferry across the Snake River close to its junction with the Clearwater. He even tacked up notices about the improvement on the doors of Walla Walla's cavernous warehouses. Soon he was rich enough that he left his tipi for a log cabin from which he oversaw the management of hundreds of new horses. Inspired by the success, John Silcott, the half-breed husband of Chief Timothy's nineteen-year-old daughter Jane, built another ferry several miles up the Clearwater.[14]

Lawyer was in the thick of things. According to C. L. Goodrich, a journalist who talked to the head chief at Lapwai in March 1861, he was busily telling all the Nimipus who cared to listen that the whites were too strong to resist. Nor, in fact, was there any need to resist them, the chief continued. The inrush was not harming the tribe. No Indian villages had ever taken form in the high, cold area that contained the gold. The place was useful only for occasional berry picking and deer hunting. So why not accommodate? Why not grant the miners permission to work north of the Clearwater—for a good price, of course—and then add to their riches by trading with the newcomers?

Agent Cain and his superior, Edward R. Geary, superintendent of Indian affairs for Washington Territory, were already thinking along the same lines.

Even before winter slacked off, reports raced downcountry of such widespread riches that a new town, Oro Fino (*sic*), had been founded two miles north of Pierce. As the influx mounted, they agreed to meet with Lawyer and his followers to see what could be done to prevent racial clashes. Apparently, the antiwhite bands led by Old Joseph, Looking Glass, Eagle-from-the-Light, White Bird, and so on were not invited to participate. Their lands were distant from the areas involved, and perhaps the negotiators did not want to risk their objections.

At the conference, which took place April 10, 1861, the countryside was marked off as Lawyer suggested. Miners could enter the reservation north of the valley of the main Clearwater as far as the trail to Weippe Prairie, and north of that trail and its extension, the Lolo Trail, as far east as the Bitterroot Mountains. The only whites who could enter the reservation south of that line were traders licensed by the agent. Troops would be stationed at Lapwai to see that the injunction was obeyed. No title passed to the miners who found claims in the permitted area. When they had exhausted the gold, they were to leave, and occupancy rights would revert to the Indians.[15]

For these concessions the Indians were to receive fifty thousand dollars. In the event, however, Congress, beset by the expenses of the looming Civil War, cut the appropriation to forty thousand dollars. Little of the amount actually reached the Indians, who could hardly have been surprised. They received none of the annuities due them under the 1855 treaty until 1861, and then only in part—shoddy shirts and cloth and no work on fencing or building schools and mills. Not even Lawyer's cabin was erected.

One curious item did arise out of the confusion. Somehow the tribe got the notion that it had been promised, in exchange for its lands, as much gold as six mules could pull in a heavy wagon. No such provision appears in any official document, but, of course, there is no telling what some zealous white bargainer might have whispered in the ears of wavering chiefs. In any event, some of the tribe fretted for years about the missing treasure.[16]

Other violations of the agreement were more immediate. One resulted from efforts to found a supply town for the mines. During May 1861, the stern-wheeler *Colonel Wright* twice entered the Clearwater River from the Snake and thrashed up against the current, aiming for the mouth of the North Fork. The boat was 110 feet long and on both trips was jammed with freight and passengers. Agent Cain was on the second trip, as was Lawyer, who was picked up at Lapwai so he would be impressed by this show of white power.

Because of the headlong curve the river describes around Rattlesnake Point, thirty-seven miles above the confluence with the Snake River, both efforts fell short of their goal. The cargo, most of it belonging to a merchant named Seth Slater, was dumped ashore on the north bank. Slater covered the freight with a tarpaulin, named the shelter Slaterville, and hoped he was proprietor of the new supply town. Not so. The river was too strenuous. A roomier, more approachable flat on the south side of the Clearwater at its junction with the Snake was chosen instead, even though the decision violated the April agreement that whites would stay north of the river. The agency staff and several Indians protested, but not Lawyer. Agog over this new evidence of the whites' might, he not only agreed to the landing, but stepped off a site for a warehouse. A hurly-burly tent city, later dignified with brick and wood and named Lewiston after the explorer Meriwether Lewis, inevitably followed. Unprovable rumor says that Lawyer was adequately compensated (bribed?) for his services in ceding the necessary land to the new proprietors.[17]

Within a year Lewiston was populous enough to be named the seat of newly formed Nez Perce County, Washington Territory. Some of the Wallowa peoples' winter villages stood near the mouth of the Grande Ronde, only thirty miles from the frenetic new town. Old Joseph must have worried—and have become still more disenchanted with Lawyer.

During the same period, the Oro Fino district was so overrun with miners that latecomers could not find claims. Strong parties of them turned illegally toward the South Fork. Straightaway they made rich strikes that burgeoned into Elk City and its satellite camps. Later, in the fall of 1861, the richest district of all, named Florence, was illegally born in the mountains just north of the Salmon River. Eagle-from-the-Light, White Bird, and other antitreaty chiefs tried in vain to halt the influx. The army offered no help, although the agreement of 1861 said it should. There were simply too many hard-case, determined whites in a country too rough to be patrolled by Lapwai's small garrison.

How many prospectors were actually involved cannot be estimated with much accuracy. Although some deep mines were developed later, the first diggings were shallow placer claims worked by a constantly moving population. Guesses about the numbers range as high as thirty thousand people roaming the various districts in the spring of 1862. Few made much money, but in the aggregate many millions of dollars were torn from the reservation in the years 1861–63.

Many Nez Perces profited also. A few mined. More acted as tenders to the growing number of pack strings that carried supplies to the scattered camps. The greatest number took up farming, as Spalding had tried so hard to get them to do twenty years earlier. They learned something of a cash economy, using gold dust and minted coins to purchase white-style clothing, blankets, household implements, and prepared foodstuffs. They also learned to drink liquor, many of them with the unquenchable thirst that is characteristic of Indian alcoholics. Helplessly, Lawyer and other leaders, the reservation agents, and responsible whites fought to keep the drug out of the area. They failed. Gold breeds greed, and too many boomers wanted profits—any profits.[18] Even Joseph's band suffered from the corruption, for many of the young men sold horses in Walla Walla and Lewiston, drank away the income, and returned to their distressed families showing all too plainly the result of their debauches. Old Joseph's son Manassa may well have been one of them, as we shall see.

As increasing numbers of whites used the trails that threaded the reservation between Lewiston and the mining camps, ugly clashes erupted. Lawless members of each race stole the others' livestock. Indian women were violated; men of both colors were robbed, beaten, and occasionally murdered. Law enforcement was almost nonexistent. The Civil War was raging in the East, and troops at garrisons had been cut to the bone. The territorial capital at Olympia, Washington, was hundreds of difficult miles away. Indian protests, led by Lawyer, brought no results, and fears grew among the isolated Americans and Nez Perces that unless some remedy was provided, a frenzied revolt might erupt.

No Horns on His Head was one of four Nez Perces who went to St. Louis in 1831 with fur traders in search of a magic book, as they regarded the Christian Bible, that might enhance their lives. During the winter two of the four died in the frontier city. In the spring the two survivors boarded the Missouri River steamer *Yellow Stone* at the start of their return trip home. Along the way No Horns on His Head died. (*George Catlin, National Museum of American Art, Smithsonian Institution, Gift of Mrs. Joseph Harrison, Jr.*)

Rabbitskin Leggins was (briefly) the sole survivor of the Bible quest to St. Louis. On the way up the Missouri aboard the *Yellow Stone*, he and his companion, No Horns on His Head, donned borrowed Lakota (Sioux) costumes so that George Catlin could paint their portraits as representative Plains Indians in full regalia. Though Rabbitskin Leggins survived the river trip, he was killed by Blackfeet the following winter. (*George Catlin, National Museum of American Art, Smithsonian Institution, Gift of Mrs. Joseph Harrison, Jr.*)

Tipis at the Nez Perce agency compound beside the Clearwater River. The circle was a typical camp formation. The site is known today as Spalding, Idaho. A unit of the Nez Perce National Historical Park is located nearby. (*Idaho State Historical Society, no. 684*)

Fort Lapwai, Idaho Territory, as seen during the early days of the 1877 Nez Perce "war" by a *Harper's Weekly* artist. (*Idaho State Historical Society, no. 3399*)

Cultural mix: The conical form of the tipi was probably borrowed in prehistoric times from the Plains Indians. The covering of mats made from tule reeds was characteristic of early-day shelters used by the Nez Perces and other Indians of the Columbian Plateau. (The man in the picture is unidentified.) (*T. L. Moorhouse photo, Nez Perce National Historical Park*)

Fourth of July parades and horse races gave the reservation-confined Nez Perce men a chance to work off their pent-up energy. Chief Joseph regularly led the parades at Nespelem, Washington State, where this picture was taken. (*E. H. Latham photo, Nez Perce National Historical Park*)

Winter camp at Nespelem, Colville Reservation. The composite tipi at the right end of the line was formed by linking several standard-size tipis together. This composite was the winter home of Joseph and his family. (Figures in picture unidentified.) (*E. H. Latham photo, Nez Perce National Historical Park*)

Close-up of Chief Joseph's winter tipi at Nespelem. It appears at the right side of the winter camp scene in the preceding photo. (*E. H. Latham photo, Nez Perce National Historical Park*)

Reputedly Chief Joseph had four wives and nine children. According to James McLaughlin, Chief Inspector for the Bureau of Indian Affairs, two of the wives were widows of Looking Glass, who was killed in 1877 at the Bear Paw battle. Joseph married the widows, as Indian custom allowed, primarily to support and protect them. The older children may have been Looking Glass's; the younger, Joseph's. The picture was taken about 1890. (*Nez Perce National Historical Park*)

General O. O. Howard, *left*, and Joseph met in 1904, after the chief had lost all hope of regaining his homeland and shortly before his death. (*Nez Perce National Historical Park*)

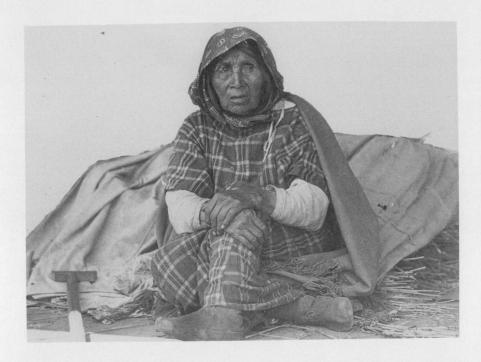

Relic of another time: Tolo in 1918. As a young woman she carried a warning of the Salmon River outbreaks of 1877 to the mining camp of Florence. A lake west of Grangeville, Idaho, was named for her. (*A. H. Hilton photo, Nez Perce National Historical Park*)

Relic of another time: Chief Joseph's daughter, KapKap Ponmi, aged fifty-nine. As a young girl she escaped from the Bear Paw battlefield during the fight that ended with the capture of most of the fugitives. (*Hutchison photo, Nez Perce National Historical Park*)

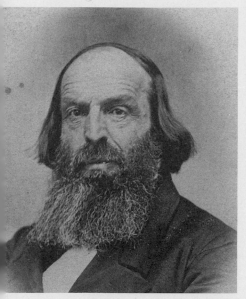

Missionary Henry Harmon Spalding built his mission station beside Lapwai Creek, Nez Perce territory, in 1836. Chief Tuekakas (Old Joseph) of the Wallowa band of Nez Perces was his second convert. Later Tuekakas recanted. (*Special Collections, University of Washington Libraries*)

A veteran of the Mexican War, Indian agent, railroad surveyor, and first governor of Washington Territory, Isaac Ingalls Stevens cajoled the Nez Perces and related tribes of the Columbian Plateau into signing their first treaty with the United States government in 1852. (*Special Collections, University of Washington Libraries*)

This sort of Romanesque pose, to which Joseph was subjected during his visits to the East as part of his effort to regain his ancestral lands, contributed to the so-called Joseph myth. (*Moorhouse photo, Special Collections, University of Washington Libraries*)

Yellow Bull, Joseph's close friend. Blind and wearing Joseph's headdress, he rode three times around the people gathered for Joseph's funeral, calling out the chief's accomplishments. (*Edward Curtis photo, Special Collections, University of Washington Libraries*)

Death-feast lodge. This composite tipi was built to hold the crowd that gathered for the potlatch—a giving away of the chief's possessions—that accompanied Chief Joseph's burial. (*Edward Curtis photo, Special Collections, University of Washington Libraries*)

Chief Joseph's gravestone in the cemetery at Nespelem, Washington. It was erected not by Indians but by white admirers. (*Special Collections, University of Washington Libraries*)

This picture of Chief Joseph was taken in Bismarck, North Dakota, by F. J. Haynes when the defeated Nez Perces paused there on their way to exile in Oklahoma. It is probably the best likeness of Joseph. (*Smithsonian Institution*)

Chief Joseph, rigged out in borrowed clothing, posed in a Washington, D.C., studio in 1879 following his famous speech in Lincoln Hall, "An Indian's View of Indian Affairs." (*C. M. Bell photo, Smithsonian Institution*)

Mounted Nez Perce warriors at Nespelem, Washington, dressed in full regalia, as are a few of the horses, for a celebration of the good old days. (*Moorhouse photo, Smithsonian Institution*)

Onetime enemies Chief Joseph and General John Gibbon met in Washington State in 1889, twelve years after the bloody battle of the Big Hole. (*Smithsonian Institution*)

Chief Tamootsin, renamed Timothy by the missionary Henry Spalding. Timothy, Spalding's first convert, remained a Christian and was loyal to the whites during the Nez Perce tribe's struggle over accommodation with the new order. (*Smithsonian Institution*)

General O. O. Howard lost an arm during the Civil War. Later, as commander of the Department of the Columbia, he led a stubborn but not very effective pursuit of the dissident Nez Perce bands as they headed toward a hoped-for refuge in Canada. (*Oregon Historical Society, neg. 11275*)

Once a fur trapper, William Craig married a Nez Perce, settled among her people, and for a time acted as the tribe's agent. Idaho's Craig Mountain is named for him. (*Oregon Historical Society, neg. 51235*)

After accepting Christianity at the Red River mission school in Canada, Spokan Garry brought religion back to the Columbian Plateau and then watched, without fully understanding it, the turmoil that followed. (*Gustavus Sohon, Washington State Historical Society, Tacoma*)

Tuekakas (Old Joseph), head of the Wallowa band of Nez Perces. He was the second member of the tribe to accept baptism at the hands of Henry H. Spalding. Years later, outraged by what he considered the flagrant dishonesty of the whites, he recanted. (*Gustavus Sohon, Washington State Historical Society, Tacoma*)

Prior to thrusting the fateful treaty of 1855 onto the Indians of the Columbian Plateau, Washington State's governor, Isaac Stevens, entertained the principal headmen at a banquet under a leafy bower. (*Gustavus Sohon, Washington State Historical Society, Tacoma*)

Although most of the autonomous bands of the Nez Perces refused to recognize a single head chief for the tribe, Lawyer, pictured here, was accepted as such by treatymaker Isaac Stevens. Thereafter Lawyer led the treaty faction of the Nez Perces. His headpiece, a mix of Indian and white styles, can be viewed as symbolic. (The combination occasionally appeared among other Indian groups as well.) (*Gustavus Sohon, Washington State Historical Society, Tacoma*)

Old Looking Glass, famed Nez Perce warrior and buffalo hunter. He was the father of Young Looking Glass, also a renowned warrior, who joined the dissident Nez Perces in 1877, after his village had been inexcusably attacked by a contingent of General Howard's troops. (*Gustavus Sohon, Washington State Historical Society, Tacoma*)

A headman of the Cayuse tribe, Five Crows (Pahkatos Qoh Qoh) followed his half-brother, Old Joseph, into Spalding's church but could not resist seizing, as spoils of war, one of the young women survivors of the Whitman massacre. (*Gustavus Sohon, Washington State Historical Society, Tacoma*)

Another of Old Joseph's half-brothers, Young Chief (Tauitau), shared the governing of one of the Cayuse bands with his full brother, Five Crows. (*Gustavus Sohon, Washington State Historical Society, Tacoma*)

Peo-peo Mox-mox (Yellow Bird) a chief of the Wallawallas. One of his sons was murdered in California while on a cattle-buying trip with Young Chief, Spokan Garry, and several others. The murderer, who was white, was not punished. Later the father was treacherously slain and mutilated by volunteer soldiers in Oregon. (*Gustavus Sohon, Washington State Historical Society, Tacoma*)

John Montieth (*standing*), the Nez Perce Indian agent, with three young Nez Perce Indians who learned enough Christianity at the reservation school to be ordained as Presbyterian ministers. *Left to right:* James Reuben, Archie Lawyer, Mark Billy. Reuben served as a scout for General Howard during the early fighting in 1877. As a preacher he later went voluntarily to Oklahoma to aid the Nez Perces in exile there, as did Archie Lawyer, son of the chief of the treaty faction of the tribe. (*Washington State University Libraries*)

A relative of one of Chief Joseph's wives, Yellow Wolf fought valiantly as a young man during the flight toward Canada. He escaped from the final battlefield but was later captured and sent to join the other exiles in Oklahoma. His reminiscences are a valuable source of Nez Perce history for that period. (*L. V. McWhorter photo, Washington State University Libraries*)

Young Joseph's brother Ollokot was the primary leader of the band's warriors during the attempt to reach Canada in 1877. (*C. W. Phillips photo, Washington State University Libraries*)

The conflict opened at the White Bird Battlefield in Idaho. American troops, very tired after forced marches in inclement weather, rode down a steep hill from the north—roughly from the point from which this picture was taken. The outnumbered but keyed-up Nez Perce warriors were concealed in declivities running horizontally across the picture. The main battle swirled across the area shown in the center of the photo. (*Bennett photo, Washington State University Libraries*)

The Indians' flight toward Canada ended at the Bear Paw Battlefield in Montana. Snake Creek winds along near the base of dark, low, flat-topped hills shown in the middle distance; the hills are rather higher and steeper than they look. Most of the Indians were camped between the creek and the center hill. Miles's first attack came from the right; the next, from the center. Both charges were aimed at the surprised camp. Joseph surrendered near the base of the lefthand slope of the draw in the right center of the picture. (*Emil Kopac photo, Washington State University Libraries*)

· 14 ·

THE BIG STEAL

T
hat part of Washington Territory's population that lived between the Cascade Mountains and the Pacific did not look kindly on the inhabitants of the goldfields. The economies of the two sections followed different roads—stable agriculture, logging, and seafaring in the west, but highly unstable placer mining in the east, along the Clearwater and Salmon rivers and (after 1863) in the Boise Basin. Politics was equally divisive. The coastal voters tended to be Republicans and strong Unionists. The majority of the miners were Democrats, many of them Southerners who had fled from the Confederate draft and yet were loud in their denunciations of Abraham Lincoln and his policies.

The situation frightened the coastal Republicans. By the end of 1861 they were outnumbered by the Democratic miners and the leeches who followed them. As time passed the imbalance was likely to increase. The only way for Republicans to stay in power in Washington Territory, the strategists in Olympia decided, was to persuade Congress to create a new unit—eventually called Idaho—whose boundaries would be drawn in such a way as to include the goldfields. The ruffian miners would then vote in the new entity.

Oregon's economic leaders supported the program for convoluted reasons of their own. They were the chief producers of goods for and transportation to the mines. But if the gold diggers remained politically attached to Washington as their numbers grew, they might try to set up programs that would challenge the Oregon monopoly. So let the bond be broken now!

The miners were not impressed. They figured they were being manipulated

181

solely for the sake of the Republicans in Washington and the fat-cat bankers in Oregon. To hell with this meretricious lure of a new and separate territory.[1]

One thing did concern the prospectors, however—the huge size of the Nez Perce reservation, which was held by the federal government in trust for the Indians and was outside the reach of white speculators in farmland, timber claims, town lots, and, possibly, deep quartz mines. Trespasses were inevitable and a leading cause of clashes. What the miners really wanted was to get rid of the savages, as they called the Nimipus, either by moving them far away into some valley where they could not interfere with the whites' desires or by jamming them into a small part of the reservation where there were few resources to tempt white intruders and where policing the natives would be easy.

The coastal voters seized the opening. Why not soften the miner's resistance to a separate territory by linking it to a shrinkage of the reservation? Not a complete elimination—that would certainly start a war—but a reduction of what had been made too big originally. Make the new proposal seem innocuous to the Indians by defining it as an amendment to the familiar document of 1855. Let the miners believe, moreover, that the compression might not occur unless a new territory was founded.

Appropriate instructions were given to William H. Wallace, who represented Washington's territorial government in the U.S. Congress and to one of Oregon's senators, James W. Nesmith. It seems certain that before the two men left for the East, they got in touch with the Nez Perce agent at Lapwai and learned from him what the miners and other whites wanted—about 90 percent of the original reservation![2] The entire Salmon River drainage was to be taken from the Nimipus. In addition, Joseph's people were to lose the magnificent Wallowa region, not because of its mineral prospects (there were none), but because the citizens of Oregon had a phobia about Indians and wanted as many as possible removed from their state.

Wallace presented the reservation part of the territorial plan to the House of Representatives in Washington, D.C., on May 14, 1862. Government negotiators, he said, would have to meet for several days with six thousand Nez Perces in a new treaty council. (In actuality the tribe numbered no more than four thousand or so.) The Indians would have to be housed, fed, and presented with many gifts. Because of the high prices that prevailed in the goldfields—beef at three dollars a pound, for one example—an appropriation of fifty thousand dollars would be needed. And, of course, though he did not say so, many of the palms that handled the money along the road to Lapwai would need to be greased. But the step was important. "I ask this," Wallace concluded dramatically, "in the name of the people of Washington Territory, in the name of the people of Oregon, and in the name of the Indians themselves."³

No congressman challenged the presentation. The American North, locked in a death struggle with the South, needed the economic stimulus of a steady inflow of newly minted precious metals. By mid-1862 the Clearwater and Salmon placer mines were churning out significant amounts of gold. So keep the elixir coming. Keep the voters of the Northwest happy, while reducing Confederate agitation. On March 3, 1863, a bill authorizing the Idaho Territory was passed, and fifty thousand dollars for a new treaty council were appropriated—by a government that was only partially meeting the obligations imposed on it by the 1855 contract.

In November 1862, well before the passage of the territorial bill, a general of the U.S. Army arrived on the reservation to confirm the siting of a permanent fort in the valley of Lapwai Creek, three or four miles upstream from Spalding's old mission and from the newer buildings that housed the Nez Perce Indian agency. The army installation was to be called Fort Lapwai. (The town that grew up around the post became known as Lapwai; the settlement at the Indian agency became Spalding.) The purpose of the fort, the general told the Indians, was to give the Nimipus fuller protection from aggressive whites than had been provided by the small unit that had been patrolling the area during the past few months.

During the course of his visit, the general also announced that the government wished to hold another council with the chiefs the next spring. The date was set for May 11, 1863. The purpose of the meeting, he or some of his entourage let slip, was further tightening of the reservation's boundaries.

The Indians were outraged. But how should they respond? Should they—could they—fight back? Confederate sympathizers who had become acquainted with some of the chiefs seized on the uncertainties. Times had changed, they said, hoping to foment an uprising that would divert funds and troops from the eastern battlefields. The South was licking the North, they told their listeners, and there was some truth right then to the statement. A hard push now could clear the whites out of the reservation.⁴

But had the times truly changed? It seemed they had not, at least according to word that now arrived of an Indian disaster in southern Idaho near the Utah line. There, beside the Bear River, where Nimipus had once ridden companionably with American mountain men, Union forces had smashed a defiant village of Snake Indians, killing 224 people, destroying 70 lodges, and capturing 160 women and children and 175 horses.

Such news brought back memories of Wright's defeat of the Yakimas and Spokans in 1858. How could strength like that be resisted? What would the great buffalo hunter and warrior, Apash Wyakaikt, Flint Necklace (Old Looking Glass) have advised? They could not know. He had died in January. Though his son took the name Looking Glass and hung his father's small trade necklace from a cord around his neck—strong magic!—it was not the same.[5] Confusions bedeviled the bands, especially those who lived outside whatever small core of land the whites were going to let the tribe keep. What did the future hold? How much of the future could they control?

May 11, 1863, the day set for the opening of the council, came and went without Old Joseph showing the least sign that he planned to attend. Some commentators believed that neither he nor any of the other dissident chiefs were notified of the meeting, but inasmuch as word of it had been out since November, this hardly seems likely.[6] Old Joseph, at least, had simply decided to boycott the affair. He was about seventy-eight years old by then and growing feeble. Probably he saw no need of taxing his strength by riding to Lapwai to state his position one more weary time to the government negotiators. The whites knew his heart. He had never taken his share of the inadequate annuities that had reached the tribe as specified by the treaty of 1855. He had sold nothing: Why should he be paid? Everything was clear. They had made their promises. No amount of talk by the government could change that now.

Old Joseph's passive resistance was jarred about May 25 or 26 by the arrival of a special messenger from Calvin H. Hale, the new superintendent of Indian affairs for Washington Territory.[7] The emissary brought surprising news and unsettling information. The council, he said, was just getting under way, although its opening had been scheduled for May 11. The presence of all chiefs was required.

He explained the delay. A long period of inclement weather had slowed the arrival of both the Indians and of one of the three white commissioners who had been selected to deal with the Indians. The Nimipus who had trickled in added another block by objecting to the two interpreters Hale had hired. One was Henry H. Spalding, who had baptized Old Joseph in 1839 and had been his mentor for nearly a decade. As Joseph knew, the missionary had moved to western Oregon following the Whitman massacre and had remarried there after the death of his first wife, Eliza, in 1851. When the Walla Walla area was opened to settlement, he took up a homestead there, but his burning desire was to rejoin the Nez Perces in some capacity. Helped by his friend, Timothy, he had been named an interpreter for the council, and that was at least a foot in the door. His associate was Robert Newell, who had once been married to a Nez Perce and had occasionally visited the country during the passing years. Joseph had received an American flag from him during the punitive expedition against the Cayuses who perpetrated the massacre.

The trouble—and Joseph knew it, too—was that neither Spalding nor Newell had an aptitude for language. Neither had mastered the Shahaptian tongue. And by this time the Nez Perces had learned the importance of accurate translations in all official dealings. They asked now that Perrin Whitman, nephew of Marcus Whitman, be brought to the council as a backup interpreter. Perrin had worked among Shahaptian-speaking tribes for more than a decade, and the Indians liked him. Unfortunately, he had moved to the Willamette Valley. Could he be sent for? The effort would eat up at least ten days, but things were at a standstill anyway, and Hale consented.

To Joseph and his advisers this didn't sound too urgent, but then the messenger added more information, probably on his own responsibility.

To fill the time until the meeting got under way, Hale had toured that part of the land on which he hoped to concentrate the Indians. The area's general location had already been determined without the Indians being informed and Joseph did bristle at that. Now the commissioner learned its exact dimensions. It stretched along the Clearwater from a short distance west of Lapwai Creek to a point some miles above the confluence where the river's Middle Fork ran into the South Fork. The area embraced several tributaries that sliced through the tablelands south and west of the river. Its bounds formed an irregular pentagon that tilted from northwest to southeast. On being surveyed later, it was found to contain 784,996 acres. The 1855 reservation from which it was to be carved, if the Indians agreed, measured 7.7 million acres. Joseph and his people did not need to grasp white mens' figures to realize how enormous the proposed reduction was. Awareness also came to them, perhaps for the first time, that the Wallowa country lay outside the shrunken reservation. This meant that the government would try to buy their homeland, even though it contained no gold to lure whites. The Indians stirred uneasily.

We can picture the messenger relishing the attention he was commanding. On he went, adding shock to shock. Hale, he said, was bubbling with excitement when he returned on May 19 from his five-day horseback tour of the reservation the government wanted. The next day the missing commissioner arrived, and the trio decided to go ahead with the council although Perrin Whitman had not appeared—and might not. They called the Indians together; by then the number of them at Lapwai had swelled to about a thousand. With Spalding and Newell interpreting and criers loudly repeating each sentence, Hale described what he had seen. There was enough tillable land in the area, he said, for each family to receive twenty acres. That was as much farming as a family unit could cope with, as Joseph knew from his experiences at the mission years before. Ample pasturage for the Nimipu horses, Hale finished, could be found on the bordering hillsides and tablelands.[8]

Joseph's people listened to the messenger's resume in horror. Open space was integral to their way of life. But if they sold the Wallowa, they would be crowded with the rest of the Nimipus into fenced plots that would be little better than the pens the whites used for their cattle. Ant-heap living with all its tensions—no!

But they did not have to sell. It was also integral to the Nez Perces' way of living that one band could not speak for another on so important a matter as this. That was why Hale was so anxious to have them attend the council. But why should they go if they did not want to sell?

The messenger explained: Lawyer himself was leading the protest to the reservation proposal. Perhaps if the Indians presented a unified front this time, they could hold the whites to the promises they had made in 1855.

Lawyer, the accommodator, speaking at last like a true Indian! Perhaps a Wallowa delegation should visit Lapwai, after all.

Unable because of illness to make the trip, Old Joseph called for his sons. Normally, the responsibilities of leadership would have fallen on Manassa, the eldest. By 1863, however, Manassa may have already been dead, killed by an arrow fired during a drunken brawl by a Nez Perce named Wayauh Yuch (Blue Legs).[9] Or if Manassa was still alive, he may have been showing signs of the weakness that would lead to his death. In any event, Old Joseph turned to his second son, Hin-mah-too-yah-lat-kekht, Thunder Rolling in the Mountains. Young Joseph, some whites were already calling him.

Young Joseph was twenty-three, serious, fluent, and probably already seeing himself as heir to the leadership of the Wallowa group, the most populous and best known of the Nez Perce bands. During their preparatory talk, Old Joseph gave a warning that Young Joseph would recall a decade and a half later when talking to newspaper reporters in the East.

"When you go into council with the white man, always remember your country. Do not give it away. The white man will cheat you out of your home."[10]

Ollokot went with his brother as subchief. Criers circulated among the villages, instructing those who wanted to attend the council to meet at an assigned rendezvous. The group, probably a large one, reached Lapwai either late in May or early in June. There was ample space for them in the tent city erected earlier in the creek valley by the six companies of soldiers stationed at Fort Lapwai—up from the normal four, as if the whites had expected violence when the Indians heard what was proposed. The camp, with its storage sheds and outbuilding, could have provided for three thousand Indians. Even counting the antitreaty bands that had come in at about the same time as did those from Wallowa, no more than two thousand were on hand. Perrin Whitman had recently arrived as well, and all the leaders and interpreters were soon surrounded by worried Indians.

The problem that staggered them was the tiny area of the reservation they were being asked to accept. At first they had refused to believe that the government was behind the insulting proposal. Crooked-tongue individuals must have hatched the plot and were trying to fool the Nimipu by pretending the Big Chief in the East was the one who wanted the agreement.

A faith in the law that is difficult to grasp today had brought about this reaction, for the Christians among the Nimipus had come to believe that the white man's law, like the white man's religion, emanated from a higher-than-human authority. Spalding and Whitman had made this idea clear to them by using the Ten Commandments as examples. Directives from the government were also commandments. This notion had been emphasized by Elijah White, who had come to them in 1842, and by Ellis, who had learned white ways at the Red River Mission School and had been elected head chief. Just before his death in the buffalo country, Ellis had told Lawyer, "Whenever the Great Chief of the Americans shall come to your country to give you the laws, accept them." For laws were sacred. Treaties were part of the law. Therefore, treaties were sacred.

Lawyer, showing a spark of the fire that had brought him his name years earlier, put the point bluntly to Hale. "In the same manner that my people receive the law of God as binding, so do we acknowledge and consider the law of your government as binding on us and on you, for the law is sacred."[11] But it was not being treated so by the people who had promulgated the treaties. So liars must be behind the proposal for a shrunken reservation.

The three commissioners, aided by the three interpreters, insisted that no lies were involved. The Big Chief, President Lincoln himself, thought that the proposed treaty was best for the Nez Perces under the new circumstances brought by the gold rush.

If that was true, Lawyer snapped back, then the president was either guilty of bad faith or was the victim of misinformation. Briskly he outlined the unstinted friendship the Nez Perces had shown all Americans since Lewis and Clark had visited them in 1805 and 1806. They had fed the explorers and had cared for their horses throughout an entire winter. They had fought beside American trappers in battles against the Blackfeet; Lawyer still bore the effects of one of those wounds. They had sent some of their young people east to learn what kind of religion was best to live under. They had helped run down the Whitmans' murderers. Later, in 1856 and 1858, they had furnished help and horses to Colonels Steptoe and Wright, but had received none of the pay promised them. Even worse, the government had failed to meet all the obligations it had assumed under the treaty of 1855. These were matters, he said, that the president and all white men should understand.

That indictment off his chest, Lawyer made a counteroffer to Hale's proposal. The Nez Perces would sell the sites where the whites had established ferries and had built such towns as Lewiston, Orofino, and Elk City. They would let the miners keep on digging gold, "but we cannot give you the country you ask for."

His followers backed him wholeheartedly. Utsinmalikin, a chief of the Kamiah region that had also been the Lawyer's home before he had moved to Lapwai, declared bitterly that the Indians had supposed the boundary drawn in 1855 was "permanent, sacred, and according to law.... You trifle with us. We cannot give you the country; we cannot sell it to you."

The blasts reduced Hale to feeble rejoinders. He admitted that the government had been dilatory in fulfilling the terms of the 1855 treaty, but insisted that since he had not been in office then, he was not responsible for the failure. Anyway, that was then, this was now. In 1855 the United States had not needed the land it was asking to buy. In 1863 it did, because the gold rush had filled it with people for whom it was responsible, just as it was responsible for the safety of the Nez Perces.

As if to underline the remark about safety, the troops at Fort Lapwai were called on to remove from the treaty grounds certain disreputable Palouse Indians from outside the reservation who were hanging around the council grounds looking as if they intended mischief. Shortly thereafter the soldiers found occasion to go to the Lewiston area, where squatters were building shanties on land that clearly belonged to the Indians. They tore down the structures, tossed the pieces in the river, and marched the trespassers back across the reservation's boundary. A small reservation, Hale pointed out, could be policed that way. One as huge as the current one could not be.

His declarations changed no minds. The antitreaty bands appeared in fitting splendor and went into conference with Lawyer's faction. They agreed to abide by the terms the head chief had already offered—sale to the United States of the scattered pockets in which the whites were ensconced but nothing else. Young Joseph's acquiescence, it should be said, cost his people nothing; there were no such enclaves in their summering or wintering grounds.

The commissioners, under orders from Washington to whittle the reservation to a splinter, rejected the offer. Later Hale wrote that the Nimipus' terms were, to use his word, "buncombe." They were made in open council, accompanied by long orations intended to impress the common people, who by temperament were averse to radical change and "did not consider their future or that of their children." Hoping to bypass the Indian politics, he arranged a series of private meetings with the white-oriented chiefs of the tribe. At these individual conferences, he reported, he set about removing their doubts and explaining to them the advantages that would accrue if they went along with his proposal.[12]

Inducements came, in a few instances, close to being overt bribery. Timothy, for instance, was told that if he signed the new treaty, he would be allowed to stay at his Alpowa home though it lay twenty miles outside the proposed boundary and that a house worth six hundred dollars would be built for him there. In most cases, however, such crassness was not necessary. Suggestions to Lawyer about his increased power and prestige on a small reservation where the antitreaty chiefs would be subservient to him were probably enough. Chiefs from the Kamiah region were told that a school, a mill, and other improvements would be built and they would receive the credit.

As their wavering became evident, the antitreaty chiefs heaped scorn on them. Hoping to patch up the differences, someone—Lawyer? Joseph?—suggested that the headmen of both factions should meet in one of the bigger lodges and talk matters over among themselves. Tempers remained short, however. Fearing that violence would erupt at the meeting, Hale sent a messenger to Fort Lapwai requesting troops. Captain George Curry responded late that night. Although Curry found the chiefs arguing hotly, he detected no indications of an outbreak. In fact, the debaters invited him and an interpreter into the lodge to witness what was happening.

Toward dawn, the chiefs agreed to disagree. Lawyer's side could sign the treaty if they wished, but Young Joseph, Ollokot, Big Thunder, and other leaders of the antiwhite faction would have nothing to do with it. Lawyer would no longer be their head chief. Rather, they would return to the premissionary, pregovernment days when each band was wholly autonomous. They would remain a friendly people speaking the same language and following the same customs, but the confederation was ended. There was handshaking all around, and Curry withdrew, reflecting, so he wrote later, that he had witnessed "the extinguishment of the last council fires of the most powerful Indian nation on the sunset side of the Rocky Mountains."[13]

There never had been a Nez Perce nation in the Anglo-European sense of the word, of course, but there had been the beginnings of a political union. Perhaps this union hadn't been in existence long enough to be able to withstand the strains. Perhaps Lawyer had tried too hard to manipulate the trends for his own gain. Perhaps the whites had made the amalgamation impossible by being insensitive to the Indians' deep attachment to their homelands. In the end, the chiefs of the bands who would not have to move were the ones who signed the agreement. The more distant bands—the ones who would have to leave the sacred places where they had experienced their visions, where they went to seek guidance from nature's unseen powers, the places where their progenitors were buried—were the ones who refused to yield.

Young Joseph and White Bird sat stony-faced and silent through two council sessions, listening to Hale and the other two commissioners argue their case. Why speak? They had given their decision to the other bands and did not want to discuss it any longer. Gathering their people together, they walked out of the meeting, satisfied they had met their tribal obligations. It did not occur to them that either the commissioners or the chiefs who stayed behind would agree, during their absence, to sell their land.

Yet that was what happened. Exact details cannot be reconstructed. Perhaps Lawyer concluded that the only way the Nez Perces could survive as a tribe was to accept whatever the all-powerful whites offered. Perhaps he wanted to save, and possibly augment, his perquisites as head chief. When none of the leaders whose bands would lose their lands consented to the treaty, he rounded up, from other bands, enough substitutes to make the list look representative. No white could tell, from the strange names beside which the signers placed their Xs, whether they were bona fide representatives or not. Certainly Hale raised no questions. As far as he was concerned, all the Nez Perce lands outside the proposed treaty lines had been sold. Within a year after Congress had ratified and the president had signed the

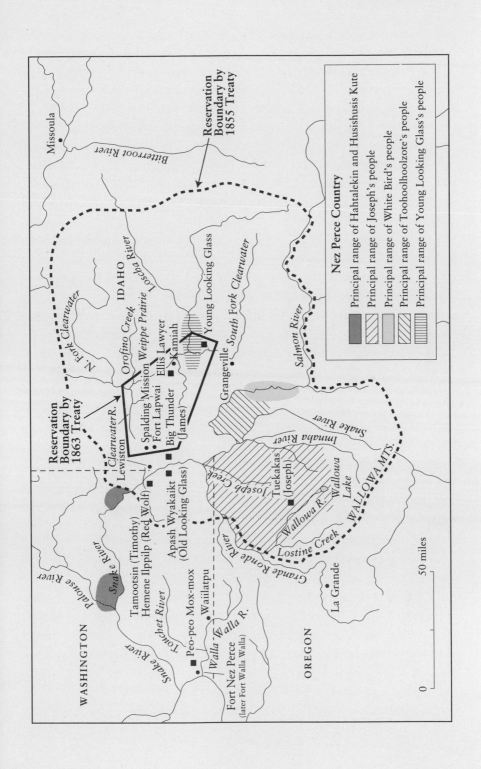

Nez Perce Country

Principal range of Hahtalekin and Husishusis Kute
Principal range of Joseph's people
Principal range of White Bird's people
Principal range of Toohoolhoolzote's people
Principal range of Young Looking Glass's people

Reservation Boundary by 1855 Treaty

Reservation Boundary by 1863 Treaty

WASHINGTON

OREGON

IDAHO

Missoula

Bitterroot River

N. Fork Clearwater

Clearwater R.

Orofino Creek
Weippe Prairie
Lošeba River

Spalding Mission
Ellis Lawyer
Kamiah
Fort Lapwai
Big Thunder
(James)

Young Looking Glass

South Fork Clearwater

Grangeville

Salmon River

Lewiston

Tamootsin (Timothy)
Hemene Ilppilp (Red Wolf)

Apash Wyakaikt
(Old Looking Glass)

Palouse River

Snake River

Snake River

Touchet River

Peo-peo Mox-mox
Waiilatpu
Walla-Walla R.

Fort Nez Perce
(later Fort Walla Walla)

La Grande

Grande Ronde River

Joseph Creek

Imnaha River

Snake River

Tuekakas
(Joseph)

Lostine Creek

Wallowa R.
Wallowa Lake

WALLOWA MTS.

0   50 miles

document, all the dispossessed bands would have to move onto the new reservation, no matter how crowded.

Joseph's people were dumbfounded. When apologists for Lawyer tried to convince them that the head chief had signed only for the band to which he belonged and that Hale was responsible for the misconception, they did not believe them. They called the document the "thief treaty" and remained forever convinced they had been sold out for a mess of potage.[14]

Old Joseph, his eyesight and his health failing, went to the parfleche trunk in which he kept articles that were, or had been, dear to him. From it he took a copy of the Walla Walla treaty of 1855, which he had been the third Nez Perce to sign, after Lawyer and Looking Glass, and the Gospel according to Matthew, which had been translated into Shahaptian and printed on the little hand press at the Lapwai mission. Once Tuekakas had sought to embrace newness, thinking it would help give him, his children, and his band the power they needed to meet the changing world. But he had been betrayed. These documents were, to him, symbols of falseness. With his family and many of his people watching, he tore them into fragments.[15]

Old Joseph needed another symbol to show he had not sold his land. With his sons he followed an ancient Indian trail to a saddle in the divide separating the Wallowa country from the Grande Ronde. White farmers and stockmen were already settling in the Grande Ronde. If any of them decided to come into the Wallowa country, they would use that trail.

To indicate the closure of the route, he and his sons set up poles at intervals in the saddle. Because postholes are hard to dig in the lava that underlies the soil in that section, they probably heaped black rocks around the base of the poles to hold them upright, much as many fence posts are still braced in parts of that country today. The builders had no nails or wire to stretch between the uprights, but the line they indicated was clear. The first whites to see the symbolic barrier understood what it said. They called it Joseph's deadline.[16]

Deadline was too tough a word, however. Basically the poles were intended not as a threat, but as a reminder. For there was still a part of the aging chief that respected the better side of some of the whites he had known, and he hoped, secretly perhaps, that they would respect what he was trying to tell them now.

· 15 ·

IMPASSE

F olklore says that in 1866 or so, during the course of surveying the Wallowa Valley and dividing it into townships and sections, one of the white workers found that he needed to drive a wooden stake into the earth inside a tipi. This he did in the face of strenuous objections from the occupants. The message was clear. As soon as the 1863 treaty was ratified—and the white settlers of Idaho and eastern Oregon had no doubt that it would be—the Indians would have no rights to this land on which they had spent their summers for untold years. They might as well prepare now to move onto the new reservation in the Clearwater country.

The reply by Old Joseph's band—it numbered perhaps 250 men, women, and children—was equally clear. Every now and then one of the warriors pulled up a stake and threw it away. They had no intention of leaving, whether the treaty was ratified or not.[1]

In exchange for the high valley where Joseph's people spent about three months each summer and for the deep, low-altitude canyons that sheltered them during the rest of the year, the government promised $265,000 to be spent on one-family, twenty-acre tracts plowed and ready for white-style rural living—on the new reservation. It also promised the Indians the right to use tribal schools, gristmills, sawmills, blacksmith shops, a white farmer to teach them agriculture, and, if the Indians wished it, a Protestant church to attend. (Catholics did not gain entrance to the Nez Perce reservation until well into the 1870s.) All this, the U.S. Bureau of Indian Affairs believed, would lead the natives to give up their uncivilized wanderings and become part of the American mainstream. The foundation of the plan was "home"—a small, privately owned farm containing a fixed domicile. What could be more American?

It was not the way Joseph's people would have defined home if they had been asked. To them home was cyclical. It was an age-old pattern of goings and comings, a seamless repetition of long familiar places, each one bringing its own elements of physical and spiritual nourishment.[2]

Each winter the band divided into small groups and returned to traditional sites in the deep canyons that swept the Grande Ronde and its tributary Joseph Creek into the massive Snake River, swollen by the awesome slit of the Imnaha. Ample food had been prepared during the previous months, and only occasional hunting was necessary to replenish the Indians' larders. Their cattle and horses, grazing on the steep slopes and grassy benches, needed little attention. There was time for dances, songs, stories, and visits to other bands and tribes. Late February and early March saw them traveling old trails across the Blue Mountains to the Cayuse-Umatilla-Wallawalla Reservation, where Old Joseph, for one, had two half brothers and several cousins. On these trips they also began to make friends among some of northeastern Oregon's pioneering whites. They raced horses with ranchers near Pendleton; Old Joseph's sons were among those who exulted in the sport. Dressed in colorful ceremonial clothes, they rode their painted horses in the Fourth of July parade at La Grande, the principal town of the handsome Grande Ronde Valley. Old Joseph actually gave a speech at La Grande's 1864 celebration.[3]

Summer came late to the high Wallowa country. While waiting for the camas roots there to mature and the red-fleshed sockeye salmon to churn up the Wallowa River into Wallowa Lake, Joseph's people joined other Nimipu bands in a traditional socializing event at Weippe Prairie. The pine-dotted expanse lay outside the new reservation, and breathing was easier there. During the root digging, feasting, and dancing, plans were laid for journeys across the mountains to hunt buffalo and perhaps do battle with the Sioux. The trips greatly vexed the government agents and religious people on the reservation, for when the braves returned and held up the trophies they had taken, the young men of the treaty bands grew envious, even disobedient.

For Joseph's people the year's climax came toward the end of July with their return from the canyons to the Wallowa. There was a special balm in the sunshine and cloud shadows that drifted across the snow-creased mountains. Glistening streams and wind-rustled meadows opened enormous visual feasts to everyone. Nimipu from other bands who could wheedle permission from their glum-faced agents came to the lake for its fishing, and after they had dried the salmon they had caught, they joined the Wallowa bands on hunts through the forests and mountains for deer, elk, and bighorn sheep. At such times they mocked the reservation Indians. A twenty-acre farm! A Sunday afternoon Bible class at the Presbyterian church! Was that the life for a warrior?

The questions were sharpened by messages coming to them from a little hunchback named Smohalla. A member of the small Wanapum tribe that lived beside the Columbia River just above its sun-blasted Great Bend in southeastern Washington, Smohalla had been so badly beaten during a fight (so the story goes) that he fled in terror, wandering throughout the West for five years before returning to his home village. He explained his absence by saying that he had died but had been sent back by the Great Chief Above to revitalize the Indians by means of a new religion. If the Native Americans followed his precepts—which included learning new songs and symbols and performing certain dances and other rituals—the whites would disappear, the buffalo would return, and all the Indians who had ever lived would be resurrected.

"My young men," he preached, "shall never work. Men who work cannot dream, and wisdom comes to us in dreams.... You ask me to plow the ground. Shall I take a knife and tear my mother's bosom? You ask me to dig for stone. Shall I dig under her skin for her bones? You ask me to cut the grass and make hay and sell it and be rich like the white men. But do I dare cut off my mother's hair?"[4]

Did Old Joseph, his sons, daughters, and wives, most of whom had been baptized as Christians, embrace the new faith? Probably. Certainly, they combed the fore part of their hair upward in the pompadour that became the new cult's badge. They may have gone to meetings directed by one of Smohalla's disciples under a flag emblazoned with the prophet's six-pointed star. Caught up by powerful drum beats, they may have danced the slow-moving *Washat* the prophet taught. They embraced his insistence on the sacredness of the earth and his abhorrence of agriculture as a violation of nature. It is less likely that they believed in an imminent millennium when all dead Indians and buffalo would be resurrected and the white race would be overwhelmed. Too many whites were too close by to be dealt with only by mystical hopes.

* * *

By 1871 Old Joseph was blind. When he rode from camp to camp, a youngster sat astride his horse with him to handle the bridle rein. But his other senses stayed sharp, and one day early in August, shortly after his people had reached the Wallowa, he caught the scent of newly mowed grass. Instantly he surmised what it meant. White men had come into the region and were making hay.

He had his young guide rein the horse over to the swale where one or two whites were working with scythes. Hadn't they seen the line of poles he had erected in 1863 as a warning?

They were unimpressed. Because of the drought in the Grande Ronde, they needed pasture. The 1863 treaty had been ratified in 1867. The government had opened the land for settlement and had sent in surveyors. They planned to take up homestead claims, as was their right, and they hoped there'd be no fuss about it.

The chief was too old, too bone weary to take on this burden. Returning to his tipi, he called his sons to him, sturdy men both. The elder, Hin-mah-too-yah-lat-kekht, was thirty-one, thoughtful and sedate. Ollokot, twenty-nine, was more ebullient than his brother, but equally dependable. They had seen the grass cutters, too, doing exactly what Smohalla counseled against, and they guessed what their father wanted to say to them.

Years later, Joseph would remember the admonition this way: "A few more years and the white men will be all around you. They have their eyes on this land. My son, remember my dying words. This country holds your father's body. Never sell the bones of your father and mother."[5]

Shortly thereafter, the blind chief died. As the women wailed and hacked off bunches of their hair as a sign of mourning, the body was interred in the little Indian burial ground between the Wallowa and Lostine rivers. The sons built a rail fence around the plot, sacrificed their father's favorite horse, and draped the still-wet hide over one of the topmost rails. Relatives and friends erected, at a suitable distance from the cemetery, a "longhouse" in which Tuekakas's death feast would be held and his possessions given away. The shelter was either a traditional Plateau structure, its framework covered with reed mats, or was made of several canvas tipis linked together in a row—canvas because manufactured fabrics were being substituted more and more for heavy buffalo hides.

On the day appointed for the feast, friends and relatives, some of them Christian Indians from the reservation, crowded into the village while the dead chief's horses were distributed. The crowd then repaired to the long-house. As the crier called out the names of the recipients, the elder of Tuekakas's widows handed out practically everything the dead chief had owned—ordinary clothing and ceremonial regalia, ornately carved and decorated pipes, tools, weapons, horse paraphernalia, keepsakes. Singing, dancing, feasting, and speech-making accompanied the distribution.[6] Acting at a separate meeting, the band council then formally elected Hin-mah-too-yah-lat-kekht head chief in his father's place.

As the eldest son, Young Joseph had expected to be chosen. Chieftain-ships were hereditary among the Nez Perces, insofar as the council and band approved. Probably Young Joseph had sought to assure approval, as was customary, by giving presents and feasts to influential men. He knew, too, that his powers were stringently limited. Although he could make suggestions (hence the Indians' emphasis on persuasive oratory), he could not compel compliance. Everyone had a voice, if he chose to use it, in whatever community matters affected his life; it was a hallmark of Nez Perce independence that white men never fully understood.

By nature Young Joseph was a diplomat rather than a warrior. He would be expected to use his considerable influence to keep the camp in order; he would take charge of the women and children during the camp's frequent, cyclical moves, an onerous task that was vital to the well-being of the band. Most important, he would act as spokesman for the group in all contacts with outsiders, including the chiefs of the other Nez Perce bands. Because white stockmen had arrived in Wallowa almost at the time of his father's death, he could anticipate that the first crucial test of his statesmanship would come from them.

Leadership on community hunts or in battle against enemy tribes would devolve on the new chief's dashing younger brother, Ollokot. Their assignments created confusion about their identities among the whites, few of whom were aware of the Shahaptian custom of having different chiefs take charge of different activities. The problem was increased by the strong resemblance between the brothers. Because of the visibility Joseph attained as spokesman for his band, white observers frequently attributed some of Ollokot's actions to the older of the pair. As a consequence they often credited—and sometimes blamed—Young Joseph for more than he deserved.[7]

Although the Joseph band, as the whites continued to call the group, did not make its annual move into the Wallowa Valley until late July, it did get early news about the high country from its restless young hunters and scouts. What they learned in the spring of 1872 alarmed and angered them. An increasing number of white stockmen, seeking relief from the persistent drought in the Grande Ronde, had ventured into the meadowlands beside the river. A few had taken their wives with them; two had brought along mowing machines. A bridge was being built to do away with the most difficult ford along the old Indian trail the first comers followed. Unless the band acted, permanent white settlement seemed certain.[8]

Young Joseph, diplomat and pacifist, decided to rely on an appeal to the law to halt the trespassers. Because the Fourth of July celebrations would concentrate most of the Grande Ronde stockmen in the town of La Grande and because the local people liked to have the colorful Indians in their parade and thus would be disposed to listen, he chose to press his claim there. With Ollokot joining in the arguments, he stated, as he would many times during the ensuing years, that his band had no wish for hostilities. Indeed, he saw no reason for conflict. The treaty of 1855 had clearly left the Wallowa country inside the huge Nez Perce reservation that Governor Stevens had outlined that year. Since the elder Joseph had rejected the 1863 treaty, the land still belonged to his band, by agreement with the whites themselves. Young Joseph and Ollokot respectfully asked, therefore, that no settlements be made in the Wallowa country and that work on the bridge and wagon road leading to the area be halted.[9]

With equal politeness the whites replied, as they would many times during the following years, that a majority of the Nez Perce tribal leaders had signed the 1863 treaty. Therefore, its terms were binding on all the bands. On that basis, the United States government had made the Wallowa country part of the public domain and had opened it to settlement. The whites did not want a war, either, and their would be none if Joseph, Ollokot, and their council recognized the legitimacy of the citizens' claims.

Unable to grope a way through the impasse, both sides agreed to ask the new United States Indian agent at Lapwai, John B. Monteith, to meet with them at another council to explain the government's views of the legalities involved. Each side believed, of course, that the agent would support its stand. After messengers had spent a good deal of time traveling back and forth between La Grande, the Wallowa, and Lapwai, the new council was scheduled to be held in the Wallowa Valley on August 22, 1872.[10]

* * *

John B. Monteith owed his job to President Ulysses S. Grant's fatuous belief that America's distressing Indian problem could be solved by encouraging the nation's churches to play a major role in the administration of policy. A radical step of some sort certainly needed taking. During and after the Civil War, when most of the U.S. Army had been engaged in the East, a widespread series of bloody Indian uprisings had terrorized the West. The ending of the War between the States left many Union Army officers unemployed. As their former commander-in-chief, Grant wanted to help them, and it occurred to him and his advisers that they would make good Indian agents. After all, their army experiences had taught them discipline, organization, administration, and devotion to the service of their country, had it not?

What actually followed was a carnival of corruption. Easterners who had grown sympathetic toward the Indians, now that the Indians had been eliminated from their neighborhoods, were scandalized. Honesty, they declared, was the best Indian policy. Clean out the stables by letting the nation's churches appoint and supervise good Christians as agents on the different reservations.

During the unseemly rivalries that followed, the Presbyterians, in the form of the Reverend Edward R. Geary, became responsible for finding the right man for the Nez Perce reserve. Geary had been superintendent of Indian Affairs for Oregon Territory from 1859 to 1861. Later, in 1867, he had joined Thomas and Walter Monteith in founding Albany College, a Presbyterian institution, in the little town of Albany in western Oregon's Willamette Valley. (Thomas and Walter Monteith had founded the town of Albany in 1850.) A third brother, the Reverend William Monteith, became Albany College's first president. Among William's progeny was his son John. Unlike his father, John was not an ordained minister, but the Presbyterian ethic ran strong in him. Geary, who perhaps had participated in the young man's education, recommended that he be put in charge of the Nez Perce reservation.[11]

Monteith reached Lapwai in the spring of 1871. He was about thirty-five and fairly tall. Tuberculosis had left its stamp on him. A scraggly beard, already showing signs of gray, emphasized the length of his pallid face. A widow's peak foretold the thinning of his hair. He had no knowledge whatsoever of Indian culture and received no briefing before he assumed office. His lack of knowledge brought no hesitations. Like his father and his father's high-minded friends, he was convinced that honest handling of the annuity payments that were due the Indians would remove suspicions; thereafter earnest exhortations, liberal doses of Bible readings, and bits of teaching by the agency's staff—a miller, a farmer, and two or three schoolteachers—would be enough to turn the Nimipus on the reservation into happy, productive, Christian agrarians. The sight of their success would draw the wandering bands outside the reserve into the agent's orbit, for surely primitivism could not hold out against the manifest benefits of American civilization. And if the outsiders should resist unduly, they could be nudged back to the path by a touch of firmness ... he hoped. The main thing was always to be honest, patient, and hardworking.

He soon found he needed those qualities. His understaffed, underfunded agency was, in effect, divided between two focal points, his headquarters compound at the mouth of Lapwai Creek, site of Henry Spalding's old mission, and a subagency, sixty miles up the Clearwater at Kamiah. Most of the twenty-acre plots the government had plowed and fenced for the Indians were clustered around Kamiah, though a fair number stretched along Lapwai Creek past Fort Lapwai to a tributary, Sweetwater Creek, where the influential Slickpoo family lived. There, to Monteith's horror, a Lewiston-based Jesuit, Joseph Cataldo, would found a Catholic mission in 1874.[12]

Ironically, part of Cataldo's success sprang from a shouting religious revival, led by Henry Spalding during the early 1870s. Spalding had come back to the reservation twice as a teacher, the second time under John Monteith. Both times his bizarre, meddlesome ways cost him his job, but Monteith had let him turn to preaching and, by capitalizing on a religious revival already under way, Spalding had succeeded in baptizing scores of Presbyterians. One was old Tackensuatis, who had led Marcus Whitman, Spalding, and their wives from the 1836 fur-trade rendezvous to their missions. Another was Lawyer, who had resisted conversion until the treaty Indians, thinking him too old for the job, had voted him out of the head chieftainship. But he kept scraps of his prestige by accepting Christ and being elected an elder of the Kamiah Presbyterian Church.[13]

The widespread religious excitement opened tipis for the Catholics, too, and there was much bickering among the different sects. Hearing of the prickly ill will, Joseph remarked dryly that his band wanted no churches. Churches fostered quarreling about God, and "we do not want to learn that." The remark was applicable to the Dreamers, too. In the end the contentions served only to exacerbate the split already existing between the treaty and nontreaty factions of the tribe—a split that in time would cause great harm to Joseph's people.

Another irritant for Monteith was the reservation Indians' treatment of their twenty-acre plots. Some plots were neglected entirely. A few families harbored milk cows, chickens, and vegetable gardens—things that required daily care and helped root the people to a single home, which was what the government wanted. The majority, however, concentrated on wheat. By and large the grain took care of itself between planting and harvesting. Flour ground at the agency's mill provided both food and a source of cash for the farmers. Other cash income came from the sale of horses that grazed on the hillsides and tablelands with a minimum of attention.[14]

Possessed of both time and money, large groups of the Nimipus frequently took their children out of school, packed up their tipis, and rode off to customary fishing stations and root grounds outside the reservation. There they consorted with the nontreaty bands—often amiably but sometimes snappishly—not just with Joseph's people, but with other antiwhite groups led by firebrands, such as Eagle-from-the-Light and young Looking Glass, and those doughty war heroes, seventy-year-old White Bird and thick-chested, belligerent Tohoolhoolzote. Furious, Monteith asked his superiors to authorize the use of troops from Fort Lapwai to keep the reservation Indians from going to the camas meadows and any Indians from going after buffalo. The army refused the request.[15]

His ugliest problems were clashes between Idaho whites and the Nez Perces. One purpose of all reservations had been to isolate the Indians until they died out—vanishing Americans, as they were sometimes called—or had been transformed into civilized Americans. The segregation of the Nimipus was not possible, however. The supply town of Lewiston and the fading mining camps of Pierce and Elk City were close to the reservation—and were filled with whiskey. Roads between the settlements crossed the reservation, as the treaty of 1863 said they could, and there were frequent rest stops along the way where liquor was obtainable. Even the trader at the post and some of the soldiers at Fort Lapwai added their bit as bootleggers. The results were predictable. Indian women were assaulted. Horse stealing and robbery were common. Fights erupted over card games, fancied insults, and ordinary braggadocio. Fatalities were investigated carelessly, if at all. Figures are elusive, but there is no question that more Nez Perces than whites died during the clashes.[16]

Other collisions erupted over trespasses by livestock, whether deliberate or accidental. For many years the reservation's boundaries remained unfenced, even unsurveyed in places. To hold back cattle and horses belonging to nearby white ranchers, the Indians sometimes set grass fires that spread outside the reservation and infuriated the stockmen who had counted on using the feed. Turn about: white ranchers sometimes castrated Indian stallions that crossed the invisible boundary and broke into paddocks holding their mares.

Land-hungry whites harried treaty Indians who were trying to hold onto small plots outside the reservation until the government got around to paying them for their holdings. As delays dragged on and the whites' aggressions went unpunished, many of the beset Indians simply gave up and let their tormenters take over. Whites who were less inclined to violence had their own proposals about land absorption: Let the government move the Indians off the western half of the reservation—the Lapwai half—relocate them in the eastern section, and open the vacated lands to homesteading. Patiently Monteith explained there was not enough arable land in the eastern section to hold the dispossessed. But some whites had a way of not listening. In 1875 a reporter for a Boise newspaper wrote, with approval, that the idea was still alive.[17]

Into these troubles rode the messenger from the Wallowa, young Moxley, "a venturesome fellow with a good horse and a good gun." Joseph's band and some would-be homesteaders from the Grande Ronde were at loggerheads over landownership, Moxley said, and they wanted the agent's opinion. Summoning Joseph's brother-in-law, Reuben, to go with him, Monteith set out promptly on the long ride—105 miles, he later estimated—to the troubled land.

Joseph met them coolly. He let them wait for an uneasy hour and then summoned them to his lodge. There they found themselves faced by about fifty Indians dressed in the kind of regalia Monteith had not yet seen in his sixteen months at Lapwai—faces garishly painted; feathers in their hair and on the long stems of their pipes; V-shaped breastplates of small, hollow bones; fringes on their buckskin clothing; porcupine quills; and beads. Somewhat abashed, the long-faced agent listened as the young chief, speaking through his brother-in-law Reuben, voiced his unvarying stand. His father had bequeathed to him, for the use of his band, the entire Wallowa region. He would say nothing more until the full council with the whites convened the following morning.[18]

The whites had built their own big canopy of canvas for the meeting. About eighty Indians, women among them, and thirty whites crowded under it, facing each other in solemn decorum. Nothing substantive was added by either side. But the whites, unaccustomed to this kind of gathering, did not show well. Joseph, by contrast, was naturally eloquent and had practiced for this confrontation. During his formal speech, he paused at telling points, whereupon his Indian listeners shouted out in approval, *aaiy*, as they were wont to do.

Although Monteith was impressed, he disappointed the Indians by saying he could not make a decision on so important a matter. He would have to consult with his own chiefs. Then, having stayed in Wallowa less than two days, he returned to Lapwai.

In October the Indians traveled back to the winter part of their homeland in the canyons. If they made their customary visit to the Cayuse-Umatilla reservation, they probably ran into anti-Indian feelings among the whites that were stirred by an explosion of warfare near the Oregon-California border. A band of Modocs led by Chief Kintpuash (the whites called him Captain Jack), had defied an army unit that was trying to put them on their reservation. Fleeing south, pillaging and murdering as they went, the rebels found refuge in honeycombed lava beds in the extreme northern part of California. When military units attacked in January 1873, the Indians beat them back with heavy losses. A shiver of fear ran through Oregon. What if Captain Jack made contact with Joseph's renegades?

It was a far-fetched notion, but for the time being, it served Joseph well. About March 20, 1873, he received, at his winter camp in the canyons, a message from Monteith, asking him and Ollokot to come to Lapwai for a talk with T. B. Odeneal, superintendent of Indian affairs for Oregon. Infinitely curious, the brothers sent criers to the different winter villages, giving instructions to those who were interested in going to the agency with them. About a hundred showed up.

The Modoc scare was behind Odeneal's winter trip from Portland. He listened carefully, and for the first time Joseph was able to explain fully, to a white man, the logic of his band's position. Always, he said, the Nez Perces had lived in separate, autonomous groups, each occupying its own clearly defined territory. When drawing up the treaty of 1855, Governor Isaac I. Stevens had recognized Old Joseph's claim to the Wallowa. Even if Lawyer were head chief—less than half the tribe recognized him as such—he had no right, in 1863, to dispose of the Wallowa land. Old Joseph had done that when he bequeathed it and the chieftainship to his oldest son.

During the talk, Odeneal jotted down notes. Young Joseph was determined to hold the valley, "it being the summer home of their childhood, and the sporting ground of their youth and young manhood." His warriors were young and well armed; only a strong force could confine them to the 1863 reservation. The situation was critical. "Each [race] considers the other a trespasser, and the rash act of some imprudent white man, or reckless Indian, is liable to produce trouble at any time. We consider prompt action important."[19]

With Monteith's help, the superintendent did his best to work out a compromise. First he asked Joseph and Ollokot whether they would move to the Umatilla reservation, where they and their people had many friends and relatives.

The brothers refused. The vast Wallowa meadows and the canyons that drained them were their home.

Well, then, would Joseph's people consider sharing the region with the whites. Surely, it was big enough for both.

The chiefs talked the suggestion over. They could not keep on saying no forever. The whites were too strong; Colonel Wright's crushing of the Yakimas and Spokans in 1858 had proved that. Since then, the Nez Perces' military situation had deteriorated. Fort Lapwai stood only three miles up Lapwai Creek from the agency. Off to the west was Fort Walla Walla. Troops could come at the Wallowa from both directions. Steamboats could bring more soldiers and endless stores of equipment up the Columbia River. Joseph's people could not count on help from the reservation Indians. The war, if any, would be waged in their own rugged country. Yes, they could hold out for a time, as Captain Jack and his Modocs were doing in their lava beds. But for how long? And at what cost?

Share their beloved Wallowa—perhaps it was the only way out of the impasse. But Joseph and Ollokot did not want a mingling of the two races. The groups should be kept apart by some sort of dividing line.

Odeneal agreed, a map was produced, and the negotiators divided the Wallowa in half by running a line due north from the Wallowa Mountains to the Grande Ronde River. The eastern half, bordered by the Snake River, was reserved for Joseph's people. The western section, which lay closest to the farming and stock-raising country around La Grande, Oregon, went to the whites.

Joseph and Ollokot were sure their people would agree to the division. Their half would embrace Wallowa Lake and the upper reaches of the river, rich in summer salmon and bordered by rolling meadows of tall grass for their horses. A few whites did live in that section, but, Odeneal predicted, the government would pay them for their houses, barns, and other improvements and help them move into the western section. The whites would like that area. The altitude was lower, and winters were less rigorous. Farming went better; isolation was not so great a factor.

As Odeneal pointed out, the brothers were, in effect, creating a reservation for themselves and their people. It would have to be run like a reservation, and they knew what that meant.

Yes, they knew. But they would be preserving their homes, which was a boon the treaty Indians along the Clearwater were enjoying, and they would have won one of the essentials of political freedom—the right to have a voice in affairs that impinged on their and their people's livelihood.

* * *

In Washington the proposed division was accepted, classified as an executive order (which did not have to be reviewed by Congress), and sent to President Grant in May 1873. He signed the document on June 10, shortly before learning that the Modoc rebels, who had been cutting a murderous swathe, had at last surrendered. (Captain Jack and two other chiefs would be hanged in October for their part in the episode.) Would the new Wallowa reservation, which had been accepted partly to placate Joseph and Ollokot, have materialized if there had been no fears of a Modoc-Joseph alliance? There is no way of telling. What did emerge with startling clarity was the division of the Wallowa country into northern and southern halves, rather than eastern and western sections as agreed by the negotiators. No satisfactory explanation for this extraordinary gaffe has ever been found.[20]

Everyone concerned was stunned. The whites' share now embraced the highest part of the region, good for grazing and salmon fishing during the short summers, but not for farming, which was a primary concern among the homesteaders. The Indians' half, the northern half, contained their wintering canyons and thick forests that were good for some hunting, but not for grazing. The Indians also had been awarded the area's choicest agricultural land, which was exactly what they did not want.

Voters in Oregon shrilled their displeasure, heaping invective on Odeneal and Monteith. The uproar quickly caught the ear of Oregon's governor, who, in a singularly misinformed letter, let the state's congressional delegation know the feelings of their constituents.[21] No longer worried by the possibility of a Captain Jack–Joseph–Ollokot alliance, the congressmen, too, began to fret. Why had the absurd division of the Wallowa region been allowed? Since it had been brought about by an executive order from the president, could It be quickly rescinded by the same means?

Joseph had no place to turn except to Monteith. The agent, squirming under the criticism being inflicted on him, was testy. If the Indians did not stop their roaming, settle down, and cultivate the land of the Wallowa Valley after the fashion of the whites—and as the government expected Joseph's people to do—then they would lose the entire region. Completely frustrated, Joseph asked for permission to go to Washington and put his side of the case before the Big Chief. Although Monteith admitted such a trip might not be a bad idea if some of the chiefs of the treaty faction went along, nothing was done. Joseph kept hoping, however. As late as the spring of 1875, he was asking General O. O. Howard, the new commander of the military Department of the Columbia, whether he had received instructions from the East about the Wallowa. Howard, however, was unable to give him any firm information.[22]

Other nontreaty bands were also having trouble with the whites. One sample atrocity, important because of the impact it would have on the future, involved an Indian called Eagle Blanket and a white squatter named Larry Ott. Eagle had given Ott permission to make limited use of a handsome, fertile cove on the east side of the Salmon River, some distance south of the present-day hamlet of White Bird. On returning from a trip in the spring of 1874, Eagle found Ott plowing a section of the cove he had been told not to touch. When the Indian threw rocks at him to stop him, Ott pulled a revolver and mortally wounded him in front of four Indian witnesses. As he was dying, Eagle sent a message to his son, Wahlitits: "Tell him for my sake, and for the sake of his brothers and sisters, and in fact for the whole Nez Perce nation, to hold his temper ... and not wage war on the whites."

Informed of the killing, Monteith had Ott bound over to the grand jury and took the four Indians who had seen the shooting along as witnesses. Saying they did not believe in the white man's God, the quartet refused to hold up their hands and be sworn in. The jury then refused to hear their testimony, and Ott was freed on a plea of self-defense.[23]

Deeply disturbed by the trend of events, the leading nontreaty chiefs met in midsummer, 1874, at a favorite camping spot, Tepahlewan (Split Rocks), near today's Grangeville, Idaho. A few leading warriors were also invited to speak up. The topic: If they could find allies among the neighboring tribes, should they declare war on the whites? Their reluctant decision: no.[24]

To Joseph, the decision involved an obligation. He must work for peace among settlers who were as angry over the Wallowa mix-up as were the Indians. Circumstances helped him. Monteith, twitching with alarm, persuaded the commander at Fort Walla Walla to send a contingent of cavalry into the valley to keep both the nontreaty Nez Perces and the white homesteaders in line. Against that background, Joseph made a point of calling on some of the settlers, reassuring their wide-eyed children, and talking to the elders in Chinook, an ancient trade lingua franca that some of them could use to an extent. Things were so quiet, in fact, that several recreationists rode up from La Grande to test the fishing in the lake. The next year, 1875, he gained more goodwill by helping save the wife and daughter of an itinerant Baptist preacher (the preacher drowned) after the family had been swept into the flooded Wallowa River.[25]

The attempted reconciliation ended abruptly with the arrival of word that the muddled presidential order of 1873 had been rescinded by the president. The entire Wallowa region was returned to the public domain. Whites could settle anywhere they chose, and the Indians could be compelled, at the whim of the government, to settle under Monteith's supervision on the 1863 reservation.

Joseph was distraught. Was war the only way to end the impasse?

· 16 ·

FLURRIES

General Oliver Otis Howard, who in time would do much to make Young Chief Joseph world famous, entered the Northwest in 1874 as commander of the military Department of the Columbia. Aged forty-four at the time, he was a battle-scarred veteran. An unresolved tension plagued his life—his profession as a warrior on the one hand and his deep piety as a Christian on the other.

Unable to find a suitable job after graduating from Bowdoin College in Maine, he had reluctantly accepted an appointment, engineered by his father, to the United States Military Academy at West Point. He was below average in size. His hair was thick and wavy, his voice high pitched. To increase his status if not his stature, he worked out hard in the gym. Tiring of the harassment he was receiving from some of the cadets because of his devoutness, he quieted it by flattening the son of Robert E. Lee with one blow. He did well in his classes and excelled in debating.[1]

Howard was wounded three times during the Civil War, once so severely that his right arm had to be amputated. At Chancellorsville, the corps he commanded was trounced by Stonewall Jackson (Jackson lost his life in that battle), but he retained the confidence of his superiors and was put in charge of the Army of Tennessee during Sherman's March to the Sea. Even in a crowd of officers, he did not drink, smoke, play cards, or utter oaths. Whenever he had a free Sunday, he visited army hospitals, prayed over the patients, and handed out religious tracts and gifts of fruit.

After the war, he served without distinction as the first and only commissioner of the Freedmen's Bureau, which was organized to protect and uplift the newly freed blacks of the South. Although honest himself, he could not root out corruption in his widespread local offices or keep the bureau from turning into a political machine devoted to registering blacks as Republicans. In 1872 its appropriations were ended, and Howard was out of a job. But not for long. At that time President Grant was struggling to reform the Bureau of Indian Affairs by introducing his ill-fated "Peace Policy." Howard was a natural recruit for the program.

His first assignment was to persuade a marauding band of Apaches, led by the dreaded chief, Cochise, to settle down on a reservation. General George Crook, whose hard-line plans for the Apaches were derailed by the appointment, wrote sarcastically: "He [Howard] told me he thought the Creator had placed him on earth to be the Moses of the Negroes. Having accomplished that mission, he felt satisfied his next mission was with the Indians."[2]

Howard confounded his detractors. Helped by the famed frontiersman Tom Jeffords, and guided by two Chiricahua Apaches, he and a single aide penetrated Cochise's rocky stronghold, something of a miracle in itself. After eleven days of feasting and talking, the negotiators won a verbal promise from the chief to move onto a special reservation in the rugged mountains of southeastern Arizona. "A lasting peace," Howard called the arrangement. "A fraud," Crook proclaimed. In a sense, both were right. Cochise kept the peace as long as he lasted—he died in 1874—but two years later, when the army ordered his band onto a different reservation, trouble erupted again.

Meanwhile Howard was transferred to Portland, in charge of a department that embraced Oregon, Washington, part of Idaho, and the newly acquired Alaska. He liked the quiet town. He and his wife attended the First Presbyterian Church, of which the Reverend A. L. Lindsley was pastor; Howard also taught a Bible class and was elected president of the local YMCA. He also began writing boys' stories in an effort to shore up his finances.

To learn more about potential trouble spots in his department, Howard sent his assistant adjutant general, Major H. Clay Wood, to confer with Joseph at the Lapwai agency in the summer of 1875—the year the presidential order creating a special reservation in the Wallowa country was revoked. The cancellation left Joseph's claim to the Wallowa exactly as it had been at the conclusion of the 1863 treaty. Howard wanted to determine, if possible, what that claim amounted to. And because Monteith feared that the ending of the Wallowa reservation might stir up the area's Indians, Howard also sent Captain Steven C. Whipple into the disputed territory with two companies of cavalry as a peace patrol.

Both Wood and Whipple were impressed by the Indians they met, finding them, in Whipple's word, "proud-spirited, self-supporting, and intelligent." Major Wood reported that, in his opinion, Joseph's title to the Wallowa country had not been extinguished by the treaty of 1863. That right could be ended only by just and legal means. Exactly what form the solution should take Wood was not prepared to say. But something needed doing quickly, he urged, both for the sake of the Indians and for the whites who had gone into the Wallowa country thinking they were entering the public domain.³

Whether by collusion or not, the Reverend Lindsley entered the debate at almost the same time that Wood submitted his report. The minister had become a close friend of the Howards. He was also one of the Presbyterians who were delegated, as a part of Grant's peace program, to oversee affairs on the Nez Perce reservation. He took it upon himself to write the general a formal letter in which he advanced sentiments that were much like those voiced by Major Wood. He went further, however. The right of occupancy held by the Joseph band should be extinguished by purchase and the Indians moved to the Lapwai reservation, where they could join in the civilizing program. If they resisted, "harsher measures" would have to be taken.⁴

Wood's and Lindsley's recommendations were in line with Howard's own thinking. As a military man, however, he could not determine policy—only suggest it. In January 1876, he forwarded Major Wood's and Captain Whipple's reports and Lindsley's letter to the Bureau of Indian Affairs, along with a proposal of his own. Let the government appoint a commission that would come West, council with the Indians, and out of the hearings formulate a fair solution to the dilemma.

It is noteworthy that none of the people involved—Whipple, Wood, Lindsley, or Howard—suggested, in writing, the possibility of buying the homestead claims of the whites in the Wallowa and reinstating the reservation there along the originally proposed lines. At the time the reserve had been created, some of the settlers had offered to sell. But that wasn't the way Manifest Destiny—as expounded by Oregon's governor, Leonard Grover; Senator James K. Kelly, who had betrayed Peo-peo Mox-Mox in the Wallawalla campaign of 1855; and Congressman Wilson—worked. They wanted the Nez Perces out of their state.

In June, while the Bureau of Indian Affairs was stodgily considering the investigative commission Howard had recommended, a part of Joseph's band began their upward drift into the high country. Their first destination was forest-girt meadows near the head of a creek called Chesnimnus. While the women were digging roots, hunters scattered out for deer. One small group of them established a base camp among white-boled aspens that fringed the meadows rolling south toward the Wallowa Valley.

On the twenty-third, two white men rode into the camp. One was a mature, respected settler named A. B. Findley. Missing some of his horses and fearing they had been stolen, Findley asked Wells McNall, one of the sons of a neighboring family, to help him look for the animals. Wells was twenty-one, wiry, quick-tempered, and cocky. Details now grow obscure. Apparently only a few Indians were in the camp at the time. One was a friend of Joseph's named Wilhautyah. Suddenly, he and young McNall were locked in hand-to-hand combat. Findley covered the other Indians in the camp with a gun to keep them from interfering. Then Wilhautyah threw the white man down. He began screaming for help, and Findley fired at the Indian.[5]

At the crash of the gun and the spurt of blood, both whites and Indians fled the scene, fearing a general explosion. One curious aspect of the episode is that after sorting through the details, both the Nimipus and the settlers felt that although Findley had done the actual shooting, McNall was mostly to blame for the killing.

Joseph's people and the settlers alike resisted the temptation to escalate the affair into a vendetta. The settlers pressured McNall into riding to the town of Union, seat of the county of Union (it then embraced the Wallowa Valley as well as the Grande Ronde) and reporting the incident to the local judge there. Unsure of his jurisdiction and incompetent at best, that worthy passed the buck to the commanding officer at Fort Walla Walla. The officer was unsure, too. Was this a civil matter, a military matter, or something for the Bureau of Indian Affairs to look into? Finally, he sent off a note to General Howard in Portland. What now?

Meanwhile Joseph helped bury his friend near the temporary summer village beside Chesnimnus Creek. A few days later he talked to Monteith at Lapwai and was persuaded to let civil officials handle the problem according to the whites' laws[6]—which was exactly what the civil officers were not doing. Up in the Wallowa the Indians began to grumble.

But perhaps the military was finally waking up. In July, just as the main body of Joseph's band was preparing to follow the deer hunters into the high valley, a message arrived from Major H. Clay Wood, Howard's assistant adjutant general. Joseph and Ollokot had talked to Wood before about the tensions in the area and liked him. Now he wanted to meet with them again, at

Lapwai. Accompanied by about forty men and women, the brothers swam their horses across the Snake River and rode through blistering hot weather to the agency's buildings, shaded by the cottonwood trees that dotted the compound at the mouth of the creek. Right away they sensed an uneasiness in the air, for by then both the reservation Indians and the soldiers knew of Colonel George A. Custer's defeat at the Battle of the Little Bighorn on June 26.

(One of the whites who attended the council with Wood was the post surgeon at Fort Lapwai, Captain Jenkins A. FitzGerald, newly arrived with his young wife, Emily, and their two children from a stint in Alaska. On July 2, before word of the Custer debacle had reached Lapwai, Emily had written her mother, "We are all very much interested in the news from the Black Hills, and as we are surrounded by Indians here, we are the more anxious that victory doesn't crown the Plain Warriors. You know, two-thirds of the Nez Perces are Non-Treaty Indians, and they are intimate with the Sioux and other tribes on the warpath.... The largest body of Indians that has ever been on the warpath is on it this summer. They should be shown no quarter!"[7] Well, she knew now who had been shown no quarter ... and soon Joseph's already restless warriors in the Wallowa would also know the story.)

The tensions at the gathering were not lightened by the presence of Joseph's brother-in-law, Reuben, who had been elected head chief of the tribe following Lawyer's death the year before. Joseph refused to recognize him. On his part, Reuben, a crusading Christian, was embarrassed and angered by his obvious lack of influence over his brother-in-law. Still, everyone was polite during the all-round, formal handshakings that opened the discussions.

In elaborating on Wilhautyah's killing, Joseph, an accomplished orator, could not resist needling the whites while resorting to a little hyperbole. If Indian chiefs failed to punish bad Indians, he said, then the chiefs were responsible for the wrongdoings. According to this reasoning, white officials, who so far had done nothing about the murder, must be held responsible. The death was a terrible thing. Wilhautyah's life had meant more to Joseph, he said, than the whole world. Now that the Wallowa earth had drunk Wilhautyah's blood, the land was sacred. As indemnity for the death, Joseph wanted the whole valley returned to him. The whites must leave so he could hold it forever more for himself and his people.[8]

To Monteith and Reuben, this speech sounded like a bold maneuver to recover the lands that President Grant had returned to the public domain the year before. If the scheme succeeded, Joseph's prestige and that of the non-treaty Indians would soar while theirs diminished, further complicating their attempts to bring the entire population on the reservation under Christian governmental control. And if the exultant nontreaty Indians were to make contact with the triumphant Sioux....[9]

Apparently, Joseph and Ollokot exchanged sharp words with Monteith and Reuben. For when the conference was resumed on the morning of July 23, it met, at Wood's request, at Fort Lapwai, three miles up the creek from the agency. This time Reuben and the angry Monteith were not invited to attend. Reports say that Joseph was "ugly" when the second session opened. Wood, however, was able to placate him by saying that Howard had proposed that the government send an impartial commission to come to the reservation and hear the Indians' side of the story. In the meantime, Joseph and Ollokot should return to the Wallowa country and make sure no violence erupted between the whites and the Indians. He promised again that American civil authorities would deal with Findley and McNall.

The brothers agreed. On reaching the Wallowa, however, they found that domestic diplomacy was not going to be easy. Stirred by reports of Custer's annihilation and by the lack of any move by the whites to bring Wilhautyah's murderers to justice, several Nez Perce warriors had set up a target threateningly close to Findley's cabin and were peppering furiously at it from the backs and under the necks of hard-running horses. At night drum beats and yells from "Indian Town" (the band's summer encampment between Lostine Creek and the Wallowa River) told of exultant war dances.

Working through the band council, the brothers warned the group: Don't do anything that would turn the white commissioners against them. As part of the calming strategy, Joseph called two or three times on the Findley family, even eating supper with them once and conversing in Chinook. (Undoubtedly Joseph knew more English than he let on, but he wanted to make no bow whatsoever toward the U.S. government.) There is no record that either he or Ollokot met with bristly young Wells McNall.

The tenuous quiet that the chiefs brought about was shattered by an extraordinary gaffe by another member of the obstreperous McNall clan, this one named John and a brother, probably, of Wells. John had created, up on the shore of mountain-bound Wallowa Lake, a seine 150 feet long and 18 feet deep—in spite of the Indians' having warned him to stay away from their fishing stations. Ignoring them, John next built what he called a fine little sailboat for handling the seine and "for the accommodations of visitors that may want to come to the red fish region." Soon he and a few sportsmen from the Grande Ronde were hauling in sockeye salmon by the wagon load.[10]

Salmon, when filletted and dried, were a principal winter food not just for the Wallowa Indians but for their friends from the Lapwai reservation. Outraged by John McNall's slaughtering of unprecedented quantities of their fish, as the Indians regarded the salmon, a party of them rode to the lake and ordered the whites to desist. McNall defied them. This was public land. He would fish as he pleased. At that, one of the Indians knocked him down with a club. The others destroyed the seine, smashed the boat, and told the white visitors from Grande Ronde to go home.

The affray could hardly have come at a more inopportune time. A month had dragged by since Joseph's and Ollokot's meeting with Major Wood at Lapwai. No word had arrived about the promised commission. No authorities had appeared to arrest Findley and Wells McNall. Patience, the hotheads growled in council, had simply led to more trampling of their rights. Look at John McNall, who thought he could get away with anything. The time had come to strike back at all the whites in the Wallowa country—but peacefully, Joseph insisted, if peace was still possible. His Indians agreed to move slowly, although they still outnumbered the whites and could have created havoc.

On September 1, Indian messengers rode from Indian Town upstream as far as Wallowa Lake and downstream to where the valley canyoned before joining the Grande Ronde River. They rode out into the fields where hay was being stacked; they knocked on cabin doors. They told every white they encountered that there would be a meeting at their encampment the following day. They missed a few of the settlers. A few others flatly refused to respond to any summons by an Indian. But seventeen white men (Findley and McNall were not among them) did show up. Included were two or three men who could speak Nez Perce and who had always gotten on well with the Wallowa band.

At the gathering, Joseph or perhaps Ollokot—the brothers looked so much alike that whites couldn't always tell them apart—delivered an ultimatum. Every white in the valley would have to be gone within a week.

The settlers flared back tumultuously. In a sense they were being reckless to argue so, but they were protecting their homes, their irrigation ditches, their hay fields, their livestock—all the hopes that had brought them to this isolated land. Their government had made treaties through the tribe's head chief, Lawyer, that had given them permission to take up claims in the valley. They regretted that an Indian had been killed and that there had been trouble about the fishing. But all of them should not be held responsible for the misdeeds of a few. They, too, loved the soaring peaks and sun-washed vistas, and they were not going to leave.[11]

The Indians remained adamant. One week.

During the next two or three days, while Joseph and scattered groups of Indians watched from strategic ridge tops, the whites galloped back and forth from household to household, trying to make plans. A few began gathering their livestock, perhaps for an exodus or perhaps to corral the animals where they would be safe if an outbreak developed. Findley, it was said, offered to give himself up, hoping for a fair hearing, but the settlers were not terrified enough yet to let him sacrifice himself.

Wells McNall did not offer to give himself up, but his family was frightened for him, nevertheless. Another member of the clan, Ephraim, somehow eluded the Indians one night and, changing horses along the way, rode hard northwest to Fort Walla Walla to ask the military for help. It was an ill-judged choice. The commanding officer at the fort had learned to mistrust all McNalls.[12] Besides, he wasn't sure of his jurisdiction. He brushed Ephraim McNall off, saying he would have to consult with his commander at Fort Vancouver.

Far too alarmed to wait for an answer, Ephraim obtained yet another horse and galloped south to the Grande Ronde, begging for volunteers to come to the settlers' aid. It was harvest time, and many said they could not leave their fields. However, about two dozen or so began gathering arms for a rescue trip to the high valley.

News that reinforcements would soon be on the way quickly reached the lower end of the Wallowa Valley. At once messengers started upstream to carry the news to the little settlement of Alder, where a majority of the beleaguered whites had clustered. (Alder sat beside Hurricane Creek, a few miles west of present-day Enterprise, Oregon.) One of the riders, an unpopular young man named Gerard Cochran, seems to have been of the same cut as Wells McNall. Along the way he and his companion encountered an Umatilla Indian who was visiting the valley and wondered what was going on. The Umatillas, whose reservation was located near Pendleton, spoke a language similar to the Nez Perces', often intermarried with them, and, as we have seen, often exchanged visits with them. This particular Umatilla, moreover, spoke English.

Cochran could not resist bragging. Reinforcements were riding in from the Grande Ronde Valley, he told the Umatilla. If the damn fool Nez Perces didn't shape up, they'd be wiped out. Cochran himself would scalp Joseph and fasten the trophy as a decoration to the head band of his bridle.[13]

The word flashed, of course. In the middle of the afternoon, Joseph led about seventy garishly painted warriors, most of them stripped to their breechclouts and mounted on hastily painted horses, up to the principal ranch near Alder. Guessing what was on the Indians' minds, young Cochran hid in the ranch's hay barn. Not that it did him any good. Joseph—or Ollokot—coldly asked why the settlers had brought the Grande Ronde people into the quarrel. The whites glanced unhappily at the mounted warriors and back at each other. For help, someone said. If help meant they were looking for a fight, the chief reportedly replied, they'd get it. As for the Wallowa settlers, there would be no trouble—if they heeded the deadline. The time was up tomorrow. The whites, heavily outnumbered, nodded. They'd go, they said, and some left the gathering to start preparations.

Then Joseph asked what was this about a scalping? Having divined already what had infuriated the normally calm chief, a couple of whites went to the barn and dragged Cochran out. Joseph dismounted and stood over him with a raised tomahawk. Who was going to scalp whom? Cochran denied uttering any such threat. It happened that the Umatilla Indian to whom he had made the rash brag was standing nearby. He slapped the young man hard across the face. Try to remember, he said, and Cochran did. Then the young man's father, who also happened to be nearby, cried out. If Joseph wouldn't hurt the boy, he'd take him out of the valley and never let him return. Joseph agreed. Probably he had not meant to do more than scare the braggart, anyway.

After repeating the deadline to the whites, he signaled to his men and to the many Indian women who, burdened with cradleboards and leading packhorses, had been watching from a distance. They rode off across the meadows to Wallowa Lake, where they camped. They may have used wood from John McNall's smashed boat for their fires that night.

Joseph's bluff about the deadline—if it was a bluff—was never called. Toward noon of that day he and his Indians saw, from a vantage point near the lake, four men approaching. One wore the gold-emblazoned blue coat of a U.S. Army officer. Two were enlisted men. The fourth was a fat, jovial settler, Tom Veasey, whom Joseph liked and who could speak Nez Perce fairly well. A parley was agreed on, and the troopers' arrival was explained.

Ephraim McNall had hardly left Fort Walla Walla after the rejection of his appeal for help when the commander there had second thoughts and ordered Lieutenant A. G. Forse, to whom Joseph was then talking, to the Wallowa Valley. Along the way the lieutenant learned that several Grande Ronde rescuers were bound for the same destination. Pushing ahead at double time, Forse overtook them at midnight, the beginning of the deadline day, camped at a ranch in the middle part of the Wallowa Valley. To get them under his control, he organized them into a militia unit attached to his own command. After resting briefly, he left half the combined force at the ranch to protect the settlers in the middle valley and rode with the rest upstream to Alder. Learning that the Indians were at the lake and fearing that if he went there with a large contingent someone might pull a trigger and start a war, he continued with the three companions Joseph had greeted.[14]

The chief liked the young officer's coolness and lack of condescension, and they talked freely. Joseph told the lieutenant of the hope he was placing in the commission that Major Wood had promised. He jumped at Forse's solution to the Findley-McNall problem. Soldiers would take the pair, along with two Indian witnesses to the murder, to the county seat, where they would be arraigned. Finally, the lieutenant demanded that to prevent clashes, the Indians should temporarily confine themselves—and their troublemaking stallions—to the Hurricane Creek area.

Penned. By a white man's order. It had never happened to Old Joseph, even temporarily. But Young Joseph agreed.

One almost has to believe that an epiphany was at work there. When only a relatively few homesteaders had lived in the Wallowa Valley, the Indians' power—their collective guardian spirits—had still seemed to be strong. But the swiftness with which the horse soldiers and the volunteers from the Grande Ronde had responded to Ephraim McNall's appeal stunned Joseph. He could not have summoned Indian allies that quickly. He could not have plucked Findley and Wells McNall out of their homes for trial, but Forse did.

It was as if a wall surrounding his lovely valley had fallen, and he looked out across the Columbian Plateau at things he had not noticed before. His world, he realized with devastating acuteness, was turning white. There were twenty-five-hundred whites in the city of Walla Walla, near the site of the old Whitman mission where Cayuse and Wallawalla Indians had once roamed. Few Indians were there now. Another thousand whites lived in the Grande Ronde. There were hundreds in Lewiston, a hub for roads that splayed out toward fading mining towns where gold seekers had turned the very earth upside down. Joseph had watched steamboats churn up the Columbia and Snake rivers, bringing power goods to the farms and ranches, the sawmills and gristmills that ringed what was left of Nez Perce country. A noisy steam engine on wheels dragged covered wagons along rails from the boat landing at Wallula to the town of Walla Walla. Bigger engines, he had heard, dragged other trains east toward the sun, to the place where the Great

Chief of the whites lived. That was where the guardian spirits had gone.

A world turned white. Most of the tribes he knew of were restive—the Yakimas, the Coeur d'Alenes, the Spokans, and the Flatheads. But what could they do? Colonel Wright's campaigns nearly twenty years before had taught them the hopelessness of resistance. Captain Jack's Modocs had succeeded in killing General Edward R. S. Canby, the highest ranking officer of the regular army ever to be slain by Indians. But afterwards the Modocs had been whipped, taken from their homeland, and thrust into a dreary reservation in a place called Indian Territory. The Sioux had crushed Colonel Custer, but no one really supposed the white people would run away because of that.

No, war was not the Indian's answer, even though some of Ollokot's young men, dreaming of the rewards for personal valor, thought otherwise. The commission that General Howard had recently gone east to implement had to be his people's hope.

And so he consented to Lieutenant Forse's request that his band confine itself to the Wallowa Lake side of Hurricane Creek. To symbolize the promise, Joseph had his warriors ride single file past the lieutenant. As each man loped by, he discharged his gun into the air. The weapons were empty now; the people were at peace.[15]

One mischance might have marred the truce. The county court turned Findley and McNall loose. It did so, Joseph was told, because the two Indian witnesses refused to testify. Their reasons have not survived. Perhaps they were intimidated. Perhaps old laws forbidding the taking of Indian testimony against whites had been invoked. Or perhaps the pair had been Dreamers and had refused to be sworn in lest the ritual be taken as signifying their acknowledgment of the white man's god.[16] Joseph did not press the matter. He had gotten the pair into court, which was at least partial recognition of the Indian's rights. And now a bigger claim concerning their basic rights was about to be heard.

· 17 ·

THE ANTAGONISTS

Fort Lapwai boasted only one residence building deemed suitable for housing General O. O. Howard and Major H. Clay Wood, the military members of the five-man commission that was charged with bringing Chief Joseph and his nontreaty Nez Perces to heel. The building in question was a white-painted, two-story duplex. Its two sections were united by a long front porch. They were separated by an entry hall, perpendicular to the porch, that pierced the structure's middle. General Howard accepted—perhaps "demanded" is a more accurate word—quarters in the apartment that sheltered the post commander, Captain David Perry, and Perry's wife. Major Wood was relegated to sleeping in the apartment occupied by the post surgeon, Captain Jenkins FitzGerald, his twenty-six-year-old wife, Emily (she generally called him John), and their two small children. The two ladies managed their feat of hospitality by pushing aside the furniture in their sitting rooms and introducing army cots and porcelain bowls for the use of their guests.[1]

The three civilian members of the commission were to be housed at the agency compound, three miles to the north where Lapwai Creek ran into the Clearwater River. Emily found the trio to be kindly, avuncular, and prosperous, but (to borrow the words of Mrs. John B. Monteith, wife of the agent) "without a speck of Indian sense, experience, or knowledge."[2] Emily liked them, nevertheless. She was charmed, too, by Major Wood's urbanity. Howard she did not like. She had met him sixteen months earlier when she and her doctor husband had been stationed at Sitka, Alaska, and Howard and his retinue had arrived on an

219

inspection trip. She found his religion "ferocious.... He is one of those unfortunate Christians who continually gives outsiders a chance to laugh."[3] Still, he was her husband's superior and had the power to assign John to any post he chose, however miserable. So Emily walked carefully while he was about.

Although Lapwai was a small post, it might become important if trouble developed. It was not protected by a stockade or bastions. Its uninspired, white-painted, loosely spaced, cubic buildings bordered a rectangular parade ground that occupied most of a broad flat formed by a widening of Lapwai's otherwise narrow, high-sided valley. All the buildings faced inward. The guardhouse crouched on the north side of the rectangle. The headquarters office, marked by a tall flagstaff, was on the south side; some distance behind the office were the stables for the cavalry contingent. The barracks, backed by huts used by the laundresses who washed the troopers' clothes for two dollars a week, partly enclosed the eastern side of the parade ground. Behind the barracks was the wagon road, which wound some sixty miles from the agency up the valley to a high camas prairie where the farming and stock-raising towns of Grangeville and Mount Idaho were taking root. Beyond the road, close to the cottonwood trees that lined the creek, was an extension of the flat where Indians camped when they had cause to visit the fort. Overlooking all this from the western side of the parade ground were the residences that housed the garrison's officers. The Perrys' and FitzGeralds' apartments occupied the building at the southwest corner, closest to the headquarter's office.[4]

Emily FitzGerald was small, pert, pretty, and thoroughly domesticated, as army wives were expected to be. Since marrying four years and eight months earlier, she had borne a daughter and a son and had suffered a miscarriage. In her literate letters to her mother, she seldom complained about the physical isolation, social loneliness, and intellectual narrowness of living in frontier army posts. She did not question army policies. When settlers and Wallowa Indians had been confronting each other in the mountains a couple of months earlier, she had described the whites as "an awful set of men." But "of course, [they] must be supported by the troops."[5]

The decision about when to put the troops into motion was not Howard's, however. That command would come, if at all, from the Bureau of Indian Affairs, and there would be no hurry about issuing it. As Emily learned from overhearing the officers talk in her converted sitting room and on the front porch, the men at the bureau were worried about what had happened to Custer during the army's attempt to push the Sioux out of the Black Hills of South Dakota onto a reservation of their own. As a result, they meant to deal cautiously with Joseph, lest he become a rallying point for all the disaffected Indians of the Northwest. The commissioners who were chosen to treat with him had been instructed to use persuasion, gently pointing out to him the advantages that would accrue to his band if they moved, of their own choice, onto the reservation. Only if they remained recalcitrant would force be used.[6]

In either event, proper channels would have to be followed. After meeting with Joseph, the commissioners would make their recommendations in the form of a written report. If the head of the Bureau of Indian Affairs accepted the recommendations, he would instruct the Nez Perce agent, John B. Monteith, about what steps to take. If Monteith thought military help was needed, he would notify Howard, who would then prepare his troops for battle. Since Howard was, at his own request, a member of the investigating commission, he might well find himself using his own muscle to enforce his own theories about the nontreaty Nez Perces.

There was a buzz phrase for this process that Emily was soon using in her letters—"bringing Joseph to terms." The expression was a euphemism. The words implied negotiations. But nothing negotiable was left to the Indians. Their only choice, after all the polite palavering was finished, would be whether they went onto the reservation in peace or under duress.

Curious about developments, Emily and her husband rode in the fort ambulance to the agency compound to watch "the wild Indians ... coming in." What they noticed first was the large number of tamed treaty Indians clustering about the mission church, where the sessions were to be held. More than idle spectatorship had brought them there. For one thing, many of them believed there was not enough pasturage and arable land inside the reservation to support all the nontreaty Indians and their huge herds of horses. That worry prompted them to be supportive of Joseph: let him stay in the Wallowa. Joseph and his non-Christian followers, some of them Dreamers, almost certainly would create pools of trouble if they moved onto the reservation.

Altogether it was a colorful event, seen through the prism of Emily's inevitable prejudices. "The squaws gathered outside in their best, brightest clothes." The men drifted inside. Reservation Indians filled the center seats and the section to the left. The Wallowa men, some sixty of them, crowded the right side of the church, "most of them sitting on the floor, horrible, dirty looking things all rolled up in blankets and robes." Nervously, Mrs. Monteith and Emily made their way up front, toward the commissioners. They were the only women inside the building, and Emily was not amused when the agent leaned over and asked her whether her hair felt on tight.[7]

The reservation Indians, she noticed, wore their hair cut off a little below their ears (relatively short hair was the missionary badge for civilized Indians), and they were clad in American-style pants, shirts, and coats. The nontreaty Indians wore—she returned to a favorite adjective—"such ferocious looking headdresses you never saw." Ollokot, "a wretched looking Indian with his hair and forehead and eyes painted red, had on a robe very elaborately painted with hieroglyphics." A few of the warriors "had all the front hair cut off but about six or eight inches and stiffened so it stood straight up from their heads like a comb, and long, black hair hanging down their backs in a braid with some kind of an ornament at the end"—coiffures that suggested the influence of the Dreamers.

For some reason Emily did not mention Joseph in her description of the gathering. She stayed only an hour or so inside the church. "The Indian smell was awful, and I wanted to get home to the children." With her husband she returned to the fort. The rest of the conference she learned about only through hearsay. Opinions varied. Mrs. Perry feared that affairs would end in war. Emily didn't. Some of the treaty Indians say "he [Joseph] is a coward, so I am not as anxious as I otherwise would be."[8]

The hopes that Joseph and Ollokot brought to the Lapwai agency soon withered under the carpings of the commissioners, particularly those of David H. Jerome, the group's civilian president. The whites, though suave and patient at first, clearly did not want to hear what the brothers said about their legal and moral rights to the Wallowa country. Rather, they kept telling the Indians why they shouldn't stay there.

The altitude, the whites said, made the area too cold for year-round farming. Joseph replied that they didn't want to farm. They went up there from the canyons only in the summer to dig camas, catch salmon, and graze their horses and cattle. They had been living that way longer than memory ran. What made the commissioners think they couldn't keep doing it—and doing it as well as the white ranchers who were crowding into the area with their livestock?

Well, maybe, the commissioners said. But wherever the Indians settled, it would have to be on a reservation where they could be protected. The state of Oregon now controlled the Wallowa and would not cede the region back to the federal government for the purposes of a reservation.

This extraordinary bit of misinformation must have made the whites who heard it swallow hard. Oregon did not own the land. It was part of the nation's public domain—if, in fact, the federal government had ever acquired it. Joseph, who had covered that point again and again during previous meetings, went at it once more. His father had not sold the Wallowa country to the United States in 1863. Nor could the government say he was bound by the actions of a majority of the other Nez Perces. According to Nimipu custom, each band was responsible for its own actions. A thousand bands could not sign away the property of one, if that one disagreed. If Joseph refused to sell one of his horses, could a potential purchaser then buy it from his neighbor? Of course not. It was the same with the land.[9]

Jerome switched approaches. Living was good on the Lapwai reservation, he said. If the Wallowa band went there, each adult male would receive a twenty-acre farm plot. The government would help with the plowing and fencing, as it had for the treaty Nez Perces. The newcomers could send their children to governmental schools, use the gristmills and sawmills and blacksmith shops the government had built, and share in the annuity goods the governmental agent distributed each year.

Joseph grew sarcastic. The members of his band were used to roaming across hundreds of thousands of acres. Should they trade that for farm plots? As long as they were free, they could cross the mountains to the Plains to hunt for buffalo. If they settled on the reservation, Monteith would try to stop the hunts and he would want them to sit stodgily on their plots while learning to live like white people. They didn't want that. The schools would take away their culture. The churches would cause bickering—Protestants against Catholics, Methodists against Presbyterians, Christians against Dreamers. As for annuities, the government was notoriously late in meeting the obligations it had already assumed. They would rather depend on themselves.

Frustrated by hours of that kind of resistance, the commissioners began to threaten. They told the listeners what had happened to other Indians who had refused to go onto the reservations that had been assigned to them—the Seminoles in Florida, the Modocs in Oregon and northern California. The Sioux would be next; fresh columns of American troops were already assembling to overtake and punish them. "What," Howard asked, "would you do if several thousand armed men came against you?"[10]

Joseph replied, "We will not give up the land. We love the land; it is our home." That was his stance throughout. He was made of the earth and had grown up on its bosom. He could not consent to sever his affections.

To the commissioners, Joseph's mystic (and to them, fuzzy) identification with the land was the result of the Dreamers' teachings. Actually, the whites had the situation backwards. It was the Dreamers who had picked up the earth-mother philosophy that was so powerful among all the tribes and had carried it to extremes that Joseph and Ollokot did not wholly accept. But railing at Dreamers, sorcerers, and followers of the hunchbacked Smohalla gave the commissioners an explanation for their failure to bring the Indians peacefully to the reservation. Rail they did.[11]

As the dispute grew more and more bitter, Joseph deliberately snubbed Commissioner Jerome. Tensions ran through the church. Years later, the daughter of Perrin Whitman, nephew of the slain Marcus Whitman and a principal interpreter for Monteith, would recall that Jerome so feared an outbreak that he abruptly terminated the council. The danger may not have been as acute as the young woman remembered, but the meeting did end on a discordant note on the second night.[12]

Blaming the deadlock on the civilian commissioners, Joseph decided to appeal directly to Howard and Wood. Both officers had been friendly during previous meetings; both had seemed to understand and be sympathetic toward the Wallowans' plight. The next morning he called on two fellow chiefs and an ancient tewat, or medicine man (their identities now unknown), and told them to dress as they would if they were going to meet with the Great Chief of all the Americans. Clad in their finery, they rode through a morning rainstorm to the fort. Avoiding the parade ground, they circled around to the back of the duplex in which, they had learned, the visiting officers were staying. A white woman saw them coming, stared, and then called for others to come and look.

Emily FitzGerald, who was the first to see the quartet, later wrote her mother, "We all stood in the rain, as we hadn't seen such a gorgeous array before. One of them who did the most talking had a headpiece for his horse that covered his horse's whole head. It was just covered with beads. There were holes for the eyes, and it really was very showy. His own costume was of some kind of skin trimmed with ermine. A fringe of ermine skins (whole skins) was around the jacket, and about the knees, and down the seams of the sleeves from shoulder to wrist, and around his cap. Their faces were all painted, and all had bows, and quivers of arrows swung at their backs. The quivers were all highly ornamented with beads. A ferocious old medicine man was with them (an old, old man). The other three were quite young chiefs. One was Joseph, himself, who is a splendid looking Indian. As far as we could understand, they had come to make terms of some sort with General Howard. They were all very smiling and pleasant and seemed very sorry about not finding him. We don't know whether this is the beginning of a settlement, but we hope it is."[13]

Apparently, the general and his adjutant had ridden down the road from the fort to the agency while Joseph and his companions had been donning their finery in their tipis. On reaching the agency, the military men had picked up their civilian counterparts and off they all went, to report the results of their conference to Washington. Unable to do more than speculate about the future, Joseph's Nimipu returned to their winter camp near the point where the Grande Ronde River runs into the Snake.

December and January 1876/77 dragged by. And then, early in February, four Indians arrived with a message from Monteith. Obviously, the quartet had been handpicked in the hope that they could keep Joseph quiet while they gave him a message from Monteith. Three of the visitors were relatives of Joseph's wife—her father, Wish-Tasket; her brother Reuben, who had succeeded Lawyer as head chief of the reservation Nez Perces; and Reuben's son, James, who was studying at the mission school at Kamiah to become a Presbyterian preacher. With the Reubens was Captain John, so-called by the whites because of his useful services during the Indian troubles of the late 1850s.

While extolling the joys of reservation life, they delivered a harsh message. The commission had decided that Joseph's people must give up their traditional homes and join the treaty Nez Perces along the Clearwater. To this ultimatum Monteith had added a date: The dispossessed must be relocated with their livestock by April 1.[14]

Joseph was thunderstruck. The long weeks of silence following the meetings at Lapwai, his own wishful thinking, and his lingering confidence in Howard and Wood had led him to believe that his guardian spirit was still strong and would lead him out of the white trap. But now he was being told that on April 1 his world would come to an end. Stricken, he refused to answer his visitors until the next day, when he said only, "I have been talking to the whites for many years about the land in question, and it is strange they cannot understand me.... I will not leave it until I am compelled to."[15]

He grasped at straws. White interpreters often had trouble with the complexities of the Nez Perce tongue, and perhaps those at the conference had given the commissioners a wrong impression. He must arrange a meeting with Howard where the truth would prevail. Also, he needed allies. He would summon the other nontreaty chiefs, whose futures were as clouded as his, to a meeting to discuss their futures. Another potential helper was the Jesuit missionary—lean, tough, weather-beaten Father Joseph Cataldo. In spite of Monteith's angry insistence that the Nez Perce reservation "belonged" to the Presbyterians, Father Cataldo had finally won the right to establish a Catholic mission beside Sweetwater Creek, a tributary stream that entered Lapwai Creek a few miles above the fort. Several dozen nontreaty Nimipus and many treaty Indians who had grown disenchanted with life as it was being directed by John Monteith had become converts. An eager proselytizer, Father Cataldo had visited Joseph and Ollokot and seemed sympathetic. Perhaps he would put in a word with Howard. Finally, there might be a possibility of making common cause with their friends, the Umatillas, and sharing a reservation with them.[16]

Ollokot took the lead in pushing for the various programs. He sought to convince Father Cataldo of the injustice of the Americans by reciting the long record of Nez Perce friendliness to the whites. He spoke in glowing terms of the Sioux's victories in many battles and said that the Nez Perces, too, would fight. Cataldo quietly replied that as a spokesman for Christ he could not interfere in political quarrels. At the same time he warned against trying to settle grievances with violent means.

The priest's advice had its effect. When Monteith learned that the nontreaty chiefs had met to decide on a course of action, he summoned Ollokot to the agency and charged him with hostile intent. Ollokot shook his head. Fighting a guerrilla war against well-equipped American troops, he now realized, would mean leaving his home and family and retreating deep into the mountains, to live like a wild animal. No, neither he nor the bulk of the Wallowa Nimipus were ready for that.[17]

Ollokot also industriously followed the chimera of uniting with the Umatillas, the two tribes living together on either the reservation currently occupied by the Umatillas or one the whites would grant them in the Wallowa country. The Americans could have whichever one was vacated. In pursuit of that last-resort plan, he arranged through Narcisse Cornoyer, the Umatilla agent, to meet with some of Howard's staff on April 1. That meeting having proved unproductive, Howard agreed to attend a second gathering at Fort Walla Walla on April 20.

To some of the Wallowans that second date offered hope. Monteith's deadline of April 1 had passed without mention by the whites. It had been a peremptory decree, and perhaps Joseph's flat rejection of it through the messengers who had been sent from Lapwai to tell him about it had given Monteith pause. Anyway, for whatever reason, the agent had not informed

Howard of the ultimatum.[18] As a result, the army people had not mentioned it during the April 1 meeting, and the lapse encouraged the Indians still further. If there had been some sort of mistake about dates, then other mistakes may have occurred because of faulty translations. They would convince the one-armed general of this when they met with him at Fort Walla Walla on April 20 and 21.

As the date neared, Joseph fell sick, and Ollokot once more acted as the band's spokesman. The antagonistic parties gathered in a big room at Fort Walla Walla, Indians on one side, army officials and civilians on the other. Howard immediately rejected the suggestion that the Wallowans and the Umatillas share a single reservation. Joseph's people would go to Lapwai. The point was not negotiable.

Lapwai? Ollokot displayed a rough pictorial map of his band's integrated canyon-high country rangeland to show how vital it was to their livestock economy. They couldn't find that kind of geography at Lapwai. Howard brushed the objection aside, answering every argument Ollokot advanced with a snap of his high-pitched voice, like a one-note bird. "You must go to the reserve."[19] He may have felt that he did not have to say more. He had already told them he was reinforcing the garrison at Fort Lapwai and was sending troops into the Wallowa area to speed the Indians along if they objected physically to moving to their new homes.[20]

After a rancorous time Howard finally did agree to another meeting, this one at Fort Lapwai on May 3 with all the nontreaty chiefs. As yet he had not talked with any of the resistant leaders except Joseph and Ollokot. Now the time had come for ordering them, too, onto the reservation.

Desperate, the Nez Perces scrambled for bits and pieces of hope. They found a few. The forgotten date of April 1, the possibility that new translations would convince Howard that the commission of the previous November had reached mistaken conclusions, and a demonstration of unity by all the nontreaty bands—surely, these portents indicated that they might yet retain their homes. Runners went to the key chiefs, asking for a general council to which Howard had agreed. Because all the chiefs would be involved with Joseph and Ollokot in the coming struggle, it is well to glance momentarily at each.[21]

The one who lived closest to the Wallowans, in the rough, high wedge of land that fills the angle formed by the junction of the Salmon and the Snake rivers, was a barrel-chested, spellbinding old orator and a true Dreamer named Toohoolhoolzote. Farther up the Salmon, due south of the reservation, were the Lamatas. Once the band had been part of a group that sprawled from the Salmon across Camas Prairie to the South Fork of the Clearwater. Their chief had been the renowned buffalo hunter, Eagle-from-the-Light. Depressed by his failure to keep miners out of his territory—his home lay on the trail to Elk City—and remorseful, perhaps, that he had let himself be coerced into signing the 1863 treaty—part of his homeland was included in the southeastern tip of the shrunken reservation—he spent most of his time in Montana with the South Fork part of his band. The rest, who clung to their territory along the Salmon River had elected as their new chief another doughty buffalo hunter and a relative of Eagle-from-the-Light, a stocky oldster named White Bird. Lately, the Lamatas had been even more annoyed by white settlers than had the Wallowans.

The best-known warrior of the Nez Perce dissidents, Looking Glass, Jr., also lived on the Clearwater's South Fork. Because he wore a small trade mirror around his neck as an identifying ornament, the assumption is that Looking Glass, Sr., was his father. The elder Looking Glass, however, had lived at Asotin, near the site of Lewiston. How the younger Looking Glass came to the South Fork is not known. Although most of his band's territory lay within the reservation, he had not signed the "thief" treaty of 1863. He had no love for the Christian element of the tribe or for agent John Monteith, who was always trying to get the buffalo hunters back onto the reserve. Looking Glass, Jr., aged forty-five or so in 1877, was with the hunters more than he was at home. He made common cause with the Crows in their battles with the Sioux, and was the only one of the Nimipus who, in 1877, had a wide reputation as a war chief.

Two lesser chiefs, Husishusis Kute and Hahtalekin, were Palouse, not Nez Perces. The Palouses were a Shahaptian group related to the Nimipus, whose reservation lay directly east of them, and to the Yakimas, who lived to the west. When Isaac Stevens had forced his 1855 treaty on the Plateau Indians, the Palouses had lost their homeland and had been told to move onto the new Yakima reservation. They ignored the order. For nearly a quarter of a century, no effort had been made to enforce their obedience. But they knew that Howard intended to treat with them as soon as he was finished with the nontreaty bands of the Nez Perces. So the dissidents sent runners to them, too, inviting them to the council. Husishusis Kute's band roamed beside the Snake River below Lewiston. Hahtalekin's people were centered on the confluence of the Palouse and Snake rivers.

At the meeting, its place and date unknown today, one stark fact emerged: The power of the whites was such that all the chiefs in attendance believed there was no real hope of gaining their ends by fighting. They would have to go to Howard's council prepared to negotiate. They rejected either Joseph or Ollokot as their spokesman, probably because both men were considered to be too young and inexperienced. (Joseph was within a few months, possibly weeks, of being thirty-seven; Ollokot was about two years younger.) There is some evidence, too, that the chiefs thought that the brothers had not been firm enough during earlier meetings with Howard.[22] In any event, they chose as their leader bull-necked, deep-voiced, recalcitrant Toohoolhoolzote.

Less than a decade and a half earlier, Oliver Otis Howard had been commanding armies and shuffling brigades. Now he sent two companies of cavalry, fewer than a hundred men, to the junction of the Wallowa and Grande Ronde rivers to check any attempt by Joseph's people to escape in that direction. Another small company started toward Fort Lapwai to reinforce the garrison there.

Less than a decade earlier, he had been director of the Freedman's Bureau, charged with finding homes and creating new ways of life for millions of newly liberated blacks. Now he was driving a handful of Indians out of homes they already had to new homes they did not want.

The shrinkage in Howard's importance was not entirely his fault. With the ending of the Civil War, the size of the United States Army had been severely reduced. Even generals were lucky to have jobs. The only battles left were with the Indians, and most of the nation considered Indians a mere bother, noticeable only when the "savages" scored an unexpected success. Acutely sensitive to his already diminished prestige, Howard dreaded being caught the way Custer had been by the Sioux or Canby by the Modocs. Even worse was an explicit warning from his superiors that the moving of Joseph's tiny band was "a very delicate and important" action and he should act only as directed by Agent John Monteith. That!—for a onetime commander of the entire Army of the Tennessee. But at least he could manipulate Monteith however he wished.

Scars left by his failure with the Freedmen's Bureau went deeper. Perhaps no man could have succeeded; the bureau was a constant reminder to the nation of a moral obligation to the former slaves that it did not want, and so the nation destroyed the bureau. Howard's mismanagement, through timidity and mistaken snap judgments rather than dishonesty, had made the destruction easier. He did not fare well when congressional investigators descended on the organization.

The struggle cost him dearly in dollars—he regarded debt with horror—and in self-esteem.[23]

Then there was the commission that had visited Joseph's people in November 1876. It had been his idea. And it had failed in its elaborately orchestrated effort to move Joseph onto the reservation. Now he was faced with the prospect of using force—delicately—to overcome his earlier shortcomings. This time things had to go right.[24]

On May 2 he was at Lapwai, getting ready for the council with the non-treaty chiefs. He helped Monteith prepare the necessary written request for military assistance. A large hospital tent for sheltering the participants, its side flaps rolled up to admit air, was erected at the south end of the fort's parade ground, close to both the headquarters office and the duplex that housed the Perry and FitzGerald families. Again Howard was billeted with the Perrys.

Joseph and Ollokot, who had arrived deliberately late at preceding councils with governmental figures, were on time for and anxious about this one. On the evening of May 2, they and their entourage camped beside Lapwai Creek above (south of) the fort and there made ready for a grand entrance the following morning. They approached single file on their variegated horses, fifty or so warriors in front and behind them the wives and children of some of them. (Other noncombatants, protected by a small guard, had remained on the Grande Ronde, a few miles above its junction with the Snake.) Nearly everyone's face was painted red. The men's hair was tightly braided and tied up with showy strings. The women, riding astride, wore bright skirts and blankets. They all sang as they circled the parade ground. The song, Howard wrote four years later, "was shrill and searching; sad, like a wail, and yet defiant in its close." Emily FitzGerald, writing only hours after the happening and feeling no need to romanticize, declared, "They circled the post three times, cupping their mouths with their hands, making the sound of Wah-Wah-Wah. When they finally stopped at the gate, they stacked their arms before entering the post. At one time during the Council ... one young brave got very excited in his gestures. As he raised his arms in emphasis, a long sharp knife fell to the ground. (They were to enter the Council unarmed.) Well, it did not make us feel any more comfortable, and we felt less so when we heard the command whispered among the officers to send out and 'double the guard.'" The whites, too, were supposed to be unarmed.

Tension. Thinking of her husband and two small children, Emily added about the Indians, "Oh, how I hate them. I wish they could be exterminated, but without bloodshed among our poor soldiers." Well, she was close by; the relatives she shocked back in Pennsylvania were far away.[25]

Little was accomplished the first day. Lingering snow in the mountains—higher mountains than Joseph had crossed—delayed the delegations from the other bands. When they did gather and Howard spoke of directives coming from Washington that all must obey, old Toohoolhoolzote challenged him aggressively. "I'd like to know who Washington is. Is he a chief, or a common man, or a house, or a place? Leave Mr. Washington, that is if he is a man, alone. He has no sense. He does not know anything about our country. He never was here.... You are a chief, Howard, and I am elected by the Nez Perces to speak for them and do the best I can for our people. Let us settle the matter between you and me."

For awhile he talked about the devotion of his people to the land. The challenge in his manner—Howard called him a cross-grained growler—led the general to adjourn the meeting (it was a Friday) to the following Monday. Howard used the intervening time to rush messengers to his reinforcing troops. The two companies high upon the Grande Ronde River should hurry down to its mouth. Those destined for Fort Lapwai should quicken their pace. The aim was to have overwhelming numbers on hand in case the threat inherent in Toohoolhoolzote's manner resulted in an uprising.

Emily FitzGerald watched him curiously. "We can all see that General Howard is very anxious ... as his orders are to have all the Non-Treaty Indians in the Department on reservations by fall.... [He] is promenading the porch quoting scriptures. Indeed, I think he is really good [referring probably to his morals], but he is awfully queer about it."[26]

When the council resumed, Toohoolhoolzote had as many objections as ever. The earth was his mother and must not be injured by plows or hoes. It was not to be separated from the Indians whom it nurtured. It could not be divided in pieces and sold, or marked off as a prison—a reservation—for people whose roots lay elsewhere.

Howard grew exasperated. "You do not propose to comply with the orders of the government?"

"You are trifling with the laws of the earth."

"Do the Indians want me to put them on the reservations by force?"

"I will not go."

There was scant hope of coming to terms with the rest of the chiefs if the cross-grained growler kept the stage with that kind of talk. Howard himself, so he wrote later, seized the chief by one arm. Captain Perry took the other. While treaty and nontreaty Indians alike watched in stunned silence, they hustled him, unresisting, across the parade ground to the guardhouse and unceremoniously locked him up.[27]

* * *

As the Indians put it, Howard had showed the rifle. They would not continue pressing their wishes without Toohoolhoolzote, but they could not liberate him without a battle. It seemed, indeed, that the one-armed general, dressed in gold braid with medals on his chest, was trying to provoke a fight—one that would engulf the women and children sitting patiently around the edges of the tent. Meanwhile, they had learned from tribal runners of the approach of more troops—troops who by then were nearing the winter village where the old people and many women and children of Joseph's band were waiting to hear the results of the talking. The people in the winter village would be seized instantly if fighting exploded at Lapwai.

The chiefs caved in. According to Howard's account, they did it with good grace, riding with the general and a small party of soldiers across the reservation to pick out lands where their people could settle. After some hesitation, Joseph joined White Bird in choosing land near the South Fork, close to Looking Glass's home.[28]

When they were back at the fort, Howard gave them their marching orders. Joseph, White Bird, and Toohoolhoolzote, whom Howard had released after five days in the guardhouse, were each allowed thirty days in which to make the move. Husishusis Kute and Hahtalekin, who had the easiest, but longest, routes to follow, were given thirty-five days. If the time limits were not heeded, the general warned, troops would be sent after the laggards.

Again, according to Howard, there were no serious objections. Joseph did say, mildly, that crossing his band's livestock over the Snake, which was roaring high with snowmelt, might take up all the time allowed, but he did not make an issue of the point.[29]

With that, the brothers and their followers packed up, returned to age-old homes full of memories, looked again at long vistas holding precious secret places, and prepared to move away with as much order and as few losses as they could.

Watching them ride slowly away, Emily FitzGerald let slip a bit of ambivalence. She had learned to identify Ollokot among the many other Indians. He was even more troublesome than was Joseph, she thought. But she felt a tug: "He is a splendidly horrible looking Indian, over six feet and straight as an arrow."[30]

· 18 ·

BLOOD FOR BLOOD

The heart of the band's winter livestock range was the lower section of Imnaha Canyon. You can look at much of it from a breathtaking viewpoint near Buckhorn Spring, 5,300 feet above sea level on the canyon's edge. From there to the canyon's bottom, four thousand feet away, the slope of the almost treeless land is, in its steepness, like the line drawn by a stooping hawk. The earth line, though, is not smooth. Promontories jut here and there. Small stream channels twist abruptly around or through occasional grassy bench lands. Down at the river there are meadows and cottonwood trees. Today there is no sound way of estimating how many grazing animals once found winter feed in the rumpled area.

Beyond the river to the east, as you can tell from above, are several sharp-backed ridges. These ridges mark the roughly parallel courses of a pair of the Imnaha's tributaries, Lightning Creek and Cow Creek. A stock trail follows the river past the mouths of the tributaries and then strikes north a ways before bending sharply east to dimly perceived gaps. Beyond the gaps is a Snake River ford later named Dug Bar. Dug Bar was one of the few places in Hell's Canyon where the Indians could cross the ever-dangerous stream.

Joseph's Nimipus had another grazing area some twenty-five mountainous miles north of the Imnaha's mouth. This one sprawled across the interlocking canyons where the Grande Ronde River, having just picked up north-flowing Joseph Creek, also penetrates to the Snake. The sparkling creek was named by whites for all the Josephs—old Chief Tuekakas; his elder son, Hin-mah-too-yah-lat-kekht, generally called Young Joseph; and Ollokot. There's a complication, however. After the death of the father, the older son was sometimes called Old Joseph, and his younger brother was then known as Young Joseph.[1] This account will dodge the issue by always referring to Hin-mah-too-yah-lat-kekht as Young Joseph and to his brother, who so closely resembled him, as Ollokot. But the creek was named for all three.

During the Joseph years, a winter village of mat-covered long houses and tipis stood near the point where the creek ran into the Grande Ronde. Many old people, women, and children gathered there in May 1877 to await the brothers' return from their conversations with the one-armed American general, Oliver O. Howard. While waiting, they were shocked by the arrival of a hundred white cavalrymen, equipped with a high-wheeled, many-barrelled, rapid-fire cannon known to whites as a Gatling gun. To reach the mouth of the Grande Ronde, the troops had ridden through very bad weather and across notably rough terrain. The movement had been part of General Howard's strategy of surrounding the Lapwai area with soldiers who were prepared to attack immediately if his conference with the nontreaty chiefs resulted in an outbreak of violence.[2] Sensing the purpose, the villagers had sent a messenger to the brothers, warning them of the cavalry's arrival in a difficult area that had never before been penetrated by a white army unit. The surprise undoubtedly helped convince the nontreaty chiefs at Lapwai that capitulation was their only recourse.

The troops had withdrawn before Joseph and Ollokot reached the village with their sorrowful message of defeat. The memory of the soldiers stayed, however, and kept the people quiet when they heard Howard's ultimatum—thirty days to move into new homes beside the South Fork of the Clearwater. Rage there was, but mostly they felt helpless, betrayed by the whites whom they had considered friends ever since their ancestors' meetings with Lewis and Clark three-quarters of a century before. Years later, during an address he made to a distinguished audience in the east, Joseph used vivid images to explain his band's predicament: "I learned ... we were like deer. They [the whites] were like grizzly bears. We had a small country. Their country was large. We were contented to let things remain as the Great Spirit Chief made them. They were not; and would change the rivers and mountains if they did not suit them."[3]

Thirty days—actually the time limit was not as severe as it is sometimes made to seem. Spring had been cold and wet. The livestock, which even in good years did not drift up to the high Wallowa Valley until well into July, had hung up in the low country, grazing the canyon bottoms and sheltering draws where new grass first appeared. Probably the most difficult animals to move were the horses and cattle in the lower Grande Ronde region. They had to be pushed up steep trails and over the divide that separates the Grande Ronde from the lower Imnaha. There they were gathered into bunches with the Imnaha animals and started toward Snake River and the ford at Dug Bar.

Meanwhile the women, long practiced in moving the mobile villages, struck the tipis and prepared family belongings for loading onto packhorses. It is said that among the baggage were iron-lidded kettles holding the metallic coins and gold dust the Indians had been paid over the years for their horses and for odd jobs they had done on ranches belonging to white settlers. The objects the packers couldn't carry were stored in carefully hidden caches, for Monteith had promised that he or whoever else served as agent for the Nez Perce tribe would give the band members permits for returning to the Imnaha on occasional hunting and fishing trips. Stored articles could be retrieved then.[4]

The relatively smooth going over trails they and their ancestors had used for ages ended at the river. The Snake was roaring with snowmelt. Here was the perilous part of their journey. Here, as they stared at the swift, muddy water, latticed with churning waves, they felt their anger grow. The white general with his hard eyes above his bushy beard! Why couldn't he have let them wait until fall when the water would have been low and the crossing easy?

They did not let their dismay cripple them. The herders in charge of the horses divided the animals into small bunches. Then, screeching wildly, they pressed them at a dead run toward a place where the river bank sloped gently toward the river. The force with which the horses hit the water and the excitement generated by the tremendous splashing carried them far out into the current, where they were less likely to try to turn back. The current at that stretch of the river, moreover, slanted toward the opposite (eastern) shore. Success, then, depended on simply keeping the swimming animals moving forward, only their heads showing above the roiling flood. Yelling, blanket-waving riders on the down sides and behind each bunch did just that. Some young colts were lost, but most of the animals—probably as many as a thousand—climbed out, dripping and snorting, about a mile farther down the stream than the point where they had entered.

The cattle proved less amenable. They balked when confronted by the water. After being crowded in, many of them fell to milling with fright in midcurrent. Scores, perhaps hundreds, were swept irretrievably downstream. Certainly, few calves reached the landing place on the opposite shore. As events developed, however, the loss made little difference.[5]

During the turmoil, the baggage was taken from the packhorses, which were driven across the flood with the loose animals. The bundles, all packed so they would be buoyant, were rearranged in several piles and lashed tightly inside tipi hides. These were wrestled into the water and towed, floating, across the river by horsemen and women. People who for one reason or another did not wish to ride across the spate on horseback were transported by clinging to the lashings of the improvised rafts. Among them was Joseph's pregnant wife nearing her time. Fortunately for her, the crossing took only two days.

From the Snake the people moved with their herds north and then east across the high plateaus of Toohoolhoolzote's country. Just before reaching the Salmon River, which they also had to cross, they dropped off such cattle as they still had in greening meadows, for they knew the plains toward which they were moving would be overcrowded with livestock. The Salmon behind them, they continued east up a rough gorge fittingly called Rocky Canyon. This canyon lifted them to the lower (southern) part of a broad, two hundred thousand acre flatland called Camas Prairie, a name borne by several other big, root-providing plains in Idaho and western Montana. (As an aid to visualizing: This Camas Prairie, along with Toohoolhoolzote's country, now called Duomecq Plain, and the Wallowa are essentially one huge wrinkled tableland, deeply incised by the Salmon and Snake River system.)

An unusual rock formation at the head of Rocky Canyon gave a name, Tepahlewan (Split Rocks) to the adjacent section of Camas Prairie. From there east and north the land was mostly rolling and open. The stretch, roamed primarily by White Bird's band, had been opened to white settlement by the 1863 treaty—a treaty not recognized as legal by Chief White Bird. Settlers were edging in and forming tiny clusters of houses and barns, dignified by such names as Cottonwood, Grangeville, and Mount Idaho. More whites were sprinkled along the Salmon River, to the south. All of them were far enough from Tepahlewan that Joseph's people did not anticipate seeing many of the intruders. What they were looking forward to was meeting with the other nontreaty bands in a last nostalgic get-together.

Tepahlewan, which lay only a few miles southwest of the reservation's boundary, had long been a traditional meeting place for bands who were gathering camas roots. Feasts, horse races, gambling games, dances to the throb of drums—all the enjoyments Agent Monteith did not like were part of the rendezvous. This would be the last time. So they hurried, arriving on June 2, two weeks ahead of Howard's deadline. The time frame had not been unreasonable, after all. What hurt was their bitter awareness that they would soon lose their freedom to wander as they chose.[6]

White Bird, Toohoolhoolzote, Looking Glass, and Red Owl's (Koolkool Snehee) bands were already on hand when Joseph's group arrived. So were representatives from the Palouse units led by Husishusis Kute and Hahtelakin. Even some treaty Indians from the reservation had shown up for the fun. Altogether some six hundred people, close to two-thirds of them women and children, were on hand with thousands of livestock. Fun, yes. But there were sudden pauses when the people fell to thinking of their wrongs, of the twenty-eight or more Nez Perces killed by the whites since 1863, of the thief treaty, of conflicts over grazing and root grounds. Every night there was war talk. But always the chiefs, even Looking Glass, the most famous warrior among them, warned that armed resistance was hopeless.

As custom decreed, Joseph's pregnant wife and her friends erected a small birth tipi apart from their group's dwellings. All males, even the prospective father, were taboo. To make use of his time, the chief, his oldest daughter, his brother, his brother's wife, and a few more men went back across the Salmon to their cattle, to butcher enough meat to tide the families over while they were establishing new homes on the reservation.[7]

As they were riding back up Rocky Canyon, early on the morning of June 15, the day of the ultimatum, driving twelve laden packhorses ahead of them, Two Moons galloped from the camp with devastating information. Two days before, the hunter-warriors of White Bird's band had decided to hold a grand parade. Its basic structure was for the participants to ride in a circle in front of the tipis, waving their weapons and boasting of their exploits. It was an inflammatory spectacle and might not have been held if Looking Glass, an advocate of peace, had not gone home with most of his people and if Joseph and Ollokot had not been absent. But nobody restrained the boasters, and soon tempers began to rise.

The rear of such a parade was a place of honor. After a battle or a horse-stealing raid, brave men rode there to watch for pursuers. On this occasion the place was usurped by two young cousins of White Bird's band, Wahlitits and Sarpsis Ilppilp, riding double on a single horse. Wahlitits in particular was known for his athletic prowess, good looks, and way with young girls, though he was already married. The sight of them showing off annoyed some of the elder people among the spectators. One shouted that Wahlitits had no right riding in a place of honor. Had he not failed to avenge the murder of his father, Eagle Blanket, by a white man named Larry Ott?[8]

Angered, Wahlitits found a bottle he had secreted in his tipi, took a swallow, and passed it to his cousin. Probably they had been drinking earlier: Why else, except from alcoholic smartaleckness, ride double in a parade? Now they brooded. Wahlitits had not followed the Indian custom of drawing blood for blood because, as was noted earlier, his father had asked him not to lest it start a war. But now … he'd show the mockers. Enlisting the services of a young cousin of theirs named Swan Necklace, he and Sarpsis Ilppilp painted their faces and rode down White Bird hill to the Salmon River, seeking Larry Ott. They did not find him, but hate and momentum carried them up the river for another twelve miles or so, past the store and sprinkling of white farms in the cove where Slate Creek entered the main stream, and on to John Day Creek, seeking other quarry. Vengeance, any Indian would have agreed, did not have to be confined to the perpetrator of a wrong; even remote associates could be made to pay. By the time they returned to Tepahlewan the next morning, they were riding new horses and brandishing new weapons. They had killed four settlers against whom White Bird's people held grudges and had wounded a fifth.[9]

A warrior named Big Dawn leaped onto one of the stolen horses, seized a plundered gun, and rode through the camp, yelling, "Now the soldiers will be after us! Prepare for war!"

Intense excitement caught up the younger men. Reputations could be achieved in any battle against any of the enemy populace. Plenty of prey lived not far from Tepahlewan, both in the curling bottomlands of the Salmon River and along the northern and eastern edges of Camas Prairie. Making a great show of coloring their faces and attaching their secret medicine bundles to some part of their bodies, seventeen braves joined Wahlitits and his companions and stormed off to continue the bloody work. With the exception of one member of Joseph's group, all the raiders belonged to White Bird's band.[10]

Behind them they left a swirl of confusion. Those wild young men! Soldiers surely would come now. Seeking to distance themselves from the peacebreakers, the treaty Indians who had come up from Lapwai to visit friends at the rendezvous hurried back to the reservation. During an agitated council, the chiefs of the remaining people decided to try a flimsy expedient. The next day, June 15, was the deadline Howard had set for their moving onto the

Clearwater lands Joseph and White Bird had already agreed, during their exploratory ride with the general, to accept as new homes for their people. They should start now. Arriving a day ahead of time would show their good intentions. Furthermore, the highly respected chief, Looking Glass, already lived close to the area in question. Although he had refused to sign the 1863 treaty, he had often spoken strongly for peace and might vouch for the other nontreaty Indians when Howard appeared, demanding explanations for the sudden bloodshed.[11]

Criers galloped among the tipis, bawling for the occupants to gather their horses, pack up, and leave this accursed spot. They were to reassemble on the other side of the plain at a cave called Sapachesap, where a group of Nez Perces had obliterated a Bannock war party many years before. Besides being close to Looking Glass's home on the South Fork of the Clearwater, Sapach-esap was a shrine of sorts and might lend steadiness to the frightened people.

Steadiness was needed. Some of the raiders who had started earlier for the Salmon had swept back during the night onto the Camas Prairie. Other people from the bands at Tepahlewan may have joined them. Whatever their identities, the renegades found easy targets. One was a wagon that turned out to be loaded with whiskey. Inflamed by it, the braves continued their ram-page, downing several terrified whites. They wounded, captured, and repeat-edly raped—a common form of dominance and revenge—at least one white woman before she was able to escape.[12]

Only a few tipis, all belonging to members of the Wallowa band, were standing when Joseph, Ollokot, and Two Moons rode into what was left of the Tepahlewan camp on the morning of June 15. It was small consolation to the chief to realize, as he passed the birthing shelter, that he had just become the father of another daughter. With Ollokot he moved from one household to the next, picking up the latest rumors, sounding out the occupants' feel-ings, and trying to decide what to do next.

Some of his followers urged him to go straightway to the fort and explain that only one member of their band had been involved in the outbreak. But during the talking, several Indians came riding back along the Sapachesap trail. They had been sent by one of the other chiefs to watch Joseph's and Ollokot's movements. The episode hurt Joseph. Were his loyalties that sus-pect? The dismay drove him to his choice. What, he demanded of his follow-ers, would the band gain by surrendering separately? All the chiefs whose people had been at Tepahlewan would be held equally guilty for the murders. Tomorrow, after he had seen his wife and baby and after the people who had been waiting for him had gathered their horses, they would pack up and go to Sapachesap, to share with the others whatever was coming.[13]

That night several relatives crowded into Joseph's tipi, with the chief, his wife, and their children. One of the visitors was Yellow Wolf, a second cousin of Joseph. (Yellow Wolf's mother and Joseph's mother were first cousins.) Twenty-one years old and already a celebrated horseman, Yellow Wolf considered himself a guard for the band's head chief. Toward midnight he heard horses' feet and what he was sure was a white man's voice. Rifles banged and bullets whistled through the shelter, luckily hitting no one. Yellow Wolf grabbed a rifle lying beside him, rushed outside, shot, and also hit nothing. But the episode showed the people that Joseph's decision was right. In the settlers' eyes all Indians were now enemies. It was wiser to avoid them and make common cause with the other bands in dealing with the soldiers.[14]

Early the next morning, June 16, the little group set out across Camas Prairie toward the new rendezvous. They did not reach the site. Although Looking Glass and his associated chief, Red Owl, had left Tepahlewan well before the first killings, they had soon discovered through the Indian grapevine something of what had happened. When White Bird and Toohoolhoolzote's bands had showed up, seeking advice and support, Looking Glass and Red Owl rebuffed them, unwilling to be swept into any conflict that developed.[15]

The rejection caused a near panic among the outcasts. However unrealistic their dependence on Looking Glass's favor had been, it had at least given them a hope to cling to during their crossing of the naked plain. Fear, disappointment, and uncertainty wracked an emergency council called by the chiefs. Like most American Indians, they were prey to their own mercurial emotions. Seldom guiding themselves by long-range considerations, whole villages were given to responding, under stress, as erratically as a flock of quail startled by a falcon. Hunt for cover—and then wait to see what happened before moving again.

At their council, the rebuffed chiefs decided to move with their several hundred people to the site of White Bird's principal village, located on a fairly broad bottomland in White Bird Canyon, a couple of miles from the creek's entry into the Salmon River. The place was snug and not easily approached. If soldiers came at them down the long hill that dropped from Camas Prairie toward the Salmon—well, they'd try to read the newcomers' attitudes and improvise accordingly.[16]

Disliking the decision, some members of Joseph's band who had gone with White Bird and Toohoolhoolzote to Sapachesap slipped onto the reservation, hoping to disappear among Looking Glass's people. The rest, swayed by the oratory of their chiefs, packed up and, late in the afternoon of June 16, headed south and west across the prairie. Along the way they met Joseph's people. When the horses being driven along by the small party were added to the rest, the herd numbered, it is said, twenty-five hundred or more head. White scouts nervously examining the plain for evidence of Indians could not miss seeing so huge a gathering. And Indian scouts, riding far out on the flanks of the migrating group, noticed the unusual number of whites hurrying along the road from Lapwai toward evident refuge in Mount Idaho. Though there were no other contacts, the sightings did nothing to calm either group.

Joseph still hoped that peace might yet be possible. If he and the other chiefs could hold a parley with General Howard before someone fired the irretrievable shot—but there was so much nervousness about. Wrapped in such uncertainties, he and the other fugitives, for that is what they had become, dropped in darkness down the steep hillside toward their last rendezvous with hope.

The Nimipus held different views of a big, tough, quick-tempered white named Arthur Ingraham Chapman, generally called Ad by his pioneer neighbors. Chapman had appeared in the region as a prospector about 1862. He had operated a ferry across the Salmon River for a while and then had switched to ranching on Cottonwood Creek, not far from Sapachesap. There he took to raising horses, using stallions of which he was very proud. He had an Indian wife from whom he learned to speak the Nez Perce language well enough that he later became a government interpreter.

Some Indians hated him, saying he had participated in the vigilante hanging of three of their people. Others complained to Monteith that he was taking their land. By contrast, still others got on well with him, inviting him and his wife to eat with them and pass the night in their tipis. Looking Glass liked him well enough that he sought him out on the afternoon of June 14, told him the Indians were on the warpath, and urged him to spread the alarm.[17]

Putting halters on his stallions, the rancher went at a run to the town of Mount Idaho. It had flourished for a time by dispensing supplies and accommodations to miners who were hurrying from Lewiston to the mines at Florence. More recently, its hotel, two stores, flour mill, and blacksmith shop had been serving the farmers who had settled in the vicinity. A rival town, Grangeville, was slowly taking form three miles to the west; its nucleus was a two-story grange hall standing tall and angular on the undulant plain.

By the time Chapman appeared, refugees were already streaming into both hamlets and were starting to throw up fortifications. At Grangeville the effort consisted mostly of leaning big timbers against the outside walls of the unfinished grange hall and stationing armed men at the second-story windows. Efforts at Mount Idaho were more ambitious—and could be. By noon on June 15, a reported 250 people were jammed into the town. First, they blocked the two streets with wagons and brush to keep mounted, rifle-firing Indians from charging through the town. Then they built a circular stockade, bounded by parallel fences five feet high, and filled the space between the barriers with rocks and sacks of flour from the mill.[18]

Chapman's contribution was to form a company of volunteers whose members promptly elected him captain. A stopgap only. At dawn on June 15, he and the town's leading citizen, Loyal Brown, began sending urgent messages to Captain David Perry, the commanding officer at Fort Lapwai. Indians—help! Not all the messengers reached the fort.[19]

The panic spread to include the settlers whose farms and occasional little stores were strung out along the Salmon River. Their place of refuge was the big cove at the mouth of Slate Creek, eight miles south (upstream) from White Bird Creek. There they dug a trench three feet deep. Into it they thrust a row of logs, upright like pickets. The cracks between the logs were closed by a second row of standing pickets placed snugly behind the first.

A side road, called the Nut Basin Road, led east up Slate Creek to its head and over a timbered divide to the mining camp of Florence. Though Florence's glory was gone, a couple of dozen miners were still poking around the old tunnels and shafts. The refugees at Slate Creek thought the miners should be warned; for one thing, some of the men at Florence might come downstream to help defend the stockade. No white man was willing to risk the twenty-six mile ride, however. So the defenders agreed to put up five dollars each if an Indian woman, a noted gambler named Tulekats Chickchamit, would carry their message through the gathering night.

A choice bit of folklore resulted. Tulekats pushed her horse so hard that when she reached the town and stepped to the ground, the animal dropped dead of exhaustion. According to legend, twenty-five armed men rushed down to Slate Creek. (Actually the number was closer to twelve.) It is also said that the settlers never paid Tulekats, or Tule, as she was commonly known, for her ride.

But in time she was rewarded. Her name, corrupted to Tolo, was given to a forty-acre lake, Tolo Lake, near Tapahlewan.[20]

Punctilious soldier that he was, General O. O. Howard wanted to be at Fort Lapwai on the day he had set for the nontreaty Indians to appear. Furthermore, E. C. Watkins, chief inspector for the Bureau of Indian Affairs, "a large, full, wholesome man"—Howard's words—had arrived in Portland on his way to impose reservation treaties on the wild tribes of the upper Columbia River. That done, he wanted to look at the Nez Perces. And, of course, he was Howard's boss; generals did what officials of the bureau told them to do. Off they went.[21]

The Columbian Indians assembled on command at Fort Simcoe on the Yakima reservation, listened passively to Watkins's harangues, and agreed to settle down. Howard was gratified. Restless Indians might join Joseph as allies, "should he be inclined toward treachery." Notice that he did not mention any other nontreaty chief by name, for in spite of Toohoolhoolzote's defiance at the May council at Fort Lapwai, it was Joseph who he felt he must watch. It was the beginning of a concentration on the Wallowa chief that would eventually becloud all America's understanding of the war that was shaping up and of Joseph's role in it. But more of that as the story progresses.

The travelers arrived at Fort Lapwai on June 14, to be engulfed that evening and the next day by increasingly desperate appeals for help from Mount Idaho. Later Howard would be severely criticized for not responding faster to the messages. But panicked settlers on the ill-defended American frontier had been known to utter loud cries of "Wolf!" when only mirages were visible, and commanders who overreacted risked career-damaging censure. Howard and Perry did send out detachments to check the rumors. Each party ran into fresh Indian and half-breed emissaries (one is said to have been a brother of Looking Glass) carrying new alarms. Each time the investigators scampered with the new arrivals back to Fort Lapwai. There the emissaries were pumped by inefficient interpreters. Once Howard and Perry had put together a reasonably clear picture of the distant situation—and who, not having been there, could say how long this task should have taken?—they acted promptly.

One lieutenant rushed to Lewiston to hire ten packers and thirty pack mules. Another lieutenant hired a special stagecoach at Lewiston and careened 110 miles to the nearest telegraph station, at Walla Walla. Contacting headquarters at Fort Vancouver, he called for reinforcements as Howard had instructed him. Meanwhile Perry ordered his cavalry to make ready to march—49 enlisted men in Company F under Lieutenant Edward Theller and 54 in Company H under Lieutenant Joel Trimble. Counting officers, the total came to 105. Add ten treaty Nez Perces hired as scouts (among them was Joseph's father-in-law, Whisk-tasket) and one interpreter, Joe Rabusco. Howard stayed at the fort with twenty men to keep order on the reservation and to take charge of deploying the reinforcements as they arrived.

Both the fort and the Indian agency three miles downstream seethed with excitement. Rumor had worked almost as well as the Walla Walla telegraph. Electrified Indians and settlers piled in for information and protection. They got in the way of soldiers who were catching and saddling their mounts, donning uniforms, and swooping up knapsacks and rifles. At the best the troopers were not a get-up-and-go bunch. Many had been recruited in eastern cities only a few months earlier and had not received enough drill to be able to handle properly either the horses or their rifles, some of which they hadn't even cleaned. Troops who had been at Lapwai a longer time had been used, according to one diarist, as "clerks, carpenters, blacksmiths, officers servants, etc." They had not drilled either and had rarely been given target practice, for expendable ammunition was limited because of the government's frugality. The horses, too, were untrained and likely to shy fearfully at unexpected sounds, such as rifle discharges.[22]

Perry and his company commanders had pulled this raw force together by twilight, which, during June that far north, came late. Although the day had been fair, rain was falling again. As yet the pack train from Lewiston had not come up; the only food for a hundred-plus men was on the backs of the five mules that had been assigned to the fort. Toward midnight the rain stopped, but the road remained slippery in some places, boggy in others. As the valley narrowed, with wet brush and dripping trees pressing close, Perry sent out scouts to guard against ambush. Nothing happened except a miserable slowing down of the column's pace.

About ten o'clock on the dull gray morning of June 16, they halted hungrily and wearily at Cottonwood, a combination ranch and stage stop the Indians had recently pillaged. They hoped the pack train from Lewiston would catch them there, but it did not, and a little after noon they were riding again, counting on better luck at supper. There was a sunset of sorts as they neared Grangeville. There they stopped, although the assigned destination was Mount Idaho.

The halt came because of the group of citizens, led by Ad Chapman, who clattered out to meet them. Wild hate was palpable in their shouts. Each individual there knew someone who had been brutalized and killed by the Indians.

(How many had died during the attacks? After a first estimate of thirty, Howard scaled his count down to fourteen, whereas Chapman insisted the fatalities numbered twenty-two. Historians of the National Park Service have pinpointed eighteen.) Their scouts had learned during the day that a large body of Indians had moved from Sapachesap down White Bird Hill toward the Salmon River. The volunteers wanted the cavalry to strike the fiends before they reached the river and vanished into the rugged mountains on the other side. Chapman promised twenty-five armed volunteers as additional strength for the attack.

Impressed by the argument, although he knew nothing whatsoever about Chapman, Perry called his officers together. What did they think?

During the discussion, the troopers unsaddled the horses, which had been ridden at least sixty miles in the past twenty-four hours. The men who were designated as cooks passed out hard bread and were heating up a thin soup of red beans when bugles sounded boots and saddles. Perry had decided to advance to the rim of the breaks that dropped into White Bird Creek. From a bivouac site there, he would move at first light against the Indian camp.

Chapman showed up with ten volunteers, fewer than half the number he had promised. Groaning and cursing, the cavalrymen resaddled and remounted. Bodies drooping, they rode from about nine-thirty to two o'clock the next morning. Finally, Chapman gave the signal to halt. Although the men were ordered to stay alert, many fell asleep as soon as they hit the ground. Several horses lay down, too, sprawling among the men. They had barely gotten comfortable, one sergeant recalled later, when "there came from the timber, the shivering howl of a coyote. That cry was an Indian signal, enough to make one's hair stand on end!"[23]

If the coyote cry the sergeant heard a little after two o'clock in the morning of June 17 really was a warning, the Indian village at the bottom of White Bird Hill must have started stirring well before the thin light of dawn began seeping out of the east. Or, more accurately, most of the people stirred. But there had been whiskey in the camp, and some who had indulged stayed dead to the world even after being struck with quirts.

Councils were called, and plans were discussed. Topography made decisions easy. White Bird Creek flowed steep and brushy from east to west before bending southwest to join the Salmon River. Stretched out along this bend were the wide, precipitously bordered bottomlands where Chief White Bird's band pitched their tipis when staying in the vicinity. This day the open places were jammed with people, tents, and animals. How the huge herds of horses were managed in those constricted spaces boggles understanding.

Due north of the village White Bird Hill rose like a big, upended, crumpled swale—a ramp, as it were, leading up to Camas Prairie. The slope was roughly four miles long, almost devoid of trees, and, in most places, steeper than it looked. The west side of the swale was a massive ridge, also treeless, that separated the ramp from the north-flowing Salmon. To the east were ravines and hogbacks. In between, small ridges rose out of the broad, four-mile stretch like welts. There were small washes, flat places, and knobs. Gripped by the panorama, a white man's eyes were likely to skip over the irregularities, but the Indians knew well enough where they were.

The dominant landmarks near the bottom of the hill and close to White Bird's encampment were a pair of stone-crested eminences, locally called buttes. Anyone who looked up through the low, rumpled saddle that connected the buttes could see most of the long slope. Men high up on the slope, however, could not see the village or its inhabitants and could see only some of the grazing herds. Fighters who occupied the tops of the eminences would be well located for enfilading any attackers who risked riding down the ramp.

Insofar as there was a head chief at the meetings that preceded the battle, it was Toohoolhoolzote. The strategy he and the others worked out and announced to the waiting people through criers took full advantage of the landforms. One group of warriors would conceal themselves behind the right-hand butte, another behind the left. More warriors would take positions in ravines and behind knobs on the lower part of the hillside.

No chain of command oversaw the implementing of this plan. Noted warriors pretty much chose their own stations. With them went their usual followers and any other braves who were attracted by their reputations. The biggest group, led by Ollokot, "tall ... on a fine, cream-colored horse" (Yellow Wolf's words) formed behind the right-hand butte. Two Moons, Yellow Wolf, and fourteen others gathered near the base of the left-hand rise. Who was in charge there? Accounts conflict. Another participant in the battle, Three Eagles, told Edward Curtis (name spellings are changed here for the sake of uniformity): "Joseph had charge at one end of the line and Ollokot at the other. I do not know what Toohoolhoolzote was doing." Still others say that Joseph fought in this battle as an ordinary Indian, not as a chief. Normally, he was in charge of the camps, but this was White Bird's village, and that aged chief was probably running affairs there.[24]

Regardless of the abilities of the various chiefs, every warrior would fight as an individual when battle was joined. He would be directed not by an outside command, but by his own sense of what needed doing for the sake of his people and his home and, above all, for the sake of his own prestige.

Weapons were assembled and handed out according to the abilities and experience of the recipients. Proven warriors and buffalo hunters received the few repeating rifles; much would rest on their shoulders. Muskets and pistols went to those who were familiar with their use. Altogether, some fifty men received firearms. The rest, possibly as many as twenty, used their own bows and arrows, war clubs, and knives. Yellow Wolf was among those carrying a bow. Although he was recognized as a fighter, he was only twenty-one, and experience was deemed a greater attribute than either courage or an athletic body.

As the whites neared, the warriors stripped down to their breechclouts— except for two of the precipitators of the war, Wahlitits and Sarpsis Ilppilp, accompanied by a friend. They, or their womenfolk, had made cloaks out of red blankets. The purpose of the blankets was to show their bravery by making targets of themselves; they perhaps hoped their medicine—their guardian spirits—would make them invulnerable, but one could never be sure.

Even when everything was in readiness for battle, the Nez Perces held their fire, clinging to their last hope for peace. To achieve peace, they had to make contact with the white officers. Tensely they watched the first opponents come into view. Most noticeable was Ad Chapman, riding a white horse and wearing a big, broad-brimmed white sombrero. With him were several of his volunteers, a few treaty Nez Perces, an army bugler, and a lieutenant. The soldiers wore blue uniforms.

Now accounts vary again. Yellow Wolf—and others—say that six Nez Perces, one of them carrying a white flag of truce, rode slowly toward the advancing column. On seeing them, Chapman fired twice but missed each time. On the other hand, Three Eagles—and others, including white narrators—do not mention the flag. According to some Indian accounts, their chiefs recognized one of the Nimipus riding with the advance guard, Jonah Hayes, a Christian Nez Perce. For some reason the chiefs believed Jonah was out front because he was charged with making contacts that might lead to a parley. But before he could give a signal, two Indians climbed onto a knoll, curious to see what was developing. Spotting them, Chapman fired twice. And missed. Whereupon, all narrators agree, a skilled warrior with a good rifle made an extraordinary and lucky long shot that dropped the trumpeter. The Indians were well aware that it was his bugle that sounded commands during the noise of battle.[25] At the collapse of the trumpeter, Chapman and the rest of the advance guard whirled their horses back toward the main column.

Perry threw a wavering line across a flat place on the sloping swale and ordered the volunteers—minus Chapman, who had disappeared—to occupy a knoll that overlooked his right flank. Before they could settle in, yowling Indians drove them off, wounding two. From the heights they poured fire on the American flank. Almost simultaneously, other Nez Perces rose out of hiding places in front of and on the left flank of the white line.

The whites never had a chance. They and their horses were exhausted. The Indians' mounts were fresh. The men of one of the army companies dismounted to fire from the ground while horse holders tried to take their frenzied mounts to the rear and hold them there. Most of the men of the other company, totally rattled, tried to shoot from the backs of their plunging animals. All this while the Indian horses were under control. If an Indian wanted to drop to the ground, take careful aim, and fire, he could count on his horse standing quietly beside him until he was ready to remount. If he wanted to hang concealed on one side of his running pony and fire his pistol under its neck, the animal never flinched. The Indians, moreover, were practiced hunters, trained to make every shot count, whereas the ill-disciplined troopers fired wildly, at random.

Perry tried to rally his men, but his second bugler had dropped his instrument in the excitement and was not about to go looking for it. A spare bugle that was supposed to have been brought along could not be found. All the captain could do was shout and gesture, but he could not be heard over the uproar, and the frenzied waving of his hands simply increased the confusion. Soon the force was in panicked retreat. Lieutenant Theller and seven men were wiped out in a single cul-de-sac. Other men dropped here and there from the briefly occupied battlefield to within four miles of Grangeville, where the belated pack train was waiting with food for the victors.

A casualty count listed one officer and thirty-three enlisted men slain, two enlisted men and two volunteers wounded. This is an unusual ratio: Generally one expects far more wounded than dead. The assumption has to be that the triumphant Indians scoured the field and exterminated, with their guns, any of the enemy who still showed signs of life. They did not mutilate or scalp the fallen, which was also unusual. Of the Nez Perces, only two had been shot with guns, painfully but not fatally. That is perhaps the most unusual ratio of all.

The Indians did plunder the dead, as a majority of soldiers of any race and era always seem to do. After Lieutenant Theller's body had been found and temporarily buried (it was later exhumed and shipped to San Francisco for reburial), his widow sent tearful letters to newspapers throughout central and northern Idaho. If Indians brought her husband's watch, rings, or other personal items to any rancher or store to swap, would the traders please buy them and ship them to her. She would pay, of course.

Other booty was of far more interest to the victors. The Indians gathered up sixty-three modern guns, which they turned over to the chiefs for distribution. They added several army horses to their herds. Afterwards they rejoiced—whoops, boasts, drum beats, and, probably, as much drinking as the small supply of whiskey allowed. In their euphoria some of the strutting young warriors, conscious of the coups they had counted, even declared they hoped the whites they had defeated would fetch their friends from the fort and come back for more.

· 19 ·

EVASIONS

The Indian camp awoke the next morning to the torment of its own uncertainties. The Indians had just won the greatest victory the Nez Perces had ever experienced. But in the light of the new day they could not see what path they should follow next. They could not fight forever, yet the Americans probably could. Certainly Howard would try to keep them from reoccupying the homelands they had been on the point of abandoning. But if they offered to surrender, would he let them go onto the reservation as scheduled? Or would he insist on punishing the chiefs by hanging them, as leaders in other Indian wars—Cayuses, Yakimas, Modocs—had been punished. Where did their path lie?

While they were wavering, they were delighted by the appearance of a small band of buffalo hunters returning from an excursion into Montana. The group's leaders were a pair of renowned warriors whose names, translated into English, were Rainbow and Five Wounds. The elder chiefs promptly asked the two to join a council concerning the future.

Much of the discussion revolved around the number of American troops in the vicinity. As far as the Indians knew, General Howard had committed most of the Fort Lapwai garrison to the attack at White Bird Canyon. A third of those men were now dead. The general could probably bring up more from Fort Walla Walla; then, too, there was the contingent guarding the western approaches to the Wallowa country. Those numbers weren't overwhelming, however, and wouldn't be even if several local ranchers joined the soldiers, as

250

Ad Chapman had. There was no reason to suppose they would fight better than yesterday's soldiers had. Some of the victorious Nez Perces wanted to tackle the whites again. But the chiefs were reluctant to risk heavy casualties—none of the fugitive bands could risk that—just for the sake of glory. What they wanted most was some sort of peace so they could settle down to the remaking of their lives. Looked at from that viewpoint, perhaps they should not have won so great a victory. Yet it was hard not to be proud.

Stay proud, Rainbow and Five Wounds said. But avoid risking everything in another great battle. The surrounding geography was well suited for ducking and dodging. If Howard came after them, the Indians could cross the Salmon, which was running high, and hide out in the rough mountains between that river and the Snake. The Americans would have their hands full meeting the challenge of the rough water and the rougher crags. While the white general was fumbling around in country totally strange to him, the bands could recross the Salmon, climb once more to the Camas Prairie, and scoot for the deep canyons where Cottonwood Creek ran into the South Fork of the Clearwater.

A good place, that junction. It lay at the southeastern tip of the reservation. It was close to Looking Glass's territory and to the lands Joseph and White Bird had agreed, with Howard, that they would settle on. If the general wouldn't let them go there now, if he still wanted to punish them, well, there were other good hiding places among the tangled ridges of the Bitterroot Mountains—as far off, if need be, as the country of the Flatheads. Friends on the Nez Perce reservation, impressed by what the nontreaty bands had already accomplished, would probably help them with food and ammunition. The main thing was to stay out of Howard's reach. Frustrate him with hit-and-run attacks. Wear down his soldiers. Such actions might bring on a stalemate that, in turn, would lead to a parley of the sort that came when warriors of one tribe found themselves fighting to a draw with warriors of another. At the parley they could hammer out the terms of a peace.[1]

Today this strategy, as propounded by Rainbow and Five Wounds, seems unrealistic. It ignored history's grim lesson that although the Native Americans had won many battles, they had lost the wars. It overlooked, as was perhaps inevitable, the potentially overwhelming resources of the whites. But it suited the Indians' psychology, which was not attuned to long-range planning and protracted campaigns. And it created a myth by leading Howard into many blunders. In trying to justify himself to his critics, Howard declared he was up against a superb tactician, whom he identified as Chief Joseph. What we need to do here is learn what Howard and his disciples never learned, although the truth has been pointed out, over several years, by various historians. And this is it:

Among the Indians, a man's most fierce loyalties centered on his tipi, his family, his small village, and the homeland from which he drew his spiritual and physical nourishments. The loss of any of those elements, whether by disease, famine, natural disaster, or enemy attack, was to be avoided at all costs. The magic powers of shamans, prophet dances, food taboos, first-feast rituals (the feast, for example, that greeted the annual reappearance of the salmon), personal wayakins, medicine bundles, and warfare were all parts of an elaborate system designed to fend off the death of the individual and, of greater import, the death of the village.

Even vocabulary bespoke the scale of values. Most Indian languages had different words for war—one for battles fought to defend the village, another for aggressive attacks on an enemy people. Honors, called coups, collected during a fight to save one's town, counted higher than honors that came from bravery shown during a raid.[2]

Howard never understood that. He supposed, probably without thinking much about it, that the Indian warriors fought for the same reason his paid soldiers fought: They had agreed, on enlisting, to obey their commanders. No Nez Perce had to obey an order, however, unless he wished to do so. When he did fight, he was fully committed—until he chose to break off the struggle. Few of Howard's men were as intensely motivated.

Each Nez Perce band, like the bands of many other tribes, had two kinds of chiefs, a war chief and a camp chief. The latter kept the village in order while it was moving from one place to another—from village to root grounds and back, for instance—or when it fell under enemy attack. Attack could, of course, precipitate incredible confusions among excitable women, crying children, bewildered elders, and panicked sick people, along with howling dogs and plunging horses. Steadying the people so they could dismantle tipis, gather up goods, pack horses, and take to the trail quickly and in good order depended on a trusted leader's knack at utilizing the ingrained habits of his otherwise volatile charges. Hin-mah-too-yah-lat-kekht—Chief Joseph— filled the role first for the Wallowa band and later for the combined groups. Failing to comprehend this distinction, General Howard, a warrior, tried to make a war chief out of Joseph—a war chief, moreover, of an exalted kind that never existed among the Native Americans. The people Howard addressed did not understand this distinction either, and so before the war was ended, Joseph attained legendary proportions. Actually, the legendary figures were all the nontreaty Indians, warring fiercely and cunningly together against extinction.

Their strategy decided on, the nontreaty Indians moved a short distance up the Salmon to a pronounced bend where the river could be forded without a horse's having to swim—at normal water levels. But in mid-June that year the stream was roaring high, and the combined bands had to spend a full day making hemispherical boats out of buffalo hides stretched over converging ribs of willows.[3] Each boat was piled high with goods and people and towed across the stream by horses. If a shuttle system was used, as seems likely, not many boats were necessary. The crossing completed, the mobile villages moved a short distance up a small tributary called Deer Creek. Finding suitable flats on which to pitch their tipis, they settled down to await the approach of the American army.

Rumors first and then official messages carried by frantic couriers brought word of Perry's disaster to Fort Lapwai. Soldiers listened with darkening memories. On June 21, 1876, almost exactly a year earlier, a combined force of Sioux and Cheyenne Indians had roughed up General Crook on Rosebud Creek in southern Montana. Five days later, on June 26, Colonel George Armstrong Custer had ridden to extinction on the Little Bighorn. Although strenuous winter campaigns were forcing the surrender of some of the participants in the Little Bighorn battle, Sitting Bull was still on the loose in Canada and threatening return. If the Nez Perce outbreak triggered his resolve and if disaffected Indians throughout the Northwest rallied behind the victorious Nimipus, the resultant combination would be hard to handle. Or so the scaremongers chattered.[4]

The Lapwai compound, both the agency and the fort, seethed with panic—"continuous and feverish," to borrow Howard's words. In retrospect he was amused by one false alarm: "ladies seizing rifles and pistols, barricading doors and cellar-ways, stepping into water-pails in dark passages." Emily FitzGerald, however, the wife of the post surgeon, was not amused by the same false alarm. "The long roll sounded, the men were all under arms, and the women and children all gathered into one house, around which there are breastworks.... I start at every unusual sound and feel the strength departing from my knees and elbows…. I wish all the Indians in the country were at the bottom of the Red Sea."[5] The Red Sea—Pharaoh's evil legions had perished there, as Emily knew. She was a Sunday school teacher.

Tremors rolling out from the reservation shook central Idaho and the adjacent parts of Oregon and Washington. Squads of volunteers appeared in the small towns as if by spontaneous combustion. Many came swaggering into Fort Lapwai to the disgust of Howard's officers, who were constitutionally contemptuous of volunteer citizenry. Some were useful, however. Eighty men patrolled the streets of Lewiston every night for a few weeks, stirred to the effort by scare stories in the town newspaper about hundreds of bloodthirsty Spokans and Coeur d'Alenes marching south to join the Nez Perce rebels.

Howard was not as imperturbable as he later pretended. In spite of his deep antipathy toward Catholics, he turned to lean, tough, militant Father Joseph Cataldo, a Jesuit, for help in keeping the Indians of northern Idaho quiet. (Missionary activity in that area rested largely with the Catholics.) With Cataldo went Bill Craig, son of the mountain man who, with his Nez Perce wife, had settled almost half a century earlier on upper Lapwai Creek. Later Howard thanked the pair for their success. But grant some credit to the northern Indians. Joining the beset Nez Perce rebels to give vent to their own dissatisfactions seemed shortsighted to most of them. In fact, some of them actually took care of the ranches of settlers who had bolted at the first breath of trouble.[6]

Howard's most acute concern revolved around military manpower. Immediately on learning of the first rampage along the Salmon, he had summoned reinforcements from all nearby stations—Whipple from his cantonment overlooking the Western approaches to the Wallowa country, others from Fort Walla Walla and from his department headquarters at Fort Vancouver. Then the news of Perry's defeat at White Bird Canyon came in and he sprayed the West with requests for troops—Fort Boise in southwestern Idaho, Fort Harney in eastern Oregon, Fort Klamath near the California border, and more in northern Nevada. Artillery regiments returning from Alaska were intercepted at the mouth of the Columbia; one of these regiments was transferred to a river steamer for the trip to the interior. Colonel Frank Wheaton in far-off Atlanta, Georgia, was ordered to load his infantry aboard a train for a hurry-up trip to garrison the interior Northwest while Howard was bringing the defiant nontreaty Indians to heel.

Part of this frantic gathering of strength was dictated by what the general conceived of as Joseph's probable strategy. (That concept—Joseph, the untutored military genius—was already gathering strength. Emily FitzGerald quickly picked it up while listening to Howard talk and pray while he paced back and

forth across her front porch. "Mr. Joseph," she wrote home, "is the smartest Indian I ever heard of, and does the most daring and impudent things."[7]) Joseph,
Howard believed, might strike south from the Salmon to contact the Shoshonis
and Bannocks. Troops assembling in Boise and marching north were to prevent
that possibility. Or the chief might drive west into the Wallowa; units headed out
of Fort Harney could deal with that situation. If somehow he curled around and
went north, Wheaton would be there—eventually. If he went east toward the
buffalo plains, which seemed to Howard the most logical alternative, the general
himself would confront him.

Underneath the trappings of strategy lay fear. Problems carrying over from
his unsuccessful years in charge of the Freedmen's Bureau had followed him
into the wilds. He simply must not fail now, as Perry had failed at White Bird
Canyon. Superior strength was the answer—an answer that may have been
implanted in him during the Civil War when union generals had failed to budge,
in spite of Lincoln's desperate urgings, until they had built up what they hoped
were insuperable numbers.

On June 22, Howard felt strong enough to move. He had gathered 227 men
at Lapwai, in a single week. Half were cavalrymen. Adding a bit of muscle were
twenty-one volunteers from the town of Walla Walla. Captain Perry, licking his
wounds at Grangeville, could add the survivors of the White Bird battle. More
soldiers were nearing Lewiston. He could even boast of artillery: a refurbished
mountain howitzer and two Gatling guns. At noon he marched, the dozens of
mules of the supply column, "unstable as water ... darting out and in, now
ahead and now behind, to catch a bite of grass; while the bell-mare kept up the
unending ding-dong call."[8]

Shortly after noon on the second day, the force went into camp at B. B. Nor-
ton's abandoned, Indian-gutted stage stop and hotel; later it would grow into the
hamlet of Cottonwood, named for the trees that flourished along the creek.
There at the northern edge of Camas Prairie, the column delayed for a day, waiting for the oncoming reinforcements to catch up. Howard sent out scouts to look
for the renegade Indians. He also conferred with Perry, who rode twelve miles
from Grangeville, uneasily one imagines, to meet his commander for the first
time since the disaster. The captain had no presentiment, of course, that he
would risk yet another drubbing at this wayside stop.

A second layover came two days later, on June 26, at another ranch, this
one located on the southern edge of Camas Prairie, near the drop-off into White
Bird Canyon. A reconnaissance into the hills overlooking the Salmon River
revealed Indians on the far side, evidently waiting for troops to appear. But the

column's main assignment that day was to find and bury Perry's dead troopers who were scattered along the trail and throughout the broad, down-sloping ramp leading toward the main canyon. It was a gruesome task. The corpses had been lying in hot sun for ten days. Coyotes had been at work on some. Digging deep graves in the rocky ground with the tools available was impossible. So was handling the decomposing flesh. Gagging at the stench, workers scooped out a shallow trench beside each body and then rolled it into the cavity with shovels. They finished during a heavy, spirit-dampening rain that turned the hike back up the hill into a muddy, slippery ordeal. The only markers they left behind were the dead men's hats (if those hats could be found), hung on stakes driven into the earth at the head of each resting place.[9]

Making no effort to conceal themselves, a large group of mounted Indians watched from high on the opposite hillside as Howard's troops moved out of the canyon and marched two or three miles upstream beside the Salmon River before going into camp. They saw—some of the chiefs had field glasses—reinforcements come in, both regular troops and citizen volunteers. The arrivals brought Howard's force to four hundred men.

There were puzzles, too. Captain Perry led a small force out of sight along the back trail. A little later Captain Whipple, who had spent several weeks before the war patrolling the Wallowa country, moved off in the same retrograde direction with a large force. Whipple's troops took with them a Gatling gun, recognizable by its high wheels and multiple barrels. Why? Where would such a weapon be needed?

Meanwhile the main body of troops had moved their camp farther up the river to a recognizable ford. Skin boats being beyond their abilities, they requisitioned, from ranches upstream, three rowboats, a rope cable, and a pulley. The idea was to stretch the rope across the stream, attach the boats to the cable by loop slings, and drag the craft across with the pulley. The pulley did not work, however. Oars and muscle power took its place, back and forth, back and forth, until all the personnel and supplies were across.

Some eighty-five nontreaty warriors greeting the opening of the performance with a headlong, show-off charge down the hill on their side of the river, hollering and shooting but, at that distance, hitting no one. Some of the soldiers shot back, also bloodlessly, while James Reuben, Joseph's nephew, who had signed on as a scout for Howard, added some choice expletives in Nez Perce. The performance finished, the warriors disappeared back up the hill, where the women of the combined bands were making ready to move camp once again. At times war could be fun.

The strategy decided on by the Indians' council now went into effect. As soon as scouts reported that Howard was across the river, the entire mass of rebels started north along the high, rugged, timbered ridges that rise between the converging Salmon and Snake rivers. Joseph, as camp chief, moved quietly among the women, children, and occasional men who were doing the packing. For the sake of the animals, he said, loads would have to be lightened. Dig holes. Cache excess quantities of roots and root flour, household utensils, and extra horse equipment. When the troubles were over, they could retrieve what they had abandoned for the sake of everyone's safety.

Joseph's handling of the big, nervous, potentially recalcitrant group—probably the largest crowd of Nez Perces ever to tackle so rough a trail—gives us the measure of the man as a leader. Several bands of individualistic people were involved in the flight. Fear of what the whites might do to them was one glue that held them together. But any family or group of families who believed some other strategy would serve them better was free to choose its own responses. Few did, largely because they desperately needed, during this time of unprecedented upheaval, something in which to trust. That sense of a realizable purpose is what Joseph, the orator, the persuader, gave them. In the opinion of Merrill D. Beal, one of the first trained historians to study the Nez Perce diaspora, Joseph's role was that of "guardian.... He became the symbol of unity, the superlative representative of the cause."[10]

During the march north, the traveling village crossed the trail Joseph's band had followed a month before on its way to the rendezvous at Tapahlewan. In the vicinity of the crossing, the Wallowans had dropped off most of the cattle that had survived the fording of the Snake. Unwilling to be burdened now by the slow-moving animals, they rode straight on, leaving them *en cache* as it were, sacrifices, like the goods they had buried earlier, to their insistence on freedom.

Assured by their scouts that Howard's entire force had struggled deep into the rain-sodden hills—several of his pack animals fell off the trail and rolled with dismayed brayings to the bottom of the precipitous slopes—the Nez Perces dropped sharply down to the Salmon, crossed it again, turned east, and began toiling up the long slopes leading back to the northern part of

Camas Prairie. Their goal now was the junction of Cottonwood Creek and the South Fork of the Clearwater.

They moved warily, worried about the detachments they had seen leave Howard's camp at the first crossing of the Salmon. Soon an advance guard led by Rainbow, Five Wounds, and Two Moons spotted a pair of white civilians who looked and acted like scouts. When the pair fled, the Indians pursued and killed one but failed to overtake the other before he had reached the Cottonwood ranch and stage stop. Part of an army was camped there. With a set of field glasses, one of the Indian leaders looked over the tents and then spotted a Gatling gun partly concealed behind some fence rails. Whipple! This must now be an important base, to be so well defended.

More Indians came up. As they were talking over the situation, they saw ten soldiers, a lieutenant, and the civilian who had escaped them ride out from the ranch. (The officer turned out to be a second lieutenant named Sevier M. Rains.) Obviously, the troops were looking for a sign of the Indians who had chased the two civilians, so it was stupid that they rode so easily into the ambush Rainbow and his warriors quickly prepared. All twelve died— thirteen, if one counts the first scout slain. Well satisfied with the results, the victors dropped back to the main body of Indians.[11]

The chiefs of the amalgamated bands, however, were alarmed. The army camp at Cottonwood was still intact. Messengers would be hurrying to Lapwai, to Grangeville, to Howard's Salmon River army—wherever reinforcements were available. The Indians' position was known now. To avoid being overtaken, they would have to press their unwieldy mass of families, pack animals, and thousands of unladen horses across those naked Camas plains as fast as possible. As protection they would have to send out flankers on all sides, to hold back threats to the mass movement.

New developments near Cottonwood soon showed the wisdom of the Indians' flanking screens. Captain Perry, whom the rebels had watched leave the Salmon crossing almost simultaneously with Whipple, had gone to Fort Lapwai for supplies. He was traveling back along the road toward Cottonwood and Grangeville at the time of Rainbow's attack on Lieutenant Rains. Fearing that Perry's pack train would draw raiders, Whipple went out with his entire contingent to meet him. After arriving at Cottonwood, the two captains put their men to work extending a line of defensive rifle pits around the ranch. While they were at it, a considerable body of warriors attacked them— a feint, actually, to keep attention away from the mobile red village on the plain. After a haphazard exchange of long-range rifle shots, the Indians galloped away. No one from the ranch followed them.

The next day the warriors guarding one flank of the long camp column saw seventeen whites riding down the road leading from Grangeville. Presumably, the newcomers had heard of Lieutenant Rains's debacle and were riding out to investigate. Their motions showed they had seen the stretched-out file of Indians. If the whites joined Whipple's and Perry's forces at the ranch, they would be strong enough to mount a charge that would create havoc among the women and children.

Warned of the danger, Joseph, aided by the aging chief White Bird, turned the noncombatants southward, farther out of range. Simultaneously, a sizable party of warriors raced out to cut the whites, who turned out to be civilian volunteers, away from Cottonwood. The collision came about a mile and a half from the ranch, but only a few hundred yards from the closest rifle pits. Although heavily outnumbered, the volunteers managed to worm into a defensive position amid a scattering of boulders. The fight, another long-range affair, lasted from about ten in the morning until three or four in the afternoon.

The dust and sound of the engagement were within sight and hearing of the detachment at Cottonwood. According to Yellow Wolf, who was with the warriors, the Indians wondered "why the soldiers in their dugout rifle pits didn't come to the fighting." They did not because Captain Perry, who as senior officer had assumed command at the ranch, for a long time gave no order to charge. Later, when being investigated by a court of inquiry on charges of cowardice, he declared his assignment was to get badly needed supplies to Howard and he could not risk any movement that would jeopardize them. The court exonerated him, but it is hard to believe that as he watched the convolutions of the distant warriors, he did not think of the trouncing he had received fewer than three weeks before at White Bird Canyon.

Be that as it may, George Shearer, a civilian who had reached the ranch earlier that morning, finally and successfully dashed to the aid of his fellow civilians. This act inspired Perry, who ordered Whipple to rescue the besieged. Seeing the soldiers racing toward them, the Indians broke off the fight. By then their people had reached lower Cottonwood Creek and were on their way down the canyon past Sapachesap to the South Fork. The cost of the affray to the Nez Perces: two wounded men, one of whom died that night. Up to that point he was the only Nez Perce slain in battle. The cost to the volunteers was higher: five horses, two men killed, three wounded, one of whom died twelve days later, and a further shrinkage of the whites' reputation as fighters.[12]

Howard was three days behind the Nez Perces when he faced his second crossing of the Salmon River. Although his cavalrymen might be able to swim their horses, the infantry and artillerymen would need transport. Accordingly, the general ordered the tearing down of a nearby cabin and the construction of a raft from its timbers. A gang of soldiers hanging onto a rope, which in turn was belayed around a tree, would ease the raft into the current, which at that point was angling toward the opposite shore. As the craft approached that shore, a soldier would leap off the raft with another line and anchor it to another tree. Presto—a ferryboat!

Alas, the current was strong, the raft heavy, and the improvised cable insufficiently strong. The cable snapped, and the raft bucked off downstream with the handful of men who were supposed to anchor the boat to the opposite shore. After a wild ride the men managed to reach Howard's side of the river and hike back to their chagrined commander. The episode produced in the general a strong case of sour grapes. Scout James Reuben had just informed him that the Indians he was chasing had reached the Camas Prairie and were heading toward lower Cottonwood Creek and the South Fork of the Clearwater. So! The army would not lose much time by returning through the mountains to the site of its first crossing. There they would once more press the miners' rowboats into service, after which they would climb White Bird Hill and hurry to Grangeville, where they would reoutfit and continue the pursuit.[13]

On reaching the little hamlet late in the evening of June 8, Howard ran into a clangor of criticism from the frightened citizens—they claimed the rebels had burned several buildings while crossing Camas Prairie—and from journalists who had arrived to report the story of this most recent great Indian war for their papers. The yappings must have been hard to take. Did this gilded veteran of the Civil War know what he was doing? For three weeks he had been outmaneuvered again and again by a rabble of primitive Indians burdened with their wives, children, and massive herds of loose horses. Did he realize that at least forty white soldiers—"our boys"—had perished, whereas only one Indian had been killed? In fact, the Nez Perces were stronger now than they had been only a few days before. Looking Glass!—in the name of all the holies, why had Howard let that happen? And with that Howard received a blast of bad news that really did shake him.

While he had been preparing for the first crossing of the Salmon, he had received from both Fort Lapwai and Mount Idaho, alarming stories about Looking Glass's people, whose village lay close to the confluence of the Middle Fork and South Fork of the Clearwater. The tales said that those reservation Indians were sending recruits and supplies to the fugitive Nimipus. Without investigating the charges—they may have been planted by ne'er-do-well whites looking for plunder if a battle resulted—Howard ordered Captain Whipple to move Looking Glass's entire band to Mount Idaho until the rebels were out of the way.[14] The nontreaty Indians at the Salmon had seen the captain who had been given the assignment march off with two companies of cavalry and a Gatling gun.

Whipple had reached Looking Glass's village early in the morning. A few Indians, seeing the soldiers start down the canyon slope in a long skirmish line, ran out to ask the cause. Surrender? But why?—and then an unnamed volunteer discharged his rifle. The whole hillside thereupon erupted with a crash of guns. The terrified inhabitants, most of whom had been in their tipis unaware of the whites' intrusion, fled in disorder, some into the forest, some across the adjoining stream. A few were killed or wounded. The troops burned several tipis, swooped up some plunder, and drove off a reputed seven hundred horses. But the band remained intact—and enraged. "A hornet's nest," Howard wrote ruefully in a later account.[15]

Looking Glass prepared to sting. He and a neighboring chief, Red Owl, left their devastated villages and moved upstream to a broad, flat alluvial bar formed where Cottonwood Creek ran into the South Fork. There they went into camp with the fugitives who had just come down from Camas Prairie. They easily persuaded Husishusis Kute to follow. Several of Joseph's and Ollokot's people who had slipped away from the Tepahlewan troubles to the safety of the reservation some weeks before now rejoined their friends.

Disgusted with the course of events, forty-three volunteers from four different squads who were loafing around Grangeville decided to combine and do a little unauthorized fighting on their own. After electing Ed McConville of Lewiston as their colonel—Ed had soldiered in the Civil War—they borrowed horses from the bunch Whipple had appropriated from Looking Glass's village and rode north along the left (west) side of the South Fork. They found the camp of the nontreaty coalition and by courier notified Howard, adding that they planned to attack if a good opportunity presented itself. Unfortunately for that ambition, the Indians also found them and attacked first, driving them to the top of a nearby hill the volunteers later named, with reason, Mount Misery. During the night Ollokot, Rainbow, and Five Wounds led a surprise raid that stampeded the white men's horses. The Indians then let the whites sit there and think things over while they grew more and more hungry and thirsty. Eventually a small party sent by Howard did reach them with orders to hang on; the army would be along soon. Howard's force did not show when expected, however, and the whites, increasingly uncomfortable, decided to sneak off their hill, to fight another day. The warriors let them go, thinking, apparently, that there was no use risking unwanted casualties at the hands of people who were no longer in shape to do the refugee camp any harm.[16]

Conjecture now. The embattled Indians had always seen the volunteer units associated with uniformed soldiers. So they thought at first that Howard's troops were somewhere close by. But he had not appeared when the whites clearly needed him. This must mean the army was not nearby. On top of that the Indians were overconfident. Each time they had fought either volunteer units or troops, they had emerged victorious. Now, with the addition of the new bands, they numbered 250 or so warriors. Surely, they were safe, at least for the time being. They could enjoy the hot day after long spells of rain. They'd swim, race horses on a meadow a little distance downstream from the camp, or just loll around their tipis. Many of them also took time to dig caches for holding family treasures, to be retrieved some joyous day after they had won peace by creating a standoff with their evasions and their challenges.

A little before noon, July 11: Howard was not west of the river, as the Nez Perces supposed, but in the rugged, heavily forested country to the east. He was there because his guide, Ad Chapman, knew that the old road from the mining towns of Pierce and Oro Fino to the agricultural and supply towns of Mount Idaho and Grangeville followed that side of the stream, albeit a couple of miles back, to head the frequent ravines that dropped steeply off the flat-topped ridges to the South Fork. The general may have been thinking, too, of a plan he had discussed somewhat superficially with McConville's couriers. He would lead his 400-plus soldiers and 150 or more packers along the road past the camp. As soon as he had gone far enough to escape detection, he would drop into the valley and swing upstream, catching the Nez Perces by surprise. Simultaneously the volunteers would strike downstream. Between them they would grind the rebels to pieces. About time![17]

On he plodded, unaware that the volunteers, having received no courier bearing word of the plan, were even then retreating toward Grangeville. He didn't know, either, exactly where the Indians were camped. He almost passed the place. In fact, the lead elements of his long column did go too far. He was checked by one of his officers who, out of curiosity, happened to ride out onto a protruding rim that gave a long view of the valley floor. There the quarry were, far below, unsuspecting but some distance upstream.

Howard halted the column. After ordering the leading companies and the forward part of the mule train to come back, he moved with his artillery to the viewpoint on the brow. Another blunder. The range was almost too far for his artillery and Gatling guns. The firing accomplished little more than to stir up another hornet's nest of surprised Indians.

Seeking a better position, Howard took the command around the head of a ravine to a big grass flat, bordered on all sides by trees—a fringe along the top of the valley slope; ruffles in the ravines that creased the north and south sides of the meadow; and, more than a mile to the rear, an almost solid wall of evergreen forest. Here and there inside the flat were lone trees and boulders strewn through tall grass that was beginning to head and turn brown.[18]

The army's maneuvering for position took time. The Indians used it to advantage. Their unwavering goal, as usual, was to save the camp with its women and children. Stripping off most of their clothing, an act that was practically a prerequisite for battle, and swinging onto the prized war horses that were always kept close to the tipis, one group of warriors clustered on the south (upstream) side of the village, the direction from which McConville had approached. A larger group raced to the north side, the area from which the cannonballs had come.

Seeing instantly that the hillside to the east was open, fierce old Toohoolhoolzote bawled for followers and lunged his horse up the nearest ravine. It was steep and rocky, but not impassable for the two dozen riders who fell in behind. The riders gained the top just as the first soldiers were emerging onto the flat at a diagonal from where the Indians were. Most of the warriors scattered along the brow of the hill. Their unexpected fire started the enemy milling. Under cover of the confusion, Ollokot, Rainbow, and Five Wounds, who more and more were acting in concert, spurred their horses toward the lead part of the pack train, just then coming into sight. They almost seized it, but there weren't enough of them and they were beaten back after killing two of the packers.

Gradually positions solidified. Dismounted Indians held the brow of the hill and the ravines that bordered the broad flat. Their line was thus shaped like a thin crescent moon. Howard was all but under siege. He sent the cavalry horses and pack animals to the forested hillock at the rear of the flat. He set up his command post in a depression not quite between the tips of the crescent and arranged his troops in a large ellipse, its back curve sparsely occupied. Upwards of four hundred soldiers and about a hundred civilians who were capable of handling guns were involved. Since the Indian camp in the valley was never left unguarded, it is unlikely that many more than a hundred Indians were ever on the firing line at one time. They were, however, cool enough and skillful enough to keep the enemy, most of them untested in battle, hugging the ground behind low, hastily created walls of rock. The Indians, too, extemporized stone shelters.

The lines were far apart, as much as six hundred yards in places. During the long night, there were occasional sorties as a company of soldiers tried to outflank the braves or a war party of Nez Perces sought to break through what they supposed was a weak part of Howard's lines. Thirst became an acute problem for the whites. (The Indian women, slipping and stumbling in the dark, lugged water up the steep hillside to their fighters.) At sunrise the Americans achieved their first success. Backed by howitzer fire, they seized a vital spring. For the most part, though, the fighting was slow and inconclusive, not attuned to Indian concepts of warfare.

Why risk casualties for nothing? Under the increasing heat of the sun, a small group here and another there began to drift down into the valley. The shift was orderly—Howard seems not to have noticed it at first—but the chiefs, meeting under an overhanging rock, understood well enough what was happening. To prevent complete disintegration, they told Joseph, who had been fighting on the lines like any other brave, to prepare the camp for another flight. By rallying the Indians who remained at the top of the slope, the war leaders would hold the troops back until the camp chief signaled that the exodus of about 550 frightened noncombatants was ready.[19]

The frantic packing started too late. About 2 P.M. a company of cavalry, which had come all the way from Fort Klamath in southern Oregon in response to Howard's cry for reinforcements, appeared on the road from Grangeville. The general, who at last had noticed the slackening in the Nez Perce fire, sent a courier racing to the newcomers. Signals were agreed on; a charge was ordered. Under its impact, the last Nez Perces on the line fled headlong. As the howitzers lofted cannonballs into the camp, the Indian women, abandoning their tipis, began climbing onto their saddle animals while the older boys rounded up the loose horses. Knots of warriors braced to cover the disorderly retreat, but what saved the Indians was the river. The whites weren't used to plunging headlong into a stream and floundering across. Most of the infantrymen, halted on the bank, waiting for the cavalrymen to realize the trouble, pick them up, and carry them across. By that time the last Indians had pulled out of the camp, and the whites fell to plundering among the tipis, most of them still standing.

Unopposed, the fugitives streamed up Cottonwood Canyon as if returning to Camas Prairie. That was not their destination, however. As the panic faded, Joseph, White Bird, and the other chiefs restored order and pulled the rebel column together. They had made a nearly disastrous mistake in allowing the white army to come upon them undetected. Sorely hurt, they needed time and space in which to re-form and face again the question, What next?

Only two areas really suited their strategy of evasion. One they had already exploited—the tumbled mountains where the Salmon and Snake rivers converged, with the Wallowa country just beyond. Going back would mean fresh exposure on the Camas Prairie, flanked by Fort Lapwai on one side and the Grangeville volunteers on the other. They had better cling to the tangled ridges east of the Clearwater, toward which they had been traveling when they had made their ill-judged pause. Unfortunately, the trail they wanted to follow into the area headed several miles to the north, close to the Christian Indian settlement of Kamiah. To get there, they would have to circle around the soldiers in their erstwhile camp. Later they would worry about the potentially hostile Indians at Kamiah.

They avoided Howard's troops by moving a short distance up Cottonwood Canyon and then swinging north along a broad, high ridge that paralleled the north-flowing river.[20] Soon they were abreast of, but high above, their abandoned camp. Surely a few of them edged to the rim and looked down with mingled relief and sorrow. The soldiers would not be following for awhile. They were too busy looting the place, even using their ramrods to probe for caches. (Later the whites would take rowboats loaded with beautifully quilled and beaded artifacts downstream for sale at Fort Lapwai and Lewiston.[21]) General Howard was doing nothing to stop them. As far as he was concerned, the Battle of the Clearwater was over—and he had won.

· 20 ·

BLUNDERS

O n reaching, after dark, the regular crossing a little upstream from the Christian Indian settlement of Kamiah, the fugitives discovered that the inhabitants had dragged away all available rowboats.[1] Except for decrying the unfriendliness of the gesture, the nontreaty Indians were undismayed. As soon as daylight came, they began devising substitutes out of hides and long, supple willow branches.

They worked with a rising euphoria. It was dawning on them that during their long battle against superior numbers, they had lost only four warriors dead and six wounded—according to Yellow Wolf, who many years later named each casualty for his amanuensis, L. V. McWhorter. Probably Yellow Wolf was close to being correct. James Reuben, Howard's treaty-Indian scout, also reported four nontreaty Indians killed and "many" wounded. (Howard gave his soldiers more credit; he stated in his final report that they had killed twenty-three Indians and wounded twenty-five.[2]) So perhaps, the chiefs thought, the time had come for them to turn on their adversary and show him there was still enough fight in them to make him think about offering them satisfactory terms.

The setting was right. Beyond the meadows that bordered the eastern shore of the Clearwater, a tangle of dark ridges rose toward the distant Bitterroot Mountains. There were swales among the lower ridges where the Indians could set up camp for their noncombatants and graze their horses, of which they had managed to retain some two-thousand to twenty-five hundred head.

The warriors would then position themselves along a protective line between the noncombatants' camp and the river. There were trees and rocks and bluffs enough to provide cover when the white soldiers attacked, as surely they would.

The Indians were hardly in place, about 3:30 P.M., when Howard's cavalry came pouring in two columns down the slopes toward the ford. Fugitives who still remained on the western shore fled either on the overloaded rafts, by horseback, or by swimming while bullets splashed up little geysers of water around them. Simultaneously the Indians who were concealed on the far side of the river opened fire. The swift response, Howard admitted later, "created a great panic, and disorder. Our men jumped from their horses and ran to the cover of the fences. [Again the range was long.] Little damage resulted, except the shame to us, and a fierce delight to the foe."[3]

The troops withdrew and went into camp. The Nimipus hunkered all night on the line they had manned. Nothing happened. Nothing happened the next day. It was not the kind of warfare the Indians relished. If the whites weren't going to fight, why stay?[4]

Quarrels, of which no clear record survives, disturbed the waiting. Some say that Joseph proposed surrendering. Others speculate that the camp chief wanted to take his followers back across the naked Camas Prairie to the Salmon River–Snake River mountains and make a final stand near the Wallowa country he so dearly loved. The war chiefs rejected that notion as too dangerous, for on the way they'd be flanked by Fort Lapwai on one side and the Grangeville volunteers on the other, to say nothing of the pursuing cavalry. Something had to be done, however. The Indians had lost many supplies during the hasty abandonment of their first Clearwater camp, and with the Americans watching, their fellow tribesmen at Kamiah were not about to help fill the gaps. Replenishment could come only in the Bitterroot Valley, from the Flatheads and from the white settlers over there, settlers who had always been friendly toward Nez Perce buffalo hunters who passed through with hides, furs, and horses to trade. Perhaps moving over there was the best choice, even though it meant exiling themselves from their cherished homelands.[5]

One-armed General Howard, whose scouts had spent the whole of July 14 poking around the vicinity to see what the lay of the land was like, soon learned of the restiveness among the rebels. The channel by which the news reached him probably went like this. Treaty Indians fraternizing with hostiles carried reports of the dissensions to James Reuben. Reuben passed them on to Howard. To them he added a conjecture: the hungry Indians would soon need to abandon their skirmish line and move a dozen or so miles northwest through the hills to Weippe Prairie, famed for its abundance of camas roots. There the women could unearth a new supply while the men hunted. Another trail to Weippe, Prairie Reuben continued, wound through the ridges farther north. If the non-treaty Indians continued as they had started, Howard could trap them. He could send half his army along that alternate trial while the rest followed the hostiles directly. Hit them at Weippe Prairie from two directions. Get them between the hammer and the anvil. Though the same sort of plan had misfired on the Clearwater, the general still liked the concept of a two-pronged attack.[6]

Reuben capped those conjectures with another, tentative but mind-boggling. His informants said they'd heard that Joseph wanted to talk to Howard about surrendering and would send a messenger to the general the following morning. Howard's pulse jumped. If that happened—he still considered Joseph to be head chief—the war would be over.

In his excitement he sent triumphant dispatches to Fort Lapwai for transmission to his superiors at San Francisco and Washington, D.C. He exulted to the Nez Perce agent, John Monteith, and to Inspector E. C. Watkins of the Bureau of Indian Affairs, both of whom had come from Lapwai to the Clearwater as observers. He nodded approval over a happy story by the newspaper correspondent, Thomas Sutherland, who had first joined him in the Salmon River Mountains.[7]

During the night, however (as nearly as we can surmise from such contradictory reports of the bizarre episode as have survived) second thoughts set in. Howard had no assurance that Joseph really would appear, and it would be foolish to let secondhand gossip from an Indian, albeit a Christian one, deprive him of his shining opportunity to set a crushing trap.

He ordered the infantry and McConville's volunteers, who had rejoined him, to prepare to pursue the Indians the moment they started moving toward Weippe Prairie. He himself marched with the cavalry, early in the morning of July 15, for the alternative trail. To hide his intent, he did not go directly down the river to a ferry at an old mining camp he would have to use, but moved up the steep Lapwai trail (today's state highway 64) as if going to the fort for supplies. Safely out of sight, he would cut back to the river.

He was not well under way when things fell apart. The Indians had packed up and were starting toward Weippe Prairie sooner than he—or Reuben—had supposed. They would reach it well ahead of the cavalry and would be in a position to wheel around and perhaps wipe out, undisturbed, the part of the army that was on their heels. He dared not risk such an attack.

Almost concurrently with the disappointment, another courier dashed up with word that a messenger from Joseph had indeed come down to the river to talk of terms. So all might be well after all. Exultant again, Howard hurried with most of the cavalry back to the riverside camp and began exchanging shouts across the water with the mostly naked emissary. Come closer, come closer! But the fellow never did. A rifle cracked and a bullet thudded into the earth between the general and his staff.

The whites thought it might have been an attempt to assassinate Howard. There is no firm evidence that an Indian pulled the trigger, however. The Indian messenger, on his part, may have supposed a bloodthirsty white was trying to disrupt the conference. Anyway, he wheeled around and mooned the general. If he was on horseback, as he almost certainly was, and riding without stirrups, as warriors almost invariably did, this was an acrobatic feat. But he managed it. As one volunteer put it, he turned, aimed, and in joyous derision, slapped "that portion of his anatomy which his leggings did not reach.[8] Then off he galloped. Whether the episode was an authentic prelude to a possible surrender, a ruse to slow down Howard's troops, an attempt to discredit Reuben, or just the antics of a young man seeking notoriety among his fellows is anyone's guess.

Frustrated and angry, Howard called his cavalry back to the scene of the humiliation and started them across the river, determined to pursue the Indians up the trail with his entire force. But then caution took over again. The Lolo Trail beyond Weippe Prairie was reputed to be one of the worst in North America—narrow, precipitous, and clogged with mazes of fallen timber. Before he let the Indians lure him into such a region, he needed to learn more about it—and about the Indians. Did they plan to pause at Weippe Prairie, or would they continue across the Bitterroot Mountains? To learn, he sent out a strong reconnoitering force made up of four cavalry companies; McConville's mounted volunteers, who had rejoined the troops; and several treaty Nez Perce scouts, including James Reuben. In command was Colonel John Mason.

Another farce resulted, although at the time it was not recognized as such. Discovering there were no Indians at Weippe Prairie, Mason pushed his big force carefully ahead. As thick timber closed around him, he sent out five scouts to examine the route. They walked into an ambush manned by eighteen men led by the famed buffalo hunter, Rainbow. One scout died. Two were wounded, one of whom perished later. A fourth, James Reuben, was shot through the right arm.

Rifles and ammunition were confiscated before the surviving scouts were turned loose. If the victors had held their fire until the main body of their pursuers came along, they might have inflicted really serious casualties. But no matter. Howard got the message. As long as determined warriors were hidden in that jungle of rock and trees, the way was not safe, especially for the cavalry. Utterly frustrated, he moved his entire command back across the river and began wondering once again what to do next.[9]

And so it came to pass that eighteen Indians, untutored in military science as taught at West Point, turned back an army of hundreds of American troops.

If nothing else, Howard was persistent. His enemy, burdened by two thousand horses and more than five-hundred noncombatants, could not move rapidly over so laborious a route as the Lolo Trail. (He underestimated the wilderness skills and hardiness of those Nez Perce women.) Besides, he theorized, if no pursuit appeared, the chiefs would let the weary fugitives lapse into their normal habit of moving along at leisurely stages. So the thing for him to do was to return to Lewiston. There he could pick up fresh supplies and some of the new troops that were scheduled to arrive any day. He could then shift the pursuit to the so-called Mullan Road, which crossed the Bitterroot Mountains at Sohon Pass, a few dozen miles north of the Lolo summit. After cutting southeast past Missoula, Montana, into the Bitterroot Valley, he could surprise his quarry by coming at them from an unexpected direction, as he had at the Battle of the Clearwater.[10]

Inspector Watkins of the Bureau of Indian Affairs abetted the plan. Watkins, it will be remembered, had first come to the Northwest with Howard to make treaties with the tribes that were not yet located on reservations. Following an easy success with the Yakimas and other Columbia River Indians, the negotiators had been on their way into northern Idaho to treat with the Spokans and Coeur d'Alenes when the Nez Perce uprising interrupted. In spite of Father Cataldo's peace efforts, significant numbers of those tribes still needed the calming down that an army passing through their territory on the Mullan Road would give them. Or so Watkins thought.

It was not a good thought. Although the Mullan Road had been built for army use just before the Civil War, it had served principally to bring hordes of prospectors, farmers, and land speculators into western Montana, Idaho, and southeastern Washington during the early and mid-1860s. Suppliers in Portland still used it, to an extent, for transporting goods to the Montana goldfields. But they did it with packhorses. In spite of its designation "road," wagons shied away from its mountainous sections. Long neglected, it had been rendered almost impassable by fallen trees, washed-out bridges, and deep bogs.[11] Evidently, Watkins and Howard were not aware of the obstacles. The general even thought he could speed the pace of his infantry by transporting them through the oppressive summer heat in wagons.[12]

Fortunately, Howard did not tangle himself in that mess. Brigands swooped across the northern and eastern sections of Camas Prairie, burned a farmhouse or two, and stole some four hundred horses from outlying ranches and from the Christian Indians on the reservation. Stories told by the nontreaty Indians claimed they stole only sixty-five horses. Later students have suspected that white outlaws committed most of the outrages, knowing the nontreaty Indians would be accused. Be that as it may, rumors that the general was planning to leave the area put the settlers and their delegate to Congress, S. S. Fenn, into such a froth that Howard was ordered to abandon all pursuit until he could provide for the safety of the Camas area.[13]

The general did indulge in a quick trip to Lewiston to meet a river streamer bringing in two companies of Colonel Frank Wheaton's Second Infantry from Georgia and to have a hurried reunion with his wife, who, he had been told, would be on the same boat. She wasn't, but his son, Second Lieutenant Guy Howard, was. In a way, the son's presence increased the father's deep embarrassment. The young man brought with him a bundle of newspapers carrying stories that were sharply critical of General Howard's handling of America's latest Indian war. He was a failure, inept and cowardly, the journals editorialized, and should be replaced.[14]

Nothing appeared to counteract the charges. The papers he saw had not yet received dispatches extolling what the authors called his vigorous activity at the Battle of the Clearwater. And those tales, too, would be turned to mockery when it became known that he had let the supposedly defeated Indians escape once again. But at least, and at last, he was free to develop a new plan for bringing Joseph, whom he still considered to be the principal source of his frustrations, to bay. Colonel Wheaton could march his Second Infantry north and, with Watkins, hold the necessary councils with the Spokans and Coeur d'Alenes. That done, Wheaton could probe the Mullan Road. Other troops that were just then dribbling in, on foot and horseback, from southern Idaho could quiet the settlers by patrolling the Camas Prairie. And Howard could set about justifying himself by pressing ahead along the Lolo Trail—with fifty hired axmen moving in front of him to clear the way.

His farewell words were a reply to his critics. He had accomplished more in Idaho than people thought: "... the Indians had been stopped in their murders, had been resolutely met everywhere, ... and the vast country freed from their terrible presence."[15] In the meantime he received instructions to follow them wherever they went, inside or outside his own Department of the Columbia. Thus, he was within his rights, as far as military protocol went, to send a dispatch that was really a command to Captain Charles C. Rawn at the brand-new army post at Missoula. Although the Indians had a long head start, the dispatch stated, they undoubtedly were traveling slowly and "my guides say that if you could move your forces this way as far as the Lolo fork, which runs into the Bitterroot River, you could prevent their escape [and] their destruction or surrender will be sure."[16]

Well, the general had made similar predictions before.

All this while the nontreaty bands were moving slowly along the Lolo Trail toward the Bitterroot Valley. Thanks to Rainbow's ambushing of Mason's scouts, they were free from harassment, at least for the time being. They had also picked up reinforcements—Hahtalekin and sixteen Palouse warriors. There was, nevertheless, a great deal of unhappiness in the camp. What had their victories brought them? Why did rumors keep circulating that they were going to abandon their original plans and flee instead to the distant land of the buffalo?

In the nightly councils Joseph became spokesman for the dissidents. Rather than foolishly walk away from success, he said, they should lead Howard back through the Salmon River mountains into the profound canyons edging the Wallowa country. Eventually the arguments he used reached one of Howard's aides, a poetic young second lieutenant named Charles Erskine Scott Wood. Wood rendered them in English as follows:

"What are we fighting for? Is it our lives? No. It is this fair land where our fathers are buried. I do not want to take my women among strangers. I do not want to die in a strange land.... We will put our women behind us in these mountains and die in our own land fighting for them. I would rather do that than run I know not where."[17]

Such romanticizing of women—if Joseph's words are correctly rendered—did not sway Looking Glass. The Nez Perces, he insisted, should keep going until they were safely beyond the reach of the antagonistic people of Idaho and their soldiers. He and Rainbow and White Bird and many others knew the advantages of the buffalo country. The people would find plenty to eat over there. They'd make many hides to trade. They'd have the Crow Indians, whom he knew well, for friends. His naivete is almost poignant today:

The nontreaty Indians' quarrel, he insisted, was with the whites of Idaho, whereas the whites of Montana had always been cordial to the Nez Perces. The whites in Montana had a different chief and council (governor and legislature) from those in Idaho. Forget Idaho. As long as the migrants did not show any hostility in Montana, all would be well for them beyond the Bitterroot Mountains, and they could move onto the buffalo plains without interference.[18]

Although Rainbow and Five Wounds were members of Joseph's group, they supported Looking Glass. So did all the other chiefs. Joseph, of course, did not have to abide by their decision; he could have withdrawn from the camp with as many of his followers as chose to join him. (A few families did depart, counting on refuge among the bands at Kamiah.) But he knew he could not reach the Wallowa unaided. The whites were too eager to lay hold of him—and perhaps hang him for the crimes of all the rebels. So he stayed with the migrants. When the settlers heard of Looking Glass's "triumph," they supposed Joseph had been forced into a subordinate position. But Indian culture did not work that way. What forced him to yield to Looking Glass were circumstances. In every other respect he remained what he had been all along, the camp chief, responsible for the well-being of the noncombatants.

The crest of the Bitterroot Mountains forms a long, spectacular, peak-studded, almost impenetrable boundary between Idaho and Montana. The eastern front of the range rises steeply out of the fertile Bitterroot Valley. To the west a series of convoluted ridges slope toward the Columbian Plateau. The Lolo Trail follows a particularly complex uplift that, with its forest-clotted laterals, towers between the Loscha and North Forks of the Clearwater River.

In places the summit ridge is little more than a narrow, crooked hogback dipping from one high knob into a deep saddle and climbing desperately out to the next rise. To avoid this constant dropping down and scrambling up—and to reach openings where there was grass and water for horses—the trail avoided the sway-backed summit and clung as nearly as possible to a level contour along the sides of the hogback and its punctuating knobs. In some places the hillsides were dense with undergrowth. In others wind-blown timber lay crisscrossed like jackstraws on the ragged slopes. Boulders protruded; ravines yawned.

No one knows how long ago the Indians first worked out a way along the ridge. They showed Lewis and Clark the route in 1805—the worst horse path they ever saw, the explorers complained later. Most fur traders avoided it, but when gold became a clarion cry in the northern Rockies in the 1860s, demands arose that in spite of winter's heavy snows, it be turned into a wagon road. In 1866 Congress appropriated fifty thousand dollars for the effort and awarded the contract to Wellington Bird of Mount Pleasant, Iowa. As matters turned out, Bird and his sixty workers made no effort to build the road and failed to do more than clear out and modify parts of the old Indian trace.[19]

The buffalo-hunting Nez Perces were used to the unimproved trail, however, and were unconcerned when neglect, snow, and wind returned the cleared portions of the trail to their original state. The route was hard on loaded horses, however. Over the years the animals lost a lot of blood from falling and slipping over rocks and snags and from scraping their flanks on thorn bushes and tree trunks. Whenever a horse broke a leg or collapsed from exhaustion, it was abandoned, for there was no way to take care of it on that mountainside. Traveling so, the fugitive Nez Perces crossed Lolo Summit on or about July 24, 1877, and started downhill along Lolo Creek toward the Bitterroot. They were in a good mood. Many of them knew, from previous visits, a great deal about the land ahead of them and its friendly inhabitants. The uncertain factor was the numerous whites who had moved into the valley. Would they upset Looking Glass's predictions by siding with the whites in Idaho? Or, as most of the nontreaty Indians wanted to believe, would the Montana whites join the Flatheads in accepting, at least for a time, the dispossessed Nimipus?

The whites. Well, yes, possibilities for trouble did exist. One sore point, as in the case of the Nez Perces, was a reservation. The Flatheads had been promised a large one that embraced much of the lovely Bitterroot Valley. What the Flathead Confederation got (the confederation was a loose composite of Flatheads and some bands of Kutenais, Kalispells, and Pend d'Oreilles, a total of about two thousand souls) was a shrunken block of land north of the valley, up toward Flathead Lake. As with the Nez Perces, many of the confederation chiefs were refusing to lead their bands into the enclosure, and so far the government was not trying to compel them. The restraint may have risen not from kindness but from a fear that angry Indians would ride to the Plains and join the Sioux. Now here came more resistant Indians—victorious Indians, to boot. What effect would that have on the Flathead holdouts? How would the Bitterroot whites respond, under those conditions, to the migrating Nez Perces?

Many white homesteaders lived in the Bitterroot Valley, drawn there by a brisk demand for farm produce emanating from the hungry gold-mining towns of western Montana—Helena, Virginia City, Deer Lodge, Bannack, and the rest. (*Bannack* as a town is spelled with an *a*; the tribal name with an *o*, *Bannock*.) The principal valley settlement was perky little Missoula, located where the Bitterroot River joined the Hell Gate to form the Clark Fork of the Columbia. (Geographers have since eliminated the name Hell Gate; the designation Clark Fork now stretches all the way to the river's source on the western slope of the Continental Divide.) Other hamlets—Stevensville, Corvallis, Hamilton—were scattered along the Bitterroot south of Missoula for fifty miles or so. Checkerboarded among the white homesteads were straggling Indian farms.[20]

Economically, most of the tribesmen were destitute. Competing with better prepared and financed white homesteaders and horse breeders was beyond their power. Now and then dissatisfaction boiled up with a thump of drums and a shrill of war dances. When that happened, the whites frantically armed themselves, threw up stockades, and dashed off appeals for help to the army posts on the eastern side of the Continental Divide. Generally, the fires were cooled by the area's Catholic missionaries working with chiefs who understood the odds against winning relief by armed conflict.

But if the Indians didn't get help with their problems, the whites eventually did. In the spring of 1877, while the nontreaty Nez Perces were doing their best to avoid their reservation, Captain Charles C. Rawn was ordered by his commander at Fort Shaw, Colonel John Gibbon, to take forty-four men across the Continental Divide and build Fort Missoula close to the town of the same name. Rawn, remember, was the officer that General Howard had urged, by special courier, to delay the Nez Perces until he could cross Lolo Summit and strike them mortally from behind.

Constant rains delayed work on the fort. Only a few sheds were up when word swept through the valley that hostile Nez Perces were moving along the Lolo Trail. The settlers reacted as usual. Some fled to their improvised stockades; some formed fire-breathing militia units. The Catholic missionaries and the new agent for the Confederated Flatheads, Peter Ronan, traveled earnestly about, giving peace talks to influential chiefs. The excitement grew so out of hand that Benjamin Potts, governor of Montana Territory, dashed off nervous telegrams to Rutherford B. Hayes, president of the United States, and Hayes's secretary of war, George McCrary. Do something![21]

Such antics had not produced significant results during earlier scares, but, nothing like the Nez Perce invasion had occurred before. On July 21, Colonel

Gibbon was ordered to take to the field. He, too, directed Captain Rawn to hold the hostiles in check until he could reach the scene.[22] It was slow going. Gibbon did not start his long march over the Continental Divide by way of Cadotte Pass until July 28. He had about 150 foot soldiers under him, all he could scrape together from Montana's seriously undermanned posts.

Beset thus by some of the most potent brass in the Northwest, Rawn took thirty-five regulars and a company of strutting volunteers from Missoula southwest across the valley to Lolo Creek. After pushing some miles into the stream's deepening canyon, he found what he considered a likely spot for a barricade. The distance from wall to wall was about four hundred yards. The mountainside to the south—that is, the one facing north—was steep and blanketed with timber. The one to the north—facing south toward most of the year's sunshine—sloped more gently and was spotted by only occasional trees and boulders. The timbered south slope, in addition, was creased, some distance upstream, by a couple of unimpressive gullies.

Later Rawn would be criticized for not building his barricade farther upstream, beyond the ravines. At the time, however, his labors were the valley's most popular show. A sizable body of Indians under the Flatheads' nontreaty chief, Charlot (his Indian name was Little Claw of the Grizzly), arrived to watch what happened. They were observers only, Charlot said, and would stay neutral while trying to keep the situation from spinning out of control. Simultaneously, a hundred or so volunteers poured in from various parts of the valley to aid Rawn, as did Governor Potts with about fifty civilians from the Helena area. Most of the volunteers lent a hand cutting and dragging logs and shoveling earth for the redoubt. None of them knew exactly where General Howard and Colonel Gibbon were on that day of growing tensions.

On July 25 the Nez Perces went into camp a few miles up Lolo Creek from the barricade, which by that time stretched a quarter of a mile across the canyon and was about hip high, pretty good protection for the whites if a firefight broke out. The prospect did not worry Looking Glass. He remained sure that the defenders would let them pass as soon as he explained that the Nez Perces' quarrel was limited to the people of Idaho and the soldiers who supported them. To make the point clear, he rode ahead with White Bird and Joseph to confer with the leaders of the soldiers and white volunteers.[23]

Rawn was stubborn. His orders were to force the Nez Perces to surrender. Gently the chiefs replied that in that case they would have to fight—a shame since all they wanted was to pass in peace through the valley to the buffalo plains.

As they talked, it became evident that the captain did not want to take on a couple of hundred determined and supremely confident warriors who had already beaten stronger forces than his. So he offered a compromise. Whether the Indians guessed his motive—he was trying to forestall a battle until either Howard or Gibbon arrived to help him—can't be said. Anyway he said that if the Nez Perces surrendered their arms and ammunition to him, they could ride past the settlements unchallenged. He suggested that he spoke for the volunteers and Charlot's Flatheads as well.

Strip themselves? Become sitting ducks? Rawn couldn't have believed the Indians would agree, even if he promised to return their arms after they had left the valley. But they did believe that they had at least to pretend to take him seriously. So they politely held another, perhaps two more, conferences with Rawn and his people. Over and over they said they would not fight the valley settlers and would fight the soldiers only if necessary. Meanwhile they went ahead evolving their own strategy.

The volunteers responded as the Indians hoped. Why force a hard and bloody fight the whites told each other, when none was necessary to protect their homes and livestock? The chiefs were right: The Indians' quarrel lay back in Idaho. Governor Potts said there was nothing useful he could do and departed with his men. The valley recruits began dribbling away.

By early morning on July 28 Looking Glass had the warriors ready; Joseph and White Bird had the noncombatants packed up and moving. They filed up one of the gulches that opened a path into the mountain that formed the canyon's south wall. Near the top they swung left—east—along a tributary their scouts had located. When Rawn heard warning yells and looked up, his barricade, ever afterwards called Fort Fizzle, was completely outflanked. The Nimipus' herd of horses, the noncombatants, and the pack strings were farthest up the hill, out of rifle range. A little below them a line of warriors formed a protective screen. In the event, no screen was needed. Here and there a few arms banged away, mere nervous twitches. Rawn ordered a pursuit, but it, too, fizzled, and the Indians entered the heart of the Bitterroot Valley without resistance.

Howard? On July 28 he was still in the Clearwater country. Word reaching the fugitives via the moccasin telegraph suggested that he might stay there. Anyway, they need not worry about him for many days yet. As for Gibbon, who on July 28 was just leaving Fort Shaw on the east side of the Continental Divide, they did not even know of his existence.

Easy going. On learning that the Nez Perces were truly peaceful and, more to the point, carried with them quantities of gold and silver coins, gold dust, currency, and jewelry, some looted but most earned through trade with white settlers in the Clearwater country, the Bitterroot people plied them with food, equipment, ammunition, and whiskey. Outsiders railed against the dealings. The merchants retorted that the Indians would have seized what they wanted, so why get shot out of pride? As for the whiskey, the chiefs kept drunkenness under control. They were as anxious to avoid trouble as the settlers were.

Meanwhile Looking Glass triumphed over a challenge precipitated by Eagle-from-the-Light. The old chief, who was then living in Montana, had carefully distanced himself from the Nez Perces when a war seemed likely. Now, however, he wanted to help his fellow tribesmen and sent messengers to them with what he considered good advice. The shortest way to freedom was straight north through the Flathead reservation to Canada.

Until then the fugitives had not seriously considered Canada as an asylum. They still respected Eagle-from-the-Light, however, even though he had cast his lot among the Flatheads. So a council was called to discuss his advice. White Bird and Toohoolhoolzote spoke in favor of the suggestion. They had heard that Sitting Bull and many of his Sioux followers had found refuge there, and perhaps the white men of Canada would welcome the Nimipus also.

Looking Glass rejected the idea. He didn't trust the Flatheads. They'd been at the barricade with Rawn's soldiers, hadn't they? And their chief, Charlot, had refused to shake hands, saying that the Nez Perces had stained themselves with white blood. Was that true neutrality? The band would be safer if they held to the plan Looking Glass had first suggested: continue to the head of the Bitterroot Valley and then cross the Continental Divide into the land of the Crows. The Crows were their friends and would help them bring order and safety back to their lives. If they wished, they could then go to Canada—or perhaps even back to their old homes. Listening to him, Rainbow and Five Wounds nodded agreement. Just hearing talk of buffalo hunts made their eyes shine.

A close argument. The chiefs looked at Joseph. He did not rise to his feet, as one generally did when addressing the council, but remarked while still seated, "When we were fighting for our own country, there was reason to fight ... but since we have left our country, it matters little where we go." Perhaps the Crows would help, as Looking Glass believed, but for himself, with the Wallowa out of reach, "I have nothing to say. ..."[24]

Looking Glass carried the argument. Easy going, south up that loveliest of valleys, the snow-streaked alpine peaks of the Bitterroot Mountains to the west and the more rounded summits of the Continental Divide to the east. They added to their strength by picking up a few lodges led by a famous hunter, Lean Elk. The whites called him Poker Joe, with reason. His father had been a French voyageur, his mother a Nez Perce. He was small and tough and carried in his head detailed knowledge of the country along the route they planned to follow to the land of the Crows.

Easy going—warm weather, good grass, cold water, short marches. No scouts watched their back trail, no sentinels guarded the camp at night. Too easy. Some of the warriors felt their nerves growing tight. They had bad dreams. A time or two there were reports of whites sighted at a distance. Looking Glass was advised to take more care. He laughed. According to Yellow Wolf, "Looking Glass was against anything not thought of first by himself." They'd left the war behind in Idaho, the chief said with assurance.[25]

They crossed the Continental Divide and chivvied their horses down through thick evergreens to the western edge of a vast open basin called Big Hole. Where Trail Creek, which they had been following, joined Ruby Creek to form the Big Hole River, they found a tranquil meadow that had long served as a resting place for parties traveling to and from the buffalo country. The Indians called it the Place of the Ground Squirrels. There the chiefs outlined a camping pattern for eighty-nine tipis—a loose V, its apex pointing upstream, or south. Between the mobile village and the mountain to the west, the stream coiled past sloughs bristling with willow brush and occasional pines. To the east the valley was bordered by low foothills sloping gently up to a tableland.

It was a good place—lots of lodge-pole pines from which the women could cut slender tipi poles for replacing those abandoned during the flight from the Clearwater battlefield. There were camas roots in the meadows, deer and elk along the edges of the forest. On the evening of August 8, the warriors started a parade of rejoicing, and the camp held its first dance since the war had started. It was good to feel free again.[26]

· 21 ·

BITTER FRUIT

ood Catholic that he was, Colonel John Gibbon decided to pay a call on the
bedridden priest, Anthony Ravalli, who was in charge of St. Mary's Mission,
just outside Stevensville, Montana, in the Bitterroot Valley. In the course of
their conversation, the Jesuit asked how many troops the colonel had.

Gibbon hesitated. Even by adding Rawn's small contingent at Missoula, he
had increased his force's strength to only 146 men and 17 officers. To make matters worse, Chief Charlot had refused to provide him with scouts. The Nez
Perces, the Indian explained, had kept their promise not to fight in the valley, so
he was going to keep his promise of neutrality. Reluctant to let word of the thinness leak out and perhaps reach the enemy, Gibbon told the ailing father a little
white lie. About 200, he said.

Not enough, Ravalli replied anxiously. According to reports reaching him,
the Nez Perce column "contained 260 warriors; they are splendid shots, are well
armed, have plenty of ammunition."[1]

After leaving the mission, Gibbon sent a courier to General Howard, who
was then toiling over the Lolo Trail, with a plea for reinforcements. He did not
wait for the addition, however. Tracks and other signs showed that the Indians
were moving slowly. By loading his infantry into supply wagons rented from
local settlers, he was able to travel, for a ways, twice as fast as his quarry. Even
though he was slowed by the execrable trail over the Continental Divide (today's
Gibbon Pass), he knew he was getting within striking distance. Then he became
too eager to wait.

The assignment of finding out exactly where the Indians were fell to Lieutenant James H. Bradley. Guided by a local rancher, Bradley rode all one night
through the forested mountains. With him were thirty regular cavalrymen and
about the same number of volunteers who had recently attached themselves to
the column, perhaps out of patriotism but more probably out of a lust for Indian
horses and gold dust to be plundered from the battlefield. At dawn they concealed themselves in an opening in the trees while the lieutenant and two enlisted men crept forward to see what they could see. By climbing a tall pine, they
spotted the unguarded camp, took careful note of its layout, and triumphantly
sent the information back to their colonel.

By dark Gibbon's troops had reached the opening where the advance
detachment was concealed. They ate and rested until shortly before midnight.
After ordering that his single noisy, big-wheel, mule-drawn howitzer be brought
up after dawn, the colonel took to the starlit trail with the tense force. As they
neared the village, the officers who were on horseback dismounted to lead their
animals. The troops formed in single file. They moved with such stealth that the
part of the Nez Perce horse herd they encountered scarcely stirred. The Indians,
tired from the celebration of the previous evening, slept soundly. Only an occasional dog barked, as if at a coyote.

Gibbon stretched out a skirmish line the same length as the village below
him—about twelve hundred yards. The reserves were put in place, and whispered orders were passed along the line that at dawn they would ease down the
hill with the utmost quiet. The signal to charge would be a rifle shot.

They crouched, waiting, on the gritty soil, behind a pine that rose here and
there and in the sagebrush, shivering with the mountain cold. As the first touch
of dawn showed the shape of the eastern horizon, a few cooking fires flickered
in the camp. Then a lone rider appeared, heading up the hill to check, apparently, on the horse herd. Time hung suspended, like a drop of water waiting to fall.
Then three or four rifles fired simultaneously at the unsuspecting rider. At that
signal, the whole line crashed with sound.[2]

To the Indians it must have sounded as if the earth had split apart: the
thunder of guns, the furious yells of the charging soldiers, the splintering of
brush, and the splash of water as the attack swept across the creek. The horses
that were tied beside many of the tipis began to plunge and neigh. The dogs
went crazy.

The Indians who woke first, many of them stark naked, seized their rifles
and revolvers and dashed instinctively for the closest cover—the banks of the

creek and the willows in the slough. Perhaps the unthinking burst was a good thing. It threw them against the charging soldiers. There were point-blank shootings, knots of hand-to-hand fighting. The moments of delay counted. But many troopers, unchecked by such encounters, did dash through into the camp proper. More individual battles resulted. Much of the whites' fury was directed at the lodges, any of which might contain snipers. Here and there a soldier rushed into one, clubbing and shooting no matter what the age or sex of the occupants.

Later the claim was made that soldiers did not attack women and children until those supposed noncombatants had first killed several white officers and men. "Then the men shot every Indian they caught sight of—men, women, and children."[3] The justification is not valid. The American officers knew perfectly well—or should have known—they couldn't send a bunch of wired-up troopers against a sleeping camp of hostiles and expect targets to be chosen with care. They knew, or should have known, that the daily dress of Indian men and women was much the same and that a soldier caught in the frenzy of battle wasn't going to pause while deciding which one to shoot. Indians acted that way, too, when making unexpected attacks on their enemies, white or red. And when a camp was overrun and filled with indiscriminate shooting, young boys, women, and elders were going to swoop up whatever guns, knives, or clubs were handy and use them. Such was the ultimate self-defense. Surprise attacks do not produce kinder, gentler wars. Ask the experts in Washington.

What Gibbon evidently had not reckoned on was the injection of these tough, outdoor-hardened Indian noncombatants into the fray. Because of that—because of the desperate and infuriated women, boys, and old men—his neatly placed skirmish line did not hold its form. In addition, sections of thick brush and unexpectedly deep pools of water in the creek created hindrances here and there. Pacing became ragged. In addition, the commanding officer on the left of the advancing line, Lieutenant Bradley, was killed early. Unguided, the movement of his troopers grew aimless. The whites tended to concentrate, leaving both flanks of the village open. Many Nez Perces escaped through the gaps, heading for either the foothills or the brush as their automatic reflexes dictated.

An extraordinary rally ensued. We can't really follow it. Most Indian reminiscences about the battle drift off, naturally enough, into tales of individual struggle, adventure, and sad descriptions of the deaths of friends and family members. But we do know the whites let themselves be diverted. Gibbon had ordered that the camp, especially the tipis, be destroyed. The gathering number of whites in the center of the village chose fire as an instrument. But the tipi covers, some of canvas but many of hide, were wet with dew and slow to ignite. The hides would be particularly resistant. The struggles drew in others, as if destruction was somehow symbolic of victory.

Even though many of the troopers were still tangling with the Indians in the soggy, willow-choked sloughs near the north end of the camp, a partial quiet settled over the central meadow. The staccato bursts of gunfire dwindled. The white officers regarded the groups of warriors who were coming together out toward the foothills as if they were of no concern. Then suddenly the warriors came charging back toward the camp. At the same time Looking Glass and White Bird began yelling at the warriors who were still grappling with the enemy in the brush to turn on the whites in the camp. A crossfire swept the area. Realizing he was in danger of being engulfed, Gibbon ordered a retreat toward a flat-topped promontory reaching out from the lower part of the steep mountainside to the west. Those who gained it heaped up logs and rocks and settled down to hold off the Indians who had been following them fiercely.

Only glimpses of Joseph appear. Early in the melee, he and a few others were seen riding across a sagebrush-covered slope to the west to cut off and drive back into the valley several hundred horses that a party of mounted white volunteers was trying to stampede. Later Two Moons saw the chief on foot, crouched near the creek with his baby in his arms. It was the child, not yet two months old, that had been born at Tepahlewan just before the war began. The chief had no gun; why we do not know. Both his wives and Ollokot's wife had been severely wounded, and he was trying to save the baby. The morning shadows were still stretching long across the meadow.

Ducking from one bit of cover to another, the Indians closed in around Gibbon's refuge. The women who had been fighting went back to the camp. Joseph reappeared; he had found someone, the wounded mother perhaps, to care for the child. Now, with White Bird helping, he prepared to move again. Salvageable tipis were packed, the wounded were searched out and treated, and those who were unable to walk were bundled onto travois. Normally, the Indians did not like to leave their dead on the battlefield, but this time there were too many to be gathered up and removed. The bodies that were out of rifle range and close to the creek were placed at the base of the banks that marked overflow channels of the stream. There the earth was caved in over them. The rest were left where they lay. By the time the sun was overhead, the noncombatants were on their way south while the warriors held the whites at bay on their uncomfortable promontory.

The Indians had one piece of luck when Gibbon's artillerymen appeared on the trail. Seeing what was happening, the whites scrambled to get their howitzer into position and lofted off a couple of harmless shots. Then a charge by the Indians rolled over them, killing one and wounding two, though not so severely that they weren't able to flee with the other survivors. The attackers dismantled the gun and returned proudly to camp with a pack mule loaded with two thousand rounds of ammunition that fitted the rifles of the dead soldiers sprawled grotesquely on the field of combat.[4]

The battle of the promontory settled into a siege marked by occasional potshots, some of them deadly. The immobilized soldiers fried under a hot sun. The wounded, including Colonel Gibbon, suffered torments of thirst. Some hunger was satisfied by the butchering and cooking of one of the officers' horses that had been killed in their midst. Fear gripped the soldiers when the Nez Perces set fire to the surrounding grass, hoping perhaps to storm the stronghold under cover of the thick smoke. Although the blaze soon died, the fear stayed, for the soldiers were running out of ammunition and might not be able to withstand a concerted assault even if it wasn't covered by smoke. But again the typical Indian reluctance to sustain unnecessary casualties took hold, and there was no assault.

As the day waned, some of the Indian fighters left the line and returned to the mostly deserted campsite (it could not be seen from the promontory) to speed up stragglers and guard them as they reined their horses along the trail taken by the main group. The departures continued after dark. Finally, only a few braves, led by Ollokot, kept watch over the huddled and miserable whites. How few the warriors actually were the besieged did not know, though Gibbon did risk sending couriers to Howard and the town of Deer Lodge with pleas for food, medical supplies, and doctors.

In essence, Ollokot's men were guaranteeing the safety of the camp, always their prime concern. Deciding finally that their purpose had been achieved, they sent a last volley crashing across the promontory and galloped off to meet, at dawn, their hurt and bewildered fellows at an assigned rendezvous. The rendezvous spot was only twelve miles away, but the cavalcade had moved slowly. Many were sorely wounded. A few—one was Ollokot's wife—died along the way. Some who could not keep up requested that they be left behind, a seeming ruthlessness common to all Indians in times of emergency.

As the numbness of terror left them, they tried to count their losses. There never was full agreement. Significantly, though, the number of veteran warriors listed—the few warriors who had fought the Sioux on the Plains and the Bannocks in southern Idaho—stayed firm. Twelve killed. Rainbow; Five Wounds; Hahtalekin, leader of the Palouse warriors; Wahlitits and Sarpsis Ilppilp, whose outburst on the Salmon had started the war; and half a dozen more of the same quality were gone. Another eighteen or twenty males had died with them. Joseph's figure of the number of men of fighting age lost to the freedom seekers was thirty-three. The number of women and children? There is no way of knowing. The body count on the field had been uncertain. Like Ollokot's wife, some of the wounded died on the trail, as, most probably, did those who had asked to be left behind. Estimates of the total range from thirty to sixty dead women and children, the bitter fruit of a simple desire to be left alone.[5]

General Howard was just coming off the Lolo Trail when Gibbon's appeal for reinforcements reached him. Leaving his infantry plodding behind, he hurried south up the Bitterroot Valley with two-hundred cavalrymen. When the closing in of the mountains slowed the group, he put a chosen cadre of twenty-five or so men on the command's best horses, added seventeen Bannock Indian scouts, and spurred ahead as swiftly as the rough trail allowed. Another messenger from Gibbon carrying a desperate appeal for medical help somehow missed him, but fortunately contacted the main body of the cavalry. With the following group rode two doctors, one of them Emily FitzGerald's husband, Jenkins FitzGerald, or John, as she called him. Accompanied by a special escort, they joined the race to the battlefield. By midday on August 10 both Howard's party and theirs had arrived.

Shocked, FitzGerald wrote his wife, "We found a horrible state of affairs. There were 39 wounded without Surgeons or dressings, and many of them suffering intensely." The official account of the casualties came to twenty-nine killed, six of them volunteers, and forty wounded, four of them volunteers.[6]

A question arises. There is no mention of any white finding a still-breathing Nimipu on the field. Either Joseph, his helpers, and the terrified women had done an extraordinary job of retrieving their wounded from the timbered hillside, the stream, the willow thickets, and the campsite. Or the burial squads who were appointed to gather dead soldiers from the battlefield for internment at the foot of the once-besieged promontory finished off whatever Indians they found still alive. Or the Bannock scouts, from a tribe that had been on-and-off foes of the Nez Perces for more years than history records, did the job. With no objection from Howard, the Bannocks hunted eagerly for Nez Perce corpses, some of which they had exhumed. Indifferent to the sex or age of the dead, they joyfully scalped the remains. Horrid, indeed, General Howard admitted, but no more gruesome than railroad accidents, major fires, or pestilences. And, he added, not nearly as bad as Indian brutalities committed on whites. Still, compunction finally got the best of the Christian general and, at the urging of one of his own men, he had the mutilated bodies buried.[7]

The battle, which came only fourteen months after the Custer massacre, attracted nationwide attention. First reactions in the nearby towns of Deer Lodge and Helena were favorable. Sympathetic citizens sent out wagons mattressed with straw for hauling the wounded back to local hospitals. With them the relief parties brought delicacies—jams, canned oysters, garden-fresh vegetables, and beef—as well as clean shirts, socks, and pajamas. Gibbon's superior officers commended him publicly and in private correspondence for a job well done against superior forces. Medals for heroism were ordered distributed. Volunteers swarmed into the camp near the battlefield to reap a belated share of glory by helping run down the beaten foe.[8]

Underneath the glitter, however, was a heavy layer of dross. After having achieved the enormous advantages of surprise, how did it happen that Gibbon had finished the battle pinned down ignominiously and precariously by untrained Indians—Indians who were also said to have lost the Battle of the Clearwater but obviously hadn't. Clearly, the critics went on, the Nez Perce war was being mismanaged, one more example of the inadequacies of America's Indian-fighting army.

Fortunately for himself, Gibbon was no longer on exhibit. He left the battle-field slightly wounded in the thigh. His troops, except for fifty men and their officers who elected to join Howard during his continued pursuit of the Nez Perces, returned to their original stations. The general appreciated the reinforcements, but was on edge about the nationwide scrutiny and about critical letters coming to him from his superiors. He dared make no more mistake and yet possible pitfalls abounded, as he became aware when he paused in the mining town of Bannack on August 14, the second day of the resumed chase.[9]

He was not operating in a wilderness. Gold rushes had swept across the area more than a decade earlier, leaving a detritus of hard-core towns fed by local farms and ranches. In turn Bannack, Virginia City, and Helena had served as territorial capitals. Deer Lodge and Butte attracted other small swarms. Freight and stagecoach roads ran south through the fat lower half of Idaho to tap the Union and Central Pacific railways in Utah. One of the roads eventually found its way up Birch Creek in Idaho and crossed a small divide into the Lemhi Fork of the Salmon River. Another, farther east, crossed Monida Pass, as it is called today, into the extreme southwestern part of Montana. That road was followed by a telegraph line. Branches from both highways led to Bannack, Montana, still the center of small mining operations and widespread ranches.

Most of the people in the area dreaded the next move of the Nez Perces. They fortified local courthouses; they built stockades; they formed militia units whose captains, elected by popular vote, considered themselves entitled by virtue of their sudden elevation to give Howard emphatic advice about what to do next. Bannack was one of those defense centers. When Howard halted at the town, he was greeted both by cheers of relief and by growls of anxiety. As he and the townspeople knew from their scouts, the Indians had fled from the Big Hole battlefield south along the edges of the hills that formed the western rim of that wide prairie. They followed the same procedure—staying close to the western hills—after crossing a difficult ridge onto the rolling plains of Horse Prairie. While skirting Horse Prairie they attacked two ranches. (The womenfolk of both places had been sent to Bannack for safekeeping.) The Nez Perces killed eight men, ransacked the two houses, and stole a reputed 250 horses. Continuing south—it was August 13, the day before Howard's arrival in Bannack—they intersected and followed the branch road that crossed Bannack Pass out of Montana into the Lemhi Valley of Idaho.[10]

Agitated militia captains from the Lemhi hurried to Howard and urged him to come to their valley. The Indians, they were convinced, planned to turn north and pass through the town of Salmon on their way to the Southern Nez Perce Trail, which would lead them back to their cherished homelands. Howard could intercept them—and spare the valley all the barbarities of which the Indians were capable—if he would cross the Continental Divide at Lemhi Pass, a gap Lewis and Clark had used on their way to the Pacific, and throw a line of soldiers across the Indians' path.

Howard did not believe the Indians intended to return home right then. In his estimation they were still planning to go to the buffalo country. Therefore, they would turn south until they could outflank the Continental Divide and swing east through the newly created (1872) Yellowstone National Park. He believed this intensely enough that on his ride from the battlefield he had stayed parallel to but well east of the Nez Perces' line of travel. That way he could, he hoped, cut them off when they swung from a southern to an eastern course.[11]

This judgment was confirmed when a new set of messages arrived telling him the fugitives had turned up the Lemhi Valley, rather than down it toward the main Salmon River. He'd had enough criticism about his strategies, however, that he was gun-shy and sought further reassurance from two treaty Nez Perces who were accompanying him as horse herders for the cavalry. They had relatives among the nontreaty Indians and were familiar with their modes of thinking. The pair agreed with the general's forecast: The middle reaches of the Yellowstone River in Montana were surely the fugitives' destination.

Howard got out his map. On it he traced his quarry's supposed route: up the Lemhi and across Gilmore Summit into Birch Creek drainage. With the mountains of the Continental Divide to their left, they would continue southeast until the range bent sharply east on its way to West Yellowstone. (Modern nomenclature goes like this: The Bitterroot Mountains merge with the Continental Divide at the head of Bitterroot Valley. The name Bitterroot clings to the Divide as far as Lemhi Pass. There it changes to Beaverhead Mountains. This name lasts as far as the range's big bend east. From there almost to West Yellowstone, the Continental Divide carries the name Centennial Mountains. All this is clearer on a map than on a printed page.) The Indians had chosen to follow the outside of this geographic arc. By following a shorter route along the inside of the curve, Howard ought to be able to cut them off at some suitable spot. His finger fell tentatively on Monida Pass. One of the main freight roads to Utah ran through the gap. That, too, would speed him on his way, and he could throw his block on the Indians somewhere near the southern exit from the pass.[12]

In spite of the command's ability to ride along roads the entire distance to Monida Pass, the trip was made unpleasant by the constant carpings of the self-appointed volunteers who accompanied Howard. Hurry!—or the Indians would get ahead of him in spite of the longer distance they had to travel. This was true, but the general refused to press his leg-weary cavalry horses; if he did, they'd be of little use when battle was joined. Exasperated and rebellious under discipline anyway, most of the volunteers left, spilling out their jaundiced views to whatever newspaper correspondent would listen. Fifty-three new militiamen from Virginia City unexpectedly replaced them. Although they were more cooperative than the original groups, the beset Howard took no joy in their coming. This war was turning into a drag.

Another addition, and this one must have made the general really nervous, was Captain Randolph Norwood at the head of Company L of the Second Cavalry. Veterans of mop-up campaigns against the Sioux, Norwood's company had been assigned as escorts for the General of the Army, William Tecumseh Sherman, who was taking an inspection tour of Northwestern forts—a tour that also included a visit to Yellowstone National Park. Knowing approximately where Howard was and feeling that Norwood would be of more help against the Nez Perces than sightseeing in the park, Sherman dispatched him to support his old friend of Civil War days.[13]

Under the circumstances the last thing Howard wanted was another jolt from the Indians. Nevertheless that was what happened. Citizens bursting with excitement galloped into his camp near the northern entrance to Monida Pass with word that Nez Perce raiders had just struck at a stage station and other buildings on the road south of Monida summit. No, the Indians had not killed anybody, but they'd cut the telegraph line and had appropriated a few horses and some grain. Drivers along the way, terrified by the reports, had abandoned their equipment and run away. Two had hidden in a cave in the lava rocks. If Howard hurried over the pass, he could probably catch the hostiles and put a stop to their marauding.[14]

But if he didn't catch them … if they reached the Yellowstone wilderness ahead of him…. He looked again at his map. About sixty miles east of him, the Continental Divide described an abrupt arc to the north, forming a pocket that was shaped vaguely, on the map, like a spearhead. A body of water called Henrys Lake filled much of the pocket. Clearly, the Indians were headed that way, on the south side of the Divide. By driving his command hard along the north side of the Divide and entering Red Rock Pass, as indicated on his map, he might get ahead of the elusive Nez Perces—for a change!—and pounce on them before they had any notion of his position.

The decision brought cries of distress from his visitors. They needed him now, south of the Continental Divide. Why continue the chase for another sixty miles through a howling wilderness when he could dash undetected through Monida Pass and come up on them, unnoticed, from behind?

Painfully aware of the weariness of his men and horses, Howard let himself be tempted into a compromise. He ordered Lieutenant George R. Bacon to take forty men and a few scouts over Red Rock Pass into the pocket. There Bacon should position himself—and this is incomprehensible—at Raynolds Pass, a low gap that led out of the pocket to the north. That was one way to the buffalo plains around the headwaters of the Missouri, but to get there the Indians would have to bypass the army's Fort Ellis. An eastern exit from the pocket, Targhee Pass (as it is known today) was the logical route for the Indians, especially if they wished to reach the land of their friends, the Crows. Nevertheless, Howard's written directions to Bacon clearly said Raynolds Pass. If the Indians arrived there ahead of the general, the order continued, the lieutenant was to harass them and slow them down as well as he prudently could. Above all, keep track of them for two days, or until Howard arrived. There must be no mistakes—not with Captain Norwood watching.[15]

The week that had passed since the Battle of the Big Hole had brought no softening of the Nez Perces' grief and hate and desire for revenge. They vented a little of it on Looking Glass, declaring that his failure to guard the camp had made the attack possible. But who should replace him as head war chief? Rainbow and the other leading warriors were dead. White Bird and Toohoolhoolzote were too old, and Ollokot was too young. Joseph lacked experience in battle and, besides, was needed as camp chief. So, in the end, the choice fell on Lean Elk, known to the whites as Poker Joe. Lean Elk had traveled to the Plains several times to hunt buffalo and was familiar with most of the country they would pass through on the way to the Crows.[16]

Habit restored some semblance of order, and there was no more traveling without guards. Many of the young warriors, however, banded together and, defying the chiefs, rode off on ill-tempered forays. They were the ones who killed the whites and stole the horses on Horse Prairie. They put on a mock, show-off charge against one of the stockades they encountered in the Lemhi Valley. Later, they surrounded a caravan of freight wagons on the road beside Birch Creek, demanded food, knocked open some whiskey barrels they found, wantonly killed five of the freighters, and fell into a murderous brawl among themselves, shooting and stabbing. One Nez Perce died of wounds delivered by a fellow tribesman during the ruckus.[17]

Somewhat sobered by the incident, the combined bands followed the cornering mountains to the east. After crossing the Monida Pass stage road, to the great fright of the whites in the vicinity, they rode eighteen miles over a dreary land, knobby with humps of lava rock, coarse brush, and occasional stunted trees. On the night of August 18 they crossed a bright stream, Camas Creek, purling down from the Centennial Mountains half a dozen miles to the north. Beyond Camas Creek and eventually converging with it was a similar stream now called Spring Creek. A shallow valley about a mile wide cupped both creeks. The space was blanketed by grass and called, as were several similar meadows throughout the mountainous Northwest, Camas Meadow.

The grass and water in the meadow were refreshing. The wounded were weary from the jolting of the travois to which they were strapped or, if they were riding, from the constant jar of the horses' feet. The babies were crying, the old people sagged. They would all have liked to stay there, but they knew their appearance at the stage station on the highway would put pursuers into motion. So the next day, August 19, on they went.

The rear guards loitered a little, and it was well they did. Investigating a cloud of dust raised by the hooves of many horses, they discovered hundreds of soldiers following their trail. Howard! It was the fugitives' first sighting of him since the Battle of the Clearwater, although they had heard that he had reached the Big Hole battlefield after their departure.

Greatly agitated, the scouts notified their own cavalcade, which had halted to go into camp fifteen miles farther on. The chiefs received the word in discouragement. Was there no way to stop that white commander's relentless pursuit?

One of the wounded, Black Hair, spoke up. The night before, at Camas Meadow, restless with pain, he'd had a vision of his fellow tribesmen stealing many army horses. Might this have been his guardian spirit revealing the future to him?

The chiefs looked at each other. The army was right then going into camp at Camas Meadow, the spot where the vision had appeared. That lent credibility. A council was called, as was always done when momentous decisions or plans had to be made. Everyone who wanted to speak up was heard, and from that meeting plans emerged for crippling Howard's advance by stampeding, just before dawn, the cavalry's horses and the supply train's mules. If the surprise and confusion were great enough, the warriors might fall on the entire camp, as Gibbon's soldiers had fallen on them at the Big Hole.[18]

· 22 ·

HANGING ON

L ots of open space and lots of grass characterized Camas Meadow. The several units of Howard's command made the most of both, spotting their camps at intervals along the perimeter of an imagined square, several acres in size. All except the tent town of the fifty-three volunteers who had recently arrived from Virginia City lay between the two streams that crossed the meadow; the newcomers camped east of Spring Creek. By stationing wagons in the gaps between the camps, the troopers formed a porous enclosure for the mules of the pack train. The bell mares the mules were accustomed to following were either hobbled or tied to the wagons. Because the Indian camp was only fifteen or so miles to the east, the cavalrymen tied their mounts with extra care to picket lines strung close to each camp, but the volunteers were more lax.

Howard's headquarters tents were pitched "castlelike"—his word—on a flat-top knoll some forty feet higher than the rest of the meadow. Sentries were stationed on the outer edges of the encampment in accord with instructions laid down in military manuals.[1]

Until shortly before dawn the camp slept soundly. Then a sentry called a challenge, a rifle answered, and the compound was filled with the screeches and war whoops of many Indians. Tied horses reared and squealed. Untied mules and released horses stampeded. Shadowy forms on horseback raced among them, waving blankets to frighten them toward one of the openings in the enclosure.

Nez Perces, of course. Apparently, a few of them had crept into the com-

292

pound with the stealth that Indians practice from childhood. There they had begun untying horses from the picket lines. When enough were freed, the plan went, the thieves' mounted companions would bring riding animals to the foot warriors and they would race away together with the herd. Fortunately, the sentry had challenged the mounted Indians and one nervous raider had fired back, releasing pandemonium, before many of the cavalry stock had been swooped up. The mules were something else. The raiders swept nearly every one of them—150 or so—out of the camp.

In the gathering light of dawn, the troopers saddled the horses that remained. Three companies took off in pursuit; the rest, including the volunteers, who had lost several of their animals, stayed with Howard as reserves. It was an unequal race, for keeping the unruly mules together in a herd slowed the Indians. After a brisk chase of seven or eight miles, approximately half way to the Nez Perce camp, the whites overtook the raiders. But luck stayed with the Indians. Contact came where the ground was rumpled with ridges of jagged lava rocks sprinkled with occasional clumps of tall brush and twisted aspens. Dismounting, they scattered out to fight off their pursuers.

Either a large number of Indians had participated in the raid or reinforcements had ridden out to meet them. Some took over the handling of the stolen herd, minus twenty or so head the attackers managed to pinch off. Others barricaded themselves in the lava. Still more threw a skirmish line across open draws, between the whites and the herd. Rifles began sputtering at long distance, a setup the Indians seemed to prefer. Under that sort of cover the warriors gradually began to outflank their pursuers. Two of the companies managed to withdraw, but Norwood's command was pinned down and endured a few miserable hours before Howard and his reserves rode to the rescue, movie-style.[2]

The Indians withdrew almost unscathed. Howard's force, by contrast, lost one man killed and eight wounded, of whom two soon died. He had, in addition, placed still more strain on his tired men and animals. And then there was the embarrassment of Targhee Pass, through which the Indians fled unopposed. It led to a revealing incident. In the first book Howard wrote about the Nez Perce campaign, he stated, with patient resignation, that Bacon's party had left Henrys Lake and Targhee Pass two days before the Indians rushed through, and so that hope of slowing them vanished. "What a disappointment!" the author sighed in print, not admitting that the lieutenant had spent the two days watching Raynolds Pass, as instructed. Bacon had then returned as he had come, along the north side of the Continental Divide, had crossed Monida Pass, and had caught up with the command after a "stern chase."

The slander might have ended there. But no. Thirty years later, in another book, *My Life and Experiences Amongst Our Hostile Indians*, Howard said the Indians escaped because Bacon lacked the heart to fight and let them "go by and pass through the narrow gateway without having fired a shot." But Bacon could not have fired. The Christian general's own mistaken orders had removed the junior officer from the scene of action.[3] Why Howard resorted to this exercise in spite many years after the event can only be surmised as follows: During this period, he received a great deal of merciless criticism, and perhaps he felt better, even in retrospect, drawing a wince or two from a blameless subordinate.

After the skirmish, the troops returned to Camas Meadow to tend to the wounded and meet the infantry and artillery companies that had been following a day behind the cavalry. By overloading the wagons and mules they brought with them, Howard was able to move forward again. Another lift to his spirits was provided by the arrival of fifty garishly beaded, feathered, and painted Bannock Indian scouts who had been recruited in southern Idaho to help run down and capture members of their own race, the Nez Perces. Their pay was to be whatever of the fugitives' two thousand or more horses they could seize. Their war chief was Buffalo Horn, one of the seventeen Bannocks who were already serving with Howard. Their white supervisor, who had enlisted for thirty days just for this service, was S. G. Fisher, a tall, competent plainsman, dressed in the obligatory fringed buckskins.[4]

Eager to utilize these fresh additions, Howard had the entire camp aroused at two A.M., and away they went, trying to cut off the enemy at the pass. The spasm not only failed but outraged his officers and medical staff. Horses and men, they pointed out, had been exhausted by more than a thousand miles of relentless marching. The infantrymen's shoes were falling apart. Although ice was forming on the water buckets in the mornings—it was late August, and they were camping at elevations of between six thousand and seven thousand feet above sea level—the enlisted men had only one thin blanket apiece and no overcoats. Rations were skimpy and tasteless. Freight horses and pack mules could scarcely plod.

The officers put these complaints in an official letter requesting a four-day rest stop. Unofficial letters were more outspoken. Dr. FitzGerald wrote his wife, Emily, "Not many officers are in sympathy with him [General Howard], and a great many think he is guilty of folly of the greatest kind to follow on at the expense of loss in men and animals in a hopeless pursuit." Howard, of course, sensed the feeling in the way the men looked at him as he went by, and when the Bannock scouts reported that the Nez Perces, having crossed the Targhee

Pass, were moving slowly through the roughest sort of country, he relented and declared the holiday.[5]

He did not rest himself. With his son Guy and a few staff officers, he rode all night in a springless wagon through Red Rock Pass and sixty-five miles farther on to the mining camp of Virginia City. There he shopped for whatever shoes, blankets, coats, socks, food staples, and fresh animals were available in the area. He encountered newspaper stories by free-swinging frontier editors who said he ought to be replaced by someone who was capable of catching an outnumbered bunch of Indians limping along burdened by women, children, and household possessions. Howard could swallow what he considered irresponsible newspaper criticism, but similar barbs from his superiors hurt. For instance, his old friend, General William Tecumseh Sherman, with whom he had marched through Georgia during the Civil War, telegraphed him in Virginia City, "That force of yours should pursue the Nez Perces to the death, lead where they may.... If you are tired give the command to some young, energetic officer."

Howard flared back. "I never flag. It was the command, including the most energetic young officers, that were worn out and weary.... Neither you nor General McDowell [in command of the Division of the Pacific, which included Howard's department] can doubt my pluck and energy.... My supplies have just come in and we will move in the morning and continue to the end."

Sherman returned a placatory answer without changing his mind about a new commander. His choice was Colonel C. C. Gilbert, to whom he gave a letter, addressed to Howard, suggesting the switch. Gilbert set off for the Yellowstone country to find the general, but failed to overtake him. The war was still Howard's to handle as best he could.[6]

At last it was beginning to look as if it could be handled. By moving into the new national park, the Nez Perces had put themselves into a huge geographic box from which few exits opened onto the buffalo plains of central Montana. The most obvious outlet was the Yellowstone River, which flowed generally northward out of the park to the site of present-day Livingston, where it slanted sharply northeast on its long journey to join the Missouri. There were difficulties, though. Not far inside the park, the Yellowstone split. The main stem was difficult to follow because of its vast, roaring, chromatic grand canyon. Far easier to traverse, as it sliced across the park's northeast corner, was the Yellowstone's east fork, known today as the Lamar River. If the Nez Perces ever managed to reach the upper Lamar, a roundabout journey to be sure, they could readily leave the park by the Livingston route.

The Lamar offered other, if harder, opportunities. Several rugged tributaries dived toward it from the Absaroka Range, whose undulant, peak-studded, mead-ow-jeweled summit formed the park's eastern boundary. Once travelers had reached the top of the divide, they could cross over to the headwaters of two key streams. The northernmost was Clarks Fork, which, after an erratic beginning, coursed due north to join the main Yellowstone about twenty miles southwest of modern Billings, Montana. The other was the Shoshone, once called the Stinking Water. The Shoshone thrust east from the Absarokas to join the Bighorn River. The Bighorn, in turn, flowed north through the Crow Indian Reservation to meet the Yellowstone, some fifty miles northeast of Billings. The Crow Indians' name for themselves, incidentally, was Absaroka, the Bird People. In 1874, doughty Looking Glass and his hunters had helped the Crows defeat a war party of Sioux. Now the Nez Perces thought they could find refuge with the Crows while they analyzed the possibilities for their future.

The rigorous campaigns the United States Army had waged against the Sioux and Cheyennes had made its officers familiar with the lower sections of that cluster of north-flowing streams—the Yellowstone-Lamar, Clarks Fork, and the Shoshone-Bighorn. As soon as the commanders were sure the fugitive Nez Perces were headed toward the national park, they set about closing the exits.

Fort Ellis, located near the site of today's Bozeman, Montana, became a staging area for troops watching the main Yellowstone River. In command there was Lieutenant Gustavus C. Doane. He was familiar with parts of the national park and had a large party of Crow scouts with him. Colonel Samuel D. Sturgis, whose son had been killed the year before in the battle of the Little Bighorn, was to keep an eye on Clarks Fork, while Major Verling K. Hart stood guard at Cody, Wyoming, over the Shoshone exit. Backup cavalry for these outposts was stationed far down the Yellowstone at Fort Keogh (the present Miles City, Montana). The commander there was Colonel Nelson A. Miles, who had once been an aide of General Howard's. Dashing, handsome, and ambitious, Miles was ready—eager—to gallop off wherever he might be needed.

That, then, was the strategy.[7] Let Howard keep pushing hard on the heels of the Nez Perces. Turn or twist as they might, they could not break free, an inevitability that suited the weary Howard. Howard had seen too many of his supposed traps fail to catch the fugitives. His burning desire now, one of his officers wrote, was to redeem himself by helping bring the Nez Perce campaign to a "brilliant end."[8]

On August 22, the Nez Perces entered Yellowstone National Park. By following first the Madison River and then the Firehold River, they reached a west-thrusting tributary since known as Nez Perce Creek. The creek opened a way onto the park's central plateau, dense with lodgepole pines. On emerging from the forest, they saw below them and off to the southeast the immense, intense blue sprawl of Yellowstone Lake.

No less than Howard's men, the fugitives were hungry and tired. They were not aware of the general's rest stop, but they did know he would be unable to harass them again until he had acquired more pack animals. So they relaxed, digging roots and hunting deer, moose, and elk in a country long famed for its game. Unhurried, they straggled out of camp late each morning and arrived in loose, ambling groups at the night's stopping place. For the most part they traveled in family groups, each unit driving its own horses with it. In open country keeping the animals in separate bunches would have been difficult, but in thick timber the division was necessary to prevent straying.

The forest in the vicinity of the Firehole River apparently confused Lean Elk. Though he was not lost, he had been in the area only occasionally and was not sure of which trails to follow to get where he wanted to go. The problem was solved when a scouting party led by Yellow Wolf brought in a prospector, John Shively, who had been looking for his own strayed horses. He said he knew the way and was taken on as a guide. A half day was long enough to straighten Lean Elk out, but Shively liked the Indians and stayed as a helper with the women's pack train. After a week or so, he "escaped," although the Indians probably would have let him go if he had asked. On reaching the town of Deer Lodge, he gave James H. Mills, editor of the *New North-West*, a pretty accurate account of the fugitives' organization. There was no head chief, he said. All tribal matters were decided in council. Joseph was about thirty-five years old (he was actually thirty-seven). Six feet tall, he wore a single eagle feather in his hair. He was always in a pleasant mood. Although the Indians would fight soldiers on the instant, they did not wish to harm citizens.[9]

The last statement does not wholly accord with some of the fugitives' actions. During the early days of the Yellowstone trek, Nez Perce outriders captured two parties of tourists numbering nineteen people; two were women. During a raid far down the Yellowstone River near Mammoth Hot Springs, Nez Perce marauders looted and burned a cabin, killed one man, chased some others off, and appropriated several horses. Altogether they killed two men and wounded two. Several captives dashed away to freedom. Others were let go. The women were not harmed. Although the Indians said they seized the

whites to keep them from giving information to the military, the random-
ness—the illogic, even—of the various episodes seems to gainsay the statement. Underneath it all one senses the tensions of ill will on the part of
young warriors who were brooding over the wrongs being inflicted on them.
The chiefs were far more responsible, knowing perhaps that when blame was
assessed, they would be held accountable.[10]

White survivors of the escapades poured out their stories to eager journalists, some of them from the East. The tales, most of them exaggerated,
made fine reading. The West, the last free-roaming Indians, Yellowstone—
such images had a resonance to them. Injustice, endurance, a cunning David
outmaneuvering the bumbling minions of Goliath—those were magic topics.
During this time a single name—Joseph—crept into prominence. General
Howard and his officers had been calling him head chief and attributing victories to him for several weeks. Partly the identification was a cultural act.
Heroes need heroic opponents. Generals fight generals, not tribal councils.
Besides, stories flow easier when a name stands for a tribe. Caesar encompass-
es all the legions of Rome. The Yellowstone captives accepted the pattern
almost instinctively. They mentioned Lean Elk and Looking Glass, but
Joseph stood strong at the core, a stereotype come to life. "'The noble red
man' we read of," wrote Emma Cowan, one of the female captives, "was more
nearly impersonated in this Indian than in any I have ever met. [How many
had she met? one wonders.] Grave and dignified, he looked a chief." A myth
was on its way to incarnation.

On August 25, the fugitives camped a few miles north of Yellowstone
Lake, beside the river. From there Looking Glass and three companions started across the Absaroka Mountains to ask the Crows to join them in fighting
the Americans, for hadn't the Nez Perces aided the Bird People in a war
against the Sioux?[11] Assuming a favorable response, the bands followed slowly, still in separate groups, up Pelican Creek, over a low divide, and down
Mist Creek to the upper Lamar River. It was hellish going. Scout S. G. Fisher,
who was following the migrants with those of his Bannocks who had not yet
deserted, summed up the route this way, "the roughist [sic] canyon I was ever
through dead and fallen timber and rocks found plenty of dead crippled horses ... the trees and logs was smeared with blood from their horses cut on sharp
stones & pine knots."[12] Emma Cowan, talking about another section of Yellowstone travel, added a touch about packhorses that got stuck trying to carry

their loads between trees that were not wide enough to admit passage. When that happened, the Nez Perce woman in charge of the errant animal dismounted, picked up a stick, and flailed the horse's face until it decided to back off and try a roomier way. After a little education of that sort, it may be assumed, the horse learned to tell how far apart two trees were.

Where Mist Creek ran into the upper Lamar, there was a fine meadow, big enough for all two thousand horses. The Indians still loitered, waiting for Looking Glass's report. In spite of a little rain, they enjoyed a few days of hunting, drying meat, patching clothes, cleaning guns, and wondering where Howard was. They did not know as yet that Fisher and his Bannock scouts were close behind, watching them. Then Looking Glass returned, and their world fell apart again. He had contacted some of the Crows' leading chiefs at the agency buildings on their reservation. From them he learned that Colonel Sturgis was somewhere up on the Clark Fork with 360 men looking for them. With the colonel were many Crow scouts, hopeful of being paid for their service with Nez Perce horses seized in battle. Chiefs at the agency who were friendly with Looking Glass said apologetically that they would try to keep as many of their bands neutral as they could. Maybe, in case of conflict, the scouts would shoot over the Nez Perces' heads and not hurt them. But, no, they could not help in any active way.

At an agitated council Joseph argued that with Clarks Fork blocked, their best alternative was to go down the Lamar to the main Yellowstone. After reaching the plains, they could cross the river and head north into Canada, where perhaps they could form an alliance with those other exiles, Sitting Bull and his Sioux.

Looking Glass objected. How would they get by Fort Ellis?

Well, Ellis was twenty-five miles or so west of the trail they would be following. The Nez Perces had been thrusting hard toward the east and the people at the fort would not be looking for them in that vicinity.

Looking Glass held out for climbing onto the Absaroka Divide. The area was big and rough—high-walled canyons, deep gorges lined with rimrock, thick patches of timber, steep talus slopes, pinnacles so crazy that the whites had given the name Hoodoo Basin to one large drainage system. Moreover, there were alternatives on the divide. If Clarks Fork was blocked, they could slip off to the North Fork of the Shoshone and go down it to the Bighorn. In the region where Joseph wanted to go, there was no alternative except fighting, and they could not afford more losses in battle.

Possibly Joseph was thinking of surrender if battle actually loomed. There is some evidence that his thoughts had turned that way, now and then, almost since the beginning of the war. Anyway, the Indian group broke apart. Looking Glass's people started up the last headwater stream of the Lamar to the top of the Absaroka Divide. Joseph pulled his Wallowans and a few others together and started down the Lamar toward the main Yellowstone. Maybe the two groups would come together again somewhere out on the open plains between the Yellowstone and Canada. Who could say?[13]

Yellow Wolf's marauders, fresh from burning the cabin near Mammoth Hot Springs, gave a quick twist to Joseph's plans. Troops were on the raiders' trail. Not many, but knowledge that Nez Perces were in the vicinity would bring more. Fort Ellis would go on the alert and close that escape route to the Plains.

The warning let Joseph postpone the decision between fighting and surrendering. Instead he went in search of Looking Glass. To save time, he and his people climbed due east up the mountain, following an ancient hunting trail that speared upward along a steep, relatively open ridge between Cache and Chalfee creeks. After gaining the erosion-shattered summit, they moved sinuously toward the southeast until they somehow made contact with Looking Glass. United again, the persistent Indians turned down what is now called Crandall Creek toward the awesome canyon of the upper Clarks Fork River.[14]

It was not possible for riders to get into the canyon at that point; it was narrow and filled with rubble, and the walls ranged from 400 to 1,200 feet high. Accordingly the fugitives rode along the tilted slopes that form a ragged border for the canyon's south rim. Now and then they had to skirt, laboriously, deep side gulches. Their goal was the point where the canyon debouched suddenly onto the plains and where they hoped to find trails that would lead them down through the mountain's spreading walls. Once the land leveled off, the going would be easy as far as topography was concerned.

In other respects affairs grew desperate. Scouts ranging out ahead discovered a large body of American troops camped beside the Clarks Fork just below the mouth of the canyon. Obviously, the enemy was waiting for the Nez Perces to appear so they could put the Indians' backs to the walls and methodically grind them up. They could not retreat, for by then they had apprehended couriers carrying messages through the badlands and knew more troops were behind them. There was a further danger—prospectors. Promising strikes of ore had been made at the northern (Montana) end of the Absarokas. (The Indians were still in Wyoming.) A smelter and a small town, Cooke City, had sprung up, and booted miners were ranging the area, looking for more leads. They would act as eyes for the military unless they were eliminated—as eight were.[15] But there was no telling how many might have slipped away.

At this critical moment an extraordinary thing happened. The troops who were camped beside the river, under the command of Colonel Samuel Sturgis, rode off toward the south—toward the North Fork of the Shoshone River, a.k.a. Stinking Water. Probably—incredibly—the reason was the Nez Perces' own loitering in Yellowstone Park.

On leaving the Crow Agency to close the eastern end of the army's trap, Colonel Sturgis had been ordered, to his discomfiture, to watch the upper reaches of both the Clarks Fork and Shoshone rivers. Since the two streams come within twenty-six miles of each other (at one point), the commanding generals, strapped for men, did not think the task unreasonable. Sturgis did. He had been given 360 men. Inasmuch as some army estimates held that the Nez Perces could throw four hundred warriors at once onto the battle line, he did not see how he could keep an adequate force beside both rivers. (Actually, there were fewer than two hundred Nez Perce warriors.) Howard was supposed to be coming along to help, but no messengers from the general had reached Sturgis, and he was reluctant, in that rough country, to rely on maybe-so. After considerable agonizing, he chose to put his force close to the point where the upper Clarks Fork breaks out of its canyon, for majority opinion held that Clarks Fork was the river the fugitives would follow. Scouts were detailed to watch the upper reaches of both it and the Shoshone.[16]

Although the spies went some distance along both watercourses, they found no Nez Perces. Time passed; Sturgis's nerves tightened. Where were those Indians? If they weren't aiming toward the Clarks Fork drainage, they must be somewhere along the Shoshone. He moved nervously ten miles in that direction and sent a cavalry squad out on reconnaissance. In the dim distance toward the Shoshone the squad saw—or thought they saw—a band of horses. That was enough for Sturgis. Off he went in pursuit. Some students of the affair think the horses were a decoy that the Nez Perces deliberately sent out. Some believe they were a phantasm conjured up by men who were searching hard for Indians. A few cynics suggest that the horses were inserted into Sturgis's report as a justification for his move. No one has any sound idea.

The Indian cavalcade—seven hundred people, two thousand horses, some packed and some snorting around unhampered—was highly visible. Along the early stages of Sturgis's route there were places where he or any of his men, especially his rear guard, could look back and see his quarry—if the Indians kept going along the high terraces. They didn't, for they discovered the hunters' presence in the nick of time.

A quandary. Sturgis's departure cleared the way onto the Plains, but if they pushed too hard on his heels, they'd be seen. Yet they were uneasy about waiting, for somewhere behind them more troops were coming up.

The scouts solved the problem. They had already noticed a deep slot, now called Dead Indian Gulch, that dropped into the main canyon at a point where it was just becoming passable. Because the gulch was narrow, precipitous, and jammed with detritus, they had dismissed it as a route. But now it *had* to do. And perhaps they could also make their abrupt switch in directions serve as a riddle for their pursuers. While considering the dilemma of routes, the chiefs and leading warriors had halted the cavalcade on a grassy slope just barely out of Sturgis's sight. During the pause, the horses had wandered around grazing and quarreling and filling the meadow with tracks. The Indians may—emphasis on *may*—have chased the animals around a little to add still more tracks over a broader area, the idea being to keep the cavalry that was following them from noticing their sudden switch in directions. If that happened, the followers would keep on plodding after Sturgis and give the fugitive still more time to reach the Yellowstone River and cross over it to the vast Plains leading to safety in Canada. Or the maze of tracks *may* just have been a happy accident. General Howard, for one, thought the confusion was deliberate—understandably, for if Joseph, to whom he attributed the scheme, was all that wily, then the army would look good if it solved the puzzle without losing time.[17]

Be all that as it may, the Nez Perces did make a sharp switch in directions on September 9, riding off through a small screen of trees on a steep hillside and then punching the whole slipping, tumbling, kicking, squealing procession down Dead Indian Gulch onto the floor of Clarks Fork Canyon. They passed almost within rifle shot of Sturgis's old camp beside the river, but the colonel was not there to detect them. Neither were any of the region's prospectors, whom the Indians' passage had scared into hiding. As for the troops behind them, the fugitives would just have to wait and see what happened.

Back in his camp beside the Yellowstone River, General Oliver O. Howard shifted his own strategy. From messengers sent him by his scout, S. G. Fisher, and by talking with James Irwin, a cavalryman who had been discharged from

Fort Ellis and then held captive for awhile by the Indians, he learned that the fugitives were leaving the upper Lamar Valley for the summit of the Absarokas. From there the Indians would have to strike for either the North Fork of the Shoshone or the Clarks Fork of the Yellowstone, probably the latter.

Fisher's courier advised further that the route the Indians had taken over the Pelican Creek–Mist Creek divide from the Yellowstone to the Lamar was a holy terror—even worse than the gully-torn land of fire-hardened trees Howard had crossed on his way east from Targhee Pass. The way down the back side of the Absarokas wasn't likely to be much better. In short, the troops should leave the Indians' trail for the time being, work north thirty-five miles to the junction of the Lamar and the main Yellowstone, and pick up the mining-camp road that had recently been scratched out between Bozeman and Cooke City, both in southern Montana. After following the Lamar upstream for a few miles, the road swung up Soda Butte Creek to the top of the mountains. For obvious reasons the fugitives hadn't followed that route—too many whites. By taking advantage of it while the Indians were thrashing through the rock piles and pine-and-spruce jungles farther south, the troops could gain a lot of ground.[18]

Following the advice brought hardship as well as gain, however. A large part of the soldiers' food, ammunition, and spare equipment was lurching along in wagons over a hair-raising road created just ahead of the wheels by the same fifty Idaho roustabouts who had cleared the way along the Lolo Trail. Wagons would be good on the Soda Butte Road, but getting them there would take too long and the Indians would slip away. Accordingly, Howard transferred a spartan amount of food and materiel to his remount herd—horses that had escaped the Indian raid at Camas Meadow and the mules he had bought at Virginia City. The wagons then groaned off with what was left to Fort Ellis, where the roustabouts were released.

The change briefly lifted the spirits of the troops. The Cooke City Road, which they picked up on September 5, was steep and twisting, but along the way they marveled at broad meadows touched with the colors of fall, at stately forests, and splendid peaks. On September 6 they topped out near the Clarks Fork mines, where Fisher overtook them. The next day they met a mixed group of men who were typical of the new land—a voyageur, half French Canadian and half Indian; a full-blooded Crow; and a white prospector. The trio had recently talked with Colonel Sturgis, who had asked them to warn the miners around Cooke City of the possible approach of the Nez Perces.

Now Howard knew where Sturgis was. Excited, he sent two of the couriers back to tell his colleague he was coming up fast. Be ready! (Days later he learned that Nez Perce raiders caught and killed the pair before they reached the colonel.) Writing in his diary on September 9, Fisher said that no opening was left for the Nez Perces to wriggle through and a fight was inevitable. "The boys," he added, "are apprehensive."[19]

What they found, however, was a maze of tracks on the grassy slopes above the canyon. No Indians. No Sturgis. By cutting sign in a wide circle, Fisher soon solved the Indian puzzle, as the Nez Perces must have suspected any competent tracker would. Probably the military were delayed more by the slot at Dead Indian Gulch than by the maze. That night, wondering somewhat about Sturgis's force, they camped almost within a rifle shot of where the colonel had been a few days before. Once more an infallible trap had failed.

The next day, September 11, they disconsolately followed plainly visible tracks down Clarks Fork. Dr. FitzGerald felt as disgusted as he had back at Camas Meadow, and many enlisted men, slumped over their leg-weary horses, undoubtedly agreed with him. Why continue this futile chase? Why not let the poor Indians go to Canada, as Sitting Bull and many of his Sioux had done? Let the army take its thumps from the public. It deserved them.

That evening Sturgis caught up with Howard. He had discovered his mistake and, as embarrassed as a colonel could be, wanted to redeem himself by taking over the pursuit. His men and horses were relatively fresh; all they had done recently was to come up from the Crown Agency, which was fewer than a hundred miles away. By contrast, Howard's animals and men were dead tired from two months of almost unrelieved pressure.

The general agreed with the plan, gave Sturgis a few scouts, a disassembled howitzer being transported on mule back, and an additional fifty men mounted on the sprightliest horses in his command. At 6:30 A.M. on September 12 off they went—"a long and weary ride" that lasted until 9 P.M., Dr. FitzGerald wrote his wife. "It rained all afternoon and my boots and everybody else's got full of water." Thus a cavalryman's life.[20]

After a wet and hungry camp, they reached the main Yellowstone, followed it downstream a few miles, and crossed to the north bank. Along the way they saw evidence that a few young Nez Perce warriors were running wild again. After seizing a two-seated mail-and-passenger wagon, they had joyfully scattered the mail during a headlong ride that ended in a splintering wreck. (The wagon's original occupants, a woman among them, had escaped into the brush on seeing the Indians approach.) The warriors had also burned some haystacks and buildings, had stolen several horses, and had shot down several citizens.[21]

What the renegades let get by was of greater significance: two messengers, one in a boat and one on horseback. The couriers carried duplicate dispatches from Howard to Colonel Nelson Miles, stationed far down the Yellowstone at Fort Keogh. At some length Howard explained to his former aide what had happened. He guessed at the fugitives' probable routes and intentions—north to the Musselshell River in the heart of what was left of the buffalo country. There they might well seek union with some band of American-hating Sioux. "As they [the Nez Perce] make extra-ordinarily long marches, it will require unusual activity to intercept them. Earnestly request you make every effort in your power to prevent the escape of the hostile band, and at least hold them in check until I can overtake them."[22]

The appeal was hardly flattering to Sturgis, who was already in hot pursuit of the fugitives. But this was no time to spare feelings. Let the colonel work while Howard caught his breath. Somehow, someday, one of these traps had to work.

· 23 ·

FROM WHERE THE SUN
NOW STANDS

By midday on September 13, the Nez Perces had broken camp and were straggling across the broad flood plain that lay between the north bank of the Yellowstone River and the boundary of the valley, a low, rim-rocked bluff five miles away. Their goal, a U-shaped trough in the bluff, was called, with considerable overstatement, Canyon Creek. Threaded by a buffalo trail, the unremarkable opening provided easy access to the immense, rolling, largely treeless plateau to the north.

The ground was muddy from recent rains; the Indians were bedraggled and tired. But they thought they had once again left their pursuers far behind and did not have to press themselves. It was a shock, accordingly, to see scouts waving blankets and riding their horses in tight circles, a sign of approaching enemies. Looking back, they soon saw hundreds of cavalrymen pouring full gallop over a slight ridge, obviously intending to overhaul the main group before it reached the sheltering walls of the dry trough.

By then the Indians were practiced at swift responses. With a minimum of confusion the noncombatants stepped up their pace. Boys and unburdened women yelled at the heels of the horse herd. Sharpshooters found secure positions among the rocks at the canyon entrance or behind the banks of the streambed where it entered the flood plain. Mounted warriors raced out to form a protective line between the fleeing families and the approaching soldiers.

Strangely, the American commander—it was Colonel Sturgis—thought the mounted warriors either intended to charge him or could be induced to charge. Bugles sounded. The blue-clad riders halted and dismounted, rifles at the ready. While one man out of every four held his own horse and those of his companions, the walkers advanced. Shooting began at long range and accomplished little. The warriors on the skirmish line stayed on their horses, giving ground as the dismounted cavalrymen winded themselves trying to narrow the gap. A belated, would-be flanking charge by a mounted company was easily beaten back. By twos and threes the Indian fighters drifted into the canyon until finally only a single expert rifleman was left to keep the opponents alert. This he did admirably until he, too, withdrew.

In their reminiscences the Nez Perces did not consider the affair at Canyon Creek a battle. No Indian was killed; three warriors were slightly wounded. An indeterminate number of horses were cut away from the unruly herd and lost. The Nez Perces themselves abandoned thirty or forty lame and exhausted animals they might otherwise have tried to nurse along. Official reports put white losses at three dead, eleven wounded. Forty-one cavalry horses were slain. Some of these horses furnished food for Sturgis's force and Howard's when he came along later. Both army groups had outdistanced their ill-directed supply trains.[1]

From the Indians' point of view, the next few days were harder to endure and more costly than was the stand at Canyon Creek. Howard's Bannock scouts and Sturgis's Crow auxiliaries, combining into a force of well over a hundred warriors, began striking hard at the laggards and rear guard of the Nez Perces. They would charge up close, whirl, shoot under the necks of the horses they were riding, and dash off. Their primary target was the Nez Perce horse herd, especially loose animals carrying packs or dragging travois. The Crows were after loot for themselves, while the army wanted them to reduce the fugitives' mobility. They made off with two or three hundred animals. (Sturgis claimed four hundred in his report.) But Indianlike, they could not maintain the high intensity, partly because of fierce countercharges from the Nez Perces' camp guards. When the fugitives reached the Musselshell River on September 17, the raiders had all departed, one small group after another.[2]

The headlong pace had been costly to the Nez Perces. Their diminishing herd was full of lame, sick, and jaded animals. The people were equally debilitated. Some who were sick and old simply gave up and, as Indians often do when they feel they are burdening the rest of the band, dropped out of the column to wander forlornly until they came to some covert into which they could crawl and die.

After crossing the Musselshell, the Indians shifted their course briefly to the northwest to pass between the Little Belt and Big Snowy mountains, two of several massifs that rise like shaggy islands, dark with evergreens, out of the high plains of central and northern Montana. There, in the once-fabled hunting ground of Judith Basin, they surprised a party of Crows who had just killed several bison. It is unlikely that the group had been involved in the attack on the Nez Perce horses. No matter. They were members of a tribe that had, in Nez Perce minds, betrayed a friendship. The nomads fell on them like thunderbolts, killing several and making off with three or four hundred badly needed, fresh horses and, presumably, quantities of dried meat.[3]

Briefly refreshed, they left the Judith River and bent northeast across a bleak, sterile land where the gumbo soil balled up maddeningly on the horses' feet. They were aiming for Cow Island Landing on the Missouri River, about a hundred miles away. This was an important point. For scores of miles in Montana the Missouri flows through a trench whose walls are from six hundred to eight hundred feet high. Crossings were—and are—few. One was at Cow Island, approachable from both south and north along steep, twisting roads through gullies whose mouths approximately faced each other across the island. Late in the year the river was low in spite of the cold rainstorms that buffeted the countryside that fall of 1877. The Nez Perces were able to haze even their pack stock to the far side without having to stop and build skin boats for ferrying.

But advantage to them was a disadvantage to steamboats carrying supplies to upriver military establishments and civilian trading posts. Unable to pass Cow Island, the boats unloaded there and stacked their goods in a depot close to a bluff on the north shore, where trains of big freight wagons would pick up the material. When the Nez Perces arrived on the south shore on September 23, the depot held less than usual—about fifty tons of miscellany watched over by four civilians and a dozen soldiers commanded by a single sergeant.

Apprised of the cavalcade's approach, the guards dug rifle pits for themselves, but, sorely outnumbered, were in no mood to offer a challenge to the Indians. The column crossed the river below the landing without incident and camped about two miles up the Cow Creek road. But when the sergeant refused to sell food to unnamed chiefs who came back and offered handfuls of coin, a few outraged warriors who had stationed themselves on a nearby bluff began shooting. The whites answered, but, as was often the case in such skirmishes, long distances and inferior weapons kept down the flow of blood. Two nicked civilians were the only casualties among the guards. A mounted soldier who chanced along the south shore was not so lucky. He was killed.

That night, covered by a handy coulee, the Indian women joined the men in frantically plundering the dump. It was the first chance they'd had since the Bitterroot Valley to replenish flour, sugar, rice, beans, clothing, pots and pans, and other everyday equipment. At dawn they set fire to what was left and rode away. As easy as playing, Yellow Wolf declared.[4]

A few miles up the steeply rising north road they overtook a train of several freight wagons. That morning they offered no harm, but the next day some of the young warriors swung back and attacked, probably in search of whiskey. They killed two or three teamsters (accounts vary), sent the rest flying, and began tearing the canvas covers off the wagons and their trailers. At that point up came Major Guido Ilgis and thirty-six mounted troopers and a lone civilian on a long reconnaissance from Fort Benton, 125 miles upstream. In another long-range shooting affair, the one civilian with the military was killed. Realizing he lacked enough strength to take on the looters who were holed up behind the wagons, let alone the entire column, which the Cow Island people had told him were somewhere ahead, Ilgis ordered a retreat.[5]

The string of easy victories was psychologically unfortunate. For a long time the Indians had been traveling under severe stress. But this time, they were sure, they had finally left all troops, other than the negligible number commanded by Major Ilgis, far in the rear. They had replenished their supplies of horses, food, and equipment, and many of them ached for enough rest to enjoy their acquistions—not a stop, necessarily, but a slowdown.

The war chief, Lean Elk (or Poker Joe) said that those who talked that way were foolish. Canada was near. Sitting Bull and his Sioux had found refuge there and would help the Nez Perces do as well. It was a mistake to dawdle with freedom so near.

Looking Glass argued with him. Whether the deposed war chief was truly hurt by the people's suffering or saw a chance to regain his prestige cannot be said. Perhaps both impulses were at work. With fierce eloquence he overpowered Lean Elk and a majority of the council. At the close of the confrontation, Lean Elk said bitterly, "All right, you can take command, but I think we will all be killed."[6]

And so that was the way they went for the next few days, starting late and camping early. Slowly they passed to the right of the long, humped ridge of the Bear Paw Mountains. On September 28, hunters riding in advance of the main group killed several bison down by a small, winding, north-flowing stream now called Snake Creek. The taste of winter comes early to northern Montana. Out on the plains occasional pellets of snow were riding on a cold wind. The sun, a dim radiance behind murky clouds, was barely overhead when Looking Glass proposed a halt. The creek channel widened up ahead, he said. They'd drop into the hollow, out of the wind, build fires of the plentiful buffalo chips, prepare a feast of buffalo meat, and rest. How did that sound?

It sounded—and looked—fine. The creek twisted sharply to the east and then resumed its northerly flow between man-high clay banks lined thickly with stunted willows and wild rose bushes. North of the twist, the bluffs bordering the little valley receded to form a cove, or hollow, about a quarter of a mile long and eighty yards wide at its southern, pear-shaped end. Those southern hills were the highest—about forty feet. The narrowest part of the cove was at the northern end. The bluffs there were marked by the only considerable outcrop of rocks in the vicinity. Snake Creek, meandering only slightly, formed a chord for the arc of the cove. West of the creek the land sloped gently up to the vast prairie that engulfed the northernmost spur of the Bear Paw Mountains. The horses, only about half as many as the fugitives had started with, would be left to graze on that western slope.

Shallow coulees dropped down the southern and northeastern bluffs into the hollow. Runoff from those coulees, together with old flood channels carved by the creek, had created gullies five feet or so deep in the floor of the cove. Those gullies made natural divisions between the camps of the different bands. Joseph and many of the Wallowans pitched their make-do shelters of canvas and blankets farthest to the south. (Many of the Indians had lost their tipis at the Clearwater or Big Hole battles.) North of them were Ollokot and Looking Glass, then White Bird, and, at the northern end, Toohoolhoolzote. The crowding made for a certain coziness as the people crouched or knelt around the little fires of dried buffalo chips. The smell of roasting meat actually seemed to give warmth to the wintery air. Looking Glass was pleased. Lean Elk had been foolish. So, too, the warrior Wottolen with his dreams of death. Canada was only forty-two miles away—an easy two-day ride. Why punish themselves now?

During the evening of September 17, Colonel Nelson A. Miles received at Fort Keogh (or Tongue River Cantonment, as the establishment was still being called) the message General Howard had sent him five days before, asking him to cut the Indians off before they reached the international boundary. His response was instantaneous. Before dawn the next morning, troops and wagons were being ferried across the Yellowstone.

Miles was that way—precipitous, competent, aggressively energetic. He had joined the Union Army as a twenty-two year old in 1861. During the Civil War, he was wounded four times, once during the same battle in which Howard lost an arm. For a time he was Howard's aide. His rise was meteoric; before the conflict ended he held the brevet rank of major general. After the war he stayed in the army as a colonel, but he desperately wanted the permanent rank of brigadier general. He sported a Prussian-style spike-ended mustache. He wore a bearskin coat during winter campaigns, a cape whenever that was appropriate. Some of his fellow officers scorned him as a glory hunter, and, in truth, he did hog credit and was not above using family connections to advance his career. (His wife was the sister of both Senator John Sherman of Ohio and General William Tecumseh Sherman.) But no one ever questioned his devotion to his profession.[7]

During the winter of 1876–77 he had pursued several of the bands of Sioux and Cheyennes that had scattered far and wide after the Battle of the Little Bighorn. Although he had forced several back to their reservations, Chief Sitting Bull and perhaps two thousand followers had escaped into Canada. An embarrassment to the Canadians, they were a continuing threat to the Americans.

There was not enough game for the fugitive Sioux in the area where they were allowed to camp, let alone enough for the Canadian tribes of the region. Of necessity bands of the Sioux kept slipping across the border to hunt on the Montana plains. The army feared, not without reason, that they would attract enough dissatisfied tribes to form a broad new confederation of hostiles, similar to the one that had been taking shape when Custer had died at their hands. One response was the formation of a United States Sitting Bull Commission. After assembling at Fort Benton on the Missouri, the commission would march north, meet with Sitting Bull, and try to persuade him to surrender. Miles, in fact, was preparing a detachment of troops to act as an escort for the commission when Howard's appeal arrived.[8]

Some of Miles's famous luck came to his aid. The northwestern route he would have to follow to get in front of the Nez Perces coincided with the route to Fort Benton. So he incorporated the escort battalion he was forming—companies F, G, and H of the Second Cavalry Regiment and K of the Seventh Cavalry—into his Nez Perce force. The rest of that force consisted of companies A and D of the Seventh Cavalry (K of the escort would march with the Seventh until after the Nez Perces had been handled), and ninety men of the Fifth Infantry Regiment, mounted on horses lately taken from enemy Indians. Forty more foot soldiers of the Fifth had to walk as guards for the supply wagons. Two artillery crews serviced two high-wheel howitzers, one a 1.6-inch caliber Hotchkiss gun, the other a twelve-pounder called a Napoleon cannon. Thirty Cheyenne and Sioux scouts rounded out the force.

When Howard learned through a courier that Miles had received his message and planned to reach the Missouri at the mouth of the Musselshell in eight days, he was enormously relieved. Gratefully, he wrote his former aide, "My command gets tired but I myself am in sound strength—all will go right now that your loyal head is awake. God bless you and yours."[9] In the event, Miles exceeded his promise. On September 24, seven days out of Fort Keogh, his advance detachments reached the junction of the Musselshell and the Missouri.

More Miles luck followed. At the same time that his first troops reached the river, so did the steamboat Fontenelle, drifting down current after having discharged a load of freight. By requisitioning it temporarily, the colonel was able to save time and preclude swimming accidents by having the steamer ferry his command across. A good thing, too, for during the process, which was nearly marred by letting the boat leave too soon, down from the Cow Island Crossing came two civilians in a rowboat. From them Miles learned that the Nez Perces had crossed and were well ahead of him.[10] Since he wanted to outdistance them and not chase them from behind, as Howard had been doing so futilely for more than a thousand miles, he obviously had to put on speed.

More luck. Once the Nez Perces crossed the river, they had slowed down, first to loot the wagon train and then to enjoy Looking Glass's decision that they take things easy. Miles, of course, did not know of the slowdown. But he did know that a force as large as his would be highly visible on the naked plain the Indians were traversing between the Bear Paw Mountains on the west and the Little Rockies on the east. To get in front of them unobserved, he would have to travel at top speed east of the latter uplift. This he did. Even the weather cooperated. As he left the Little Rockies behind and turned west—it was September 29—drenching rains fell. Mists closed in, reducing visibility, but his scouts had worked out a route in advance and were able to lead the soldiers without a hitch to that night's miserable camp.[11]

Unhappily, as the scouts soon learned from the Nez Perces' broad trail, they were still behind the Indians—but by no more than nine or ten miles. Wanting to strike before his quarry had saddled up for another days' ride toward Canada, Miles ordered reveille sounded at 2:00 A.M. The sky had cleared and cold air had pooled around the campsite. The ground and nearby creek were frozen.

After attending to their horses and gulping breakfast, the troops swung into their saddles, leaving the wagons and cannons to follow as best they could.

After they had ridden about five miles, the scouts gave a signal and they paused while the colonel laid down the order of the charge. The three units of the Seventh Cavalry were to lead the way in columns of four—A to the left, D in the center, K (of the Sitting Bull escort group) to the right. The three units, F, G, and H of the Second Cavalry were to swing to the left well above the camp hollow and strike for the horse herd. The mounted infantry, A and D, was to stay behind as a backup for the Seventh Cavalry units. It was about 9:00 A.M. of September 30.[12]

They trotted for a time, then galloped easily, pieces of thawing mud flying from the horses' hooves. About a mile from the hostile camp, which was still invisible because of the abrupt drop of the southern bluffs, Miles paused again, this time to survey the scene ahead—dead north—through his field glasses. The land seemed to skip easily over the still-invisible cove to the prairie where the horses were. A few Indians were already moving among them.

Bugles sounded. Pistols out, sabers aloft, carbines ready. Charge! The three companies of the Second Cavalry, led by the frenzied Sioux and Cheyenne scouts, swung left for the horse herd. The others went straight ahead, full tilt. Major Henry Remsen Tilton, the surgeon of the Seventh, remembered the exhilaration: "To be astride a good horse, on the open prairie ... one of four hundred horsemen, galloping on a hot trail, sends a thrill through your body which is seldom experienced."[13]

A hundred days of stressful traveling had brought little change to the Nez Perces' age-old cultural habits. A council of chiefs could make decisions about routes, campsites, and battle strategies, but they could do little to enforce compliance. The Indians remained highly individualistic, cooperating with each other, the band chiefs, and the group as a whole only when it suited their sense of fitness, often as revealed to them by their private guardian spirits.

So it was on the cold morning of September 30. Although Looking Glass had prevailed on the council to slow down the daily pace, the families knew there would be another day of marching, and each was getting ready for it in its own way, a lack of imposed discipline that a white army officer would have found intolerable. Some were lingering over breakfast, others were packing, a few were looking for their horses in the restive herd being assembled by the older boys and their mentors.[14]

There were warnings. A rider who had spent the night on the plains with a party of hunters galloped in with word of buffalo stampeding away from some sort of alarm. A kind of lassitude kept the report from spreading. Looking Glass was so little impressed that he told the mothers around him to take their time finishing whatever they were doing. Meanwhile, another scout had taken the trouble to ride far enough south to glimpse a large body of riders in the distance. Pushing his horse to the top of a hill from which part of the Indian camp was visible, he waved his blanket frantically and then spurred full speed to the village.

Of a sudden, listlessness burned into panic. Several warriors, accompanied by women and children, ran toward the horse herd. Crashing through the brush that lined the creek, jumping down the five-foot cut bank, and scrambling out the other side took time. Meanwhile the white riders had found an easy crossing upstream and were thundering toward the herd, rifles banging. There was a hideous melee as the charge crashed into the bunch. Indian horses plunged and squealed. Family groups that had already caught and saddled their animals fled in terror toward the north. Warriors who were able to swing onto their mounts fell in behind to cover their flight. Riding wildly, bonneted Sioux and Cheyenne scouts for Miles's army hurled themselves against the berserk Nez Perce horses that were to be their pay for their services and tried to drive them onto the prairie where they could be brought under control.

Joseph grasped the threat early. Shouting, "Horses! Horses! Save the horses!" he jumped onto the pony he had kept tied near his lodge and dashed across the creek. Yellow Wolf followed on foot. Yellow Wolf's mother and one of Joseph's daughters, Kapkap Ponme ("Sound of Running Feet"), somewhere between twelve and fifteen years of age, had already gone ahead to start catching the pack animals the family would need for the day. Joseph tossed her a rope. Gesturing frantically, he told her to join the people, many riding double, who were fleeing north. Probably, he supposed he would follow with the rest of his extended family when the battle was over. He did not know yet how terrified the village was. Later it would be estimated that as many as two hundred people joined the route. Under the circumstances they felt no obligation to stay and fight.

Whirling back across the creek, Joseph joined the defenders. As he told the story later, "It seemed to me there were guns on every side, before and behind me. My clothes were cut to pieces and my horse was wounded, but I was not hurt. As I reached the door of my lodge, my wife handed me my rifle, saying: 'Here's your gun. Fight.'"—a remark whose tenor suggests that as camp chief he had not, up to that time, participated in many of the fugitives' battles. But now he was catapulted into violence.

Rifle in hand, he joined the warriors who were rushing to find positions from which to fight—in the gullies that wrinkled the edges of the cove, behind occasional rocks, even inching up to the brows of some of the hills. Friends fought together or joined a favorite chief. There was no concerted plan. No one gave orders except as a natural leader emerged in one of the knots that had come together like magnetized iron filings. The noise increased the sense of confusion—yells, gun blasts, and the pounding hoofs of the charging cavalry, "a rumble like stampeding buffalo," Yellow Wolf remembered.

As the battle opened, Colonel Miles's luck deserted him. While the three companies of the Second Cavalry peeled away to the left after the Indian horses, those of the Seventh drove straight ahead toward the village. Then the ground roughened in front of Company K, led by Captain Owen Hale. To avoid the insecure footing, Hale swung his riders still farther to the right and emerged hell-bent on a long tongue of prairie land bordered by steep bluffs on the left and a shallow coulee on the right. Near the base of the bluffs was Joseph's section of the camp.

As Hale hesitated, his opponents materialized like hornets, rushing up the steep slope from the camp. More ran up the ravine at the troopers' back. Hale ordered his bugler to signal "Dismount!"—a bullet stung Hale to death immediately afterward—and a savage battle at close quarters erupted, well away from the Indian village. Nothing like that had been any part of Miles's intentions.

Similar troubles engulfed companies A and D. While K was veering to the right, companies A and D kept their horses pounding straight ahead. Unexpectedly, a forty-foot hill, too steep to ride down, yawned in front of them. Its tawny slopes were peppered with the figures of Indian warriors, many stripped almost naked in spite of the cold and all of them scrambling upward for the kill. To keep the front ranks of the cavalry from being pushed over the hill, the way Indian hunters sometimes pushed stampeding buffalo over a deadly drop, the captains signaled for a sharp U-turn to the right. The maneuver could not be executed smoothly, and for several moments the overconfident troopers found themselves tangling together in frightened confusion. Discipline prevailed. The troopers retreated behind the shield of a slight rise over which the Indians who had gained the top of the main bluff could not shoot. Dismounting swiftly, the cavalrymen counterattacked on foot, forcing the Indians to seek protection just below the brow of the hill. There the Indians stayed, refusing to be dislodged.

As positions stabilized, the army surgeons established a "hospital" in the depression behind the rise, treating emergency cases on the ground without tents, for the supply wagons had not yet arrived. Establishing his headquarters in the same depression, Miles contemplated an evolving stalemate that brought him no happiness.

His first problem was Company K. Because it was closest to the village, most of the defenses had concentrated there. To relieve K's beset men, Miles ordered the dismounted troopers of the other companies to turn their horses over to designated holders and to go on foot to the relief. Although the exposure was acute in places, most got through. Their arrival broke up the hand-to-hand fighting, and the Indians slid back down the slope to take positions in the rock-fronted shelters and shallow pits the women had helped prepare. None of the exhausted whites were inclined to follow.

The Indians farther south had noticed the movement of the troops toward K and had scurried to match it. The shift in their firing enabled Miles to move his infantry into the positions vacated by the cavalry. The infantry's job was to hold back any flanking thrust in the direction of the hospital.

It had not been a long battle—little more than half an hour so far—and now Miles, who had anticipated a swift sweep through the village, found himself facing the embarrassing possibility of being defeated as soundly as Howard, Gibbon, and Sturgis had been. Indeed, his situation was worse. The advantage of surprise had been his. So was the advantage in numbers. He knew many warriors had been drained away from the camp by the rout that had followed the attack on the horse herd. How many fighters remained to face him he could not tell. Whatever the figure (it was about 75) he had thrown the full strength of the Seventh Cavalry, about 125 men, and 90 infantrymen against them. Although he had accepted heavy losses, as had the Nez Perces, the enemy had fought him to a standstill.

In all probability the Indians would try to contact Sitting Bull and tell him what was happening. The old chief, of course, knew that a commission of high-placed government officials was assembling at Fort Benton preparatory to march north to propose a treaty of capitulation to him. He didn't know that part of the commission's escort was Company K of the Seventh Cavalry, but he would find out. He would find out, too, that the Nez Perces had cut Company K to pieces while outfighting yet another American army—Miles's army. How would Sitting Bull and his Sioux respond to that news? How soon? And how soon would the commission learn?

To make matters worse, Colonel Sturgis and General Howard were advancing toward the battlefield from Cow Island. If Sturgis, Miles's counterpart in rank, arrived first and added soldiers to the attacking force, Miles would have to share with him the credit for whatever success ensued. If Howard arrived first, he would take command and receive the glory. Somehow Miles had to break the stalemate and produce a victory or the rank of brigadier general he yearned for would be further away than ever.

Impetuously he decided on another risky charge. An infantry company, commanded by Lieutenant Henry Romeyn, was sent to the tongue of land above the village. There it reinforced Company K and the other dismounted cavalrymen. At a given signal, all were to charge down the slope onto the south portion of the village. While the Nez Perces were concentrating on that threat, Lieutenant Mason Carter was to race with nineteen foot soldiers down one of the southern coulees to the creek and, sheltered by its banks, work toward the main fight, subjecting the Indians to a crossfire that might break them.

Joseph later told of the two-pronged attack this way in the April 1879 issue of *The North American Review*. "The soldiers kept up a continuous fire. Six of my men were killed in one spot near me. Ten or twelve soldiers charged into our camp and got possession of two lodges, killing three Nez Perces and losing three of their men, who fell inside our lines. I called my men to drive them back. We fought at close range, not more than twenty steps apart, and drove the soldiers back upon their main line, leaving their dead in our hands. We secured their arms and ammunition."

Of the 125 men in the Seventh Cavalry, 53 died or had been wounded during the two charges. Glumly, Miles realized he would have to do by siege what he could not do by direct attack. After sending couriers to Sturgis and Howard—"Please move forward with caution and rapidity"—he carefully extended a thin line completely around the Indian camp.

The light rain changed to snow. There was some shelter. During the day, the women and children, using camas sticks, knives, and pots and pans, had dug caves into the banks of the creek bed and the ravines. Warriors who had to stay on guard deepened the rifle pits with some of the trowel-shaped bayonets they had picked up on earlier battlefields. A few tiny fires smoldered in the caves, but wet buffalo chips did not burn well and sufficient quantities of dead willow twigs were hard to get. The children whimpered from cold and hunger. There was stocktaking. At least eighteen people had been killed, three of them women. Ollokot was dead. So were Lean Elk, Toohoolhoolzote, and such notable warriors as Pile of Clouds. Forty or more were wounded. Women wailed softly. Some warriors began to chant their death songs.

Unable to endure more, some families slipped away through the pickets. A few others, already outside but finding the dangers of the camp preferable to the dark loneliness of the Plains, crept back in. The ease of their passage led their chiefs to ask for volunteers to carry an appeal to Sitting Bull. How the messengers traveled, whether by foot or with some of the few horses remaining in the camp, is unknown. It doesn't matter. Before reaching their destination they were killed by Assiniboin Indians who wanted to convince the whites they were not aiding the enemy.

Emptiness and the whine of the wind. Yellow Wolf remembered for them all: "Thoughts came of the Wallowa where I grew up. Of my own country when only Indians were there. Of tipis along the bending river. Of the blue clear lake, wide meadows with horse and cattle herds.... Then with rifle I stood forth, saying to my heart, 'Here I will die, fighting for my people and our homes.'"

Toward midday a white flag appeared and a voice called from the army line, asking for a parley with Joseph. A myth was in the process of crystallizing. Miles did not know which chiefs remained alive, but in Howard's dispatches Joseph had always been the astute leader of the fugitives, and so Miles supposed he was the one who could pronounce the future for all the enemy. After some anxious discussion, a hastily summoned council agreed that Joseph should talk to the colonel. Joseph's friend Yellow Bull walked across the meadow with him to the meeting, as did Tom Hill. Half Delaware and half Nez Perce, Hill knew enough English to relay interpretations Joseph could trust.

Very plainly Joseph told Miles he could not speak for the entire camp.[15] Nevertheless, they did talk of a general surrender. Miles pointed out the hopelessness of the Indians' position. If Joseph countered by mentioning Sitting Bull, there is no record of it. Emphasizing his generosity, Miles said that if the Nez Perces would surrender all their weapons, he would take the surviving Indians to Fort Keogh for the winter. In the spring when travel was again possible, they could return to the Nez Perce reservation in Idaho. And that, he might have said with a little twist of the knife, was all the whites had wanted in the first place, before the shedding of so much blood.

Joseph shook his head. The Indians would need at least half their guns for hunting. He would, however, tell the others what had been offered. As the little party was moving toward the camp, Miles called Joseph back and, in gross violation of the flag of truce, seized him. Yellow Wolf says that the chief was then bound hand and foot, rolled tight in a blanket, and deposited in a mule corral. Joseph himself never mentioned, at least for the record, any ill treatment.

About the time the chief was seized, young Lieutenant Lovell H. Jerome wandered, astoundingly, into the Indian camp. Why not, he may have thought. A truce was in effect, and he was curious. Then the truce ended abruptly and the Indians laid hold of him. Some wanted to kill him, unpleas-antly perhaps, but Yellow Bull recognized the captive's value. The Indians treated him well, under guard, while awaiting Miles's response. Exasperated and wondering afresh what had happened to his vaunted luck, the colonel agreed to an exchange. That done—it was midday, October 2—the battle resumed, mostly sniping by well-concealed sharpshooters on both sides.

As snow began to fall again the next day, Indian sentries watched Miles's wagon train lumber into the military camp. The Napoleon cannon arrived, too, but kept overshooting its mark until the artillerymen elevated the muzzle by dropping the gun's tail into a hole. Shells could then be lobbed into the valley as if by a mortar. One lucky hit on a cave shelter buried a woman and child alive, but in the main the explosion of the shells caused harm only to the nerves of the besieged. Meanwhile the Indians could not help knowing, partly by the smell of cooking food, that the wagon train had brought fresh supplies to the military camp—meat, flour, ammunition, and tents for all but the most remote pickets to sleep in during the cold, wet nights. Would any relief ever come to the Indians? Driven by anxiety, they peered again and again toward the north, wondering whether any of their people had reached Sitting Bull yet. On one such occasion, when Looking Glass raised himself to look, a bullet tore off the top of his head.

Sturgis, Howard, and their troops were paused beside the Missouri River when Miles's appeal that they come with caution and rapidity reached them. They traveled in two columns, Howard's men in the lead. As they approached the battlefield, the general wanted to go even faster, intent, perhaps, on being in on the long-deferred victory. When the weary troopers couldn't keep up, he pushed ahead with a small escort, composed of his two aides, Lieutenants Guy Howard and Charles Erskine Scott Wood; interpreter Ad Chapman; seventeen cavalrymen; and two treaty Nez Perce Indians known to the whites as Captain

John and Old George. The pair of Indians had served faithfully as horse herders throughout the campaign. Both had daughters married to nontreaty husbands. As far as the fathers knew, both young couples were in the belligerent camp. Howard hoped that the familial connection would enable the parents to make contact with the nontreaty leaders and explain to them, in their own idiom, the wisdom of surrendering.

Fearing that General Howard would take command and reap the glory of the coming victory, Miles greeted his superior stiffly. Howard, however, ignoring the advice of his own staff, chose to be generous and let Miles continue in charge. The general also agreed with the terms Miles had already offered the Nez Perces. If the Indians surrendered, they would be housed and fed at Fort Keogh during the winter. As soon as the Bitterroot trails were free of snow the following spring, they could return to the Lapwai Reservation. Inasmuch as Howard had been intending to push the nontreaty Indians onto the reserve when the war broke out, it is unlikely he said anything about Joseph's people returning to the Wallowa-Imnaha country. Wishful thinking, though, apparently gave some of the band that idea.

On the morning of October 5, Captain John and Old George rode down the steep slope into the valley under a flag of truce. The effusiveness of their greeting irritated Yellow Wolf and Joseph, but the pair got their points across, not least the warning that the main body of Howard and Sturgis's troops was only a day away. The soldiers' arrival would make the odds against the Nez Perces insuperable even if Sitting Bull did arrive, a hope that was growing steadily dimmer. (As matters developed, no Sioux appeared. The impending visit by the U.S. Sitting Bull Commission kept the chief quiet, and parties of young warriors who might have responded received the appeal too late.)

At the Nez Perce camp considerable unhappy talk about the state of affairs was undoubtedly mixed with discussions about terms of surrender. Things were bad, all right—most of the principal chiefs were dead, and a lot of people, Joseph's family with them, were wandering forlornly through the hills. Children were hungry and freezing. Joseph was heart-weary—but not too weary to send greetings to his old adversary, General Howard. Naturally, Old George and Captain John carried summaries of all they had heard back to the military camp. At the camp, twenty-five-year-old Lieutenant Charles Erskine Scott Wood, who had literary ambitions and an active imagination, listened with fascination to it all.

While Looking Glass had been alive, he had sided with White Bird in an adamant refusal even to think about surrender. Now White Bird stood alone, but his determination did not slip. He did not trust the white army officers or their promise, delivered through the emissaries, that no Indian would be punished for the war. The outrages at White Bird Canyon that had precipitated the conflict had been committed by members of his band. He knew of chiefs in other tribes, Captain Jack of the Modocs for one, who had been hanged in retaliation for the misdeeds (as defined by the whites) of a few of the band's members. So when Joseph told Old George and Captain John that the surrender terms were acceptable, White Bird stayed silent, as was his prerogative. One Nez Perce chief could not impose a binding commitment on another, as Lawyer had sought to do at the signing of the 1863 thief treaty.

So Joseph went alone to meet the victors, and that circumstance—no other chief with him—seemed to prove what Howard had been implying in his dispatches all along. Joseph was chief. The sole leader. The red Napoleon.

As befitted a chief, he rode, probably on a borrowed horse, to the meeting place at the foot of the bluffs. He carried a rifle across the pommel of his saddle. He leaned down talking to the four or five friends who, lacking horses, walked beside his mount.

Howard, Miles, interpreter Ad Chapman, Lieutenant Wood, and a few others waited motionless. They, too, were standing. Joseph dismounted and adjusted his blanket. Carrying his rifle cradled in the crook of one arm, he walked up to the officers. He started to hand the weapon to Howard. The general gestured him on to Miles, who accepted the symbol of capitulation.[16]

The chief spoke in such a soft voice that some of those who were present did not hear him. Indians, of course, possessed neither clocks nor calendars and generally used the imagery of sun or moon to indicate the passage of time. Resorting to a common idiom meaning "from now on," Joseph brought the story of a once-free people to a close:

"From where the sun now stands I will fight no more forever."

· 24 ·

INTERLUDE: FANCY FREE

L ieutenant Charles Erskine Scott Wood, who added appreciably to the Joseph legend, left behind a remarkable but not always reliable legacy. Born in Erie, Pennsylvania, he graduated from West Point in 1874. On returning from duty in Alaska, he was assigned to Howard's force and caught up with the general near the Salmon River shortly after Perry's defeat at White Bird Canyon. The timing was unfortunate: a day of heavy rain, the burial of the dead and bloated soldiers, a sudden midnight shot at a shadow at the edge of camp that might have been an Indian, but was an American sentry. Wood always insisted he was not the one who fired the fatal shot. He was never brought to trial. Nevertheless, his fellow troopers thought he was responsible for the death, however inadvertently.[1]

After leaving the army in 1884, Howard's onetime aide became a prosperous lawyer in Portland. His avocations were writing, painting, and supporting programs of social radicalism. He loved the high sage deserts and cool mountains of eastern Oregon, the background of much of his poetry. He considered himself a friend of Joseph and sent his adolescent son to live with the chief during parts of two summers. His greatest notoriety attached to his relationship with Sarah Bard Field with whom he fell in love when he was fifty-eight, she twenty-eight. When Sarah's husband, a Baptist preacher, refused to grant her a divorce, she obtained one under Nevada's then-scandalously lenient laws. When Wood's wife, a devout Catholic, also denied her spouse a divorce, he and Sarah simply set up open housekeeping in San Francisco, where they became the center of the city's bohemian, artistic, and politically radical community. All of which is not necessarily irrelevant to the Joseph story.

It is not possible to determine how many Indians surrendered to the whites after the Bear Paw battle. Of the 700–750 men, women, and children who began the flight, about 120 were killed, 55 of them women and children. (In return, the Indians managed to slay 177 soldiers and civilians while wounding 147 more.) One historian states that 233 Nez Perces fled from the battlefield, most of them during the rout of the first day. Seventy-year-old White Bird, who refused to surrender, led the last group to Canada. With him were his two wives, fourteen other women, Yellow Wolf, and a few warriors. Along the way they picked up Yellow Wolf's mother and Joseph's daughter, Kapkap Ponme. Not all who tried to escape succeeded, however. Troops scouring the plains near the battlefield brought back an unrecorded number of fugitives. The best we can say statistically about the ending of the war is that somewhere between 405 and 431 people gave themselves up to the government forces. One commonly accepted median, 418, breaks down into 87 men, 184 women, and 147 children.[2]

By October 13, victors and losers had reassembled on the north bank of the Missouri River near the mouth of the Musselshell. There they met two steamboats that Howard had requisitioned for a double purpose. First the craft ferried troops, prisoners, and baggage to the south shore of the river. That done, they were to transport Howard's footsore infantry and some unhorsed cavalrymen downstream to Omaha, where they would catch the train to San Francisco and, eventually, the Pacific Northwest. Meanwhile Miles's contingent and the prisoners, their wounded in wagons or on travois, would travel overland to Fort Keogh beside the Yellowstone, where, the commanders had agreed, the Indians would spend the winter before returning to Idaho.[3]

As for himself, Howard planned to ride one of the steamboats as far as the railhead of the Northern Pacific at Bismarck, the raw new territorial capital of North Dakota. From Bismarck he, his son Guy, his aide-de-camp, Charles Erskine Scott Wood, and a few other officers would hurry by train through St. Paul, Minnesota, to Chicago, where he would report directly to his superior, General Phillip Sheridan, on the outcome of the Nez Perce campaign and on his and Colonel Miles's decision concerning the captive Nez Perces. A written report also had to be prepared for the secretary of war, who would present the document and all other reports relative to the military events of 1877 to the Congress of the United States.

Howard, who rather liked writing, prepared the first pencil draft of his report to the secretary of war while the steamer he was on moved down the river toward Bismarck. He then handed the draft to his aide, Lieutenant Wood, for polishing and copying. Many years later an amateur historian and assiduous researcher, Mark H. Brown, found that penciled draft. He noticed that three paragraphs had been inserted in a hand different from Howard's. The first intrusive paragraph stated that on surrendering his rifle, Chief Joseph had delivered a speech that Wood, standing nearby with pad and pencil, had taken down verbatim as it was translated by interpreter Ad Chapman. The second paragraph, which presents the speech, is strange in view of the know fact that only a few officers, an interpreter, and half a dozen Indians, none a chief, were present at the actual surrender. Yet the paragraph ends, "Hear me, my chiefs...." The final paragraph of the insertion purports to describe Joseph handing over his rifle to Miles.[4]

The speech (paragraph two) begins: "Tell General Howard I know his heart." Possibly, just possibly Joseph did speak those words to Ad Chapman at the moment of surrender and Ad passed them on to Howard. Or possibly he spoke them to Captain John and Old George when those two Nez Perce horse herders visited the besieged camp to urge surrender of the Indians. If the latter event is accepted as true, we don't have a speech but a message intended for General Howard—a message first spoken in front of a council of the Indians—"Hear me, my chiefs." Captain John and Old George then returned to the military camp and repeated the message to General Howard, presumably in Wood's hearing. Touched by the pathos and drama of the words, Wood later took the liberty of inserting them into the report for the secretary of war under the fiction that they had been spoken directly to Howard at the act of surrender.[5]

The trouble with that interpretation is that Indians do not have the same thought patterns that whites do. In the minds of the Nez Perces at that last, critical council they were not giving themselves over in toto to the whites— were not surrendering as the whites would have described surrendering. What was important to the Nez Perces—a point of deepest honor—was the recording of which side first offered to quit fighting.[6]

Yellow Wolf was at that key council. According to him, Miles and Howard had directed the messengers to say to Joseph, "We will have no more fighting." At that Joseph grew excited. Some of the Indians had accused him of saying, "Let's quit!" while Miles had been holding him prisoner. Not so, he cried triumphantly. "I did not say, 'Let's quit!' ... General Miles said 'Let's quit!' And now General Howard [who had arrived after the brief imprisonment] says 'Let's quit!'" Thus, Joseph was justified: The Indians had not given up. The whites had. To which Yellow Wolf added in his reminiscences, "We were not captured. It was a draw battle.... We expected to return to our homes. That was promised us by General Miles. That was how he got our rifles from us. It was the only way he could get them."[7] Joseph confirmed this point of view two years later in his article in *The North American Review*: "General Miles had promised that we might return to our country with what stock we had left.... I believed General Miles, or I never would have surrendered"—for by then Joseph knew what *surrender* meant.

But Charles Erskine Scott Wood wanted drama and pathos. So he invented, first, a message to General Howard, using as raw material some of the details brought to the military by Captain John and Old George after their visit to the Indian camp: cold, hunger, exhaustion, death, grief. But filtering sentiments, however pathetic, through a messenger wasn't good storytelling. Accordingly Wood, who wasn't particular about the truth—remember that sentry at White Bird Canyon—turned his literary talents into creating a speech. First came Joseph's gesture toward Howard: *Tell him I know his heart*. Readers could easily visualize the listening general ramrod straight and resplendent in full-dress uniform. Then the nod toward the chiefs: *Hear me*. What reader, having absorbed the romantic paintings of stately Indian councils then flooding the country, would picture Joseph's entourage as it really was: half a dozen weary fugitives, muddy, cold, gaunt, dressed in tattered clothing. *My chiefs*: feathered headdresses, fringed and beaded buckskin jackets; no chiefs were there, but that was the scene to imagine.

Wood had a chance to give his effort a trial run when a reporter interviewed Howard and him in Bismarck, North Dakota, during their brief stop on the way to Chicago. He wanted it done right, so he almost surely handed the journalist a written copy. This is the way it appeared, somewhat belatedly, in the *Bismarck Tri-Weekly Tribune* of October 26, 1877:

Tell General Howard I know his heart. What he told me before I have in my heart. I am tired of fighting. Our chiefs are killed. Looking Glass is dead. Tahool-hool-shoot is dead. The old men are all dead. It is the younger men who say yes or no. He who leads the young men [Ollokot] is dead. It is cold and we have no blankets. The little children are freezing to death. My people, some of them, have run away into the hills and have no blankets, no food; no one knows where they are—perhaps freezing to death. I want time to look for my children and see how many of them I can find. May be I shall find them among the dead. Hear me my chiefs; I am tired. My heart is sick and sad. From where the sun now stands I will fight no more forever.

Now notice: Wood and Howard were interviewed again in Chicago. The resultant story, entitled "The Bible Chief," appeared in the *Chicago Times*, by coincidence, on October 26, the same day that Joseph's alleged speech was printed by the Bismarck newspaper. The *Times* allotted a single awkward line to Joseph's surrender statement: "From where the sun stands, forever and forever, I will never fight again."

Back to honesty? Not for long. On November 17, *Harper's Weekly* reprinted the long version exactly as it had appeared in the *Bismarck Tri-Weekly Tribune*. *Harper's* had been running a series of articles on the Nez Perce war, and its reporter in the field might well have picked up a copy of the *Tribune*. Or Wood might have graciously provided a copy. Or Howard might have. Or Miles.

Howard and Miles have a role here. Howard, who was sensitive about his reputation, almost surely was perusing the accounts in *Harper's Weekly*. Miles, who was feted in Bismarck on November 19, certainly could have picked up a copy of the *Tribune* for October 26, since he featured in it. And it is not possible to believe that they skipped reading the long version of the speech as it was printed on page 630 of *The Report of the Secretary of War for 1877*. Yet there is no record that either man ever repudiated the account, which both knew to be technically false. Why? Perhaps they didn't think it worth the bother. Or perhaps there was a more profound reason they sensed even then.

Joseph's surrender speech has been reprinted many times with only slight variations.[8] Its impact was immediate and helps explain the extraordinary reception the little frontier North Dakota town extended the chief when he appeared in November, of which more in a moment. The reason: the poet in Charles Erskine Scott Wood had plumbed deep. He probably knew it; hence, his manipulations. Whatever the actual provenance of his words, he had touched with them the infinite sadness of a race's defeat and death. And so the fiction stood unchallenged.

On October 23, to a salute of cannons and the tune of the fort's band blaring "Hail to the Chief," Colonel Miles reached Fort Keogh on the Yellowstone River with his Nez Perce prisoners and such soldiers as had not descended the Missouri by steamboat. For the better part of six days, the list-less Indians went about trying to establish themselves in what was, to them, a foreign land. The effort ended abruptly with the arrival of unsettling orders from Alfred H. Terry, commanding general of the Department of Dakota. Maintaining four hundred Indians at so distant and isolated a spot as Fort Keogh, Terry declared, would be prohibitively expensive. Consequently they should be sent eight hundred miles farther down the river to Fort Abraham Lincoln near Bismarck, North Dakota.[9]

To get down the river before its annual freeze-up, Miles had to act quick-ly. He told Joseph and the other leading men to make up a cavalcade of the healthiest Nez Perces, whatever their gender and age. They'd ride horseback the eight hundred miles to Fort Lincoln. But close to half the prisoners—the very young, the very old, the sick, and the wounded and their caretakers—could not make such a journey into the teeth of winter. Fortunately, there was a way out. The commissary department had been stockpiling, for winter use at the fort, garden vegetables, butter, eggs, some hay, and even a little fire-wood produced on pioneer ranches far up the Yellowstone's fertile valley. The supplies had been floated downstream on flat-bottom mackinaw boats made of whipsawed lumber. Some of the craft were as much as thirty-two feet long and eight feet wide. The army had bought the ponderous flatboats at bargain prices—they would have been difficult to drag back upstream—and had tied them to the riverbank for whatever use might develop. Just what Miles need-ed, once he'd found rivermen who were capable of handling them. The boat-man who concerns us here was Fred Bond, aged twenty-five.

In his reminiscences Bond remembered himself as "tall dark and power-full of true English blood."[10] Like Charles Erskine Scott Wood, he was staunchly romantic, and the twenty-two Indians placed under his charge pro-vided his imagination with the fodder it needed. His spelling mirrored his character: rough hewn.

They started their journey on October 31, when slush ice was already beginning to form in the river. The young captain quickly won the coopera-tion of the Indians by setting up a hierarchy that enabled them to run their own affairs within the limits of their circumstances. He appointed as director of the party a noble-looking Indian who could speak a little English, and named him Chief George Washington. In charge of the women was a tall, rawboned, dark-skinned, white-haired female whose wrinkled face "would put to shame an age[d] alligator of the Florida glades." For unstated reasons he called her Shades of Night. The leaders assigned other women to gather wood, to cook, and to wash and care for the wounded. The older boys became crewmen charged with wielding the heavy oars and, when necessary, the long poles that would help heave the flatboat across sandbars or thrust it through the gathering ice. Bond handled the great sterrr sweep, with occasional relief in smooth water from a most delectable fifteen-year-old maiden dressed in fine deerskin, her hair plaited with five-dollar bills as ornaments. "her cheeks was tinted with Erythrite (pink cobalt bloom) ... a picture of true wild human nature." When she was teased, "you could see the youthfull blush rais through the Erythrite polish on her dimpled cheek." He named her Viola because of her dark eyes. Her mother was along but seems not to have interfered unduly with the burgeoning romance.

So they could vary their diet of hardtack, rice, beans, and flour, Bond entrusted Chief Washington with a rifle and "caretiridges" so he could hunt deer. He let the boys make bows and arrows for shooting beaver, whose skinned and roasted tails were a great delicacy. On spotting stands of ripe bull berries, he eased the flatboat against the banks and let the Indians gather fruit. They were so greedy for the taste of freshness that Washington had to threaten them with a whip to herd them back on board. Viola dodged him, "so I go and run down Viola and cary her to the boat." There they feasted, though it was "sad for our sugar ration."

When bureaucratic red tape held them up for a time at Fort Buford, where the Yellowstone River runs into the Missouri, and the people were confined in log huts guarded by rough soldiers, "I gave Viola my dirk to protect her honor." After they resumed their journey—all this while they were far ahead of the other flatboats—Bond caught a severe cold. It was endurable, though. "I felt soft hands press my brow and gentle hands moist now my parched lips."

As they neared Fort Lincoln on November 16, they were welcomed by a cannon blast and three whistles from a switch engine. Although Bond had told his passengers of "the great Iron horse that had the speed of a hundred ponies that lived on wood and water," the sight and clatter of the locomotive filled them with fear. "They became so helpless I had to work the boat across the river all alone to the Fort landing. They set up a moaning chant no doubt their death chant."

They had more reason for fear than either they or Fred Bond had any way of knowing. The people of Idaho remained icy with hate over the White Bird murders, which Joseph had not committed any more than he had led the warriors in battle. Learning of the surrender of the fugitives on October 5, public prosecutors had obtained indictments for murder against him and thirty-four other Indians—probably as many tribesmen as they could find names for. As early as September 3, E. C. Watkins, inspector for the Bureau of Indian Affairs, who had been with Howard prior to and during the beginning of the outbreaks, wrote his superiors that the nontreaty rebels should be sent "so far away that they can never return," for if they did come back the vengeful whites would set on them and kill them.[11]

The top generals of the army, Sherman and Sheridan, agreed. Neither Howard nor Miles, they snapped, had any authority to make arrangements concerning the disposition of the prisoners. Miles, who reached Fort Abraham Lincoln with the mobile part of the Nez Perces shortly after the flatboats arrived there, was ordered to requisition a train for taking the dispossessed Indians via Chicago to Fort Leavenworth, Kansas, where they would be held until a permanent site could be decided on.

This action, of course, violated promises made to the Indians by Howard and Miles that they would be returned to Idaho in the spring. Howard sought to clear his skirts in the prisoners' eyes by arguing that White Bird's flight to Canada just after the surrender invalidated the agreement. Miles, pompous though he could be at times, was made of sterner stuff. For years he did what he could to help the Nez Perces return home.[12]

Waiting for Miles to arrive in Bismarck took awhile. Fred Bond used the time to look over the town's resources for himself and then to show them to Chief Washington and wide-eyed Viola. The place was only three blocks long, but those blocks were crowded with scouts, trappers, miners, gamblers, soldiers, and rivermen. Bond thought it magnificent. "There was law and order because there was no lawyers. Great respect was shown to the gentler sex. Every person was more or less jolley because money was plenterfull and each person was robust and strong for the week had not yet appeared."[13]

While Chief Washington and he were eating breakfast in a restaurant one morning, they heard a band playing the "star spangle banner." They rushed outside. "Shore enough ... coming down the slope was Gen. Miles with Chief Joseph on is left." Behind them marched the command. One reaching the center of town, the troops formed a hollow square around the Indians who had traveled overland and had been greeted just outside town by many of those who had arrived by flatboat. "The appearance of all heart rending very sad." Then "the stampeed commenced. Women children even men rushed the hollow squar with all kind of cooked food.... The command had to halt till each Nez Perce prisoner and even the over land guard was furnished with food of good kind."

Miles and his staff were entertained with a banquet on the evening of November 19. Meanwhile interest in Joseph mounted, in part because of a eulogistic toast Miles delivered in his honor at the banquet and because of the Wood-manufactured speech that had been printed in the triweekly paper nearly a month before. The upshot was an invitation, unique in the history of Indian warfare, that was delivered publicly on the front page of the paper the morning of November 21.

TO JOSEPH, HEAD CHIEF OF NEZ PERCES

Sir:

Desiring to show you our kind feelings and the admiration we have for your bravery and humanity, as exhibited in your recent conflict with the forces of the United States, we most cordially invite you to dine with us at the Sheridan House in this city. The dinner to be given at 1½ P.M. today.

At a reception held in the hotel salon before the dinner, Joseph and a few other leading Indians greeted the ladies of the town, who were dressed to kill and intensely curious. He also had his picture recorded by F. J. Haynes, soon to be recognized as one of the foremost photographers of the American West. Perhaps the best picture of the chief ever taken, it became a best-seller throughout the nation.[14] Through it all the chief conducted himself with quiet dignity, though it is said he murmured sadly at one point, "When will the white men ever learn to tell the truth?"

If we are to believe Fred Bond's account, he joined in all the festivities. Using part of $323 he won playing faro, he bought a red silk head scarf for Viola's mother and then enlisted her help in outfitting the girl. Viola couldn't dance at the ball because her shoes turned out to be too big, and she did not know white-style dancing anyway. At the ladies' reception "she sat like a stone, dazed by the splendor." Evidently other aspects of the celebration were more entertaining. They stayed up all night taking in the shops and gambling halls. In the morning when the train was loading the weeping Indians, he went with her to the depot. The guards wouldn't let him on. His farewell was a note he pressed into her hand. He told her that after she had learned to read English, she would discover she could find him "near the headwaters of the two mighty rivers that flows toward the risen sun." She never appeared, though he says he learned she became a government nurse and saw service in the Philippines during the Spanish-American War.

Chief Joseph stood on the rear platform of the train to wave good-bye to the crowd of townspeople who had come to wish the Indians well. The whistle blew, the bell clanged, and "the Belle of Bismarck" (unidentified) kissed him on the cheek, a farewell from all the people of the Northwest.

"And," finished Fred Bond, "I turned my face towards the setting sun to join once more the winners of the golden West."

The golden West: wherever there are winners, there also have to be losers.

· 25 ·

AN AMERICAN TRAGEDY

The Nez Perce prisoners of war reached Fort Leavenworth in northeastern Kansas on November 24 and were sequestered on a piece of bottomland about two miles above the military establishment. The Missouri River was on one side, a frozen swamp on the other. In spite of the winter cold, they got on fairly well. The army rations issued to them were adequate, and no one complained when they resorted to their heathenish dances to keep up their spirits. Best of all, they rested after months of battles, forced marches, grief, and uncertainty.[1]

New terrors came with spring. Mysterious fevers and chills began inflicting people of all ages. Whites called the disease ague, or malaria, and knew that when mosquitoes began to swarm with the first hot weather, epidemics would sweep through the lower Missouri and Mississippi valleys. Quinine would help, but no one at Fort Leavenworth seems to have thought of requisitioning quinine for the Nez Perce prisoners. Desperately, the people turned to the tribal medicine men, but they could no more cope with the onslaught than the tewats of a century before had been able to handle smallpox. By the end of spring, half the group were seriously debilitated, and twenty-one, mostly children, had died.

Meanwhile control over the prisoners had passed from the War Department into the hands of the Bureau of Indian Affairs. Fearful of what that change portended, Joseph insisted again that Generals Miles and Howard had promised to return the Nez Perces to Idaho when summer came. Captain

332

George Randolph of Fort Leavenworth added recommendations that the Indians be treated with consideration. Wasted words. The bureau and the Congress of the United States, which voted appropriations for carrying out the nation's Indian programs, decided that the prisoners should be resettled on a seven-thousand-acre tract in the Quapaw Reservation in southeastern Kansas.

Various justifications were given. The Modocs, who had been relocated in the same area after their uprising in 1873, were doing well. In Idaho, where indictments for murder were still in force, the whites' hostility would be hard to handle. After May 1878, another excuse was raised. The Bannocks and Northern Paiutes had erupted, and Howard was pursuing them through southwestern Idaho and eastern Oregon, much as he had pursued the Nez Perces. The Sioux, too, were still restless, and if Joseph appeared in the Northwest, he might become a rallying point for a new series of Indian wars.[2]

They moved south by train and wagon in July 1878, a time of extreme, humid heat. Many, including Joseph and the interpreter, Ad Chapman, were prostrate. Three children died along the way. Persons already infected with malaria took the disease with them, in their blood stream. During their first two months on the Quapaw Reservation, another forty-seven perished. Not understanding the disease or the mechanics of its transmission, the Nez Perces blamed the land, saying it was uninhabitable, though in reality it was a pleasant woodland region.

In spite of the deaths, there was no immediate drop in population. Army units scouring the Plains kept picking up driblets of bedraggled fugitives they sent on to the reservation. Most of the captives had fled from the Bear Paw battlefield at the time of Miles's first charge and then had found themselves wandering forlornly they knew not where. Some found refuge among sympathetic Plains tribes (and a few were slaughtered by unfriendly captors). Some surrendered in despair at various army cantonments or trading posts. Others just gave up and died.

Many of those who fled immediately after Joseph's surrender were lucky enough to find shelter for the winter at Sitting Bull's camp in Canada. During those cold and hungry times, they did some second thinking. They knew the American officers had promised to send those who surrendered with Joseph back to Idaho. Homesick, a mixed group of twenty-five or thirty decided to rejoin their friends and relatives on the Lapwai Reservation. Among them were Yellow Wolf and Joseph's teenage daughter, Kapkap Ponme, who had fled from the Bear Paw at the first charge of the white cavalry against the

Indians' horse herd. The Sioux gave the returnees horses, a few guns, and ten bullets each. But it was hard to kill game enough to feed twenty-five people with so little ammunition. Of necessity, they said later, they raided a few ranches along the way for horses, beef, and other supplies. Scuffles resulted. They killed at least one white and skirmished with one small army unit. Rumor inflated their progress to a bloody rampage. White hostility flared, but what was worse, they found no welcome on the reservation.[3]

Exhausted and helpless, most surrendered. Kapkap Ponme and several other women were allowed to remain with the Christian Indians at Kamiah. The warriors were sent eventually to join the other Nez Perce exiles on the Quapaw Reservation. "No mountains, no springs, no clear running water," Yellow Wolf grieved. "We called where we were held Eeikish Pah [Hot Place]. All the time we suffered from the climate.... All the newborn babies died.... We were always lonely for our old-time homes."[4]

Joseph remained determined to take his surviving followers back to those old-time homes. He harped constantly to every white official he saw about Miles's promise. (He knew by then of Howard's back-pedaling.) He said that the Quapaw lands assigned the band were unacceptable; the Indians were supposed to support themselves by farming, but the soil was too poor, the water supply insufficient. (Would he and the other Dreamers in his band have torn the bosom of Mother Earth in order to farm?)

Agents from the Bureau of Indian Affairs offered a new tract farther south. Joseph refused to move. To the exasperated whites, it looked as if his intransigence was deliberately calculated to wear them down until finally they gave in to his wishes. They thought, too, that his stubbornness was sustained, in part, by his Dreamer religion, which preached, among other things, that a savior would appear, the whites would vanish, and every Indian who had ever lived would be resurrected to enjoy a reinvigorated paradise.[5]

In the fall of 1878, the commissioner of Indian affairs himself, Ezra Hayt, and one of his board members, E. M. Kingsley, traveled from Washington, D.C., to the Nez Perce camp to try to break the stalemate. Their appearance, of itself, suggests something of Joseph's powers of persuasion—and perhaps something of the prodding Miles was exerting on his behalf, for, in general, Indians had to accept whatever the government was willing to hand them. Hayt, however, wanted to be fair. A return to Idaho, he said, was out of the question because of intensified hostility resulting from the Bannock War, just then winding down. But if Joseph would pick a companion, Kingsley and he would show them a place they had heard of—one they were sure the Nez Perces would like.

Joseph chose as a fellow traveler Husishusis Kute, the only surviving chief of the Palouse rebels. Ad Chapman went along as interpreter. By wagon the four men traveled about 175 miles west along the Kansas-Oklahoma border and then dipped south to the neighborhood of present-day Tonkawa, Oklahoma. A hot, fine tract of some ninety-thousand acres sprawled there, boxed on two sides by the merging Chikaskia River and the Salt Fork of the Arkansas. The land was part of the Ponca Reserve, but Hayt said that if Joseph agreed to settle there, the government would purchase it for the Nez Perces.

With considerable reluctance Joseph did agree and then sat at a table with Husishusis Kute and the Ponca chiefs while a deal was hammered out— some $18,000 for 90,000 acres, which, if governmental custom prevailed, would be paid to the sellers in the form of shoddy, overpriced goods and equipment.[6]

The trip brought him a new friend, the Indian commissioner, who afterwards wrote with just a touch of condescension, "I found him to be one of the most gentlemanly and well-behaved Indians I have ever met. He is bright and intelligent and is anxious for the welfare of his people.... When he gives up hope of returning to Idaho, I think he will choose the location I have named."[7]

Hope was not yet gone, however. Hayt had also noted in his report that "the present unhappy condition of the Indians' appeals to the sympathies of a very large portion of the American people." Taking cognizance of that sympathy and undoubtedly working with Hayt's approval, Inspector General John O'Neill of the Bureau of Indian Affairs made arrangements for Joseph to travel to Washington, D.C., and plead his case directly to President Rutherford B. Hayes, Secretary of the Interior Carl Schurz, and such other persons of influence as he could reach. Accompanying him on the trip were his friend Yellow Bull and, once again, the government-appointed interpreter, Ad Chapman.[8]

The idea of taking red delegations to the capital so they could be awed by seeing for themselves the power and the glory of the whites was not new. Several pliant treaty Nez Perces had joined the ritual during the days when the reservation was being diminished. Neither Joseph nor Yellow Bull had approximated such an experience, however, even though they had ridden a crowded train through Chicago on the way to Fort Leavenworth. They would need shepherding, but the records are so sparse that we don't know who the shepherds were. If Joseph had not said, almost in passing, that he had indeed spoken to President Hayes and Secretary Schurz, one might doubt that the meetings actually took place. In fact, memory of the entire trip focuses on a single event, the speech Joseph delivered in Lincoln Hall on January 14, 1879, and there is much about it we wish we knew but don't.

Who conceived the notion of putting him in front of so distinguished an audience? Who arranged for the hall, prepared the publicity, and sent out the announcements? Most of all, who was sure that once he was on that strange platform, he would strike the right note between fawning, clowning, boasting, and defying? What white man knew him that well?

Because the press had followed the closing phases of the Nez Perce war with some thoroughness and because Joseph's alleged surrender speech, along with the unusual reception at Bismarck, had attracted considerable attention, a large crowd was anticipated. An audience drawn by those lures would expect to see a military genius bearing the burden of defeat and yet standing tall for the sake of his people. How did the principal actor dress for such an occasion?

We know that C. M. Dell, a photographer well-known for his portraits, took a picture of Joseph while the chief was in Washington. He is posed beside a stack of fake studio boulders. He is wearing a horizontally striped blanket coat. Concentric necklaces of shells and beads show between the coat's wide lapels. Another blanket, this one fringed, is draped across his left forearm. His right arm rests easily against his side; in his right hand is a fur of some sort. He wears beaded moccasins. The front part of his hair, which he never cut, is combed upward in a Dreamer-style pompadour. Two tightly bound braids drop over his upper chest.

The clothing is not Nez Perce clothing, which may mean only that Joseph borrowed it for an incidental picture. Or, as seems more likely, the promoters of the speech dressed him that way because the getup brought him, in their minds, an air of aboriginal stateliness. In a stereotyped way they succeeded. Except for the chief's braids and forelock, he does look, in the picture, and would have looked on the platform, more like an ancient Roman senator sporting a toga than like an Indian. And yet … Joseph's innate dignity does shine through. So perhaps the promoters knew what they were doing—if, in fact, they were the ones who dressed him for the performance. We'll never know.

At least we know the mechanics of the delivery of his speech. He spoke a few sentences and then paused while Ad Chapman (dressed how?) translated. The process didn't allow for many tricks of voice tone or gesticulation. It also dragged the performance out for two hours. Joseph, illiterate, could not have read the talk or even have used notes. The talk came off the cuff and yet for two hours moved inexorably toward the end he wanted. He must have thought a great deal about it before he spoke. Perhaps he talked over parts of it in advance with Yellow Bull and even, though it seems unlikely, with Chapman. Were any other whites involved in the prior studies?

Quite possibly there were polishings after the fact. We do not know what Joseph's exact words were. Chapman, a rough frontiersman, gave his substandard brand of English to Joseph's Shahaptian vocabulary and grammar. Some unidentified reporter took down the interpreter's renderings and passed them on to the staff of an influential journal of the time, *The North American Review*. Having undergone who knows what sort of editorial polishing, the speech appeared in the April 1879 issue as "An American Indian's View of Indian Affairs." It has been reprinted a few times since under the title "Chief Joseph's Own Story." As for style, Indian oratory in general tended to exhibit the modes of expression in favor among whites at the time of translation. Even granting all that, however, a question remains: To what extent did Joseph himself manipulate the truth for the sake of effect?

To some extent, almost surely. One instance is his narrative of the Isaac Stevens treaty of 1855, the first to draw a boundary around Nez Perce territory. In the Lincoln Hall account, Joseph's father (Tuekakas) stands as a mighty patriot, a freedom lover. In spite of urgings by the missionary Henry Spalding, Old Joseph refused (his son said) to sign the document. As a matter of record, however, Spalding was not at the council and Old Joseph's X clearly appears as number three in the list of signers. More serious was Young Joseph's angry accusation during the speech that General Howard had refused to give the nontreaty bands a reasonable amount of time for moving their livestock onto the Lapwai reservation. Howard flatly denied the charge in a later issue of the *Review*. Whom do we believe? The Christian general? Or the red Napoleon?

Although Joseph admits the tribe was split between bands who favored and opposed entering into agreements with the whites, he is silent about the crucial part Christianity played in the division. After all, it would not have been politic for him to admit anti-Christian feelings in front of the Lincoln Hall audience. Therefore he stayed silent. Nor was that the only discreet omission. Nowhere in the speech does Joseph claim to have been *the* leader of the Nez Perce warriors. He says "we" in talking of decisions. But he seldom names any other chief, and he never mentions the role he played as camp chief in keeping the noncombatants united and moving in order. War chiefs had more glamor, and it was his reputation as war chief that had brought this audience together. Now was not the time to reduce himself in his listeners' minds. He needed all the support he could rally if he was to regain living space in the Wallowa country for his people. Under such circumstances, moreover, memory could have failed him at times. Expediency occasionally could have assumed control, perhaps without his conscious awareness.

He challenged his audience immediately. "Some of you think an Indian is like a wild animal. This is a great mistake. I will tell you all about our people, and then you can judge whether an Indian is a man or not." ("Wild animal" is a curious comparison. Indians respected all animals. Why did Joseph use this phrase here?)

After speaking of a few basic Indian values, he shifted his theme to the Nez Perces' historic contacts with the on-thrusting whites—fur traders, Lewis and Clark, missionaries, and representatives of the United States government. He told of Lawyer selling the Wallowa country without authority, of growing pressure from white gold miners, farmers, and ranchers. He described his and the other nontreaty chiefs' clashes with Howard; he admitted candidly the part some of their wild young men had played in precipitating the war. He also pointed out the wrongs the whites had committed, particularly at the Battle of the Big Hole. "The Nez Perces never make war on women and children; we could have killed a great many women and children while the war lasted, but we would feel ashamed to do so cowardly an act." Shame had not restrained the whites, however.

He spoke of negotiating with Miles for an end to the conflict. Ever afterwards he felt betrayed. "I could not bear to see my wounded men and women suffer any longer; we had lost enough already. General Miles had promised we might return to our country with what stock we had left…. He could not have made any other terms with me at that time. I would have held him in check until my friends came to my assistance [he meant the Sioux, who, of course, would not have come], and then neither of the generals nor their soldiers would have ever left the Bear Paw Mountain alive…. We gave up all our horses—over eleven hundred—and all our saddles—over one hundred—and we have not heard from them since."

He spoke bitterly of their exile and of the government's refusal to honor its commitments. "I cannot understand how the Government sends a man out to fight us, as it did General Miles, and then breaks his word…. I have heard talk and talk and nothing is done.... Good words do not last long until they amount to something.... Words do not pay for my dead people. They do not pay for my country, now overrun by white people. They do not protect my father's grave.... Good words will not give me back my children."

And then, standing close to the nation's capitol in a hall named for Abraham Lincoln, he adroitly turned America's ideals back on the nation itself. "I know my race must change. We cannot hold our own with the white men as we are. We only ask an even chance to live as other men live. We ask to be recognized as men. We ask that the same law shall work alike on all men....

"Let me be a free man—free to travel, free to stop, free to work, free to trade, where I chose, free to choose my own teachers; free to follow the religion of my fathers, free to think and talk and act for myself—and I will obey every law or submit to the penalty.

"Whenever the white man treats the Indian as they treat each other, then we shall have no more wars. We shall be all alike—brothers of one father and one mother, with one sky above us and one country around us, and one government for all. Then the Great Spirit Chief who rules above will smile upon this land, and send rain to wash out the bloody spots made by brothers' hands upon the face of the earth. For this time the Indian race are waiting and praying....

"In-mut-too-yah-lat-lat [which was the *Review's* rendering of his name] has spoken for his people."

The Lincoln Hall audience responded with a thunderous ovation. They had assembled that evening because they had read of the Nez Perce Joseph in the newspapers. They had gathered because Indians had been almost eliminated from their part of the country, and they were detached enough to be concerned over American Indian policy. What they heard from the speaker was, in its general tenor, pretty much what they expected to hear—endurance outlasting continued injustices, valor in the face of overwhelming military odds, pride and dignity unsullied by defeat.

But there was more. However unconsciously, Joseph was plumbing the depths of what it meant to be a white citizen of the New World—and, simultaneously, what it meant to be a Native American standing in the way of a race obsessed with different ideals and different prospects. Where did rightness lie? In trying to answer, he turned to archetypal images. "My father's grave." "One sky above." A symbolic rain washing out bloody spots made by brothers' hands.

His words became mythic: the reassertion, by a child of nature, of universal human hopes. Here in a fruitful land that white poets were calling the Garden of the World, the roots of a new civilization were seeking nourishment. But eternal temptations—lust for power, land, money—were dimming the ideals. A savior was needed to restore the nation's primal innocence—a native sailor who, of necessity, must shed his own blood, as thousands of Indians were doing, before the bloody spots of the evil brought to the new continent by thoughtless white invaders could be washed away.

Joseph, of course, did not think of himself as that sort of savior. He simply wanted help in getting his people home. If he became a mythic hero, those qualities would be transmuted from the outside, and he would then be a different, static, almost totally unhistoric Joseph. Meanwhile, of course, his audience had no idea they were listening to an incipient myth, American in tone, but based on emotions that reached farther back than that of Homer's *Odysseus*. Those thoughts, if they occurred at all, would come later, after the nature of the Indians' sacrifice was more fully recognized. Yet even while Joseph was speaking, there was a perception of substrata of meaning that touched the listeners profoundly, at least for a little while.

There was no immediate gain from the speech, and Joseph and Yellow Bull returned empty-handed to the Quapaw tract. A little later, in July 1879, the exiles once again loaded their possessions into wagons and on horses and moved to the newly purchased, ninety thousand-acre reserve beside the Chikaskia River. There the civilizing process, as defined by the Bureau of Indian Affairs, took over again, seeking to remodel its charges as American citizens—without the rights of citizenship. Since most whites of the time were still farmers, the captives were also supposed to become agriculturists, capable of supporting themselves despite inadequate training, the vagaries of weather, and erratic market prices that they did not understand. It is surprising to note that Joseph and his family, followers of a Dreamer cult that objected to any laceration of the earth, were listed in 1883 as having produced 150 bushels of wheat, 150 melons, and 50 chickens.[9]

Late in 1879, three Presbyterian Indians arrived from the Lapwai Reservation to help their Chikaskia brethren by building a church and opening a school. James Reuben, who had worked industriously for Howard as a scout during the war, was one. Archie Lawyer, son of the chief who had been primarily responsible for the "thief treaty" of 1863, was another. The third was

Mark Williams, who eventually became a career missionary to various Indian tribes. As usual, the appearance of treaty Indians resulted in divisiveness. After deciding that accommodation with the whites was the only hope left to them, about a third of the defeated accepted the newcomers and moved away from the main band. The larger portion clung to Joseph, who was growing increasingly resistant toward white ways.[10]

A couple of years of Oklahoma climate bested Archie Lawyer and Mark Williams, and they returned to Idaho. James Reuben hung on, devoting himself mostly to teaching school. Meanwhile, important changes were gathering force outside the reservation. American reformers, having seen the end of slavery, were turning their energies more and more to the cause of the Indians, thanks, in part, to Joseph's widely circulated Lincoln Hall address. Both Miles, who had won a brigadier general's star and had been put in charge of the Department of the Columbia, and Howard's onetime aide, Charles Erskine Scott Wood, had embarked on letter-writing campaigns to governmental officials, urging the return of the Nez Perces to their homeland. The Presbyterian Church and the Indian Rights Association, founded in 1882, added their muscle. Activists circulated petitions, not least the widow of President James Garfield; she collected five hundred signatures in Cleveland, Ohio, alone.[11]

One sorrowful aspect of life in the Hot Place was the war-created "surplus" of widows and orphans among the exiles. Those without close relatives to look after them had a desperate time getting along. Working energetically through white friends of the Indians, Reuben persuaded the authorities to let him take thirty-three of those forsaken ones to Idaho. No funds were provided for the trip, and the exiles had to raise money by making and selling handicrafts and surrendering some of their cherished native clothing to collectors. Anonymous donors added more dollars. Comforted along the way by the ministrations of one of the most toothsome of his charges (or so the rumor said) Reuben took twenty-nine persons, two of them elderly men, home to a supercharged emotional welcome at Kamiah, the religious center of the Lapwai Reservation.[12] The downward shift in numbers remains unexplained.

The trip cost $1,625. Congress's stinginess in not providing the funds and its hardheartedness in not releasing all the exiles raised a great hue and cry among reformers. Chastened, the lawmakers passed a bill that awarded Reuben $1,625 (presumably he repaid the original donors) and granted discretionary powers about the rest of the captive Nez Perces to the secretary of the interior. In other words, get those troublesome Indians off the government's back the best way possible.

Troubles immediately arose about how to dispose of them. Many of the Christian Nez Perces on the Lapwai Reservation were reluctant to make room for hard-core Dreamers who, in their opinion, had surrendered all claims to real estate on the reservation by taking to the warpath, rather than accepting what had been offered them in the first place. Still, word was dropped among the exiles that conversion to a civilized religion, whether Catholic or Protestant, might make a difference as far as the Lapwai Reservation was concerned. But there was a second problem—the indictments for murder and other war crimes that were still outstanding against Joseph and several members of the Wallowa band. Whites along the Salmon River and in the Wallowa Valley might be hostile toward those criminals, as they were regarded. So the Wallowa was ruled out as a haven. A substitute was found in Washington State, shaggy Colville, a catchall reservation, bounded on the east by the Columbia River and on the north by the Canadian province of British Columbia. The Indians, it is reported, agreed to the choice.[13] Anything to get closer to home, away from the hell hole of Eeikish Pah.

In the spring of 1885, the euphoric Indians drove their laden wagons into Kansas to board the first of the railroads that would zigzag them into the Northwest. Between 260 and 270 people were involved, a figure that does not include the 29 who had already gone to Lapwai with James Reuben. The unemotional figures held a terrible store of heartbreak. Close to 500 survivors of the war had been incarcerated in Indian Territory: the original bands who had been sent south through Leavenworth plus small groups of wanderers who had been picked up here and there, now and then by the military. Fewer than 300 of those people started north, which means, still as a matter of statistics, that roughly 40 percent of the fugitives had perished in little more than seven years. The terrible reality of the blow came back to them as they were loading their baggage into freight cars—some 35,000 pounds, or about 130 pounds per person. The miscellany of life—tipi canvases, colored beads, warbonnets, brass kettles. Suddenly, a heartbreaking wail arose, a lament for the dead they were leaving behind.[14]

The number of the returnees who stopped at Lapwai and the number who continued up the Columbia to Colville was so nearly the same that one wonders whether, at the end, convenience rather than reason dictated the divisions. One hundred and twenty-one adults, including those taken north by Reuben, and twenty-six young people went to Lapwai. One hundred and twenty adults plus thirty children and infants were destined for Colville. Almost all Joseph's band, the exact number unknown today, accompanied the Colville contingent, for that seemed to them the surest route to the Wallowa country.

Although the terrain of the Colville country was mountainous and the valleys held ample streams of cold water, the place was imbued with a gritty bleakness the new arrivals did not like.[15] On top of that, tribes already settled in the Nespelem section allotted to the Nez Perces by the government were so hostile that troops had to be called from Fort Spokane to restore order. Winters were fierce; agriculture was chancy. Cash money became a new necessity. Scrambling for it, men and women found seasonal jobs picking hops in the Yakima Valley to the south. Others turned their hands, when they could, to poorly paid jobs constructing roads, sawmills, and other government buildings, and the ferries that were needed to cross the Columbia to the outside world. In the end, though, they always had to swallow their self-respect and go to the government for handouts.[16]

The Indians were adroit at mocking the whites with the whites' own traditions. From somewhere, several northwestern tribes picked up the custom of celebrating the Fourth of July, America's Independence Day. (Old Joseph had participated, during the 1860s, in such ceremonies in La Grande, Oregon.) To assert their Indianness that day and for the week or so that followed, the Nez Perces on the Colville Reservation, reinforced by many visitors from Lapwai, pitched their tipis in a huge circle on a meadow in the Nespelem Valley. Joseph invariably led the opening grand parade, on horseback; behind him came every mobile male, single file, horses and humans garish with the feathers and paint of olden times. Women and girls held a separate parade. Afterwards there were horse races, war dances (purely social events now), gambling games, and far too much drinking. Teetotaler Joseph, trying to set an example for the young men, stayed sober. Meanwhile white agency personnel, intent on proving their contention that he exerted a malign influence on the people, watched his every movement and demeaned him in every little way they could.

The ultimate blow delivered by the government as part of the Indians' civilizing process was Congress's passage of the Dawes Severalty Act in 1887. The aim was to make the Indians "intelligently selfish" by instilling in them a knowledge of and respect for private property, specifically real estate. (Missionary Henry Spalding had launched his own version of the campaign along those lines half a century earlier.) Communal ownership of the reservations was to end. Each tribal member was to be allotted his very own plot. These plots varied in size from 40 acres for a minor to 160 acres for heads of families.

Some grazing allotments were as much as 320 acres. Whatever land was left unallotted would be sold at bargain rates to interested whites. Representatives of the whites, of course, lobbied intensely for the bill, and the reformers who joined them in pushing it through Congress under the leadership of Henry Dawes of Massachusetts were too addlepated to discern their allies' "intelligently selfish" motives.[17]

The dismemberment of the Lapwai Reservation began in 1889. Every tribal member, including the exiles, was entitled to an allotment. If the members did not pick plots for themselves, the parcels would be picked for them by government overseers. Among the few Indians who moved from Colville to Lapwai to obtain allotments were Yellow Bull and his family. Most of Joseph's Wallowans did not. They recognized some of the fallacies of the bill; for instance, 320 acres were too few to be a viable grazing unit. They sensed who the main gainers would be. And they were right: All told, 175,000 acres of the Lapwai Reservation were allotted to the tribal members; 542,000 "surplus" acres were then put up for sale to white ranchers and speculators.[18] But the main reason Joseph and his followers held back was their realization that by accepting an allotment in Lapwai, they would forever lose their claim to any portion of the Wallowa country.

Joseph's driving purpose remained the reacquisition of his ancestral lands. In 1897 he thought he saw another chance. With the head chief of the Sinkiuse (Columbia) Indians—the whites called him Moses—he journeyed to Washington to protest the intrusion of white prospectors onto the southern part of the Colville Reservation. While in the capital, he spoke about the Wallowa to another president, this time William McKinley. He met again with General Miles and rode with him in a buggy during a parade connected with the dedication of Grant's tomb in New York City. He posed for pictures with Buffalo Bill Cody, who valued the publicity enough that he paid for the chief's stay at the Astor House hotel. Impressed by the widespread acclaim, the Bureau of Indian Affairs promised to review the Wallowa case.

As usual, nothing happened. Thinking perhaps that he could stir the bureau into action if he presented its commissioners with concrete figures about the cost of land in the Wallow Valley, he traveled there with a few leading members of the tribe to talk to the settlers. A few of the whites, it is said, were willing to deal with him. Most were not. When he spoke of the injustice of their not even letting his people pay to reacquire lands they had never sold, they returned a logical riposte. He and his people had relinquished those lands when they had started for the Lapwai Reservation in response to General Howard's orders. And even if they had any right to the land after that, they lost it by going to war against the United States.

Back to Washington Joseph went, riding still on the swell of popularity engendered by his previous visit. This time he pressured the Bureau of Indian Affairs into sending its chief inspector, James McLaughlin, west to study the feasibility of the land transfer. McLaughlin spent several weeks in the Nespelem area. He decided that sustenance hunting was good there and that the farming potentials were higher than the Indians realized. He talked to the Colville agent, who disliked Joseph and speculated that the chief's prime motive in seeking a return to the Wallowa was to restore his slipping prestige among the Indians.

After traveling to the Wallowa with Joseph (details of the trip were noted in the first chapter of this book), the inspector listened gravely as the settlers pointed out their accomplishments in turning raw land into prosperous, irrigated farms. Why hadn't the Indians done that? It wasn't as if the savages hadn't had a chance to learn, first from the missionaries and then from the government teachers at the agency. They were lazy and improvident. Turning the land back to them would be a retreat into barbarism.

A curious point, not touched on by either side in the dispute, arises here. The Nez Perces had always been seasonal nomads, moving from high country to low and back again to avoid the rigors of winters and the soaring temperatures of summer. In historic times, at least, the Wallowa bands had not occupied the upper valleys more than three or four months a year. Yet there is no record that Joseph ever mentioned, when asking for the return of his lands, the canyons of the lower Grande Ronde, Joseph Creek, the Imnaha, or the Snake—areas that Agent John Monteith had generally referred to during the early 1870s as the home territory of the Joseph bands. Did Joseph suppose that rights to graze livestock and hunt on those canyoned ranges somehow attached as well to the Wallowa farms? Did he suppose that he and his people could learn to subsist throughout the winter in the snow-piled high country as the whites did with their towns, improved roads, and active marketing systems?

Or had the Wallowa become a symbol of a beloved way of life that would not quite disappear as long as those who called it home—who had called it home for millennia—held onto a piece of it? Just a piece. If they retained that, they could master (they thought) whatever demands were imposed on them by either man or nature.

Be that as it may, McLaughlin's report was strongly adverse, and the bureau dismissed the case. Joseph lived four more years, until he was sixty-four, traveling to address whatever audiences would listen to his appeals, delivered in words grown increasingly piteous. On September 21, 1904, while sitting in front of his tipi—not a white-style cabin, never that—he died of a massive heart attack.

The next year Indian and white friends, the latter led by a young professor of history from the University of Washington, Edmond S. Meany, erected beside Joseph's grave on a gentle slope in the Nespelem Valley, a classically styled monument of white marble not much taller than a man. A temporary platform shaded by a striped awning was built for the speakers at the dedication. Yellow Bull, nearly blind with age and wearing Joseph's magnificent head dress, its tail reaching behind him to the ground, represented the Indians. He had heard Joseph's Lincoln Hall speech in Washington, and now he said, out of that memory:

"Joseph is dead but his words will live forever. This monument will stand for many, many years. Joseph's words will stand as long as this monument."[19]

Some of the women wailed and covered their faces with their hair.

In 1952 several citizens of Anadarko, Oklahoma—once Indian Territory—decided to incorporate what they called, awkwardly, the National Indian Hall of Fame for Famous American Indians. The next year a building arose on a ten-acre grant of land from the state, and complicated eligibility rules for nominees were composed. Electors were drawn from among college faculties, judges of appellate courts, authorities on Indian affairs, and notable living Native Americans. No one who had not been dead for fifteen years before nomination was eligible for election. There are also rules about how much Indian blood a candidate's veins must carry.[20]

The first Indian honored was Black Beaver, a noted Delaware guide and scout for American exploratory and military expeditions and a dependable interpreter at many important American and Indian councils. The third was Allen Wright, a Choctaw who was graduated first from Union College, Schenectady, New York, and then from Union Theological Seminary, New York City. Wright translated many Choctaw and Chickasaw government documents into English, and many Biblical texts from Hebrew into Choctaw. He also served for some years as principal chief of the Choctaw Nation.

In between those two came Chief Joseph, the second Native American elevated to fame by vote. The program at the dedication of his bust in 1957 declared that he was chosen for his military skills. "During the [Nez Perce] retreat toward Canada, Chief Joseph displayed such generalship as to be remembered along with the classical retreat of Xenephon's Ten Thousand. His military and tactical skill won unlimited praise from his conquerors." To which the principal speaker at the ceremony, General Hugh Milton, assistant secretary of the army, added, "The feat of Chief Joseph is unparalleled in American History." This remark out of the way, the speaker went on to say that we, as a nation, can learn much by studying closely the United States government's relations to the American Indians.

Clearly neither the writer of the program notes nor the assistant secretary had studied Joseph's relations with the government of the United States. A military hero? Duncan MacDonald, a half-blood Nez Perce who had investigated the "war" for an obscure Montana newspaper in 1878, had strongly implied that Joseph had not been one of the nontreaty group's military leaders. Edward S. Curtis made the same point more bluntly in volume eight of his twenty-volume account *The North American Indians*, published in 1911. L. V. McWhorter reached the same conclusion in *Hear Me, My Chiefs!*, issued in 1939. So did Francis Haines in his 1939 study, *Red Eagles of the Northwest*, reissued with small changes in 1955 under the title *The Nez Perces*—time enough for the assistant secretary or his speech writer to have reviewed it.[21]

The clarion call of militarism was louder, however. First, General Howard in *Nez Perce Joseph* (1881); then a flock of books about our Indian-fighting army (J. P. Dunn's, *Massacres of the Mountains*, Colonel Cyrus Brady's *Northwestern Fights and Fighters*, and Paul Wellman's *Death in the Mountains*, among others); fictionalized biographies (Chester Fee); popularized deep-breathers (Helen Addison Howard), plus numerous stories and articles in adventure-story magazines and newspaper supplements—all ladled on a laud that became irresistible during the decades following the success of World War II. Military heroes were again in style. Dwight D. Eisenhower was president, following precedents set by George Washington, Andrew Jackson, William Henry Harrison, Zachary Taylor, and that accidental militarist, Theodore Roosevelt. An Indian who could be put on a level with whites, such as those listed (and especially an Indian who had lived for a time in Oklahoma), definitely suited the needs of the new National Indian Hall of Fame for Famous American Indians.

Here's a question to play with: If the electors had realized Joseph was not a military hero, would they have nevertheless voted him in because of his other characteristics, chiefly the symbolic ones?

Next question: What really is the significance of the National Indian Hall of Fame?

One rationale for it is said to be our generation's—every generation's—need for heroes. But, surely, the roots go deeper. The hall of fame at Anadarko is comparable to the applause of the audience at Lincoln Hall in Washington, D. C. Both are saying, in large part, that we are sorry for the wrongs we have done. But they were wrongs of execution, we imply, not of intent. We wanted the Indians to be saved by means of assimilation into white culture—the familiar Anglo-Saxon assumption of superiority.

Joseph was aware of that intent. He admitted in his Lincoln Hall speech, "I know my race must change," but he did absolutely nothing to create change. In one letter to Professor Edmond S. Meany, dictated on May 27, 1901, he stated, "If the Government would only give me a small piece of land for my people in the Wallowa with a teacher that is all I would ask."[22] With a teacher. But he never accepted any teacher the church missions or the Bureau of Indian Affairs sent to the Lapwai, Chikaskia, or Colville reservations. Like most American Indians, he wanted to find salvation by staying away from the whites. He clung first to the isolation of the Wallowa area and the profound canyons that drained it. The attempt of the nontreaty bands to flee to a haven in Canada was another effort to stay away. So was turning to the Dreamer religion, with its hopes that all whites would disappear and all Indians would be resurrected. Joseph sensed all this, but the entire weight of Nez Perce tradition and culture kept him following the immutable patterns set by generations of ancestors.

Similarly, the weight of tradition and culture kept the white men from really encouraging Indian assimilation. In theory we subscribed to the tenet that all men are created free and equal, but, as Chief Joseph reminded us, we do not always act that way when someone with a skin of a different color or an exotic religion moves into the neighborhood. It's an old story. On whatever part of the frontier the two cultures came into contact, brutality on both sides was the order of the day, with the whites winning because they could be more brutal, more corrupt, more hypocritical, more careless of their own stated standards of justice. Then the spasm passed, and we looked afresh at our lapsed ideals, built halls of fame, applauded eloquent Indian speakers, reveled in Indian handicrafts. We grieve a little, pay our respects, and think we are settling a debt. But the resonances stirred by the symbols we have created go deeper, down to the red streak of savagery that runs, like blood, in everyone's veins. We need saviors—military ones, religious ones, political ones, Indian ones—and so we create them out of our own aspirations, our own fears, hoping that by civilizing our foes, whoever they are, we will also civilize ourselves.[23]

But the Indian problem still hasn't gone away, as the Vanishing Americans of Chief Joseph's era were supposed to do through the kindly processes of decreed assimilation.

As the Nez Perces would say, *Kopet*. Which means, That is all.

NOTES

Full bibliographical data for the references that appear below can be found in the bibliography.

1. THE GRAVE

1. Information for this chapter was drawn primarily from Josephy, *The Nez Perce Indians and the Opening of the Northwest* (hereafter *NPNW*), 449–50; McLaughlin, 344–46; Thomason; Butterfield, 70–73; Chief Joseph, "An American Indian's View," 419; McWhorter, *Hear Me*, 958–99; Rodeffer, 125–26; and Spinden, 251–53.

2. Gidley, *Kopet*, 63.

3. Quoted in ibid., 15–16.

4. Rodeffer, 125–26.

2. WE, THE PEOPLE

1. My generalized cultural picture of the tribe is based primarily on Spinden; Curtis (vol. 8); Haines, *Nez Perces*; Josephy, *The Nez Perce Indians and the Opening of the Northwest* (hereafter *NPNW*) and *Nez Perce Country*; Slick-

351

poo; Ray, *Cultural Relations* and *Ethnohistory;* Walker, *American Indians of Idaho* and *Conflicts and Schisms.* See also, works on related tribes by Daugherty, Ewers, Fahey, Point, and Ruby and Brown. Broad overviews of Indian culture in general are in Spicer, Farb, and composites such as Brandon, Hodge, and Waldman.

Because the Nez Perce and related tribes speak Shahaptin, they are sometimes called Shahaptins. The Nez Perces accept that term but object to *Nez Perces,* saying their people never wore nose ornaments, even though Lewis and Clark reported such adornments. In spite of tribal dislike, however, *Nez Perce* had become ineradicable and in this book will be used interchangeably with a phonetic rendering of the tribe's name for itself, *Nimipu,* a word that is spelled in several ways.

2. Coleman, 85–86.

3. Aoki, "Nez Perce Texts," 14–17.

4. Ibid., 23–29. Variants of this most famous Nez Perce myth appear in Curtis, vol. 8, 162–63; Josephy, *Nez Perce Country,* 17; and McBeth, 151–59.

5. Conversation with Allen Slickpoo, Sr., at the Big Hole Battlefield, Montana, August 7, 1989.

6. Fishing: Chalfant, 110; Relander, 57; Spinden, 208–09.

7. Rollins, 52–55. For the great trade emporium at The Dalles, see Johansen and Gates, 18–19, Josephy, *NPNW,* 22–23; and Lahren and Shultz, 159. The first whites who encountered The Dalles Indians did not leave flattering pictures. See, for example, Ross, *Adventures,* 89–94; Thwaites, *Original Journals,* 3, 150, 6, 182–88.

8. Corning, 53.

9. Government: Josephy, *NPNW,* 32–33; C. L. Miller, "After That," 7–12; Ray, *Cultural Relations,* 19–24; Riley, passim; Waldman, 63–65; Walker, *Indians of Idaho,* 105–07.

10. Camas: Haines, *Nez Perces,* 11–12; Josephy, *NPNW,* 18–19, and *Nez Perce Country,* 23–30; Slickpoo, 35; Spinden, 201–02. The illness suffered by members of the Lewis and Clark expedition and other whites from eating too much camas root is described in Cutright, 218–19.

11. Branch; DeVoto, *Across the Wide Missouri,* 37–43; Ewers, *Blackfeet,* 14–15, 72–78; Lamar, 135–37; Point, chap. 3, including photographs, and chap. 4 passim.

12. Guardian spirit: Because the quest was intensely personal and grudgingly revealed to curious outsiders, accounts differ markedly. My rendering is a composite of several presentations and is not meant to be definitive. See

Beal, 12; Curtis, vol. 8, 62–64; Josephy, *NPNW*, 21–27; Miller, "After That," 46ff; Randolf; Ray, *Cultural Relations*, 68–69, 102–09; Slickpoo, 58–61; Walker, *Conflicts and Schisms*, 18–23. Yellow Wolf's guarded explanation of the phenomenon is in McWhorter, *Yellow Wolf*, 295–300.

13. For the dark side of shamanism see Michael Forbes Brown.

14. As in note 12, plus Curtis, vol. 8, 71–75.

15. Slickpoo, 6.

16. Curtis, vol. 8, 62–63.

3. The First Intrusions

1. Horses: Ewers, "Horses in Blackfoot Culture"; Haines, "Northwest Spread"; Jablow; Josephy, *Indian Heritage*, 118–20; Webb, 52–67.

2. Brandon, 335–36, touches on the migrations. See also, Jablow; and White.

3. Trade guns: Ewers, "Blackfeet," 21–23. Jablow, 12; Russell, 64–75.

4. Organization of hunting trips: Josephy, *The Nez Perce Indians and the Opening of the Northwest* (hereafter *NPNW*), 32–33.

5. Gidley, *Kopet*, 65.

6. Point, 110. There are fine examples of costumes in the Nez Perce Historical Park visitors center, Spalding, Idaho.

7. Disease: Burns, 13; Ewers, *Blackfeet*, 28–29; Fahey, 127–29; Josephy, *Nez Perce Country*, 44–45; Lehmer, 136–58; Sheehan, 227–30; Trenholm and Carley, 21.

8. Sweat baths: Hodge, vol. 2, 660–62; Spinden, 198.

9. Ross, *Fur Hunters* 155; Beckwourth, xxxvi.

10. There are variations in detail and uncertainty about dates among scholars who support the Prophet Dance hypothesis. Not all do. See Aberle; Burns, 17; Curtis, vol. 8, 75–76; Daugherty, 83–85; C. L. Miller, 157–72; Spier; Suttles, 353–54; Walker, *Conflicts and Schisms*, 32–38, and "New Light," 245–47. Josephy, *Nez Perce Country*, 44–45, among others, is skeptical.

11. Lewis and Clark's first stay among the Nez Perces: Thwaites, vol. 3, 84–98. There are summaries in Lavender, *Way to Western Sea*, 269–74, and Ronda, 157–62.

12. Ronda, 159; Josephy, *NPNW*, 37–38; Thwaites, vol. 3, 81–82. Curtis, vol. 8, note 5, gives a different story: The Nez Perces had heard of whites, feared them, and called them *paiyowit*, a name used in myths for strange creatures who caused destruction. But a wise chief recognized the visitors as

friends and stopped the murder some of the Nez Perces proposed.

13. Lewis and Clark's second stay: DeVoto, *Journals*, 372–402 condenses the original accounts. Lavender, *Way to Western Sea*, 328–35, summarizes the events.

14. For numerous references to Twisted Hair in the Lewis and Clark journals, consult the indexes in either Thwaites or Moulton. For the six guns: Josephy, *NPNW*, 38; Thwaites, vol. 5, 23.

15. Drury, *Chief Lawyer*, 16, 26, 289–90.

4. RIVALRIES AND SEDUCTIONS

1. Josephy, *The Nez Perce Indians and the Opening of the Northwest*, 40–46, 651–63, contains fine summaries about the Canadians who crossed the Continental Divide to the sources of the Columbia in the early 1800s and about Americans who tried to push up the headwaters of the Missouri against the Blackfeet during that same period. The route used by the white overlanders in 1811 is speculative, but cannot be far from the one suggested in the text.

2. DeVoto, *Journals*, 248.

3. Chalfant, 94.

4. Franchere, 110.

5. The basic account of Astoria is, of course, Washington Irving's two volumes. See also Porter, 164–247, and Lavender, *Fist*, 118–77. Wilson Price Hunt's account of the overland trip is in Rollins, 281–308.

6. Glover, 305–6.

7. Ibid., 350. My account of Astor's dealings with the agents of the North West Company and of Thompson's trip to Astoria, which differs from the standard version, is in *Fist*, 123–50 passim and, esp. 443.

8. Ross, *Adventures*, 214, 226, 234–36.

9. Chittenden, 205–6.

10. See Ross, *Adventures* 234–44, for incidents related to the Indians' refusal to trap, the arrival of the Nor'Westers' first canoes, and the withdrawal of the Astorians. See also, Porter, 221ff.

11. Porter, 531–32.

12. Ross, *Fur Hunters*, 126–27.

5. MINGLINGS

1. My account of the meeting at the mouth of the Walla Walla is based primarily on the reminiscences of one of the white participants, Alexander

Ross (*Fur Hunters*, 163–75). Ross wrote many years after the events he describes, he is given to exaggeration, and his details are often fuzzy. But he is the only source we have for much of the material in the chapter; so, to fill in some of the gaps he left, I have resorted to my own imagination.

2. Ibid., 86–88; Porter, 577–78.

3. Morgan, *Jedediah Smith*, 117–18.

4. Ross, *Fur Hunters*, 166–70.

5. Josephy, *The Nez Perce Indians and the Opening of the Northwest* (hereafter *NPNW*), 58n.

6. Merk, *Fur Trade*, 55–57.

7. This description of Wallowa life is swiped with only minor changes from Ray, "Ethnohistory," 87.

8. The genealogy is swiped from Josephy, *NPNW*, 668–69.

9. Quoted in Glover, 152.

10. Merk, 45–46; Morgan, *Jedediah Smith*, 118–26. Merk's presentation of George Simpson's 1824–25 journal of a trip to the Columbia, preceded by an acute introduction and followed by many pertinent documents, is a fur-trade classic, as is Dale Morgan's biography of the American hunter and explorer, Jedediah Smith. I am deeply indebted to both, as are all other historians of the early periods of Northwestern history.

11. Merk, 108.

12. Ibid., 181.

13. Ibid., 108.

14. Ross's troubles are summarized in Morgan, *Jedediah Smith*, 125–30.

15. Merk, 351–52. Josephy, *NPNW*, 83, quoting original sources from the Hudson's Bay Company archives.

16. Morgan, *Ashley*, 166.

17. Morgan, *Jedediah Smith*, 133–42, 148–51.

18. Josephy, *NPNW*, 69.

19. Merk, 102.

20. Ibid., 132, 136.

21. Josephy, *NPNW*, 85, quoting Orin J. Oliphant, "George Simpson and the Oregon Missions," *Pacific Historical Review*, 6 (1937).

22. Christopher L. Miller, *Prophetic Worlds*, 41–45. This book is a condensation and refinement of the same author's doctoral dissertation (see bibliography). The way Miller links his causes and effects is pretty pat, but the ideas are nevertheless stimulating and controversial.

23. Point, 15.

24. Big Head, or Silimxnotylmilakobok (renamed Cornelius by later mis-

sionaries) told the story in 1842 to Lieutenant R. E. Johnson of the United States Exploring Expedition during the years 1838–42, Captain Charles Wilkes commanding, in 1842. When Big Head was ten years old—about 1790—volcanic debris raining on his village from an eruption of Mount Saint Helens terrified the people. What was happening to the world? Could it be straightened out? A Spokan medicine man assured them: There was a magic book with all the answers. Inasmuch as the Spokans could hardly have known of books in 1790, one suspects that Big Head added the detail for effect after he had seen the wonders of print—talking leaves, as it were. See Wilkes, *Narrative*, vol. 4, 439, and Christopher L. Miller, *Prophetic Worlds*, 41–45.

25. Glover, 341, 343, 344, 346, 348, 349 ff; Ross, *Adventures*, 138.

6. THE QUEST

1. Josephy, *The Nez Perce Indians and the Opening of the Northwest* (hereafter *NPNW*), 88–92.

2. Drury, *Diaries ... Spalding and Smith*, 107.

3. Ferris, 85–90.

4. Yards of print have been expended on the makeup of the delegation and its reasons for undertaking the trip. In general, I follow Josephy, *NPNW*, 93–96, with the added thought that the expedition was an ad hoc affair that unfolded slowly as opportunities arose during the Indians' stay with Fontenelle's group from the American Fur Company.

5. Donald Dean Jackson, *Yellow Stone*, 33.

6. Ewers, "Light."

7. Jackson, *Yellow Stone*, 47.

8. Josephy, *NPNW*, 98. Morgan and Harris, 306.

9. Irving, *Bonneville*, 47–48.

10. Readers who are curious about the battle can check summaries of it in DeVoto, *Wide Missouri*, 81–86, Gowans, and Hayden and go from there to the contemporary accounts they cite.

11. Josephy, *NPNW*, 77–78.

12. Ibid., 98; Irving, *Bonneville*, 138–42.

13. A moving account of the Indians' removal and the harsh policies prompting it is Van Every's *Disinherited*.

14. Many accounts describe the Nez Perce–Flathead Indian delegation and the white missionary efforts that it prompted. Secular writers are likely to be

skeptical of William Walker's story. Malcolm Clark, *Eden Seekers*, is a bit extreme; see also, DeVoto, *Wide Missouri*, 6–15, Haines, "Nez Perce Delegation," Josephy, *NPNW*, 97–101. Religious writers, notably Drury in his many books about the first missionaries in the Northwest, are inclined to accept the story quite literally; see, for example, Drury, *Chief Lawyer*, 27–32.

7. REJECTION

1. Morgan and Harris, 137. This admirable edition of Anderson's *Journal* and *Narrative* of his trip west with William Sublette brings together most of the known records of the 1834 rendezvous. See pp. 128–60, June 19 through July 4.

2. Ibid., 139; and Townsend, 86.

3. Townsend, 83.

4. Morgan and Harris, 134–35.

5. Ibid., 330–31.

6. Ibid., 139.

7. What little is known of Christy's unlucky trip can be put together out of Morgan and Harris, 228–89 and 318–19. See also *McLaughlin's Fort Vancouver Letters, First Series*, cx and 131. For Bonneville's Wallowa adventure, see Irving, 218–75. See also, Josephy, *The Nez Perce Indians and the Opening of the Northwest* (hereafter *NPNW*), 108–16, esp. 110.

8. DeVoto, *Wide Missouri*, 199.

9. Morgan and Harris, 100, 231–32; and Josephy, *NPNW*, 121–23.

10. Josephy, *NPNW*, 123 and 126, quoting Lee's diary. For Shepard, see Malcolm Clark, 87.

11. Morgan and Harris, 172–73.

12. *Nez Perce Indians* (Garland), 74–75, 293, 299. A missionary of a later date, Asa Smith, also believed that war contributed significantly to the decline in the Nez Perce; see Drury, *Spalding and Smith Diaries*.

8. THE ENERGIES OF HOPE

1. The rendezvous of 1935: DeVoto, *Wide Missouri*, 226–31; Drury, *Marcus and Narcissa*, vol. 1, 133–38; Gowans, 152–61; Parker, 80–82.

2. Parker's journal, published in 1838, went through several editions that year. Paginations differ. The fourth edition, which I used, covers his trip between pp. 89 and 178 and pp. 273–89. Astute comments on his exploratory

journey are in DeVoto, *Wide Missouri*, 235–38, and Josephy, *NPNW*, 133–42.

3. Chalfant, in *Nez Perce Indians* (Garland), 99–100, and Josephy, *NPNW*, 668–69, present different accounts of Joseph's genealogy. In general, I follow Josephy.

4. For band politics, see Chalfant, in *Nez Perce Indians* (Garland), 96–102.

5. Parker, 289.

6. Drury, *Marcus and Narcissa*, vol. 1, 69.

7. Drury, *Spalding*, 29.

8. Quoted by Pearce, 65.

9. Burns, 31–33; and Billington, *Protestant Crusade*, chap. 5.

10. Drury, *Marcus and Narcissa*, vol. 2, 333.

11. Elliott, *White Women*, 3–10.

12. Drury, *Marcus and Narcissa*, vol. 1, 192. Whitman's charge may have been a recrimination brought on by disparaging remarks made about him by Parker on returning to civilization. See Drury, *Spalding*, 141; DeVoto, *Wide Missouri*, 258–61.

13. Drury, *Marcus and Narcissa*, vol. 1, 196.

14. Elliott, *White Women*, 19. For the 1836 rendezvous in general, see DeVoto, *Wide Missouri*, 244–59; Gray, 118–30.

15. Drury, *Marcus and Narcissa*, 195–96.

16. Drury, *Spalding*, 147–48.

17. Josephy, *NPNW*, 156. Josephy gives a good summary of the settling process on pp. 153–57.

9. THE STRUGGLE FOR SOULS

1. Drury, *Diaries … Spalding and Smith*, 240. Josephy, *The Nez Perce Indians and the Opening of the Northwest* (hereafter *NPNW*), 669.

2. Drury, *Diaries*, 250. Before the sermon ended [on December 23, 1838] Timothy [Tamootsin] was before the pulpit to bear witness, but when he tried to describe his spiritual awakening, he "was overwhelmed with grief and cried aloud." Tuekakas won attention by urging two weeping young Indian girls to visit Spalding and learn the ways of Christ. Spalding himself was pretty well dissolved, finishing the day's record: "Oh God of love what a Sabbath this has been."

3. Quoted in Drury, *Spalding*, 205.

4. Fort Colvile, with two "l"s was named for Andrew Colvile of the Hudson's Bay Company, but Americans, thinking of villages, persistently added a third "l"—Colville. Even Spalding did so, although he had ample reason to know better.

5. Drury, *Diaries ... Spalding and Smith*, 171.

6. Josephy, *NPNW*, 161–64.

7. Brosnan, 95. Drury, *Marcus and Narcissa*, 276–77.

8. Josephy, *NPNW*, 173–79.

9. Drury, *Lawyer*, 47, 51–52.

10. Drury, *Walkers*, 99.

11. The involved story of the horse-cattle scheme is treated in Josephy, *NPNW*, 164–65, 167–71, and Lavender, *Westward*, 310–16. Gray's sanitized versions are in his journal, 62–71 and *History* (which doesn't always agree with his journal), 173–74.

12. Drury, *Spalding*, 201, 422; Josephy, *NPNW*, 181.

13. Josephy, *NPNW*, 189. Drury, *Diaries ... Spalding and Smith*, 142.

14. The trip: *Diaries ... Spalding and Smith*, 269–72.

15. Ibid., 279–80.

16. Ibid., 279–80.

17. Ibid., 288. See also, Josephy, *NPNW*, 190–91, 669. Josephy's list of family names, drawn from tribal legend, is unlike Drury's. I follow Drury because Spalding jotted them in his diary at the time of their bestowal.

18. Drury, *Diaries ... Spalding and Smith*, entries from August 26–30, 1840.

19. Ibid., 304–6.

20. Josephy, *NPNW*, 293–94, 273. Drury, *Diaries ... Spalding and Smith*, 267. Wilkes, vol. 4, 459–62.

21. Josephy, *NPNW*, 189.

22. Ibid., 210, 212.

23. Smith to Greene, September 3, 1840, quoted in Christopher L. Miller, *Prophetic Worlds*, 92–93.

24. Josephy, *NPNW*, 213.

25. Ibid., 307.

26. Ibid., 202–4.

27. Drury, *Marcus and Narcissa*, Vol. 1, 454.

28. Spalding to Green, February 12, 1846, quoted by Christopher L. Miller, *Prophetic Worlds*, 95.

29. White's career is covered, not altogether satisfactorily, in Allen.

30. Whitman's motives for going east and a summary of the round trip are covered thoroughly, if somewhat ponderously, in Drury, *Marcus and Narcissa*, vol. 1, 445, through vol. 2, 86.

10. Catastrophe

1. The assaults: Drury, *Spalding*, 294; Drury, *Marcus and Narcissa*, vol. 2, 14–19.

2. Elijah White's first trip to the interior: Allen, 177–90; Josephy, *The Nez Perces and the Opening of the Northwest* (hereafter NPNW), 122–27; Victor, 44–50.

3. Rich, 348.

4. White's rules as printed in Josephy, *NPNW*, 229:

1) Whoever wilfully takes life shall be hung.

2) Whoever burns a dwelling house shall be hung.

3) Whoever burns an outbuilding shall be imprisoned six months, receive fifty lashes, and pay all damages.

4) Whoever carelessly burns a house, or any property, shall pay damages.

5) If any one enter a dwelling, without permission of the occupant, the chiefs shall punish him as they think proper. Public rooms are excepted.

6) If any one steal he shall pay back two fold; and if it be the value of a beaver skin or less, he shall receive twenty-five lashes; and if the value is over a beaver skin he shall pay back two fold, and receive fifty lashes.

7) If any one take a horse, and ride it, without permission, or take any article and use it, without liberty, he shall pay for the use of it, and receive from twenty to fifty lashes, as the chief shall direct.

8) If any one enter a field, and injure the crops, or throw down the fence, so that cattle or horses go in and do damage, he shall pay all damages, and receive twenty-five lashes for every offence.

9) Those only may keep dogs who travel or live among the game; if a dog kill a lamb, calf, or any domestic animal, the owner shall pay the damage, and kill the dog.

10) If an Indian raise a gun or other weapon against a white man, it shall be reported to the chiefs, and they shall punish him. If a white person do the same to an Indian, it shall be reported to Dr. White, and he shall redress it.

11) If an Indian break these laws, he shall be punished by his chiefs; if a white men break them, he shall be reported to the agent, and be punished at his instance."

5. Allen, reprinting Spalding's undated letter to White, 201–12.

6. Drury, *Spalding*, 303. Josephy, *NPNW*, 235.

7. Allen, 213–14.

8. White's second trip: Allen, drawing primarily on Hines, 52–70. For a strongly antimissionary, antiwhite stance, see McWhorter, *Hear Me*, 50–74.

9. Drury, *Marcus and Narcissa*, 107n.

10. Quoted in Josephy, *NPNW*, 237.

11. Mrs. Lawyer's name was given to me by S. Ross Evans, professor of Native American history at Lewis-Clark State College, Lewiston, Idaho. For the Indians' performances at Lapwai, See Victor, 62–63, drawing on Hines.

12. Josephy, *Nez Perce Country*, 47, 64. McWhorter, *Hear Me*, 18, says the Indian name of Lewis and Clark's Twisted Hair was Wellammottinin. Or just possibly the name was Sahayah (McWhorter, 101n). Drury, *Lawyer*, 27, 289, following agent John Montieth, who knew Lawyer, gives the chief's commonly used name as Hallalhotsoots. Indians often had several names.

13. Drury, *Marcus and Narcissa*, Vol. 2, 108.

14. Fee, 20. Josephy, *NPNW*, 191.

15. The growing dissatisfaction in the missions is covered in Drury, *Marcus and Narcissa*, vol. 2, 132–98 passim, and Drury, *Spalding*, 299–328.

16. *Marcus and Narcissa*, vol. 2, 127.

17. *Ibid.*, vol. 2, 109.

18. Josephy, *NPNW*, quoting Gray, 490. There are a plethora of accounts about the Whitmans' massacre. As thorough as any is Drury's in *Marcus and Narcissa*, vol. 2.

19. Josephy, *NPNW*, 259.

20. McWhorter, *Hear Me*, 602–3. In a companion statement on those pages, McWhorter, quoting remarks by Indians, says that Joseph left the mission because a U.S. government agent insulted him in front of his people by giving him shoddy goods. The only government agent to reach Nez Perce lands during the first part of the 1840s was Elijah White; he appeared there late in 1842 and in the spring of 1843. Joseph was at Lapwai as late as the summer of 1844. It is possible, of course, that the chief was still nursing grievances against White in 1844, but it is hardly likely that they were serious enough to turn him against his mentor, Spalding. In other words, I do not think Joseph left the mission permanently until after the mission ceased to exist.

21. Drury, *Spalding*, 343; and Josephy, *NPNW*, 257.

22. Drury, *Spalding*, 346.

23. Morgan and Harris, 346.

24. Victor, 170–71; Bancroft, vol. 1, 713n; Josephy, *NPNW*, 267. Chief Joseph's name appears in Victor's reproduction of the note, but not in

Bancroft and hence not in Josephy. I think Bancroft's omission was inadvertent.

25. Data concerning the commission and its activities are taken from Newell's *Memoranda*, 96–140.

26. Ibid., 121.

27. Ibid., 122.

28. Ibid., 112.

29. Josephy, *NPNW*, 273.

30. Newell's *Memoranda*, 135. Punctuation has been altered slightly.

31. Josephy, *NPNW*, 280–81.

11. BACK HOME

1. Drury, *Spalding*, 362–67.

2. Drury, *Walker*, 230.

3. Ibid., 231–33.

4. McWhorter, *Hear Me*, 128n.

5. Johansen and Gates, 305–9.

6. *Reports of Explorations* vol. 12, 107–82, is the source of most of the material presented herein about Stevens's railroad work. See also Hazard Stevens's biography of his father, *Isaac Ingalls Stevens*, vol. I, 238ff. Useful summaries are in Fuller, 206–11; Josephy, *The Nez Perces and the Opening of the Northwest* (hereafter *NPNW*), 292–94; Goetzmann, *Army Explorations*, 278–83; and Lavender, *Land of Giants*, 287–91.

7. Josephy, *NPNW*, 294–99.

8. Ibid., 300.

9. Winther, 130–31.

10. Drury, *Lawyer*, 92.

11. Slickpoo, 77–144, presents excerpts from the official account of the Walla Walla Council, a document stored in the Nez Perce tribal headquarters. Lawrence Kip's diary gives an outsider's view of daily events. Detailed summaries are in Stevens, vol. 2, 34–58, and Josephy, *NPNW*, 315–87. McWhorter, *Hear Me*, 87–96, is, as usual, intemperate.

12. Slickpoo, 104; Josephy, *NPNW*, 322.

13. Drury, *Lawyer*, 96–97. The sketch of Lawyer by Gustavus Sohon is reprinted in Drury, *Lawyer*, facing p. 106; Stevens, facing p. 55, and Josephy, *NPNW*, illustration no. 3.

14. Kip was sure there was a plot (pp. 13, 24), as was Stevens, 47–48. Josephy, *NPNW*, 322–23, and *Nez Perce Country*, 83, is dubious.

15. Drury, *Lawyer*, 121; Josephy, *NPNW*, 328.

16. Slickpoo, 130–38 passim; Josephy, *NPNW*, 328–33.

17. Estimates of the size of the reservation the Nimipu ended with in 1855 range from 5,000 to 90,000 square miles. Belated surveys suggest 12,000. See Josephy, *Nez Perce Country*, 106.

18. Stevens, 61; Cram, 85.

19. Beal, 27–28. Ray, "Ethnohistory" in *Nez Perce Indians*, (Garland), 15–16.

12. UPHEAVAL

1. Josephy, *The Nez Perce Indians and the Opening of the Northwest* (hereafter *NPNW*), 337–38. There was one small exception to the general rule against trespassing. Until December 1, 1855, settlers filing under the Donation Land Claim Act could make entries before Indian titles had been extinguished. Dread of the warlike tribes of the interior restrained the whites' activity on the Plateau, however, until Stevens's premature announcements implied that everyone would be welcome—and protected.

2. Ibid., 344–45. Ruby and Brown, *Indians*, 140.

3. Trimble, 15–17.

4. Gulick, 122–23, drawing on McWhorter's "Tragedy of the Wahk-Shum." Wahk-Shum was the name of a spring near the scene of the killing. Meany, 179, says Bolon's corpse was burned.

5. Meany, 181.

6. For Pearson, see Stevens, vol. 2, 101–2, 121–23; Josephy, *NPNW*, 343n.

7. Stevens, vol. 2, 107.

8. Josephy, *NPNW*, 386–87.

9. Or so Governor Stevens said he was told by a half-breed messenger. Stevens, vol. 2, 132.

10. Ibid., 143. Stevens's trip back from the Blackfoot council is covered in ibid., vol. 2, 132.

11. Adapted from Josephy, *NPNW* 355–56.

12. Josephy, *NPNW*, 356n, quoting from "The Proceedings of the Lapwai Council" (1863), pp. 66–67.

13. Stevens, vol. 2, 143–44. The author, Hazard Stevens, believed that Looking Glass had actually been plotting against the governor's life but had done a swift about-face on seeing how sentiment in the tribe was running in favor of the whites.

14. Official white reports tend to excuse the slaying of the hostages on the grounds that they were being treacherous: Victor; Fuller, 228–29; Glassley, 119–20. Stevens vol. 2, 148, says only that Peo-Peo Mox-Mox "had been captured and slain while trying to escape." Frank Gilbert, after collecting as many eyewitness accounts as he could a quarter of a century after the battle, reaches a contrary conclusion: the slaying was a military offense. (See Gulick, 125–28.) Josephy, NPNW, 359, the Nez Perces' most thorough historian, agrees and adds that Peo-Peo Mox-Mox was not a war chief at all but a peace chief, who was earnestly trying to end the confrontation.

15. The muster roll is in Horace Austin, auditor, to Carl Shurz, secretary of the interior, April 11, 1875, in connection with a request for payment of the bill long due the Indians for service in 1855–56. See "Letters Received by the Office of Indian Affairs, Idaho Superintendency, Lapwai Agency," micropsy copy 234, Roll 345. A copy is in the library of the Idaho State Historical Society, Boise.

16. Ibid., plus Stevens, vol. 2, 144–45, and Josephy, NPNW, 362.

17. C. Monteith to H. Price, December 16, 1882, Lapwai Agency files, loc. cit., note 15 above.

18. Ibid.; Stevens, vol. 2, 169, 200; and Josephy, NPNW, 368n.

19. Josephy, NPNW, 364, 367–68.

20. Ibid., 368–70; and Ruby and Brown, Indians, 156–57.

21. Josephy, NPNW, 369; and Stevens, vol. 2, 201.

22. Josephy, NPNW, 371; and Stevens, vol. 2, 202.

23. For the council, see Josephy, NPNW, 373–76; and Stevens, vol. 2, 209–20.

24. Stevens, vol. 2, 220–24.

25. Governor Stevens's side of the controversy with General Wool can be followed in ibid., 224–31.

13. A Touch of Gold

1. Sergeant Michael Kenney of the dragoons gives an eyewitness account of the Steptoe expedition; a copy is in the library of Washington State University, Pullman. Reconstructions of the disaster are in W. C. Brown, Indian Side, 185–97; Dozier; and Victor, 485–89.

2. Kip, Army Life.

3. Wright's campaign is treated in Victor, 489–99; and W. C. Brown, 229–329. Brown goes into detail about the punishments.

4. Drury, Lawyer, 162.

5. Aoki, "Nez Perce Texts," 81–85.

6. Josephy, *The Nez Perces and the Opening of the Northwest* (hereafter *NPNW*), 388, drawing on the *Report of the Commissioner of Indian Affairs* for 1859, p. 420.

7. McWhorter, *Yellow Wolf*, 42.

8. Howard, *War Chief Joseph*, 24.

9. Henry Miller, 20.

10. Henry Clay Wood, *Status of Young Joseph*, 23.

11. Gidley, *Kopet*, 63. Henry Steele, a subagent at Nespelem, Washington, where Young Joseph lived out his last years in exile, declared that he measured the chief in 1898 when he was 58 years old and found that he stood "5 ft. 9 in. in moccasins." People do shrink with age, but hardly five inches before reaching age 60.

12. Josephy, *NPNW*, 450, says that in 1871, when Young Joseph was thirty-one, he had a six-year-old daughter, so he must have been married sometime before 1865. I suggest 1862 or 1863 and imagine Joseph had known his bride prior to that. Fee, 48–54, says, in a partly fictional account of the marriage, that Joseph wed at nineteen.

13. For the early years of the gold rush, see Burcham's editing of Pierce's memoirs in *Idaho Yesterdays*, Fall, 1960. Conley, 62–63, gives a good profile of Pierce. See also, Trimble, 65–66; and Josephy, *NPNW*, 390–96.

14. See Beal, 19; Conley, 76; Goodrich, 23; and Josephy, *NPNW*, 397.

15. Josephy, *NPNW*, 402.

16. Slickpoo, 148.

17. Bancroft, 235–38; Conley, 93; Josephy, *NPNW*, 402–03; McWhorter, *Hear Me*, 100–102; Tallkington, 1–18.

18. Wells, "Farmers"; Josephy, *NPNW*, 408–9.

14. THE BIG STEAL

1. Johansen and Gates, 327–28.

2. Drury, *Lawyer*, 178–85, passim. During the negotiations of 1855, Stevens had let the Indians express their opinions about boundaries. The courtesy did not hold in 1863.

3. Bird, 12–21.

4. Ray, "Ethnohistory," 26–27, in *Nez Perce Indians* (Garland).

5. Trenholm and Carley, 195–96; Josephy, *The Nez Perces and the Opening of the Northwest* (hereafter *NPNW*), 413–14.

6. Slickpoo, 147; Zucker and Hogfoss, 89.

7. Drury, *Lawyer*, 182. Drury names only White Bird as receiving a special message, but since Joseph's band was the largest and most influential in the tribe, he surely received one also.

8. Ibid., 185.

9. McWhorter, *Hear Me*, 128. Manassa bled to death from an arrow wound that opened an artery in his thigh. Yielding to the Indian imperative for revenge, Young Joseph tried twice to kill Blue Legs but failed both times— or so McWhorter's informants told him.

10. Chief Joseph, "An American Indian's View," says flatly that his father was not at the 1863 council. Verne Ray, a respected anthropologist, agrees (Indian Claims Commission, Docket, 186). See Ray "Ethnohistory," 20, in *Nez Perce Indians* (Garland). I go along with Joseph and Ray, although this view puts me at variance with several able historians.

11. The quotation (the speech containing it was interpreted orally by Spalding and recorded by the council's two scribes in language that probably wasn't Lawyer's) is from Drury, *Lawyer*, 188. Josephy, *NPNW*, gives an abstract of the same speech. Both authors summarize the negotiations at length but from radically different viewpoints (Drury, 176–216; and Josephy, 415–32.) Merle Wells, long-time director of the Idaho Historical Society, supports Drury's pro-Lawyer leanings. Allen Slickpoo, Sr., a Nez Perce historian, and L. V. McWhorter, tireless collector of Nez Perce folklore, are angrily anti-Lawyer.

12. Josephy, *NPNW*, 423–25; Drury, *Lawyer*, 199–200.

13. Josephy, *NPNW*, 426.

14. Drury, *Lawyer*, 205–16; Josephy, *NPNW*, 426.

15. The tale of Old Joseph's destruction of the documents first surfaces, as far as I can learn, in a letter written nine years after the event by Indian Agent John B. Monteith to F. A. Walker, commissioner of Indian affairs, August 27, 1872 (Slickpoo, 179–80). Some historians (see, for example, Beal, 31; Drury, *Lawyer*, 204; Josephy, *Nez Perce Country*, 105), evidently caught up by the drama of the act, state that the destruction occurred at the council. But if, as I believe (see note 10 above), Old Joseph did not attend the conference, the tearing did not occur there but took place in the Wallowa country. To suppose that Young Joseph took the papers to the council and tore them up as the agent for his father strains credulity.

16. Bartlett, *Wallowa Country*, 13. See also that book's endpaper maps.

15. IMPASSE

1. Bartlett, *Wallowa Country*, 15.
2. Ibid., 41. Haines, *Nez Perces*, 190–91. Also conversations with Steven Ross Evans of Lewis-Clark State College, Lewiston, Idaho, and his Nez Perce wife, Connie.
3. Bartlett, *Wallowa Country*, 22n.
4. Mooney, vol. 2, 708. Click Relander devoted an entire book, *Drummers and Dreamers*, to Smohalla and his teachings. See also Walker, *Conflicts and Schisms*, 48–52; and Aoki, "Nez Perce Texts," 81–85.
5. *North American Review*, April 1879. Young Joseph's account of his father's deathbed plea was, of course, filtered through an interpreter, a stenographer, and a magazine editor, who undoubtedly polished it. The sense remains accurate, however.
6. Gidley, *Kopet*, 73–78 passim, gives details of Young Joseph's death feast in 1904. The ceremonies following Old Joseph's death could not have been much different.
7. Evans, 18.
8. Bartlett, *Wallowa Country*, 20–21.
9. Ibid., 22.
10. Ibid.; and Josephy, *The Nez Perces and the Opening of the Northwest* (hereafter *NPNW*), 452–54.
11. Corning, 6, 9, 169.
12. Irwin Thompson, "Cataldo."
13. Haines, *Nez Perces*, 157–71; Drury, *Spalding*, 402–07; and Drury, *Lawyer*, 267–70. For Monteith's troubles with Spalding, see the agent's correspondence as printed in Slickpoo, 159–64.
14. Monteith's correspondence with both church people and government officials contains a long litany of his troubles. I have made no effort to cite each and every letter. The Lapwai agency has most of his files. I used the typed transcripts of those letters, which are in the library of the Idaho Historical Society, Boise. See also, Mark H. Brown, *Flight*, 44–67; Haines, *Nez Perces*; Henry Clay Wood, *Status*.
15. Haines, *Nez Perces*, 171–72.
16. For various views on the violence in the area, see Josephy, *NPNW*, McWhorter, *Hear Me*; 118–26; Henry Clay Wood, 24–27.
17. Goulder, 7–8. For the shortage of suitable land for the Indians, let

alone for whites, see Monteith to E. S. Parker, September 18, 1871, Idaho Historical Society, Boise.

18. Monteith described his Wallowa experience to F. H. Walker, commissioner of Indian affairs, August 27, 1872, transcript, Idaho Historical Society, Boise. The letter has been widely reprinted: Bartlett, *Wallowa Country* 24–25; McWhorter, somewhat abridged in *Hear Me*, 132–34; and Slickpoo, 178–80.

19. Ray, "Ethnohistory," 30–34, in *Nez Perce Indians* (Garland), quotes at length from Odeneal's report of the March meeting.

20. Bartlett, *Wallowa Country*, 39–44 passim; and Josephy, *NPNW*, 456–57. Maps of the two different divisions are in Gulick, 176–77.

21. Josephy, *NPNW*, 459.

22. Monteith to Edward Smith, commissioner of Indian affairs, April 10 and 28, 1873; November 23, 1873; and June 15, 1874. Typescripts, Idaho Historical Society, Boise. See also, O. O. Howard, *Nez Perce Joseph*, 30.

23. Monteith to Smith, April 7 and 28, May 14, and June 4, 1874, typescript, Idaho Historical Society, Boise; Mark, H. Brown, 65–66.

24. Josephy, *NPNW*, 464.

25. Bartlett, *Wallowa Country*, 48–49, 52. Josephy, *NPNW*, 464–65.

16. FLURRIES

1. For Howard's youth, see W. S. McFeeley. Carpenter, *Sword and Olive Branch*, is a broader, more admiring biography.

2. Utley and Washburn, 218.

3. Henry Clay Wood, *Status*, 49.

4. Josephy, *The Nez Perces and the Opening of the Northwest* (hereafter *NPNW*), 474.

5. Ibid., 469–72; Bartlett, *Wallowa Country* 60–62; McWhorter, *Hear Me* 129–31, 611–13.

6. Monteith to Commissioner J. Q. Smith, July 31, 1876, typescript, Idaho Historical Society, Boise.

7. FitzGerald, 201–2.

8. Henry Clay Wood, *Supplementary*, 2–4.

9. Monteith to J. Q. Smith, July 31, 1876, typescript, Idaho Historical Society, Boise. This angry letter from the agent to the commissioner does not specifically mention the Sioux, but the thought could hardly have escaped Monteith's mind. True, the Sioux and Nez Perce buffalo hunters often fought each other on the Plains, but a common enemy could bring them together. In

1875, a year before the meeting with Wood, Monteith himself reported to Smith (March 1, 1875) that the Sioux had urged the nontreaty Indians to join them in war against the whites. It is also said that Joseph, Looking Glass, and Eagle-from-the-Light were all on the Plains that year (Haines, *Nez Perces*, 251). Though they turned down the approach then, they might reconsider now that the Sioux had so graphically demonstrated the possibility of defeating the whites.

10. Bartlett, *Wallowa Country*, 63–64.

11. Ibid., 64–68; 89–108; and Josephy, *NPNW*, 479–83.

12. Bartlett, *Wallowa Country*, 65.

13. Ibid., 67.

14. Ibid., 101–4, reproduces Forse's report on his assignment. Ibid., 93–94, reproduces a long letter by one of the settlers.

15. Joseph, *NPNW*, 482.

16. Ibid., 483.

17. THE ANTAGONISTS

1. FitzGerald, 217.

2. Josephy, *The Nez Perces and the Opening of the Northwest* (hereafter *NPNW*), 484.

3. FitzGerald, 140.

4. Ibid., photograph facing p. 218. Mark H. Brown, 33, drawing on an article by Howard, gives a somewhat different description, perhaps because the photograph, though dated 1876 in FitzGerald's account, was probably taken later.

5. FitzGerald, 206.

6. Wooster, passim, points out the many problems of split jurisdiction in military matters affecting Indians. The American philosophy of civilian control over the military meant that the Department of the Interior, which embraced the Bureau of Indian Affairs, called the shots and army units were summoned only to implement strategies already decided on.

7. FitzGerald on the council, 219–21.

8. Ibid., 223.

9. Chief Joseph, "An American Indian's View."

10. FitzGerald, 222; and Josephy, *NPNW*, 489, drawing on *Annual Report, Department of the Interior* (1877).

11. Josephy, *NPNW*, 485–86.

12. Mark H. Brown; and McWhorter, *Hear Me*, 145–47. Commissioner Jerome was housed by the Whitmans during the conference.

13. FitzGerald, 223.

14. The *Report of the Secretary of War, 1877* (House Executive Document No. 1, V.I, pt. 2, 45th Cong., 2d sess., serial 1794, pp. 115–116, 585–96) carries much of the correspondence about matters immediately preceding the removal. Duplicates of many of Monteith's letters, written during the same period to Commissioner James Q. Smith, are at the Idaho Historical Society, Boise.

15. Monteith to Smith, February 2, 1877, loc. cit.

16. Burns, 373, 375.

17. Josephy, *NPNW*, 495.

18. McWhorter, *Hear Me*, 150.

19. McDonald, "The Nez Perces," 10–11. McDonald's account, prepared from interviews with Indians involved in the war, is often almost incoherent. (The son of a Scotch trader and a Nez Perce mother, McDonald was by no means a trained reporter.) His account differs in many ways from Howard's official report (see *Report of the Secretary of War, 1877*, vol. 1, 590) and from the same general's reminiscences (*Nez Perce Joseph*, 42–43). For other variations on the theme, see Mark H. Brown, 76–80; and Josephy, *NPNW*.

20. *Report of the Secretary of War, 1877*, 590.

21. Ibid., 587.

22. MacDonald, 12.

23. McFeely; for an incisive characterization of Howard and the Freedmen's Bureau, see his introduction.

24. Mark H. Brown, 75; and Evans, 37–40.

25. FitzGerald, 246–47. Accounts of the council are contradictory. Mine is a composite of the following primary sources, in addition to the FitzGerald letters: *Report of the Secretary of War, 1877*, 593–94; Howard, *Nez Perce Joseph*, 57–71; MacDonald, *Idaho Yesterdays*, Spring, 1977, pp. 12–13; McWhorter, *Yellow Wolf*, 37–41.

26. FitzGerald, 248–49.

27. Howard, *Nez Perce Joseph*, 67.

28. Haines, *Nez Perces*, 212.

29. In January 1879, Joseph gave a speech in New York City to a distinguished audience. He used the talk to stir sympathy for his people, hoping they would be allowed to return to Idaho from their exile in Oklahoma. In the course of the address, he complained, "General Howard refused to allow me more than thirty days to move my people and their stock.... We left many of our horses and cattle in Wallowa, and lost several hundred in crossing the

[Snake] river.... We had not complied with General Howard's order [about time limits] because we could not." Howard, in short, had demanded the impossible, and it had cost the Indians dearly—or so Joseph implied.

Joseph's speech was translated, edited according to the literary tastes of the time, and printed as "An American Indian's View of Indian Affairs" in the *North American Review*, April 1879. On reading it, Howard took immediate exception to some of Joseph's statements, including the one about the time limit, and replied in the same magazine, July 1879 issue, with "The True Story of the Wallowa Campaign." Joseph had not asked for more time, he said, and therefore it was wrong to pillory him for not granting it.

A letter written by Howard's aide, Lieutenant W. C. Wilkinson, on May 12, 1877, at the time the deadline was set, supports Howard's contention (See Carpenter, "General Howard," 132.) Opposed to this contention is a statement by Duncan MacDonald in the newspaper, *New North-West*, in the summer of 1878 (reprint, *Idaho Yesterdays*, Spring 1977, p. 12) expressing Joseph's outrage at the demand. That's close to contemporary evidence, but does not make a prevaricator out of Howard. In my opinion, the Indians' anger began when they encountered the Snake River and *then* they blamed the general for their troubles (see chap. 18). From there to saying that Joseph protested in advance was but a step—a step unfortunately taken by nearly every historian of the Nez Perce outbreak. Howard, I admit, isn't always likable, but in this case he's had bad press.

30. FitzGerald, 250.

18. BLOOD FOR BLOOD

1. Bartlett, "Ollokot and Joseph."
2. Bartlett, *Wallowa*, 71.
3. Chief Joseph, "An American Indian's View."
4. A small detachment of soldiers who were stationed in the Wallowa that spring saw neither cattle nor Indians because neither were that far up in the mountains. (Bartlett, *Wallowa*, 72–73, notes this fact and describes the lateness of the spring and the kettles of coin.) What all this means is that the roundup was not the dreadful chore described by McWhorter (*Hear Me*, 175) as "half a year's task crowded into a thirty-day limit" and repeated by several other authors.
5. Gulick, 197, quoting Gerald J. Tucker, "The Story of Hell's Canyon," 112; and Haines, *Nez Perces*, 217–18.
6. Various accounts, marked by the usual discrepanices, cover this event and those that immediately followed: Haines, *Nez Perces*, 218ff; Josephy, *The*

Nez Perces and the Opening of the Northwest (hereafter *NPNW*), 514–15; Mac-Donald, 14; and McWhorter, *Hear Me*, 195–97.

7. McWhorter, *Hear Me*, 196–97.

8. Differing tales deal with the events that brought scorn on Wahlitits. For examples: Mark H. Brown, 99–101; McWhorter, *Hear Me*, 190. I follow McDermott, 3–4.

9. Some accounts say Wahlitits was a teetotaler. I follow Curtis, vol. 8, 23, 164; Curtis talked to some of the participants. As for the murders, see esp., McDermott, early pages.

10. Curtis, vol. 8, 24, 165; McDermott, 15–31. It is not possible to reconstruct precisely what did go on among either the settlers or the Indians during the beginning days of the outbreak. McDermott's study probably comes the closest of many studies.

11. McDermott, 11.

12. Ibid., 15–31; Michael Forbes Brown, 98–117; Josephy, *NPNW*, 513–15.

13. Curtis, vol. 8, 24–25. Mark H. Brown, 16–17; Chief Joseph, "An American Indian's View."

14. McWhorter, *Yellow Wolf*, 46.

15. MacDonald, 14.

16. Mark H. Brown, 131.

17. McWhorter, in *Hear Me*, 215, condemns Chapman, but in *Yellow Wolf*, 55, speaks well of him. See also McDermott, 73–74, and Monteith's 1871 correspondence with Chapman, transcripts, Idaho State Historical Society, Boise.

18. McDermott, 37–43.

19. Howard, *Nez Perce Joseph*, 90–97, reprints the messages that were received.

20. McWhorter, *Yellow Wolf*, 52. Aoki, "Nez Perce Texts," 100.

21. Howard, *Nez Perce Joseph*, 74–85.

22. Mark H. Brown, 128, drawing his quotation "clerks ..." from the manuscript diary of Michael McCarthy. That diary plus Sergeant Schorr's "Narrative" and the other reminiscences in McWhorter, *Hear Me*, 231–61, with added material from McWhorter, *Yellow Wolf*, 54–612, and Howard, *Nez Perce Joseph*, 107–18, are the basis of all later accounts. More data are in "Claims of the Nez Perce Indians," 56th Cong., 1st Sess., Document 257. By far the most thorough synthesis is McDermott, who also prints the transcript of Captain Perry's first Court of Inquiry.

23. Mark H. Brown, 133, again quoting McCarthy, and McWhorter, *Hear Me*, 233, again quoting Schorr.

24. McWhorter, *Yellow Wolf*, 55; Curtis, vol. 8, 26.

25. McWhorter, *Yellow Wolf*, 54–55; Curtis, vol. 8, 26.

19. EVASIONS

1. Yellow Wolf (McWhorter, 62–63, 69) makes it clear that the strategy of evading Howard by crossing back and forth over the Salmon River was devised by Rainbow and Five Wounds. My elaborations are assumptions based on the Indians' war psychology. Nothing else satisfactorily explains the Indians' roundabout march during the early days of the flight. See also, Haines, "Chief Joseph and the Nez Perce Warriors," p. 4.

2. Hodge, "War and War Discipline," in Hodge, vol. 2, 914–15.

3. McWhorter, *Yellow Wolf*, 62, describes the kind of craft called bull-boats by fur trappers. These boats differed, it is supposed, from the ones Joseph's band had used in crossing the Snake River because satisfactory willows did not grow on the flood-scoured bars of that stream.

4. Burns, 382–83.

5. Howard, *Nez Perce Joseph*, 127; FitzGerald, 262–66 passim.

6. Burns, 385–405, goes into exhaustive detail about the situation among the Indians of northern Idaho during the opening weeks of the Nez Perce conflict.

7. FitzGerald, 270.

8. Howard, *Nez Perce Joseph*, 128–31.

9. Mark H. Brown, 159–60.

10. Haines, "Chief Joseph"; Beal, 63.

11. The Rains affair: Mark H. Brown, 173–75; Josephy, *The Nez Perces and the Opening of the Northwest* (hereafter *NPNW*), 537–38; and McWhorter, *Hear Me;* 280–86; McWhorter, *Yellow Wolf*, 71–76.

12. The second Cottonwood affair: Haines (ed.), "Skirmish"; McWhorter, *Yellow Wolf*, 75–77, and Randall's "Memoir" in *Yellow Wolf*, 80–83 (the latter to be sprinkled with salt). See also, Mark H. Brown, 178–83; Josephy, *NPNW*, 539–40; McWhorter, *Hear Me*, 287–89.

13. Mark H. Brown, 185–86; Howard, *Nez Perce Joseph*, 154–55; Sutherland, 3–4.

14. Mark H. Brown, 164–66; Josephy, *Nez Perce Country*, 131.

15. McWhorter, *Hear Me*, 262–74. Howard, *Nez Perce Joseph*, 149.

16. Beal, 70–72; Mark H. Brown, 186–88; Josephy, *NPNW,* 544. Hendrickson and Laughly, 161.

17. Josephy, *NPNW,* 546.

18. The battle: Howard, 157–66; *Report of the Secretary of War, 1877,* 122–24; McWhorter, *Yellow Wolf,* 85–101; Mark H. Brown, 188–96.

19. McWhorter, *Yellow Wolf,* 101.

20. Hendrickson, 43.

21. FitzGerald, 290.

20. BLUNDERS

1. Mark H. Brown, 200.

2. Figures compiled from Mark H. Brown, 196–97; *Report of the Secretary of War, 1877,* p. 124; Howard, *Nez Perce Joseph,* 166–67; and McWhorter, *Hear Me,* 323.

3. Howard, *Nez Perce Joseph,* 167.

4. McWhorter, *Yellow Wolf,* 104.

5. Beal, 77.

6. Josephy, *The Nez Perces and the Opening of the Northwest,* (hereafter *NPNW*), 553.

7. Beal 312n; Mark H. Brown, 200–201; FitzGerald, 278–79; *Report of the Secretary of War, 1877,* p. 124; Sutherland, 11.

8. McWhorter, *Hear Me,* 329. Josephy, *NPNW,* 554.

9. McWhorter, *Yellow Wolf,* 106.

10. *Report of the Secretary of War, 1877,* 125.

11. W. T. Jackson, 268–78.

12. Beal, 84.

13. Mark H. Brown, 206, Josephy, *NPNW,* 260. MacDonald, *Idaho Yesterdays* (Spring 1977), 30.

14. Howard, *Nez Perce Joseph,* 172. Brown, 208–9.

15. Howard, *Nez Perce Joseph,* 170.

16. Sutherland, 19–20.

17. Charles Erskine Scott Wood, "Chief Joseph," 138.

18. Josephy, *NPNW,* 556.

19. Space, 43–45, W. T. Jackson, 312–18.

20. Burns, 410–34, covers the situation in the mountains at the time the Nez Perces took to the Lolo trail. See also Fahey, 167–86.

21. Beal, 96–97; Mark H. Brown, 216; Burns, 439. Letters covering the developing crisis are in Phillips, ed., "The Battle of the Big Hole," in Hakola, *Frontier Omnibus*, 363–75. Hakola also reprints some of Rawn letters in "Early Days at Fort Missoula."

22. Burns, 441; Fahey, 194.

23. *Report of the Secretary of War, 1877*, vol. 1, 548, contains Rawn's official report of the affair. Chief Joseph, "An American Indian's View," gives his version. MacDonald, *Idaho Yesterdays*, Winter 1978, summarizes his interviews with survivors. Other reminiscences are in McWhorter, *Hear Me*, 343–56. The stories are full of discrepancies. The most judicious summary is Josephy, *NPNW*, 567–72.

24. Yellow Bull in Curtis, vol. 8, p. 166. MacDonald, Winter 1978, 7. A careful summary of the Bitterroot traverse is Burns, 441–48.

25. McWhorter, *Yellow Wolf*, 108–10.

26. Ibid.

21. BITTER FRUIT

1. Burns, 450–51.

2. Gibbon's approach: Beal, 112–16; Mark H. Brown, 246–53; Josephy, *The Nez Perces and the Opening of the Northwest* (hereafter *NPNW*), 578–81; *Report of the Secretary of War, 1877*, 501–5; Sherrill, 3–7.

3. Quotation, Dr. FitzGerald to Emily in FitzGerald, 304.

4. I have drawn much of my account of the battle from *Report of the Secretary of War, 1877*, 68–78, 501–5, 520–23. See also, Indian reminiscences: McWhorter, *Hear Me*, 366–403, McWhorter, *Yellow Wolf*, 115–60; Yellow Bull, Curtis, vol. 8, 167; MacDonald, *Idaho Yesterdays*, Winter 1978, 9–10, 18–19. White histories: Howard, *Nez Perce Joseph*, 202–08; Sherrill, 8–12; Sutherland, 23–25. More recent summaries, Beal, 117–23; Brown, 253–62; Josephy, *NPNW*, 582–87.

5. Beal, 128–30; Chief Joseph, "An American Indian's View," 23–24; McWhorter, *Yellow Wolf*, 159. Mark H. Brown, 264–65, presents a variety of estimates.

6. FitzGerald, 303. See Beal's thorough accounting, 131–34.

7. Howard, *Nez Perce Joseph*, 211.

8. Mark H. Brown, 269.

9. Beal, 140–41; Carpenter, "General Howard," 137–38.

10. Beal, 145–46; Howard, *Nez Perce Joseph*, 213–14; Josephy, *NPNW*, 590–91. Mark H. Brown, 270–85, is highly detailed but hard to follow.

11. Josephy, *NPNW*, 592.

12. Ibid., 593; Howard, *Nez Perce Joseph*, 215–16.

13. Josephy, *NPNW*, 594.

14. Mark H. Brown, 287, quotes newspaper reports describing the purported depredations. Beal, 151, drawing on a different newspaper, says there were no depredations. Take your choice.

15. *Report of the Secretary of War, 1877*, 128. Davison, 11–12. Howard's years-later statement (*Nez Perce Joseph*, 219) about what he told Bacon is not to be trusted.

16. Beal, 144, 252; Josephy, *NPNW*, 590.

17. McWhorter, *Yellow Wolf*, 164–65.

18. McWhorter, *Hear Me*, 417, and Josephy, *NPNW*, 595, say the vision that launched the raid came from a warrior named Black Hair. Duncan MacDonald, who talked to White Bird about a year after the incident, ascribes the vision to Grizzly Bear Youth (*Idaho Yesterdays*, Winter 1978, 20–21). MacDonald, *ibid.*, is the source of statements that the Indians planned to engage Howard's whole force in battle during the confusion caused by the horse stampede. Yellow Bull agrees. Yellow Wolf says "all" warriors went on the foray. Josephy and Haines, *Nez Perces*, 260, disagree and think the raid was to be carried out in deep quiet by a small group of chosen men. Either way, there was quite a scramble, as the text indicates.

22. HANGING ON

1. Mark H. Brown, 290; Howard, *Nez Perce Joseph*, 223–25; *Report of the Secretary of War, 1877*, 611.

2. Beal, 155–61; Howard, 226–29; *Report of the Secretary of War, 1877*, 612; Sutherland, 28–30.

3. Davison, 11–12; Howard, *Nez Perce Joseph*, 234; and Howard, *My Life and Experiences among our Hostile Indians*, 292–93.

4. Mark H. Brown, 298–300.

5. Carpenter, *Howard*, 138–39; FitzGerald, 303. Howard, *Nez Perces*, 234. *Report of the Secretary of War, 1877*, 130–31.

6. Part of the Sherman-Howard exchange is in *Report of the Secretary of War, 1877*, 12–13. See also, Howard, *Nez Perce Joseph*, 237, and Carpenter, *Howard*, 139.

7. Josephy, *The Nez Perces and the Opening of the Northwest* (hereafter *NPNW*), 600–601.

8. Davison, 12.

9. McWhorter, *Yellow Wolf*, 170–71. Mark H. Brown, 318, quoting the *New North West*.

10. Beal, 177–79. Principal sources for the Yellowstone trek are McWhorter, *Yellow Wolf*, 172–80, and McWhorter, *Hear Me*, 427–47. See also, *Report of the Secretary of War*, 616–20; Howard, *Nez Perce Joseph*, 239–54; Mark H. Brown, 313–54; Josephy, *NPNW*, 601–5; Sutherland, 33–34; Goodenough, 16–29. Particularly valuable is Lang, 14–45.

11. Lang, 20. Mark H. Brown, 346–47, quoting Thomas Marquis, *Memoirs of a White Crown Indian*. The dates of Looking Glass's ride to appeal to the Crows are speculative only. A few historians question whether Looking Glass ever visited the Crows to make his pitch.

12. Lang, 25, quoting Fisher's unedited journal, which later was unfortunately polished for publication.

13. I assume the arguments from what the Indians actually did. The hitherto unrecognized fact that the fugitives split and that Looking Glass's followers went up the headwater stream of the Lamar comes from Lang, 28ff.

14. I do not agree with Mark H. Brown's interpretation of the trails the Indians used in breaking out of Yellowstone. (No one can be completely sure of just where they went.) But his maps (322–23, 352–53) certainly help clarify the region's complex terrain.

15. Beal, 324, n. 5; Brown, 351.

16. Sturgis "explains" his misadventure in *Report of the Secretary of War, 1877*, 509–10. Mark H. Brown picks it apart, 247–49. See also, Haines, *Nez Perces*, 264–65, and McWhorter, *Hear Me*, 451–52.

17. The notion that the Nez Perces deliberately added hoof prints to the maze their two thousand horses had naturally left originates with Fisher and is followed by most commentators. Though Josephy, *NPNW*, goes along, he is somewhat skeptical (605–6), as I am. The Nez Perces, expert horsemen, couldn't have seriously believed that simply piling up prints would fool an experienced tracker for long.

18. Josephy, *NPNW*, 604; Lang, 25–26.

19. Mark H. Brown, 349, quoting Fisher's diary.

20. FitzGerald, 311–12; Howard, *Nez Perce Joseph*, 255–56.

21. Mark H. Brown, 357–59.

22. *Report of the Secretary of War, 1877*, 623.

23. FROM WHERE THE SUN NOW STANDS

1. The most satisfactory account of the skirmish is McWhorter, *Hear Me*, 461–66. The most detailed is Mark H. Brown, 359–63. See also Sturgis's official statement in *Report of the Secretary of War, 1877*, 511–12. Either Sturgis thought his men had inflicted more damage on the Indians than was the case or he deliberately inflated his figures: 16 Indians killed; 900–1,000 horses stampeded away. Howard reduced the total considerably, but the figures were still far too high.

2. McWhorter, *Hear Me*, 467–68. See also, Beal, 199; Josephy, *The Nez Perce Indians and the Opening of the Northwest* (hereafter *NPNW*), 611. If Yellow Wolf (McWhorter, 187–94) is to be believed, and Indians are careful not to make boasts that can't be confirmed, he was practically a one-man army in fighting off the raiders.

3. Beal, 201; Mark H. Brown, 367.

4. McWhorter, *Yellow Wolf*, 199; Mark H. Brown, 372–74.

5. *Report of the Secretary of War, 1877*, 557; McWhorter, *Hear Me*, 472–73; Beal, 203–4; and Josephy, 614, agree that three teamsters were killed. Mark H. Brown, 375–76, names two of them. Yellow Wolf (McWhorter, 202) blames whiskey for the bloodletting.

6. Two Moons to McWhorter, *Hear Me*, 473–74.

7. Utley and Washburn, 261–65, and Wooster, 168, succinctly characterize Miles. See also, Pohanka, 105–26.

8. Mark H. Brown, 380; Wooster, 167, 172–73, 180.

9. Pohanka, 106.

10. Mark H. Brown, 384; Kelly, 188.

11. Mark H. Brown, 386; Kelley, 192.

12. I follow Ege here. A more detailed account of prebattle troop movements is in Mark H. Brown, 390–91.

13. Mark H. Brown, 388, quoting Major Tilton.

14. Various controversial items cling to the battle at Snake Creek. For instance, did the Indians prepare rifle pits and shelters before the battle began or during the fighting? Were the Indians or was Miles the first to raise a white flag of truce? How did Looking Glass happen to be shot? Did Chief Joseph deliver his famed surrender speech at the time of surrendering or before or not at all? And so on. Rather than thrash out these questions in front of the reader, I have reached my own conclusions and incorporate them into the narra-

tive without comment. Readers who are interested in developing interpretations of their own can begin by delving into the accounts listed below.

For Indian points of view: *Chief Joseph's Own Story*, 24–27; McWhorter's duo, *Yellow Wolf*, 205–26, and *Hear Me*, 478–90. Joseph's friend Yellow Bull and Tom Hill, half Delaware and half Nez Perce, add bits in Curtis, vol. 8, 168–69 and 171–72. See also, Duncan MacDonald, *Idaho Yesterdays* (Winter 1978), 24–25. White views: Miles and Howard in *Report of the Secretary of War, 1877*, 512–15, 528–29, 629–34. See Miles, *Personal Recollections*, 265–74. Two useful white historians: Beal, 213–26; Mark H. Brown, 388–410. Brown quotes extensively from reminiscences and diaries by U.S. Army participants in the battle. Highly useful in understanding the battle are explanatory plaques affixed to boulders at Bearpaw State Park, eight miles south of Chinook, Montana. One can study the maps on the plaques while actually looking over the terrain.

15. Mark H. Brown, 400, quoting Major Tilton, who attended the conference.

16. A wide variety of statements purport to describe the handing over of the gun. McWhorter (*Hear Me*, 497), who examined most of them, chose to follow Wood, as I do.

24. INTERLUDE: FANCY FREE

1. Beal, 230–31 and 246; Mark H. Brown, 160–61.

2. Mark H. Brown, 410–11; Haines, *Nez Perces*, 281; Josephy, *Nez Perce Country*, 151–52; McWhorter, *Hear Me*, 50; and McWhorter, *Yellow Wolf*, 230–31.

3. Brown, 417–18; *Report of the Secretary of War, 1877*, 631.

4. Mark H. Brown, 407–8.

5. Haines, *Nez Perces*, 279–80.

6. Wells, "Nez Perces."

7. McWhorter, *Yellow Wolf*, 224–25, 234–35.

8. For an exhaustive analysis of the various versions of the speech and the context of its delivery, see Aoki, "Chief Joseph's Words."

9. Mark H. Brown, 424.

10. Bond's entire account is the primary basis for this section of the "Interlude."

11. Mark H. Brown, 424–25.

12. Ibid., 429–30.

13. Bond, 21.

14. Josephy, *The Nez Perces and the Opening of the Northwest*, 636.

25. AN AMERICAN TRAGEDY

1. Principal sources for this account of the Nez Perce exile in Indian Territory are Beal, 274–93; Stanley Clark, 214–31; McWhorter, *Hear Me*, 525–40; Ray, "Ethnohistory," 63–79, in *Nez Perce Indians* (Garland).

2. Haines, *Nez Perces*, 293.

3. McWhorter, *Yellow Wolf*, 229–90.

4. Ibid., 289.

5. Stanley Clark, 216–17.

6. Beal, 293.

7. Ray, "Ethnohistory," 68–69, in *Nez Perce Indians* (Garland).

8. Stanley Clark, 218.

9. Ibid., 219–25.

10. Ibid., 222–23.

11. Beal, 288–89.

12. Ibid., 292; McBeth, 99–101.

13. Beal, 293–94; Haines, *Nez Perces*, 296; McWhorter, *Yellow Wolf*, 290; Slickpoo, 200–201.

14. Stanley Clark, 230–31.

15. Yellow Wolf disagreed. There was enough space, he said, for hunting deer, fishing for salmon, and digging for roots. See McWhorter, *Yellow Wolf*, 290.

16. See M. Gidley's duo, *One Sky* and *Kopet*, for affairs at Colville.

17. E. Jane Gay, *With the Nez Perces*, tells of the government's allotment activities on the Nez Perce Reservation as directed by that formidable anthropologist, Alice Fletcher.

18. Josephy, *Nez Perce Country*, 164. See also Riley, 50–51, and Slickpoo, 219–24.

19. Gidley, *Kopet*, 79, gives Yellow Bull's speech as translated by Camille Williams.

20. "Dedication Ceremonies ... Indian Hall of Fame."

21. Steven Ross Evans examines the Red Napoleon myth in detail in his master's thesis.

22. Gidley, *Kopet*, 37.

23. Pearce, *Savagism and Civilization*, passim.

BIBLIOGRAPHY

Aberle, David. "The Prophet Dance and Relations to White Contacts." *Southwest Journal of Anthropology* 15 (Spring 1959).

Alcorn, Rowina. *Timothy, Perce Chief* (with corrective appendix by Glen Adams). Fairfield, Wash., 1985.

Allen, Miss A. J. *Ten Years in Oregon: The Travels and Adventures of Dr. Elijah White and Lady.* Ithaca, N.Y., 1848.

Aoki, Haruo. "Chief Joseph's Words." *Idaho Yesterdays*, Fall 1989.

———. "Nez Perce Texts." In *Linguistics*. Berkeley, Calif., 1979.

Bancroft, H. H. *The History of Washington, Idaho, and Montana.* San Francisco, 1890.

Barry, J. Nielson. "Lieutenant Jeremy Pinch." *Oregon Historical Quarterly* 33 (September 1930).

Bartlett, Grace. "Ollokot and Joseph." *Idaho Yesterdays* (Spring 1977).

———. *The Wallowa Country, 1867–1877.* Fairfield, Wash., 1984.

Beal, Merrill D. *"I Will Fight No More Forever": Chief Joseph and the Nez Perce War.* Seattle, 1963.

Beckwourth, James. *Life and Adventures.* Introduction by Bernard DeVoto. New York, 1931.

Before the Indian Claims Commission. Docket nos. 175, 180-A. 1967. See *Nez Perce Indians*, below.

Berkhofer, R. J., Jr. *Salvation and the Savage: An Analysis of Protestant Missions and the American Indian Response.* Lexington, Ky., 1965.

Berreman, Joseph B. *Tribal Distribution in Oregon.* (Memoir no. 73) Menasha, Wis., 1937.

Billington, Ray Allen. *The Protestant Crusade.* New York, 1938.

———. *Westward Expansion: A History of the American Frontier.* New York, 1960.

Bird, Annie Laurie. "Portrait of a Frontier Politician." *Idaho Yesterdays,* Fall 1958.

Boas, Franz. "Language" and "Religion." In *Handbook,* edited by F. W. Hodge (*q.v.*).

Bond, Fred G. "Flatboating on the Yellowstone." New York, 1925.

Branch, Douglas E. *The Hunting of the Buffalo.* Lincoln, Nebr., 1962.

Brandon, William. *The American Heritage Book of Indians.* New York, 1961.

Brosnan, Cornelius. *Jason Lee.* New York, 1922.

Brown, Mark H. *The Flight of the Nez Perce.* New York, 1967.

Brown, Michael Forbes. "Dark Side of Shamanism." *Natural History,* November, 1987.

Brown, William Compton. *The Indian Side of the Story.* Spokane, Wash., 1961.

Burcham, Ralph. "Oro Fino Gold," *Idaho Yesterdays,* Fall, 1960.

Burns, Robert Ignatius, S. J. *The Jesuits and the Indian Wars of the Northwest.* New Haven, 1966.

Butterfield, Grace. "Old Chief Joseph's Grave." *Oregon Historical Quarterly,* 41 (1945).

Carpenter, John A. "General Howard and the Nez Perce War of 1877." *Pacific Northwest Quarterly,* October 1958.

———. *Sword and Olive Branch: O. O. Howard.* Pittsburgh, Pa., 1964.

Chalfant, Stuart A. See *Nez Perce Indians,* below.

Chief Joseph. "An American Indian's View of Indian Affairs." *North American Review,* April 1879. This account has been reprinted various times as "Chief Joseph's Own Story."

Chittenden, Hiram M. *The American Fur Trade of the Far West.* Reprint. Stanford, Calif., 1954.

Clark, Malcom, Jr. *Eden Seekers: The Settlement of Oregon, 1818–1862.* Boston, 1981.

Clark, Stanley. "The Nez Perces in Exile." *Pacific Northwest Quarterly,* July 1945.

Coleman, Michael T. *Presbyterian Missionary Attitudes toward American Indians, 1837–1893.* Jackson, Miss., 1985.

Conley, Cort. *Idaho for the Curious: A Guide*. Cambridge, Idaho, 1982.

Corning, Howard, McKinley. *Dictionary of Oregon History*. Portland, 1956.

Coues, Elliott., ed. *New Light on the Early History of the Great Northwest: The Manuscript Journals of Alexander Henry and of David Thompson*. 2 vols. Minneapolis, 1965.

Cram, Captain T. J. "Topographical Memoir of the Department of the Pacific." *House Executive Document*, no. 114, 35th Cong., 2d sess. Washington, 1859.

Curtis, Edward S. *The North American Indians*. Vol. 8. Norwood, Mass., 1911.

Cutright, Paul Russell. *Lewis and Clark, Pioneering Naturalists*. Urbana, Ill., 1969.

Daugherty, Richard P. *The Yakima People*. Phoenix, Ariz., 1973.

Davison, Stanley A. "A Century Ago." *Montana, The Magazine of Western History*, October 1977.

"Dedication Ceremonies of Bronze Portraiture in the Indian Hall of Fame, 1957." *The Chronicles of Oklahoma*, Winter 1957–58.

DeVoto, Bernard. *Across the Wide Missouri*. Boston, 1947.

Bernard de Voto, ed. *The Journals of Lewis and Clark*. Boston, 1953.

Dozier, Jack. "The Coeur d'Alene Indians in the War of 1858." *Idaho Yesterdays*, Fall 1961.

Drury, Clifford M. *Chief Lawyer of the Nez Perce Indians, 1796–1876*. Glendale, Calif., 1979.

———. *First White Women over the Rockies*. Glendale, Calif., 1963.

———. *Henry Harmon Spalding*. Caldwell, Idaho, 1936.

———. *Marcus and Narcissa Whitman and the Opening of Old Oregon*. 2 vols. Glendale, Calif., 1973.

———. *The Diaries and Letters of Henry H. Spalding and Asa Bowen Smith....* *1838–42*. Glendale, Calif. 1958.

———. *Elkanah and Mary Walker*. Caldwell, Idaho, 1940.

Ege, Robert J. *After the Little Bighorn: The Battle of Snake Creek, Montana Territory*. Greeley, Colo., 1982.

Elliot, T. C. *The Coming of the White Women*. Portland, Oreg., 1937.

———. "The Strange Case of David Thompson and Jeremy Pinch." *Oregon Historical Quarterly* 40 (1939).

Evans, Steven Ross. "Chief Joseph and the Red Napoleon Myth." Master's thesis. Washington State University. 1969.

Ewers, John C. *The Blackfeet: Raiders on the Northern Plains*. Norman, Okla. 1958.

———. *The Horse in Blackfoot Culture*. Washington, D.C., 1955.

———. "When the Light Shone in Washington." *Montana, The Magazine of Western History*, Autumn 1956.

Fahey, John. *The Flathead Indians*. Norman, Okla., 1971.

Farb, Peter. *Man's Rise to Civilization: The Cultural Ascent of the Indians of North America*. New York, 1978.

Fee, Chester Anders. *Chief Joseph: The Biography of a Great Indian*. New York, 1936.

Fenneman, Nevin M. *Physiography of Western United States*. New York, 1931.

Ferris, W. A. *Life in the Rocky Mountains*, edited by Paul C. Phillips. Denver, 1940.

FitzGerald, Emily. *An Army Doctor's Wife on the Frontier: Letters from Alaska and the Far West*. Pittsburgh, Pa., 1962.

Fletcher, Alice C. "Agency System." "Governmental Policy." "Land Tenure." "Oratory." In F. W. Hodge, *Handbook* (q.v.)

Franchere, Gabriel. *The Journal of Gabriel Franchere*, edited by W. Kaye Lamb. Toronto, 1969.

Fuller, George W. *A History of the Pacific Northwest*. New York, 1947.

Gay, E. Jane. *With the Nez Perces: Alice Fletcher in the Field, 1889–92*. Lincoln, Nebr. 1981.

Gidley, M. *Kopet: A Documentary Narrative of Chief Joseph's Last Years*. Seattle, 1981.

———. *With One Sky Above Us: Life on an Indian Reservation at the Turn of the Century*. New York, 1979.

Glassley, Ray H. *Pacific Northwest Indian Wars*. Portland, Oreg., 1953.

Glover, Richard, ed. *David Thompson's Narrative, 1784–1812*. Toronto, 1962.

Goetzmann, William H. *Army Explorations in the American West*. New Haven, 1959.

———. *Exploration and Empire*. New York, 1966.

Goodenough, Daniel. "Lost in the Cold." *Montana, The Magazine of Western History*, Autumn 1974.

[Goodrich, C. L.] "News from the Nez Perce Mines." *Idaho Yesterdays*, Winter 1959–60.

Goulder, William A. "The 'Statesman' in Northern Idaho." *Idaho Yesterdays*, Winter 1984.

Gowans, Fred R. *Rocky Mountain Rendezvous: A History of the Fur Trade Rendezvous, 1825–40*. Provo, Utah, 1977.

Gulick, Bill. *Chief Joseph Country: Land of the Nez Perce.* Caldwell, Idaho, 1981.

Gray, William H. *A History of Oregon.* Portland, Oreg., 1870.

Hafen, LeRoy. "Robert Newell." In *The Mountain Men and the Fur Trade of the Far West,* edited by LeRoy and Ann Hafen, vol. 8, Glendale, Calif., 1972.

Haines, Francis. "Chief Joseph and the Nez Perce Warriors." *Pacific Northwest Quarterly,* January 1954.

———. "The Nez Perce Delegation to St. Louis in 1831." *Pacific Historical Review,* 6 (1937).

———. *The Nez Perces, Tribesmen of the Columbia Plateau.* Norman, Okla., 1955.

———, ed. "The Skirmish at Cottonwood, by George Shearer." *Idaho Yesterdays,* Spring 1958.

———. "The Northwest Spread of Horses among the Plains Indian." *American Anthropologist* (40) 1938.

Hakola, John W. *Frontier Omnibus.* Missoula, Mont., 1962.

Hayden, William C. "The Battle of Pierre's Hole." *Idaho Yesterdays,* Summer 1976.

Hendrickson, Borg, and Linwood Laughly. *Clearwater Country.* Kooskia, Idaho, 1987.

Hewitt, J. N. B. "Mythology" and "Dance." In *Handbook,* edited by F. W. Hodge (q.v.)

Hodge, F. W., ed. *Handbook of American Indians North of Mexico,* Bureau of American Ethnology, Bulletin no. 30. 2 vols. Reprint. New York, 1959.

Hogan, William T. *The Indian in American History.* New York, 1963.

Horsman, Reginald. "American Indian Policy and the Origins of Manifest Destiny." In *The Indian in American History,* edited by Paul Prucha. New York, 1971.

———. *Expansion and American Indian Policy,* Lansing, Mich., 1967.

Howard, Helen Addison, assisted by Dan L. McGrath. *War Chief Joseph.* Caldwell, Idaho, 1941.

Howard, O. O. *My Life and Experiences among Our Hostile Indians.* Hartford, Conn., 1901.

———. *Nez Perce Joseph.* (Reprint). New York, 1972.

———. "The True Story of the Wallowa Campaign." *North American Review,* July 1879. This article is a rebuttal of certain charges made by Chief Joseph in the April issue of the same magazine.

Irving, Washington. *Astoria*. 2 vols. Reprint. Philadelphia and New York, 1961.

———. *The Adventures of Captain Bonneville, USA*. Norman, Okla., 1961.

Jablow, Joseph. *The Cheyenne in Plains Indian Trade Relations, 1795–1840*. New York, n.d.

Jackson, Donald Dean, ed. *Letters of the Lewis and Clark Expedition*. 2 vols. Urbana, Ill., 1978.

———. *The Voyages of the Steamboat Yellow Stone*. New York, 1985.

Jackson, W. Turrentine. *Wagon Roads West*. Berkeley and Los Angeles, 1952.

Johansen, Dorothy O., and Charles M. Gates. *Empire of the Columbia: A History of the Pacific Northwest*. New York, 1957.

Johnson, Virginia Weisel. *The Unregimented General: A Biography of Nelson A. Miles*. Boston, 1962.

Joseph, Chief. See Chief Joseph.

Josephy, Alvin M., Jr. *The Indian Heritage of America*. New York, 1968.

———. *Nez Perce Country*. Washington, D.C., 1983.

———. *The Nez Perce Indians and the Opening of the Northwest*. New Haven, 1965.

———. *The Patriot Chiefs*. New York, 1961.

Kelly, Luther S. *Yellowstone Kelly: Memoirs of Luther S. Kelley*. New Haven, 1926.

Kenny, Michael. Untitled account of Steptoe's 1858 campaign. Copy in Washington State University Library.

Kip, Lawrence. "Army Life on the Pacific: A Journal of the Expedition ... in the Summer of 1858." New York, 1859.

———. *The Indian Council at Walla Walla*. Eugene, Oreg., 1897.

Kopper, Philip. *The Smithsonian Book of North American Indians Before the Coming of Europeans*. Washington, 1986.

Kroeber, A. L. "Nature of the Land Holding Group." *Ethnohistory* 2 (Fall 1955).

Lahren, S. L., and John L. Shultz. "New Light on Old Issues: Plateau Political Factionalism." *Northwest Anthropological Notes*, Fall 1973.

Lamar, Howard, ed. *The Reader's Encyclopedia of the American West*. New York, 1977.

Lang, William L. "Where Did the Nez Perces Go in Yellowstone in 1877?" *Montana, The Magazine of Western History*, Winter 1990.

Lavender, David. *Land of Giants: The Drive to the Pacific Northwest, 1750–1950*. New York, 1958.

———. *The Way to the Western Sea: Lewis and Clark across the Continent*. New York, 1988.

————. *The Fist in the Wilderness.* New York, 1964.

————. *Westward Vision.* New York, 1963.

Lehmer, Donald J. *Introduction to Middle Missouri Archeology.* Lincoln, Nebr. 1971.

Mark, Frederick. "William Craig." In *The Mountain Men and the Fur Trade of the Far West,* edited by LeRoy Hafen and Ann Hafen, vol. 2. Glendale, Calif., 1972.

McBeth, Kate C. *The Nez Perces Since Lewis and Clark.* New York, 1908.

McDermott, John D. *Forlorn Hope.* Boise, Idaho, 1978.

McDonald, Duncan, "The Nez Perces; The History of Their Troubles and the Campaigns of 1877." *Idaho Yesterdays,* Spring 1977 and Winter 1978. This is a reprint of McDonald's articles that appeared in the *New North-West* of Deer Lodge, Montana, April 26–December 20, 1878.

McFeely, W. S. *Yankee Stepfather: General O. O. Howard and the Freedmen.* New Haven, 1968.

McLoughlin, James. *My Friend, the Indian.* Boston, 1926.

McWhorter, L. V. *Hear Me, My Chiefs: Nez Perce History and Legends.* Caldwell, Idaho, 1952.

————. *Tragedy of the Wahk-Shum, the Death of Andrew J. Bolon, Indian Agent.* Yakima, Wash., 1937.

————. *Yellow Wolf: His Own Story.* Caldwell, Idaho, 1940.

Meany, Edmond S. *History of the State of Washington.* New York, 1909.

Merk, Frederick, ed. *Fur Trade and Empire: George Simpson's Journal, 1824–25.* Cambridge, Mass., 1931.

Miles, Nelson A. *Personal Recollections and Observations.* Chicago and New York, 1897.

Miller, Christopher L. "After That the World Will Fall Apart." Ph.D. diss., University of California, Santa Barbara, 1981.

————. *Prophetic Worlds: Indians and Whites on the Columbia Plateau.* New Brunswick, N.J., 1985. This volume is a compression and revision of the same author's dissertation.

Miller, Henry. "Miller's Letters from the Upper Columbia." *Idaho Yesterdays,* Winter 1960–61.

Mooney, James. *The Ghost Dance Religion and the Sioux Outbreak of 1890.* Washington, D.C., 1896.

Morgan, Dale L. *Jedediah Smith and the Opening of the West.* Indianapolis, 1953.

————. *The West of William H. Ashley.* Denver, Colo., 1964.

Morgan, Dale L., and Eleanor Towles Harris. *The Rocky Mountain Journals of William Marshall Anderson: The West in 1834.* San Marino, Calif., 1967.

Morrill, Allen C., and Eleanor D. Morrill. *Out of the Blanket.* Moscow, Idaho, 1978.

Moulton, Gary E., ed. *The Journals of the Lewis and Clark Expedition.* Lincoln, Nebr., 1986–.

Mulford, Ami Frank. *Fighting Indians in the Seventh Cavalry.* Corning, N.Y., 1878.

Newell, Robert. *Memoranda,* edited by Dorothy Johansen. Portland, Oreg., 1959.

Nez Perce Indians. New York: Garland Publishing Co., 1974. This compilation contains Stuart A. Chalfant, "Aboriginal Territory of the Nez Perce Indians"; Verne F. Ray, "Ethnohistory of the Joseph Band of Nez Perce Indians"; and "Before the Indian Claims Commission, Dockets No. 175 and 180-A."

[Ogden, P. S.] *Traits of American Indian Life and Character.* San Francisco, 1933.

Parker, Samuel. *Journal of an Exploring Tour Beyond the Rocky Mountains.* Ithaca, N. Y., 1838.

Pearce, Roy Harvey. *Savagism and Civilization, A Study of the Indian and the American Mind.* Baltimore, 1965.

Philbrick, Francis S. *The Rise of the West, 1754–1830.* New York, 1965.

Pohanka, Brian C., ed. *Nelson A. Miles: A Documentary Biography of His Military Career.* Glendale, Calif. 1985.

Point, Nicholas. *Wilderness Kingdom: Indian Life in the Rocky Mountains, 1840–1847.* New York, 1967.

Porter, Kenneth Wiggins. *John Jacob Astor, Business Man,* 2 vols. Cambridge, Mass., 1931.

Prucha, Francis Paul. *American Indian Policy in the Formative Years.* Cambridge, Mass. 1962.

Prucha, Francis Paul, ed. *The Indian in American History.* New York, 1971.

Randolph, June. "Witness of Indian Religion: Present-day Concepts of the Guardian Spirit." *Pacific Northwest Quarterly,* 1957.

Ray, Verne F. *Cultural Relations in the Plateau of Northwestern America.* Los Angeles, 1939.

———. See *Nez Perce Indians,* above.

Relander, Click. *Drummers and Dreamers.* Reprint. Seattle, 1986.

Reports of the Secretary of War, 1877. 45th Cong. 2d sess., House Executive Document. (Serial 1794) Washington, D.C., 1878.

Reports of Explorations ... for a Railroad from the Mississippi River to the Pacific Ocean, vol. 12. Washington, D.C., 1859.

Rich, E. E., ed. *McLoughlin's Fort Vancouver Letters, 1st Series, 1825–38* Toronto, 1941.

Riley, Robert J. "The Nez Perce Struggle for Self-Government: A History of Nez Perce Governing Bodies, 1842–1950." Master's thesis, University of Idaho, 1961.

Rodeffer, Michael J. "A Classification of Burials in the Lower Snake River Region." *Northwest Anthropological Research Notes*, Spring 1973.

Roe, Frank G. *The Indian and the Horse*. Norman. Okla., 1955.

Rollins, Phillip Ashton, ed. *The Discovery of the Oregon Trail: Robert Stuarts's Narratives.*" New York, 1935.

Ronan, Mary. *Frontier Woman*, edited by H. G. Merriam. Helena, Mont., 1973.

Ronda, James P. *Lewis and Clark among the Indians*. Lincoln, Nebr. 1984.

Ross, Alexander. *Adventures of the First Settler on the Oregon or Columbia River*, edited by Milo M. Quaife. Chicago, 1923.

————. *Fur Hunters of the Far West*, edited by Milo M. Quaife. Chicago, 1924.

————. "Journal of Alexander Ross—Snake Country Expedition, 1824." *Oregon Historical Quarterly*, June 1913.

Ruby, Robert H., and John A. Brown. *The Cayuse Indians: Imperial Tribesmen of Old Oregon*. Norman, Okla., 1972.

————. *Indians of the Pacific Northwest*. Norman, Okla., 1981.

Russell, Carl P. *Firearms, Traps and Tools of the Mountain Men*. New York, 1967.

Schwantes, Carlos A. *The Pacific Northwest: An Interpretive History*. Lincoln, Nebr., 1989.

Scott, Leslie M. "Indian Diseases as Aids to Pacific Northwest Settlement." *Oregon Historical Quarterly*, 1928.

Sheehan, Bernard W. *Seeds of Extinction: Jeffersonian Philanthropy and the American Indian*. Chapel Hill, N. C., 1973.

Sherril, T. C. "Battle of the Big Hole," edited by Ella Hathaway. N. P., 1919.

Slickpoo, Allen P., Sr. *Noon-Nee-Me-Poo: Nez Perce Culture and History*. Lapwai, Idaho, 1973.

Smith, Sherry L. *The View From Officers' Row*. Tucson, 1990.

Space, Ralph S. *The Lolo Trail*. Lewiston, Idaho, 1972.

Spier, Leslie. *The Prophet Dance in the Northwest and Its Derivatives: The Source of the Ghost Dance*. Menasha, Wis., 1935.

Spinden, Herbert Joseph. *The Nez Perce Indians*. Lancaster, Pa., 1908.

Stevens, Hazard. *The Life of Isaac Ingalls Stevens*. 2 vols. Boston and New York, 1900–1901.

Sutherland, Thomas A. *Howard's Campaign against the Nez Perce Indians*, Portland, Oreg., 1878.

Suttles, Wayne. "The Plateau Prophet Dance among the Coast Salish." *Southwest Journal of Anthropology*, Winter 1957.

Talkington, H. L. *History of the Nez Perce Reservation and the City of Lewiston*. Boise, Idaho, 1938.

Teit, James A. *The Salishan Tribes of the Western Plateau*. 45th Annual Report, Bureau of American Ethnology. Washington, D.C., 1930.

Thomas, Cyrus. "Reservations." In *Handbook*, edited by F. W. Hodge (*q.v.*).

Thomason, Caroline Wasson. "Chief Joseph's 'Return' to His Beloved Wallowa." *The Spokesman-Review* (magazine section). Spokane. Wash., August 16, 1953.

Thompson, Irwin S. "Joseph M. Cataldo, S.J. and St. Joseph's Mission." *Idaho Yesterdays*, Summer 1974.

Thwaites, Reuben Gold, ed. *The Original Journals of the Lewis and Clark Expedition*. 8 vols. New York, 1904–05.

Townsend, John Kirk. *Across the Rockies to the Columbia*, edited by Donald Jackson. Lincoln, Nebr., 1978.

Trenholm, Virgina C., and Maurine Carley. *The Shoshoni, Sentinels of the Rockies*. Norman, Okla., 1964.

Trimble William J. *The Mining Advance into the Inland Empire....* Madison, Wis., 1914.

Turney-High, Henry H. *The Flathead Indians of Montana*. Menasha, Wis. 1973.

Tyrell, J. B. "Letter of Roseman and Perch, July 10, 1807." *Oregon Historical Quarterly*, December 1937.

Underhill, Ruth M. *Red Man's America: A History of Indians in the United States*. Chicago, 1953.

Utley, Robert M., and Wilcomb E. Washburn. *Indian Wars*. New York, 1977.

Van Every, Dale. *Disinherited: The Lost Birthright of the American Indian*. New York, 1966.

Victor, Frances Fuller. *Early Indian Wars of Oregon*. Salem, Oreg., 1894.

Waldman, Carl. *Atlas of the North American Indian*. New York, 1985.

Walker, Deward E., Jr. *American Indians of Idaho*. Moscow, Idaho, 1973.

———. *Conflicts and Schisms in Nez Perce Acculturation*. Pullman, Wash. 1968.

———. "Ethnology and History." *Idaho Yesterdays*, Spring 1970.

———. "New Light on the Prophet Dance Controversy." *Ethnohistory*, Summer 1969.

Warren, Robert Penn. *Chief Joseph of the Nez Perces, Who Call Themselves the Nimipu—the Real People*. (A poem.) New York, 1983.

Webb, Walter Prescott. *The Great Plains*. New York, 1931.

Wells, Donald W. "Farmers Forgotten." *Idaho Yesterdays*, Summer 1958.

Wells, Merle W. "The Nez Perces and Their War." *Pacific Northwest Quarterly*, January 1964.

White, Elijah. See Allen, Miss A. J.

White, M. Catherine, ed. *David Thompson's Journals Relating to Montana ... 1805–12*. Missoula, Mont., 1950.

White, Richard. "The Winning of the West: The Expansion of the Western Sioux...." *Journal of American History*, 1978.

Wilkes, Charles. *Narrative of the United States Exploring Expedition During the Years 1838 ... 1842*. 5 vols. Philadelphia, 1845.

Winther, Oscar Osburn. *The Old Oregon Country: A History of Frontier Trade, Transporation, and Travel*. Stanford, Calif., 1950.

Wood, Charles Erskine Scott. "Chief Joseph, the Nez Perce." *Century Magazine*, May 1884.

Wood, Major Henry Clay. *The Status of Young Joseph and His Band of Nez Perce Indians and the Indian Title to Land*. Portland, Oreg. 1876.

———. *Supplementary to the Report on the Treaty Status of Young Joseph*. Portland, Oreg., 1878.

Wooster, Robert. *The Military and United States Indian Policy, 1865–1903*. New Haven, 1988.

Zucker, Jeff, Kay Hummel, and Bob Hogfoss. *Oregon Indians: Culture, History, and Current Affairs*. Portland, Oreg., 1983.

ACKNOWLEDGMENTS

For help in understanding the physical geography covered in this account, I thank first Cort Conley, Idaho river runner, writer, historian, and environmentalist. He led the way, on different occasions, through what is left of the Nez Perce Reservation and its historical sites. We looked over the giant tilt of the White Bird Battlefield and the labyrinth of forests and canyons threaded by the Lolo Trail. Alvin Josephy, Jr., long recognized as an authority on North American Indians, especially the Nez Perce tribe, joined forces with a Wallowa Valley rancher, Biden Tippitt, to lead Conley and me through that extraordinarily rugged area, beloved by Chief Joseph and his people. Dr. Charles Kirkpatrick of Bozeman, Montana, took my wife, Muriel, and me through the Big Hole Battlefield; from there we followed the fugitives's trail through Horse Prairie, over the Continental Divide, south down Birch Creek, and east across Camas Prairie to West Yellowstone. Sherm Ewing of Great Falls unlimbered his new plane and, with his wife, Claire, flew Muriel and me above much of the upper Missouri River and over some of Montana's once-fabled buffalo country to a landing in Chinook. That in turn made possible a careful scrutiny, on foot, of the climactic Bear Paw Battlefield.

Long conversations with people who are familiar with the Nez Perces helped me map the inner landscapes the book covers. Among them were Susan Buchel and Superintendent Franklin Walker of the Nez Perce National Park, Spalding, Idaho. Tim Nitz, photo archivist of the same park, pointed the way toward images that were pertinent to the study. Allen Slickpoo of the Nez Perce Tribal Council; Beverly Coolbaugh, a descendant of Chief Joseph, now living in Santa Barbara, California; Steven Evans of Lewis-Clark State College, Lewiston, Idaho, and his Nez Perce wife, Connie, appreciably broadened my understanding of a culture that is very different from my own. Aubrey Haines, retired historian of Yellowstone National Park, and Dr. Merle Welles, director emeritus of the Idaho State Historical Society, added still more to my grasp of the material.

Libraries and librarians were, as usual, indispensible. Elizabeth Jacox, M. Gary Bettis, and Judith Austin, the latter the editor of *Idaho Yesterdays*, aided by others whose names I never knew or regrettably have forgotten, guided me through the resources of the state's historical society. Additional boosts came from Christian Burn and the staff of the Department of Special Collections, University of California at Santa Barbara, and from the Thacher School library, Ojai, California. John Little of Bear Mountain Books, Redding California, graciously loaned me several volumes, some of them hard to run down, that I was able to use at home—a considerable boon.

Sue Cherrie of Ventura proved to be an alert and able typist. Although Muriel arrived a little late on the scene, she quickly showed how essential wives are to the creative process.

INDEX